Prophecy and Progress

The Sociology of Industrial and Post-Industrial Society

Krishan Kumar

Allen Lane

ALLEN LANE
Penguin Books Ltd
17 Grosvenor Gardens
London SW1W 0BD

First published 1978
Published simultaneously in Pelican Books

ISBN 0 7139 1146 8

Set in Monotype Times by
Richard Clay (The Chaucer Press) Ltd.
Printed in Great Britain by
Billing & Sons Ltd, Guildford, London and Worcester

Contents

Preface

This book, probably inevitably with a theme such as it has, has been strongly affected by recent history, both intellectual and political. To take the intellectual first. At the suggestion of my colleague Ray Pahl, who knew of my interest in theories of social change, I began some time in 1972 to explore the newly re-opened vein of speculation on the future of industrial society. I found myself, somewhat to my surprise, in an unsuspected world of scenarios, 'surprise-free' projections, Delphi forecasting, commissions on the year 2000, and institutes of futurology. An initial hope that I might be able to combine my liking for science fiction with more sober academic pursuits was, alas, soon disappointed. Even the most routine science-fiction writer has more imagination and understanding than was revealed in the technocratic, jargon-ridden, commission reports, think-tank projections, and social forecasts through which I dutifully plodded. If we were indeed facing 'future shock', the most shocking thing about the future seemed to be its prose, and its ponderousness. Innumerable 'Mankind 2000s' and 'Plan 2000s' later, it was quite clear to me that it would be unprofitable to devote a whole book to the phenomenon of futurology. It would be too dispiriting a business.

There was one exception. It was not long before I came across Daniel Bell and his theory of the 'post-industrial' society, first elegantly and powerfully stated in some notes of 1967. Here was an idea that had a good deal of plausibility, and seemed well worth further examination. It was intellectually bolder and tougher by far than anything else I had hit upon in the literature of futurology. Industrial society, he proposed, was increasingly departing from its nineteenth-century base. We needed to take stock of its present, and think about its future, with quite different intellectual concepts from those inherited in the traditional theories of industrialism. This view therefore also had the special attraction of being quite consciously and explicitly linked to the classic sociological theories of industrialism. Indeed it depended for much of its force on the contrast with those analyses, and the history subsumed by them.

This then suggested the pattern of investigation. As an essential step in assessing its worth, the post-industrial idea directed the student of industrial society back to the historical past of that society and the theorizing that accompanied its origins and evolution. If we were moving into a 'post-industrial society', what was the 'industrial society' which it was replacing and from which it was being so sharply distinguished? What were its principles of structure and development, and how might these have changed in the course of the last two centuries? How in particular had the great European sociologists of the last century – Saint-Simon, Marx, Tocqueville, Weber, Durkheim – conceived the new society that they saw forming before their eyes? For it was evident that the post-industrial theory was constructed very much with those figures in mind, and in one aspect aspired to do for the late twentieth century what they had done for the nineteenth: that is, to create a powerful vision or 'image' of a society in the making. The possibility arose that the force of the post-industrial idea might derive as much as anything from a contrast, not so much with the real history, as with the image, of industrial society, to which the nineteenth-century sociologists had made their influential contribution. A further step in the analysis therefore involved setting the 'image of industrialism' against the historical developments of the times. In the final conception, what seemed the most helpful way of proceeding was to counterpose the image of the post-industrial society to that of the industrial society, and to see both as related in an intellectual tradition which had produced a special and at times seriously distorting vision of the history of industrial society. To get a better sight of our present condition, we had first to define and dissect that tradition.

Logically, at the beginning of this tradition, I came to the figure of Saint-Simon, the first prophet of the industrial society; and here a further theme offered itself. Saint-Simon's thought straddled the eighteenth-century Enlightenment idea of progress and the nineteenth-century idea of industrialism. His sociology of industrialism explicitly linked 'progress' and 'the industrial society': the idea of progress was to find its fulfilment and end in the establishment of industrial society. Later sociologists inherited this fusion of ideas, although with varying degrees of confidence. As part of the exploration of the sociology of industrial societies, therefore, I have sought to trace the varying fortunes of the idea of progress, up to and including its embodiment in the contemporary theory of post-industrialism.

The idea of progress also provides a bridge between these themes, which occupy the main part of the book, and the ideas developed in the last two chapters. I have indicated the intellectual currents which stimulated this study. The impact of the political history of our times came just after I had started serious work on the book. In the winter of 1973–4 the actions of the oil-producing states quadrupled the price of oil, the staple of the industrial system, and the world woke up to the energy crisis. Of course there had been people – E. F. Schumacher was one of them – who had been issuing warnings about energy for some time before that. But it took the dramatic events of that winter to make energy part of the consciousness of the world, and to alert it to the dependence of the industrial system on fuels and resources which were finite, dangerously depleted, and unevenly distributed across the globe.

What followed was a remarkable and highly educative debate, in all the industrial countries, on the current condition and future prospects of the industrial societies. For months the correspondence columns of *The Times* made for fascinating daily reading. The *New York Review of Books*, with characteristic intellectual pungency, published a whole series of articles on resources and technology, amongst which the contributions of Emma Rothschild and Geoffrey Barraclough were outstanding. In all this, the energy crisis was rightly seen as symptomatic of a much deeper crisis of industrial society. The confident progressivism of the post-1945 era was checked. The mood of anxiety and uncertainty was extended backwards to bring into question the whole mode of development of the industrial societies to date. Some proclaimed the 'end of the hydro-carbon age', some even 'the end of industrialism'. Small was rediscovered to be beautiful. Serious attention was paid to alternative forms of technology, powered by alternative, renewable sources of energy such as sun, sea, and wind. The whole structure of work and bureaucratic organization, as this had taken shape over two centuries, was declared to be in need of re-examination. To most reflective people it was evident, at the very least, that certain assumptions built into the pattern of development of industrial societies were now very shaky. Rapid and continuous economic growth was one of these. Some fundamental readjustment, some shift of direction, seemed urgent and necessary.

My thinking during these years was undoubtedly affected by the new mood, although I can honestly say that I was predisposed to go along with it in any case. The post-industrial idea was now more firmly seen in perspective as a product of an epoch of exceptional growth and abundance (although I have never thought that it can be dismissed just because of this, any more, say, than Marx's theory of capitalism can be dismissed because of the end of the epoch of *laissez-faire*). It may well in fact turn out to be the last, and by no means the least, theory of industrial society which is still basically couched in the terms of classic industrialism. At any rate, I certainly felt the need to pose the question: if not the post-industrial society *à la* Bell, what then? What alternative lines of development are conceivable, what emerging, in the last three decades of the twentieth century? The last two chapters offer some thoughts on this. They are very preliminary and tentative, and some are bound to find them unduly fanciful. But it seemed to me that some effort had to be made in this direction, in rounding off this account of the theory and practice of industrial society.

*

Preface

I should like to offer my grateful thanks for help and support to Jill Norman, of Penguin Books. To Ray Pahl, Professor of Sociology at the University of Kent and the general editor of Penguin Sociology, I owe a good deal more than is usually owed to series editors. He was not only responsible for suggesting the initial idea for this book but, as a colleague and friend, has over the years been very generous with both his time and his thoughts, in discussing its themes. This book can only have profited from those conversations with him. Thanks are also due, I suspect, to the members of the Acton Society, London, especially (probably) Edward Goodman and Trevor Smith; although what ideas have actually been stolen from the Society's very convivial seminars and dinners could only be determined by someone with a stronger head than mine. Finally I should like to thank John Goy, of the University of Kent library staff, for preparing the index.

KRISHAN KUMAR
Canterbury, February 1977

1 New Worlds

The History of the Human Species as a whole may be regarded as the unravelling of a hidden Plan of Nature for accomplishing a perfect state of Civil Constitution for Society . . . as the sole State of Society in which the tendency of human nature can be all and fully developed.

Immanuel Kant, *Idea of a Universal History on a Cosmopolitan Plan* (1784).

Poetic imagination has put the Golden Age in the cradle of the human race, amid the ignorance and brutishness of primitive times; it is rather the Iron Age which should be put there. The Golden Age of the human race is not behind us but before us; it lies in the perfection of the social order. Our ancestors never saw it; our children will one day arrive there; it is for us to clear the way.

Henri de Saint-Simon, *The Reorganization of the European Community* (1814).

1. The Ideologues of Progress

When sociology arrived in Europe early in the nineteenth century, it marked the culmination of a strand of thinking about man and society that was increasingly directed towards the future. Strictly speaking, western social thought had felt the pull of the future ever since, in the fifth century, St Augustine produced his grand work of synthesis, *The City of God.* In this Christian apologia he fused the Greek and Hebraic traditions into a philosophy of history, a theory of development, that looked forward to the end of secular history, and a movement from life in the earthly to life in the heavenly city. Such eschatological preoccupations continued to affect thought and action throughout the subsequent centuries. But the backward-looking spell of the memory of the world of classical antiquity remained, to bewitch thinkers into a sense that the great, golden age of man was really in the past, by comparison with which present times were mean and second-hand. This spell was decisively broken only towards the end of the seventeenth century. It came in the victory of the 'Moderns' over the 'Ancients', following a long-drawn-out literary controversy, and the conviction thereafter that modern philosophy and modern science were not only the equal of that of the ancient world, but immeasurably more pregnant with great and far-reaching developments for mankind.

With this victory, as J. B. Bury was the first to point out a long while ago,[1] the idea of progress became firmly established in the European mind. Mankind could now be seen as advancing, slowly perhaps but inevitably and indefinitely, in a desirable direction. In a sense it was illogical to try to determine the happy end-point of this progression; but the attraction to do so proved irresistible. However dimly perceived, the future was seen in terms of the triumph of some existing quality or principle deemed to be of supreme worth, or as constitutive of man's or society's very nature. It might be reason, science, or liberty. But whatever it was, the principle whose fulfilment was predicted and sometimes promoted cast its light back on to the present and the past. The end, the future, became the vantage point, from which to view the present and past states of mankind; since it was only at the end of man's development that the principle would be seen in its clearest and fullest expression. No doubt, contrariwise, discerning that future would depend on the most fundamental analysis of present trends. But, just as in human biology our interest and the focus of our investigations is on the developed organism and not intrinsically, for themselves, on the materials and processes that produce it, so in social biology, or sociology, the thing that has to be kept in mind, the informing principle of our inquiry, must be the social forms that were in the making, and whose future outlines could only roughly be seen. The chronological line – past, present, and future – was barren as well as deceptive. Only the perspective of the future revealed what was important in the past, and linked it to our lives in the present. The future was the guiding thread. Pascal said it, in the *Pensées*, in a spirit of irony; but what he said would have been taken as a solemn statement of intent by the ideologues of progress: 'The present is never an end, the past and the present are our means. Only the future is our end. Thus we never live; but we hope to live . . .'

The eighteenth century produced numerous, more extended and developed, statements of this sort. Two were especially important to the versions offered by the later sociological tradition: those of Turgot and Condorcet. To these thinkers were later linked two others, also French, and key figures in the establishment of the 'new science' of society: Henri, Comte de Saint-Simon, who was the first to analyse systematically the new industrial society that was emerging, and to suggest a plan for its organization; and Auguste Comte, who gave the new science its name, 'sociology', and laid down an elaborate programme for it to follow which has had a profound influence both in Europe and America. These four – 'the prophets of Paris', their biographer Frank Manuel has called them[2] – were linked by more than the ordinary bonds of intellectual influence. They were disciples and friends, strong bonds even when the friendships turned to bitter enmity. Condorcet was the self-confessed disciple and devoted admirer of Turgot, and in many respects his own work was a fulfilment and a development of the unpublished sketches of the latter. Saint-Simon's work reveals a close reading of Condorcet's writings, down to the existence of a manuscript in which Condorcet's *Progress of the Human Mind* was analysed under explicit headings – 'ideas to be adopted', 'ideas to be rejected'. Comte was for some years Saint-Simon's secretary and his acknowledged pupil, though he later broke sharply with his former master; he, too, wrote of Condorcet as '*mon prédecesseur immédiat*'.

There was therefore an exceptionally strong line linking the eighteenth-century *philosophes* of progress and the nineteenth-century fathers of sociology. And what gave the group its distinctiveness was its fascination with movement and change, its profound impression that human life had experienced a vast and varied succession of different modes of thinking and behaving in the course of history. That succession was of course continuing – such was the discoverable law of social development – and these men felt themselves witnesses to yet another momentous mutation, one which was lifting human life to a newer and higher plane, and whose basic principle and promise could be discerned by all unprejudiced thinkers. Such men could not but be struck by the conviction that the contemporary equals the merely temporary. The tribulations of their private and public lives – amounting, in Condorcet's case, to his condemnation to death by the Jacobins – could be borne on the missionary belief that these were but the travails of the new order. As Manuel says,

> they were intoxicated with the future: they looked into what was about to be and they found it good. The past was a mere prologue and the present a spiritual and moral, even a physical, burden which at times was well nigh unendurable. They would destroy the present as fast as possible in order to usher in the longed-for future, to hasten the end.[3]

In the movement of thought towards the future, Turgot played a particularly significant part. His lectures on the successive advances of the human mind, delivered at the Sorbonne in 1750, constitute by general agreement the first important statement in modern times of the ideology of progress. Progress for him was not simply a fact, written into the past records of mankind; it was the very principle of the human as opposed to the natural order, and it was for this reason that the future promised a happier and more perfect state. The bare statement of this view, repeated a hundred times in the century following,[4] conceals the really radical, and necessary, departure accomplished by Turgot. For what Turgot was doing was to reassert the autonomy of the human world, as against the very influential contemporary efforts to assimilate the human to the natural order. The triumphant success of Newtonian physics dazzled the eighteenth-century philosophers. They hoped to discover in human society a principle of order, of equilibrium, equivalent to the operations of gravity in Newton's mechanical universe. Montesquieu's great masterpiece of the mid-century Enlightenment, *The Spirit of the*

Laws, was conceived basically in mechanistic terms; the good polity was subject to technical breakdown because of a failure to operate in accordance with its true character. The genius legislator, by fathoming the spirit of a nation's laws, could effect a restoration, and set the machine working once more so that it might continue its regular motions. Similarly, Adam Smith's model of the 'natural' economy, in *The Wealth of Nations*, was conceived in the image of a self-balancing machine: man's propensity to truck, barter, and exchange gave rise to actions obeying impersonal laws – such as the law of supply and demand – which, if not distorted by 'unnatural' interventions on the part of the political authority, maintain the system in a state of mechanical equilibrium.

Turgot chafed under this static conception, with its motif of regularity and recurrence. Against it he posited a primary, more or less innate, human tendency to *movement*, which led to a principle unique to the human world, that of progress, and which was directly antithetical to the principle of recurrence in the physical world. As he put it in the opening statement of his second lecture, the *Tableau philosophique des progrès successifs de l'esprit humain*:

> The phenomena of nature, subject to constant laws, are enclosed in a circle of revolutions which are always the same. Everything is reborn, everything perishes, and through successive generations in which vegetation and animal life reproduce themselves time merely restores at each instant the image which it has caused to disappear. The succession of men, however, presents a changing spectacle from century to century. Reason, the passions, liberty, produce new events without end. All ages are linked to each other by a series of causes and effects which binds the present state of the world with all those which have preceded it. The conventional signs of language and writing, affording men the means of assuring the possession of their ideas and communicating them to others, have fashioned of all detailed forms of knowledge a common treasury, which one generation transmits to another like a legacy that is ever being augmented with the discoveries of each century, and thus the human race, considered from its beginnings, appears to the eyes of a philosopher to be one immense whole which, like every individual, has its infancy and its progress.[5]

There was a special historical oddity in this striking and original separation of the natural and the human worlds. Firstly it went sharply against the grain of what is generally thought to be one of the deepest tendencies of the thought of the Enlightenment: the striving to find a total philosophy whose principles were so fundamental and so general that they were applicable to the whole of creation. Some form of social Newtonianism was an easy, and popular, resolution of this endeavour. But secondly, Turgot's conception marked the beginning of what was to be only a very temporary phase in which the distinctiveness of the natural and the human or social was insisted upon. Early in the nineteenth century the world of nature and the world of man were reunited, thereby continuing and intensifying the dominant intellectual tendency inaugurated by the scientific revolution of the seventeenth century. The point is that Turgot's conception was essential for the development of the science of man, so long as the reigning scientific 'world-view' was the mechanistic universe of Newtonian physics. Such a view simply did not allow for the change, the temporality, the novelty, in a word, the progressiveness, of the human world. But by the mid-nineteenth century the scientific influence was of a quite different kind. Not physics now, but geology and especially biology were at the centre of attention. And the work of Buffon, Lamarck, Lyell, and Darwin had introduced into the world of nature precisely those elements of change and novelty that Turgot had insisted on as the principles of the human order. The theory of the evolution of the natural world squared uncannily well – too well, as it turned out – with the conception of change and progress – 'from infancy to maturity' – in the social world. Indeed it isn't far-fetched to suppose that the attention to change brought by the idea of progress stimulated inquiries in an evolutionary direction in the natural sciences. At any rate, to complement the theory of social evolution – which is what Turgot more or less invented – there was now a highly satisfactory theory of natural – geological and biological – evolution. The natural and the social worlds could now be seen as continuous; human social evolution was a special case of biological evolution in general; the principles of order and change in the one applied equally to the other. The ghost raised by Turgot, of an utterly divided order of creation, was, for some time at least, laid. The curiosity is that Turgot should have perpetrated the scare while preparing the ground for one of the most total, most monistic intellectual systems of all time – that of the 'positive philosophy' of Saint-Simon, Comte, Spencer, and a host of other theorists of the nineteenth century.

Turgot raised the flag of the future on the ideal plane. The French Revolution did so on the plane of actuality. No other event in the history of modern times has so powerfully aroused the sentiments of novelty, transformation, and the creation of a new order. As Alexis de Tocqueville later wrote, 'no previous political upheaval, however violent, had aroused such passionate enthusiasm, for the ideal the French Revolution set before itself was not merely a change in the French system but nothing short of a regeneration of the whole human race.' Edmund Burke, severely critical of its course as he was, was drawn to say that 'all circumstances taken together, the French Revolution is the most astonishing that has hitherto happened in the world.' 'How much the greatest event in the history of the world and how much the best,' Charles James Fox greeted the fall of the Bastille. Goethe declared that the victory of the French revolutionaries at Valmy in 1792 marked a new era in man's history. And Hegel waxed ecstatic over the fact that the French Revolution had revealed the great secret of human history, as the progressive realization of Reason: 'Never since the sun had stood in the firmament and the planets revolved around him had it been perceived that man's existence centres in his head, i.e., in Thought, inspired by which he builds up the world of reality . . . This was accordingly a glorious mental dawn. All thinking beings shared in the jubilation of this epoch.'[6]

The very word 'revolution' was re-charged, and given a new significance. Since classical times the uses of the word in political and social life had reflected pretty faithfully its clear etymological root. Revolution meant a turning back, or a turning round, as in the motions of a wheel. Plato and later classical writers used the term to mark the various stages of the cyclical progression that they saw as the inevitable pattern of human affairs, as much as it was the pattern so clearly revealed in nature by the revolutions of the seasons. Later in Europe astronomical usage heavily influenced political applications of the concept. The associations with the natural world were hence retained. When applied to the affairs of men, revolution could only connote the stages of the recurrent, cyclical patterns of government that were the human analogue of the regular, lawfully revolving motions of the planets and stars.

This conception conspicuously lacked any idea of novelty. It was in this that the French Revolution was so decisive. It was in the course of the French Revolution that the word 'revolution' acquired its modern meaning, its modern associations of novelty and fundamental change. It was only then that 'revolution' ceased to be a phenomenon of the natural or divine order, made by non-human, elemental forces, and became part of a man-made conscious purpose to create a new order based on reason and freedom.[7] No matter that this particular attempt failed to make and secure the new world. Henceforward the idea of fundamental transformation, of the whole restructuring of human society, became deeply lodged in the European mind and, by a later export, in the consciousness of the rest of the world.

Nor was it necessary that this transformation should be brought about by violence, in the manner of the French attempt. The lesson drawn from the course of the French Revolution – particularly by those thinkers whom we are considering – was that revolutionary violence was at most an expedient, necessary perhaps in the conditions of particular societies, to hasten on the changes already being effected by more fundamental, long-term social and intellectual forces. The new society matures in the womb of the old, as Marx was later to put it; 'force is the midwife to the old society pregnant with the new.' Against which Lenin later pencilled in the laconic comment, 'Some births are difficult, others are easy.' Political revolution was to become an obsession for some of the self-styled disciples of the early sociologists. But for the masters themselves it was always a secondary matter. The revolution that absorbed them, that they saw working itself out before their eyes, that they sought to analyse and promote with all their strength: this revolution had altogether grander dimensions. It was nothing less than the coming into being of an entirely new order of society, one based on reason and science, whose realization would necessarily have as a consequence the fullest extension of human freedom.

It is an irony not uncommon in history, that one of the most powerful and influential statements of this view should have been written by a man fleeing from the agents of that very French Revolution that did so much to further this conception. In 1793 the Marquis de Condorcet, one of the earliest and most enthusiastic supporters of the Revolution, and a fervent disciple of Turgot, was in hiding in Paris, condemned to death by the Jacobins for his former Girondist stance. In the shadow of the guillotine he composed the *Esquisse d'un tableau historique des progrès de l'esprit humain* (*Sketch for a Historical Picture of the Progress of the Human Mind*). Condorcet has been described as 'the last of the *philosophes*', and his *Esquisse* as 'a dramatic paean, a passionate affirmation of rationalist faith, the climactic expression of the eighteenth century quest for reason in history'.[8] In it he synthesized and bodied out the ideas of Turgot and of the other eighteenth-century ideologists of progress, giving however to those ideas a form and an utterance vastly bolder and more appealing than any of his predecessors. The *Esquisse* was the form in which the eighteenth-century idea of progress was generally assimilated by western thought. It was a consciously written manifesto, which was necessarily referred to both by those who affirmed allegiance to its message – such as Saint-Simon and Comte – and by those who denounced it. Malthus' pessimistic *Essay on Population* appeared as a formal refutation of Condorcet's ideas. The influential conservative school of de Maistre made the tenets of the *Equisse* the main target of their war on the ideology of the eighteenth-century Enlightenment; de Bonald anathematized it as the 'Apocalypse of the new Gospel'.[9]

Much of what Condorcet had to say expressed in a terser, more self-evident way, Turgot's idea of the inherent capacity of man for change and progress, and thus of his history as the progressive realization of that capacity. Man had so far progressed through nine stages; the tenth, of which the French Revolution was the herald, lay in the future. But in a number of ways Condorcet significantly modified the tenor of Turgot's thought, and introduced elements which were to feature centrally in the sociological schemes of Saint-Simon and Comte.

Condorcet radically secularized the philosophy of history that he inherited from Turgot. What Turgot offered was still a theodicy – one, it is true, couched in concrete, historical terms, but still penetrated by the idea that behind the laws of history there lay a transcendental sanction, corresponding to the unique, divinely-ordained quality of human history as opposed to natural history. Providence was still the guiding force of history, as it had been for St Augustine. Condorcet, atheist and passionate secularist, not only took God out of the story, he injected his account with a virulent anti-religious bias. The laws of human history were seen as the products of that history itself, the results of the activities of men and not of God. Progress was an autonomous human creation, not the expression of the divine purpose working itself out on earth.

With this ejection of a residual theology, Condorcet could begin the process of reuniting the worlds of man and of nature, so impressively pulled apart by Turgot. He could do so because he kept the basic idea that the laws of human society were not the laws of a static system, like the laws of equilibrium, but dynamic, temporal and historical. The fact of progress, and of its necessary continuation into the future, could be demonstrated from the facts of history with the same degree of probability, and with the same lack of any absolute certainty, that Hume had shown characterized the laws of nature. The idea of progress and the methods of science could be reconciled. The phenomena of the human and of the physical worlds were all on the same plane, all susceptible to observation and explanation by the same method. 'They are equally susceptible of being calculated,' wrote Condorcet, 'and all that is necessary, to reduce the whole of nature to laws similar to those which Newton discovered with the aid of the calculus, is to have a sufficient number of observations and a mathematics that is complex enough.'

Peace having been made with the methodology of the future, it was possible to ask what this new science of history could deliver with regard to the society of the future. And here Condorcet made claims strikingly similar to those soon to be advanced by Auguste Comte, the designator if not the founder of sociology, the new science of society. History, thought Condorcet, was 'a science to foresee the progression of the human species', a science of social prediction which could be a source of great power. For by foreknowledge it was possible to 'tame the future' (Comte's '*prévoir pour pouvoir*'). The careful study of history revealed the central developmental tendencies of the evolution of society, and by the extrapolation of these we were in a position to see something of the future stages of that evolution. 'These observations on what man has been and what he is today will later lead to the means of assuring and accelerating the new progressions which human nature still permits him to hope for.'

'A science to foresee the progression of the human species' – one hardly dared hope to find so apt and complete a description of the intellectual enterprise later embarked upon by the pioneers of sociology. For here is Comte's pronouncement of the aim of the new science, sociology:

> The aim of every science is foresight [*prévoyance*]. For the laws established by observation of phenomena are generally employed to foresee their succession. All men, however little advanced, make true predictions, which are always based on the same principle, the knowledge of the future from the past . . . The foresight of the astronomer who predicts with complete precision the state of the solar system many years in advance is absolutely the same in kind as that of the savage who predicts the next sunrise. The only difference lies in the extent of their knowledge. Manifestly, then, it is quite in accordance with the nature of the human mind that observation of the past should unveil the future in politics, as it does in astronomy, physics, chemistry, and physiology. The determination of the future must even be regarded as the direct aim of political science, as in the case of the other positive sciences. Indeed, it is clear that knowledge of what social system the

elite of mankind is called to by the progress of civilization – knowledge forming the true practical object of positive science – involves a general determination of the next social future as it results from the past.[10]

The overriding commitment to the prediction of future states of society was one element in Condorcet's legacy to nineteenth-century sociology. The other was equally influential, in touching on an aspect of the idea of progress that haunted the minds and affected the actions of many a nineteenth-century thinker. If the progress of mankind was inevitable, stretching in a continuous chain from man's infancy to the furthest point of his development, what then should be the role of the individual at any given stage? In a strict sense there should really be nothing for him to do but acknowledge the inevitability of change, welcome it when it came, and commit himself to the direction of its currents as they pulled him along. But few were willing to rest on this position, for the good reason that very few thinkers, and none of the important ideologists of progress, held to a view of progress as mechanical as this sketch implied. They were none of them mindless Panglossians, accepting all the features of any given society, at any stage, as the necessary germs of the next stage. They realized that there were distortions, lags, retardations, powerful counter-progressive forces, at all stages in the progress of man. While none of these could ultimately halt that necessary progress, they could put mankind to much suffering in the process of trying to do so.

There was therefore a special merit, argued Condorcet – and others after him – in promoting the tide of progress, easing the birth-pangs of the new society. Indeed on a rational understanding of history it became the duty of every enlightened being to throw his energies into shaping and developing the forces of progress. Especially was this true at this point in time when, as indicated by the French Revolution, mankind was on the verge of a passage to an order of society marked by the highest utilization of its capacity for reason and freedom.

And who were in the vanguard of the advance of reason? To whom should one most be looking, as the prime agency of the transition to the new order? Condorcet's answer was again pregnant with consequences for the whole, more systematic discussion of just this issue in nineteenth-century sociology. It was the scientists who, as a group, carried the seeds of the future within them. Science was the fullest embodiment of the principles and tendencies of the European Enlightenment. It represented the distillation, as it were, in its purest form of the rationalist philosophy with which the Enlightenment had fought the superstitious and unregenerate forces of Church and State. Therefore the new society, whose whole informing principle was to be rationality, should be guided and shaped by the men of science.

There is no need here to go into detail about Condorcet's schemes for the organization of scientists, and the application of scientific techniques and solutions to social problems. We shall find essentially the same conceptions, in a more full-blooded form, in the plans and designs for society of Saint-Simon and Comte. All we have from Condorcet is, in any case, a fragment, in the form of a commentary on Bacon's *New Atlantis*. Briefly, he envisaged a body of scientists constituting the supreme body within the state, separate from and above all other political institutions. The spirit of science would infuse itself into the thought and behaviour of all citizens of the new order. Instead of the old pursuits of power, riches, and military glory, men of talent would pour their energies in the direction of scientific achievement. Judgements of worth, status, and honour would now turn on scientific promise and the practical fulfilments of that promise, which would be aided by all the resources of the society. 'The love of truth assembles there the men whom the sacrifice of ordinary passions has rendered worthy of her; and enlightened nations, aware of all that she can do for the happiness of the human species, lavish upon genius the means of unfolding its activity and its strength.' Scientific reasoning and calculation would be applied to all problems of values and ethics, so that social conflicts could be resolved by appeal to criteria which were universally accepted.

Frank Manuel's comment points up admirably the long-ranging significance of these tentative figurations:

In Condorcet's last manuscripts there continually obtruded grave misgivings about the decisions of any public bodies which were not technically competent as experts. With the accumulation of sufficient data and the application of the calculus of probabilities the state could be run by social mathematics – without debates. With one leap the first sociologist of scientific creativity traversed the age of middle-class parliamentarism and arrived at the ideal of the all-knowing scientific technician as the ruler of society.[11]

And with such a leap Condorcet rounded off the eighteenth-century legacy. His sociological successors of the nineteenth century now possessed the main elements for elaborating a systematic theory of social development, and for situating the society of their own times within this framework. There was the postulate of mankind's evolution, from infancy to maturity, and of its necessary progress. There was the notion of stages of development, each stage leading upwards on an ascending scale, and each being more or less continuous with the last and the next. There was the perception that the transition from one stage to the next was not a regular and mechanical process, but needed to be aided and promoted: by individual men of genius, or whole groups which could discern the emerging future shape of society and devoted themselves to realizing it. Crucially, perhaps, there was the sense that man stood on the edge of one of the most momentous transformations of all his history, that in the ideas and the events around him could be seen innumerable witnesses to this fact. The future beckoned urgently, and the promise it held out could only adequately be gauged by the chaos that might result if the forces of progress were not all combined in the task of bringing the new society into being. Of those forces the most important were science, the men of science, and all those who could see in the achievements of the scientific method the highest fulfilment of the Enlightenment, and the key to the future direction and organization of society.

2. Saint-Simon: The Science of Society and the Society of Science

The philosophy of the eigteenth century was critical and revolutionary, that of the nineteenth will be inventive and organizational.

Saint-Simon, Motto for a projected *New Encyclopaedia* (1810).

If the society of the future was the society of science, then the science of society, sociology, had to be considered the master guide to that future. The eighteenth-century theorists had already indicated the need for a systematic philosophy of history by which each age could comprehend its place in the continuum past, present, and future; and by which it could adjust its institutions and practices to the requirements of its current stage of evolution. It was the claim of the early sociologists to have found such a systematic science of society.

The word 'sociology' itself, coined by Comte, did not make its appearance until 1838, after which it passed into general currency; but the thing clearly existed much earlier. Earlier writers, such as Saint-Simon, talked of 'social physiology', or social, moral, or political science, or 'the science of man'. The intent was the same in these cases as in the later 'sociology'. It was to put the study of human behaviour and human society on the same sound footing as had been achieved in the sciences dealing with the natural world. The social sciences, by assimilating the well-tried and well-proven methods of the natural sciences, were to become as objective, as precise and predictive, as they were. The scientists of the Institut de France, the self-styled 'idéologues' of the Directory period of the French Revolution, were apparently the first to apply the term 'positive' to the triumphantly successful methodology of contemporary natural science. Saint-Simon adopted the term in 1807 to express the common denominator, in a methodological sense, of all the modern sciences, natural and social. Thereafter the term, and the ambition that went with it, was widely diffused. 'Positivism' became the creed of all those who believed that there was but one science. It had many branches, embracing all the phenomena of the natural and social worlds, and they were not all equally well developed. But there could only be one method, that general one which – or so it was thought – had allowed Newton to calculate the movements of the heavenly bodies, and Lavoisier to isolate oxygen; and which was to account for the triumphs of Lyell in geology and Darwin in biology. Hitherto the science of man and society had limped behind those of physics and chemistry; soon it would not only equal but crown their achievements. This was the common theme of the writings of the major early sociologists, Saint-Simon, Comte, Spencer, Marx. Later Marxists were inclined to jib at the positivism of Engels' pronouncement at Marx's graveside, that 'just as Darwin discovered the law of development of organic nature, so Marx discovered the law of development of human history'. But it is doubtful if Marx would have taken offence – he did after all wish to dedicate *Capital* to Darwin – and in any case it is certainly in keeping with the spirit not only of his own endeavours but that of a host of other nineteenth-century social theorists.

Of all the early expounders of the idea of a science of society, there is one who has special claims on our attention: Henri, Comte de Saint-Simon. He is not perhaps the best of them, certainly not the best known, and his influence was diffuse rather than direct. But his was the earliest, and in many ways still the most powerful, vision of a new order of society, corresponding to which would be an entirely new way of thinking about society. Saint-Simon was the immediate descendant of the philosophic tradition that included Turgot and Condorcet. Indeed much of the force of his often bizarre life and writings stems from the fact that he had one foot in the aristocratic *salons* of the eighteenth-century Enlightenment and another in the bourgeois *cafés* of the nascent industrial age. As a liberal aristocrat of the eighteenth century, he fought in the French Army against the British in the American War of Independence; later he was a radical republican and Dantonist in the early stages of the French Revolution. Imprisoned and almost executed by the Jacobins during the Terror, he survived to be the patron and associate of the brilliant circle of scientists who flourished during the Directory. The

Empire found him urging Napoleon to be a new Charlemagne and to unite Europe on the basis of the emerging scientific and industrial order; with little need of alteration, he was urging substantially the same thing on the statesmen gathered at the Congress of Vienna, when he proposed the integration of the states of Europe and the establishment of a European Parliament. In his later years he emerged in his most important and characteristic role, as the champion and ideologue of the scientists, bankers and industrialists whom he saw as the creative force of the new society; while from his sayings and writings his disciples, the Saint-Simonian sect, gleaned enough material to turn his doctrine into one of the earliest forms of socialism.

Even this very brief recital of his activities gives some indication of Saint-Simon's interest to us, as a striking and original figure transitional between the two ages of feudalism and industrialism. Some further idea of this can readily be got by considering some of the words that Saint-Simon or his immediate disciples introduced into the vocabulary of European social thought. Between 1800 and 1832 they coined: 'individualism', 'positivism', 'industrialism', 'socialism'. They originated the phrase and concept of 'the organization of labour'; and the contrast between the 'bourgeoisie' and the 'proletariat' in the special technical sense of the terms are Saint-Simonian creations. No wonder that, surveying Saint-Simon's contribution from the vantage point of the late nineteenth century, Émile Durkheim was led to conclude that 'in him we encounter the seeds already developed of all the ideas which have fed the thinking of our time';[12] or that George Lichtheim should more recently have observed that 'all told, Saint-Simonism has probably done more to shape our world than any other socialist school except the Marxian (which took over some of the Saint-Simonian inheritance).'[13]

Although Saint-Simon has figured often enough, in histories of social thought, as the founder of positivism and a precursor of modern socialism, this treatment has tended to obscure his real interest to us in our time. Saint-Simon speaks especially forcibly across a century and a half to us because he tried to grasp, and act in, a period of crisis and transformation. In this day it is widely believed that the industrial societies, whose birth he witnessed, are undergoing a parallel process of crisis and transformation, and not a few prophets have been willing to come forward to act the Saint-Simon of the new age. Whether or not the parallel is apt we shall leave for later discussion. But it cannot be denied that there is a sense of profound changes affecting the nature of contemporary industrial societies; and this goes some way to explaining the renewed interest in Saint-Simon.

For there was not a word that Saint-Simon wrote, and almost not an act that he performed, that was not infused with a sense of urgent mission, a conviction that a critical moment had been reached in the development of European societies. More than any thinker before or since, Saint-Simon's writing, and his life, convey to us this powerful impression of standing at the dawn of the industrial civilization of the modern world, of seeing out one age and ushering in the next. What is particularly remarkable about this vision is its precocity, almost its prematureness. In the first two decades of the nineteenth century the Industrial Revolution in England was only just beginning to have perceptible effect on the general life of society; in France the systematic introduction of industrial technology had started only in Saint-Simon's own life-time; in the rest of Europe industrialization was almost entirely a future prospect. And yet without a tremor of doubt or hesitation Saint-Simon seized on the idea that the new world of the nineteenth century was to be *industrial*. In a striking passage he fused the eighteenth-century idea of progress with the perception that the future age was to be the age of the machine:

> The most absurd of beliefs places the golden age in the past. It is the future alone which holds it in store. Giants will return, not giants in stature, but giants in the power of reasoning. Machines will replace the arms of men. The seven-league boots of the fairytale are ordered for humanity by the great captain of the army of workers. Industry is the only politics of peace, because peace is the only politics of nations . . .[14]

Saint-Simon modified Condorcet's rather mechanical conception of the progression of humanity through ten stages.

Progress there certainly was, and he gave nothing to the eighteenth century in the fervour of this conviction: '. . . the supreme law of progress of the human spirit carries along and dominates everything; men are but its instruments . . . it is no more in our power to withdraw ourselves from its influence or to control its action than it is to change at our pleasure the primitive impulse which makes our planet circle the sun.'[15] But Saint-Simon introduced an element of conflict and discordance lacking in Condorcet's account. Without using or apparently being aware of contemporary notions of the 'dialectic', he arrived at the notion that mankind's (inevitable) progress had taken place through a dynamic alternation of 'organic' and 'critical' epochs. Both sorts of epoch were necessary: antagonistic yet complementary forces in a movement that spiralled ever upwards. The 'organic' periods, such as those of the classical civilization of Greece and Rome, or of the feudal societies of medieval Europe, were stable, constructive periods. The societies of those periods were integrated around a single ideal, propounded and developed by élites who were the intellectual vanguard of their time, and whose ideas governed the prevailing political institutions. Such organic periods were always followed by 'critical' periods, in the face of the attempt by the dominant élites to freeze the flow of history, and to cling to power on the basis of outmoded understanding and ideals. Critical epochs were fundamentally transitional between two organic ones. They were periods of doubt and criticism, of conflicts between the old and the new ideologies and élites, of war and revolution. Inevitably they were succeeded by organic epochs, in which societies were once more integrated, but now on the basis of a new ideal and under the leadership of a new élite.

In the final form of his philosophy of history Saint-Simon identified three organic epochs linked by two transitional, critical, epochs. There was first the age of classical antiquity, with an ideology of polytheism and a social order based on slavery. Somewhere around the third and fourth centuries A.D. occurred the disintegration of the ancient world, expressing the passage of a critical epoch which led ultimately to a new level of integration in the Christian states of medieval Europe. This second organic epoch had a 'theological' ideology and a social order based on feudalism. From about the twelfth century new forces were already undermining this civilization; by the eighteenth century it was on its deathbed, sapped by a critical period that had reached its extreme point in the destructive-creative onslaught of the Enlightenment *philosophes*. Now, in Saint-Simon's own life-time, the third organic civilization was coming into being. Its ideology was that of science, or positivism; its social system was industrial.

Saint-Simon returned again and again, to the point almost of obsession, to the parallel between the crisis of the ancient world, at the time of the later Roman Empire, and the crisis which European feudal society had as yet barely surmounted, and whose most explicit manifestations had been the Enlightenment and the French Revolution. In each case the turmoil was both spiritual and temporal; and in each case there had to succeed an order of society based on new philosophical (or religious) and political principles.

The transition which is now taking place is composed, like the preceding one, of two elements: one philosophical, the other political. The first consists in the passage from the theological to the terrestrial and positive system; the second, in the passage from a regime of arbitrary rule to a liberal and industrial regime. The philosophical revolution has long since begun, because we should trace its origins back to the study of positive sciences introduced into Europe by the Arabs more than ten centuries ago. To complete this revolution we have to accomplish only one more thing: we must finish the comprehensive work necessary for the organization of a positive system, whose elements now exist isolated. The transition in its political form can be said to date from Luther's Reformation. Although this political transition has been less catastrophic than the political transition from polytheism to theism, it has already produced great misfortunes; it was the issue behind the Thirty Years' War, the two English revolutions of the seventeenth century, and the French Revolution.[16]

It is scarcely necessary to stress how influential this schematic outline of European history has been. More important perhaps is the implication, equally influential, that systems of thought do not prosper until the social conditions appropriate to their appearance and spread have 'ripened', and that theorizing, consequently, is an activity closely tied to the stage of social development of the society. For

first a system of social order has to be established, comprising a very numerous population and being composed of several nations, lasting over the whole possible period for that system, before a theory can be grounded on that great experience. Only then can we be capable of 'distinguishing', as it were, at first glance, which improvements are part of the natural stages of development of the social state and which are not, and in what order.[17]

A 'positive' science of society, then, could not have emerged earlier, before a 'positive' order of society had appeared, at least in its distinctive outline. It was idle to berate past ages for not having established a true theory of society when their social conditions had not suggested such a theory. The thought of each age had a necessary part to play in the progression towards a full understanding of the laws of social development. To each age its own task. 'The philosophy of the eighteenth century was critical and revolutionary, that of the nineteenth will be inventive and organizational' – so ran the motto of Saint-Simon's project of 1810 for a *New Encyclopaedia*. But equally this implied that each age would not let itself be seduced by the preoccupations of the preceding one. It would acknowledge and acclaim the promulgation of the new philosophy of the age. It would reform its social organization and political institutions in accordance with the new economic forces and intellectual ideals, under the leadership of the most creative class.

Saint-Simon had no doubt that all these things would ultimately happen: such was the law of progress. But he was disturbed and perplexed by the failure of his contemporaries to seize the opportunities so clearly offered to them by the recent developments in Europe. The social and intellectual forces that were to bring in the new world of industrialism had been maturing since at least the twelfth century. In most European states, especially those of the west, these forces had become patent by the eighteenth century. But the class that should have inherited had failed to do so. The course of the French Revolution, in particular, was an instructive example of the fact that progress was not mere mechanical progression. It depended upon a perception of the true tendencies of the time, together with a willingness to act upon that knowledge.

The French Revolution, according to Saint-Simon, was the culmination of two broad currents of change that had their origins deep in the period of European feudalism. The first was the development of science, as against the system of revealed religion, and a corresponding growth to influence of the class of scientists as against the authority of the priests. The second development was the progressive emancipation of the medieval communes which, developing beyond the confines of feudalism proper, had given rise to a dynamic and economically expansive class. This comprised first the traders and bankers of the era of commercial expansion; later the workers and industrialists of the new workshops and factories. These two revolutionary developments represented ultimately the triumph of the industrial society over the feudal state. Together they progressively undermined the social order of feudalism, creating over a period of six centuries a state of society 'which engendered and necessitated a political revolution . . .' Thus, 'if one insists on attributing the French Revolution to one source, it must be dated from the day the liberation of the communes and the cultivation of exact sciences in western Europe began.'[18]

These social forces contained all the ingredients of the new scientific industrial society. It was open to them not simply to deliver the final blows to the old system but to found the new. They should have shrugged aside the failing power of the old élites, military and aristocratic. The industrial society is a society of production. It consists of 'two great families: that of intellectuals, or industrials of theory, and that of immediate producers, or scholars of application'.[19] Saint-Simon later added the artists to these two groups, as fulfilling necessary expressive functions in the new society. This three-part élite, of scientists, industrialists, and artists, is the natural manager of the industrial society. Political rulers in the old sense will be unnecessary. Not only can the political class be dispensed with, but also the military, since the politics of industrialism are the politics of peace, both nationally and internationally. In addition there are other groups of non-productive 'idlers', mere consumers: courtiers, the owners who do not work and so are unproductive, lawyers and career politicians, and the whole army of clerks and administrators who staff the state bureaucracies. All these could have been put to useful, productive work, or suppressed. The producing class, which in any case is the numerical majority of the population, could then have reorganized the political constitution of the society in such a way that they in their own persons, acting through organs which they themselves constituted, would have taken on the necessary managerial roles of the industrial society.

But what in fact happened? The industrialists and scientists, far from stepping in to take power, allowed the course of the French Revolution to be dominated by a ruthless but shallow and parasitical group, the lawyers and professional politicians, the 'metaphysicians'. It was this group, the real basis of the Jacobin phase of the Revolution, who misled the nation into thinking that the problems of society could be resolved by a politics of power, a mere rearrangement of the forms of government. They could not see, and the industrialists did not force them to see, that the politics of power were the politics of the old regime. The new society, which was straining to be born, could not come into existence until 'government', rule over men, had been replaced by 'administration', the self-management of society by the productive classes who essentially constituted the society. Thus:

> The men who brought about the Revolution, the men who directed it, and the men who, since 1789 and up to the present day, have guided the nation, have committed a great political mistake. They have sought to improve the governmental machine, whereas they should have subordinated it and put administration in the first place. They should have begun by asking a question the solution of which is simple and obvious. They should have asked who, in the present state of morals and enlightenment, are the men most fitted to manage the affairs of the nation. They would have been forced to recognize the fact that the scientists, artists and industrialists, and the heads of industrial concerns are the

men who possess the most eminent, varied, and most positively useful ability, for the guidance of men's minds at the present time. They would have recognized the fact that the work of the scientists, artists, and industrialists is that which, in discovery and application, contributes most to national prosperity. They would have reached the conclusion that the scientists, artists and leaders of industrial enterprises are the men who should be entrusted with administrative power, that is to say, with the responsibility for managing the national interests . . .[20]

From Saint-Simon's point of view, then, the French Revolution was a revolution *manqué*. It should have inaugurated the new world of the industrial society. It should have been the political expression of the rise to their proper influence of the producers. Instead it had continued the politics of the old order. By an unnatural twist, against the tendencies of the time, it had forced France, and the whole of Europe, into a false, wasteful and bloody path. The Revolution, which was fundamentally a European one, had still to be terminated. And 'only the industrial doctrine, when adopted, can end the revolution.' Most of Saint-Simon's life, intellectual and practical, was dedicated to making the world see this. In his writings he tried to show that there could be a true science of man and society, one that could uncover the principles of change and persistence in human society. Such a science, which was only possible because the social forces underlying its development had sufficiently matured, made it clear that an era of epoch-making transition was under way. Therefore that science – 'sociology' – had essentially to be about the making of the new society. Sociology, the science of society, had to take as its subject matter the forces dissolving the old society and bringing in the new, the society of science. It had in effect to suggest the principles of reorganization of European society on the eve of the coming scientific and industrial order.[21] This, in his sketch of the future society under the management of the scientists, industrialists, and artists, was what Saint-Simon tried to do. In practical terms, it meant making the scientists and industrialists conscious of their mission, and spurring them on to action. This Saint-Simon signally failed to do.

Saint-Simon died in 1825. In some obvious ways, had he returned at the end of the century, he might have been very satisfied with the uses to which his legacy had been put. There was scarcely a European intellectual, or European school of thought, that had not been influenced, sometimes profoundly, by his ideas. Saint-Simonism became a key ingredient of the positivist sociology of Comte, Spencer and Durkheim; Continental socialism everywhere, especially in France, Germany and Russia, was heavily indebted to it; it even crossed the Channel and modified English individualism, through its decisive influence on Thomas Carlyle and John Stuart Mill. At the practical level, Saint-Simonism became the leading ideology of industrialization on the Continent – 'the religion of the engineers', F. A. Hayek calls it. The temple of this religion was the Ecole Polytechnique, devoted to the cultivation of the applied sciences, which had been founded at the height of scientific enthusiasm in 1794. It became the centre from which was diffused the Saint-Simonian influence throughout nineteenth-century France and Europe.[22] Comte himself was described as 'a Saint-Simon who had been through the École Polytechnique'; many of Saint-Simon's friends and disciples were students there; and many of the leading French scientists, engineers, bankers and financiers had their Saint-Simonian baptism either at the École or by close contact with the Saint-Simonian movement that developed from there after Saint-Simon's death.

The English editor of Saint-Simon's writings, Felix Markham, comments that 'it is not too much to say that the Saint-Simonians were the most important single force behind the great economic expansion of the Second Empire, particularly in the development of the banks and railways.'[23] It was a prominent Saint-Simonian, Prosper Enfantin, who organized the formation of the Paris–Lyons–Mediterranean railway in 1852; it was two Saint-Simonian brothers, the Pereires, who founded the Crédit Mobilier, also in 1852, and so established the basic type or model of Continental capitalism, 'finance capitalism', with the banks as an organizing and controlling centre, directing under a coherent programme industrial concerns, railway systems, town-planning activities, and public utilities. Hayek writes of these Saint-Simonians that it cannot be denied that they succeeded in changing the economic structure of Continental countries into something quite different from the English type of competitive capitalism . . . Even if the *Crédit Mobilier* of the Pereires ultimately failed, it and its industrial concerns became the model on which the banking and capital structure in most of the industrial countries of Europe were developed, partly by other Saint-Simonians.[24]

Perhaps we might add as a final spectacular example of Saint-Simonian activity the construction of the Suez Canal, a project thought up by Enfantin, whose 'Société d'études pour le Canal de Suez' provided de Lesseps with the results of all its research.

It is an impressive list of intellectual influences and practical activities. And yet the ghost of Saint-Simon, hovering over Europe at the end of the century, might still have turned away in disappointment. For in many ways crucial to his thought, it was *not* Saint-Simon's century. True, industrialization had gone on apace, but it had nowhere produced 'the industrial society' – the society managed by and in the interests of the producers, the 'industrials of theory' and the 'scholars of application'. To only a very small extent had the men of the nineteenth century realized that the important requirement of industrialism was *organizational* philosophy and an *organized* social order. Instead the crude working ideologies had been liberalism, constitutionalism, individualism, utilitarianism, *laissez-faire*. The practice of states too had been irrational and out of keeping with the fundamental postulates of the industrial society. Industrialism was a supranational system and could only find its fulfilment within an international order. Yet the states of Europe, after the briefest of experiments, had reverted to the worst and most destructive type of competitive nationalism. The politics of the past, the struggle for power, had dominated the national and international arena, under the leadership of the career politicians and militarists who had no natural place in the body of industrial society. Even socialism, the philosophy that most continued the Saint-Simonian emphasis on science, reason, and organization, had been destructive and divisive. For by introducing the doctrine of class warfare *within* the industrial realm, between workers and industrialists, it had destroyed the natural harmony of interests that linked the members of all the producing classes against the idlers and parasites who lived off their productive enterprise. In this way socialism too postponed the day when the new organic order of industrialism could come into being.

If not the nineteenth, what then of the twentieth century? Markham makes the interesting point that 'it cannot be a matter of chance that Saint-Simon's ideas seem in many ways more relevant to the present day than they did to the nineteenth century.'[25] And indeed one of the reasons for concentrating on Saint-Simon, rather than on other more systematic theorists of industrialism, is that he seems so much more our contemporary than other better-known nineteenth-century figures. His fascination lies in the fact that not only does he give us glimpses of the old era of feudalism and the new order of industrialism, but that in some important ways he seems also to jump over both these ages to peer down, however dimly, on a third: our age, the age of the technocratic, planned, administered societies of the late twentieth century, increasingly pushed into supranational groupings by the logic of technological and commercial developments. Out of his writings can be got the elements not just of early capitalism, Marxian socialism, and anarchism, but the more characteristically twentieth-century ideologies of syndicalism, corporatism, managerialism, and state socialism (or state capitalism) – not to mention Europeanism and internationalism. Not just Marx and Proudhon can be held to be in some sense his disciples but Mosca, Pareto, Sorel, Mussolini, Stalin, Burnham.[26]

To be the parent of such diverse offspring might appear to make Saint-Simon the woolliest thinker of the nineteenth century, all things to all men. But in fact it really does the opposite. For what these doctrines have in common are certain elements which are consistently present in Saint-Simon's work, and which can be seen to be the most permanent part of the Saint-Simonian legacy. Two of these in particular seem worth drawing out: the idea that industrialism entails socialism; and the profound hostility to politics as an independent activity, beyond economic life.

Saint-Simon did not himself make the equation between

industrialism and socialism, and indeed it cannot be got from his writings if we think exclusively of the humanist, libertarian socialism, of Marx. But if we think of that central aspect of socialism, in all its varieties, which is concerned with the rational, scientific, efficient organization of society and its natural environment, then it is not difficult to see how his later followers could find the equation in his thought. For according to Saint-Simon, modern society is the society of production. Its most vital trait, its single organizing principle, is the progressive increase of control by man over things. Instead of being preoccupied, like past societies, with the goals of power and domination, it addresses itself exclusively to the goal of increasing the well-being of its members through the peaceful cultivation of the arts, science and industry. Its unique function is the production of useful things. And, since no society can survive long which is based on conflicting principles, all social life must converge on the principle of production. The only normal form that collective activity can take is the industrial form. Society will be fully in harmony with itself only when it is totally industrialized. 'The production of useful things is the only reasonable and positive end that political societies can set themselves.' Society must become a vast production company. 'All society rests on industry. Industry is the only guarantee of its existence. The most favourable state of affairs for industry is, for this reason, the most favourable to society.'[27]

We are already half-way to socialism here, with the vision of modern society as a vast productive enterprise, all its members collectively engaged in the fullest realization of the potential of the scientific industrial society. All that was needed to complete the move was to elevate the 'industrials', the producing classes – scientists, artists, industrialists and proletariat – above the 'idlers', the non-producing classes, and to offer the latter the choice of either accepting the direction of the former or being extinguished. The important principle here was to make the producers, those directly involved in economic activities, the sole directors and managers of the industrial society. At various times in his life Saint-Simon had different ideas of how precisely this was to be done, the main problem being how to get the right combination and balance of the industrialists, the scientists, and the artists. In his most complete scheme he envisaged three Chambers, composed exclusively of the producing classes, which were to constitute the Parliament of the industrial society. Earlier, in his period of infatuation with the scientists, he had proposed a 'Council of Newton' as the supreme directing body. But the variations never affected the main principle. As Durkheim, his most lucid follower, pointed out, the ultimate tendency of Saint-Simon's system was 'to bind economic life to a central organ that regulates it – which is the very definition of socialism'.[28]

It is important to see here how Saint-Simon's analysis of industrialism differed from that of the classical economists, such as Adam Smith. They too argued that the essential principle of modern society was industry, and that economic relationships are the substance, *par excellence*, of collective life. But they saw economic actions as private matters, with the public agency, the state, superimposing as it were a framework of law within which these private activities could be most vigorously pursued. Hence they were led in the direction of the political theory of liberalism. Saint-Simon could never accept this distinction between private and public. Since economic life constitutes the whole of social life, it is unthinkable that the central public organ should play so marginal a role. Indeed the central public organ can have no more important function – if it has any other at all – than the regulation of economic life. Just as in the 'military' societies of the past, all ambitions, activities, and institutions were 'militarized', so in the industrial society of the future all institutions, including the political, must be 'industrialized'. The industrial system is at one with the entire social system of modern societies: it is not just an 'economic' part, separate from 'political' and 'legal' parts. Consequently any directing influence, the necessary action exercised by the whole of the industrial system over its parts, must emanate from society itself; it is the collectivity that must control this activity. As Durkheim put it:

Saint-Simon, having established that henceforth the only normal manifestation of social activity is economic activity, concludes that the latter is a social thing, or rather that it is *the social thing* – since nothing else is possible – and that it must be regarded as such. It must indeed have a collective character unless there is something else that has – unless there is something more common among men. Society cannot become industrial unless industry is socialized. This is how industrialism logically ends in socialism.[29]

From this deduction easily followed, as a corollary, the second idea: the basic irrelevance of politics as a separate science and a separate activity. Since economic life is co-terminous with social life generally, it must form the whole substance of politics. Not only is there a politics of economic interests and activities, there is no other. 'Politics,' says Saint-Simon, 'is the science of production, that is, the science which has for its object the order of things most favourable to all sorts of production.'[30] In that case there cannot be a science of politics as such, neither a class of political theoreticians nor of political practitioners. Politics, the queen of the sciences, Aristotle's master-science, must be dethroned. The state must be subordinated to society. The political realm must be recognized for what it is, a 'superstructure', and all political activities must be absorbed into the industrial base, where they can be directed by those involved in and knowledgeable about production. The problems of industrial society could not be dealt with by a separate class of politicians, rearranging the parts and powers of government on the basis of abstract constitutional theories. That had been the mistake of the lawyers of the French Revolution; and the same mistake was being perpetrated by the liberals of the early nineteenth century, with their endless constitution-mongering. Only the class of 'industrials' could conceive, resolve, and execute the tasks of the industrial society.

In all this Saint-Simon was proclaiming the end of political rule, the exercise of political power, as such. Industrial society had no need of coercion. The men who direct, the scientists and industrialists, do so not because they possess superior political or diplomatic skills, but because they have knowledge. They do not give orders, they only declare what conforms to the nature of things. The scientists state what is known on any particular question; the industrialists apply and execute . longer a case of men controlling men. It is thir. through the mediation of those who understanc indicate the manner in which they should be handled. system,' says Saint-Simon, 'society is governed essentiall in the new it is governed only by principles.'

Basically Saint-Simon takes his model or political rule from the management of large industrial concerns. These, as he sees them, are not governed, they are administered. The managerial bodies that direct them do so in accordance with scientifically-gathered information about the market, pricing, the state of the labour force, and so on. Industrial organizations are not command hierarchies, they are cooperative ventures. The populations of the industrial societies were already being accustomed to 'the administrative mode of conducting affairs' by their experience of participation in industrial life. It would not therefore be a radical innovation to introduce the same methods in regulating the general affairs of society. 'Humankind has been destined by nature to live in society. It was summoned, first, to live under governmental rule. It is destined to pass from governmental or military rule to administrative or industrial rule.'[31] Small wonder that European anarchists could later adopt as their own slogan the Saint-Simonian motto, 'from the government of men to the administration of things'.

It is impossible to overestimate the influence of this conception of politics – or of anti-politics – on European social thought of the nineteenth and twentieth centuries.[32] It is of course a utopian conception, although to say that is to say very little about the source of its great appeal to minds that can hardly be described as naive. Nor was Saint-Simon the only or even the earliest elaborator of the idea. It is contained in Rousseau, and implied in the anatomy of 'civil society' carried out by the classical British economists. Nevertheless it is through Saint-Simon's system that it seems to have affected the major currents of European social thought. It is the line linking Marxist socialists, anarchists, syndicalists, corporatists, and managerialist ideologies of all kinds, including the technocratic élitism of the current prophets of the post-industrial society'. It implied the subordination of the state to society, political life to social and especially economic life, political theory to political economy and sociology. Its great appeal was the possibility of eliminating chance and capriciousness in human life, of bringing instead order and predictability. The great tool for this was to be science, especially social science. The social agency was to be the experts, the men of knowledge, the scientists, engineers, mathematicians and economists, with a leavening of those – bankers and industrialists – who could claim to be honest men of affairs with no political axes to grind and with special skills to offer. Theory, scientific theory, was to govern social practice, thereby eliminating much of the human and material waste caused by the old order of political debate and political conflict. Society would then have completed its long-drawn-out transition to a new organic stage which would be its final one; the revolution would have been terminated at last.

John Stuart Mill, re-encountering Saint-Simon in the form of Comte's *Systeme de Politique Positive*, was driven at the last to denouncing the positivist programme as 'the most complete system of spiritual and temporal despotism that ever issued from the brain of any human being – except, perhaps, Ignatius Loyola'. Be that as it may, the future was to be more accommodating to Saint-Simon's Jesuits than to Mill's liberals.

2 The Great Transformation

> The revolution which broke out between 1789 and 1848 . . . forms the greatest transformation in human history since the remote times when men invented agriculture and metallurgy, writing, the city and the state.
>
> Eric Hobsbawm, *The Age of Revolution 1789–1848* (1962).

> It has lengthened life; it has mitigated pain; it has extinguished diseases; it has increased the fertility of the soil; it has given new securities to the mariner; it has furnished new arms to the warrior; it has spanned great rivers and estuaries with bridges of form unknown to our fathers; it has guided the thunderbolt innocuously from heaven to earth; it has lighted up the night with the splendour of the day; it has extended the range of the human vision; it has multiplied the power of the human muscles; it has accelerated motion; it has annihilated distance; it has facilitated intercourse, correspondence, all friendly offices, all despatch of business; it has enabled man to descend to the depths of the sea, to soar into the air, to penetrate securely into the noxious recesses of the earth, to traverse the land in cars which whirl along without horses, and the ocean in ships which run ten knots an hour against the wind. These are but a part of its fruits, and of its first fruits. For it is a philosophy which never rests, which has never attained, which is never perfect. Its law is progress. A point which yesterday was invisible is its goal today, and will be its starting-post tomorrow.
>
> Thomas Babington Macaulay, *Essay on Bacon* (1837).

> The bourgeois period of history has to create the material basis of the new world . . . Bourgeois industry and commerce create these material conditions in the same way as geological revolutions have

created the surface of the earth. When a great social revolution shall have mastered the results of the bourgeois epoch, the market of the world and the modern powers of production, and subjected them to the common control of the most advanced peoples, then only will human progress cease to resemble that hideous pagan idol, who would not drink the nectar but from the skulls of the slain.

Karl Marx, *The Future Results of British Rule in India* (1853).

1. The Revolution as Myth

The eighteenth-century idea of progress had been in the main abstract and speculative. It postulated stages of development whose actual content was only lightly sketched in, as progressive instalments of reason, or happiness. With Saint-Simon the idea was concretized and given a more substantial body. It was linked firstly to the progress of science and then, in a more directly Baconian tradition, to the progressive applications of science, to the process that Saint-Simon himself caused to be known as *industrialization*. As the nineteenth century developed, the scope and dimension of the change connoted by the term 'industrialization' swelled to gigantic proportions. It came to be seen in apocalyptic terms, as a revolution transforming every aspect of human life and thought. Progress, if the concept were to sustain itself, could now only mean industrialization. And if, as in past ages, there was a dark side to the current phase, this was a remediable phenomenon, necessary but temporary. The logic of industrialism would drive societies forward to a new point of stability: to a new plateau, on a higher plane, where all the dynamic contradictions of the past would be resolved.

The changes which were the first obvious and visible evidence of this revolution were those which took place in England in the first half of the nineteenth century. It was the French who, by analogy with their own Revolution of 1789, were the first to hail these changes as an 'Industrial Revolution', and to make the influential bracketing of the two as a single, all-embracing, world-historical phenomenon.[1] In the earlier years of this century

British academic historians, digging away at the causes, premonitions and characteristics of their industrializing period, became somewhat coy about the term 'revolution', and were inclined to stress the continuity with the past. Such reserve seems to have disappeared, largely no doubt due to a new reflectiveness stimulated by the world-wide efforts at industrialization in this century, and a startled awareness of just how extraordinary was England's achievement in becoming the first industrial society in the history of the world. As Eric Hobsbawm rightly says, 'if the sudden, qualitative, and fundamental transformation, which happened in or about the 1780s, was not a revolution then the word has no common-sense meaning';[2] while Carlo Cipolla, echoing Hobsbawm's remark at the head of this chapter, discourses as follows:

> Between 1780 and 1850, in less than three generations, a far-reaching revolution, without precedent in the history of mankind, changed the face of England. From then on, the world was no longer the same. Historians have often used and abused the word Revolution to mean a radical change, but no revolution has been as dramatically revolutionary as the Industrial Revolution – except perhaps the Neolithic Revolution. Both of these changed the course of history, so to speak, each one bringing about a discontinuity in the historic process. The Neolithic Revolution transformed mankind from a scattered collection of savage bands of hunters . . . into a collection of more or less interdependent agricultural societies. The Industrial Revolution transformed man from a farmer-shepherd into a manipulator of machines worked by inanimate energy.[3]

The causes, course and consequences of the Industrial Revolution are, at one level, a matter for historians to discuss and dispute. But just as with the French Revolution, from the very start the Industrial Revolution was taken out of the realm of history proper and equipped with the mantle of ideology, or myth. It became not just a description of certain linked structural changes in society, but a rallying-cry, a programme for action, a justification of the inevitable harshnesses that must accompany the effort to industrialize. It was celebrated in painting and poetry, as in the factory paintings of Joseph Wright and Philip de

Loutherberg, and Turner's euphoric 'Rain, Steam, Speed'. The Saint-Simonians performed the *Chant des Industriels*, an 'Industrial Marseillaise' composed for them by Rouget de Lisle, the aged author of the famous 'Marseillaise' of the French Revolution. The best architecture of the age was industrial: bridges, canals, railway constructions.[4]

Out of the discrete units making up the Industrial Revolution – the movement from the land to the cities, the massing of workers in the new industrial towns and factories, the separation of work and family life – was compounded a powerful *image of industrialism*, as a social system and a way of life, that was part fact, part fabrication. In the consequent idea of 'the industrial society' lay not a little of the intellectual's longing for logical purity and the artist's longing for aesthetic unity.

This point emerges more strongly if we consider some of the sources of the nineteenth century's image of industrialism. While it was left to sociology to turn that image into a 'model', it is clear that both in the popular consciousness and in the sociologist's model there were ideas and feelings that had their roots in artistic and literary representation, rather than in scientific investigation. A host of writers and thinkers contributed their distinctive responses to the new culture of industrialism, often without any intention of being representative or at all complete in their presentation. In a real sense our notions of industrialism, especially in England, are made up of an amalgam of the novels of Dickens, Mrs Gaskell, George Eliot, Charles Kingsley, and perhaps, at a more rarified level, Balzac; together with the passionate moral and cultural criticism of the industrial society offered by writers such as Thomas Carlyle, Matthew Arnold, and John Ruskin.[5] As Raymond Williams says, such writers, living through the period of transformation, were involved in 'a creative working, a discovery; . . . they were defining the society, rather than merely reflecting it; defining it in novels' – because no one yet had been able to give an adequate sociological definition of it.[6]

Thus, for instance, Dickens' use of London in *Oliver Twist*, *Dombey and Son*, and *Bleak House* became the source of crucial defining experiences of urban life in a new order of society, and one that was highly influential on later European attempts to comprehend the same phenomenon. Even more accessible, and more easily popularized, was his artful evocation in *Hard Times* of a typical northern factory town of the early Industrial Revolution, 'Coketown', which speedily became and long remained a generic symbol of the industrial town.[7] Or there was Carlyle's early and vivid characterization of the way in which industrialism was transformative not just of the external environment of man, but of his internal one too, his innermost values, feelings and beliefs:

> Not the external and physical alone is now managed by machinery, but the internal and spiritual also . . . The same habit regulates not our modes of action alone, but our modes of thought and feeling. Men are grown mechanical in head and heart, as well as in hand . . . Their whole efforts, attachments, opinions, turn on mechanism, and are of a mechanical character . . . Mechanism has now struck its roots down into man's most intimate, primary sources of conviction; and is thence sending up, over his whole life and activity, innumerable stems – fruit-bearing and poison-bearing . . .[8]

Even where the sources were documentary in origin, they tended to enter the consciousness of the time largely through highly selective mediation by writers intent on propagating a particular view of, and a particular solution to, the problems of industrialism. During the 1830s and 1840s in England there appeared a flood of official reports on what following Carlyle came to be known as 'the condition-of-England' question: reports on the conditions in the new factories by the Factory Commissioners, on the employment of children in the mines and factories, on the condition of the dying class of handloom weavers, on the workings of the new Poor Law and the system of workhouses, on the health and housing of the labouring classes. The reports were shocking enough in their own right, especially perhaps for the factuality and sobriety of the presentation. But few people read them in the original, and the versions that did get wide circulation were either directly fictional in form or allowed themselves a good deal of 'poetic licence' in the manner of their reworking of the original material. Thus the reports became the documentary basis for the best-known of the 'industrial' novels, Mrs Gaskell's *Mary Barton* (1848) and *North and South* (1855), Dickens' *Hard Times* (1854), Disraeli's *Sybil, or The Two Nations* (1845), Charles Kingsley's *Alton Locke* (1850), George Eliot's *Felix Holt* (1866). This was of course a quite proper use; but we should not look to these authors for a historically accurate account of the process of industrialization, or even only of the sufferings it produced. As Williams says, such authors, in observing and informing themselves of the conditions of early industrialization, transmuted their materials in such a way as to turn themselves into 'generalizing rhetoricians of human suffering'.[9]

Much the same was true even of many of the purportedly objective and factual versions that were offered. Perhaps the most influential of these, on a European scale, was Engels' *The Condition of the Working Class in England*, first published in German in 1845. Although England was not to receive a translation until 1887, the book was immediately hailed on the Continent as a classic, influencing decisively the generation of early socialists as well as social thinkers of other political persuasions. Fritz Mehring, Marx's celebrated biographer, called it 'one of the foundation stones of socialism'. Marx himself referred to it extensively in *Capital*, and Lenin later wrote that 'it made a profound impression upon the minds of all who read it. Everywhere Engels' study came to be regarded as the best available contemporary account of the condition of the proletariat; and indeed, neither before 1845, nor after, has a single book appeared that presented an equally striking and true picture of the misery of the working class.'[10] It was widely held to be the first systematic account of the social effects of the Industrial Revolution, and many were the later attempts to 'do an Engels' on the effects of industrialization on the Continent.

And yet, as his latest English editors remark, the book is in the nature of 'a brilliant political tract', persuasive by very reason of its high selectivity, compression, and passionate one-sidedness.[11] Although drawing heavily on the official reports and other English investigations, Engels' use was so selective as often to be severely distorting. Evidence from dates as widely scattered as 1801 and 1841 were quoted as illustrative of the same point.[12] Minor movements within the working class, isolated crimes against property reported in the daily newspapers, were all built up into a quite misleading picture of the development of a 'social war' of revolutionary proportions. This, paradoxically, was set down side-by-side with an account that so emphasized the brutalized and degraded condition of the working classes that it was inconceivable that they could play the role of revolutionary liberators written in for them in Engels' epic drama.

Again, given Engels' purpose, there cannot be great reason to complain. The book indeed remains a vivid, superbly written and in many ways remarkably accurate account of the social conditions of early industrialism in England. But to make this rhetorical and dramatized account a main ingredient in a model of the industrialization process in general, as later sociologists were to do, is to give it a status it did not earn.

These remarks are not made to score points off the nineteenth-century novelists and writers of political tracts. Their responses must always form an essential component of any acceptable picture of the social impact of the Industrial Revolution. What needs stressing is the fund of ideas and associations that they deposited in the social consciousness, such that when social theorists came to construct an abstract, general model of the transition to industrialism they drew almost naturally and, as it were, unthinkingly on these deeply-lodged images and sentiments. Quite simply, there really were no other accounts that had penetrated so deeply the surface of the new industrial society in the making. The ideology of industrialism, the expression of its tendencies at the level of culture and political doctrine, preceded the full working out of its structural features (this is strikingly clear in the case of Saint-Simon). This is hardly surprising: it is a normal feature of social change. What makes its implications more troublesome, however, is that the sociologists who were constructing their models were themselves still living in the midst of the revolution, and had an urgent need to make sense of it, to master it. The powerful images supplied by earlier writers, from other societies, became a convenient short-hand for typifying their situation, and abbreviating the actual movement of history. In the course of doing that it was easy to forget, or fail to explore, the particular visions and particular preoccupations that had generated those images.

The developing sociological tradition of the nineteenth century was to make its own important contribution to the image of industrialism, even though it saw its task as largely analytical and scientific in character. For, as with the earliest theorist of industrialism, Saint-Simon, no subsequent thinker was able or prepared to stand aside from the transforming currents of his time and merely describe and explain them, in an 'objective', neutral manner. Living in a revolution, they sought in some way to influence its outcome. This was not necessarily a conscious purpose – though it was clearly so in the case, say, of Saint-Simon and Karl Marx. Even where it was conscious, such thinkers were genuinely convinced that in their analyses they had anatomized the 'core' characteristic of industrial society, and had discerned the rhythm of its pulse. Such being the case, the schemes of action and reorganization that they proposed followed, in their view, from the inherent logic of the developing industrial system, and were not a matter of particular values or particular choices.

But merely to glance over a few pages of the writings of the nineteenth-century sociologists is sufficient to dispel this complacent view. In the very language they use, in the whole style and manner of presentation, it is obvious that they are in the business not just of scientific explanation but of exhortation.[13] For whatever reasons of personal, class or national circumstances, they are concerned to urge upon us a particular interpretation of the industrializing process, to put upon it a peculiar colour, bias, and pressure. This was so even when, and perhaps especially when, the interpretation went against their own personal interest or scale of values, as most obviously with Alexis de Tocqueville and Max Weber. Often, too, the source of that interpretation seems to lie as much in artistic intuition, and in particular glimpses and insights, as in the scientific accumulation and examination of evidence. No one can avoid that impression when reading, say,

Max Weber on the rise of the 'Protestant ethic' in Europe, Georg Simmel on 'the metropolis and mental life', Marx on the alienating and dehumanizing effects of the capitalist economy, or Émile Durkheim on the disturbing state of *anomie* produced by the transition to the industrial society. In each case we are dealing with thinkers who have had a particular vision of the newly-emerging order, a vision which has vividly lit up particular features of the landscape while relegating others to the shadows.

To put it like this is not of course necessarily to question the truthfulness of their accounts, or to suggest that there were covert motives leading to deliberate distortion. We know enough, from the work of Karl Popper and others, about the form and history of scientific progress to acknowledge the supreme importance of intuition, imagination, and speculative hypothesis. And indeed it is the very quality of vision, of a powerful and satisfying one-sidedness, that makes the writings of Marx, Weber, Durkheim and other nineteenth-century sociologists such magnificent accounts of the social process of industrialization, the models still of sociological thinking. But we must be careful for that very reason in taking any of them as definitive and complete accounts, even in gross structural terms, of the model and type of industrial society 'as such'. Even more must we be suspicious of the wide-spread practice later of bundling together all these particular versions of the industrial society into a composite stereotype of modern society: as if a good painting could be produced by pasting on to one canvas a Braque, a Matisse, and a Picasso. The attempt to identify the principal structural characteristics of the society emerging in England in the course of the Industrial Revolution was one thing, and a commendable one. It was also immensely valuable to see the extent to which these features were replicated as the Industrial Revolution spread and was imitated, first by the rest of Europe, then by the rest of the world. But it was bound to be dangerous to start off, as many twentieth-century sociologists did, with a preconceived model of 'modern industrial society', put together out of the bits and pieces of nineteenth-century European development; and to judge the progress to 'modernity' of other societies in its terms. Still more was it so when in practical political terms the attempt was made to force those societies to conform to the model.

2. Sociology and the Industrial Society

The 'founding fathers' of sociology all lived, wrote and theorized under the overwhelming impression that a 'terrible beauty' was born. A new society, the industrial society, was in the making, fraught equally with hope and despair. We can group them to some extent in terms of their perceptions of the central problems of the new society: Saint-Simon, Comte, Spencer and Durkheim concerned with the dangers arising from the disintegration of the old order, and the need to bring about a speedy reintegration along new principles of social organization and social morality; Marx and Weber preoccupied by the fact that the new society was capitalistic in its form, with deep-lying tendencies towards dehumanization and mechanization; Tocqueville and John Stuart Mill on the 'passion for equality' characteristic of the new society, and the consequent drive towards a uniform mass society. But all of them, whether inspired more with hope or more with gloom, could not but conceive their task as the description and explanation of the great transformation taking place before their eyes, and in their lives. Philip Abrams aptly reminds us that

> the generation that gave birth to sociology was probably the first generation of human beings ever to have experienced within the span of their own lifetime socially induced change of a totally transformative nature – change which could not be identified, explained and accommodated as a limited historical variation within the encompassing order of the past.[14]

Following the lead given by Saint-Simon and certain other writers,[15] the early sociologists accepted the view that the crisis was a general one. It affected all aspects of European society, economic, political, and cultural. The French Revolution, dramatic and explosive as it had been, was seen as but one expression of an overall transforming tendency affecting all European societies. It belonged therefore, as it willingly acknowledged, not just to France, but to Europe and indeed the whole world. The Industrial Revolution of the English was another, more profound expression of the same movement: slower in its operations but ultimately far more subversive of traditional institutions and ways of life. A crucial step was taken, and a critical distinction lost, in the later sociological agreement to subsume these and other related changes under the general rubric of 'industrialization'. Industrialization became the generic term encompassing all the major changes in the movement to 'the industrial society'; and the industrial society came to be identified as the distinctive type of *modern* society, incorporating therefore common features which went well beyond those of a simply economic and technological character. Industrialization meant, certainly, the transformation of the productive forces of society through the application of a machine technology and the factory system; but it also meant urbanization, secularization, the 'rationalization' of thought, institutions, and behaviour, the individualization of consciousness and conduct, and a host of other changes in family life, politics, and culture. Later still the term 'modernization' was applied to this set of changes; and while compared to this helpless admission of conceptual defeat the notion of 'industrialization' is a positive model of precision, to talk of a movement to 'modernity' at least keeps us in mind of the very wide range of changes which the nineteenth-century sociologists sought to order and comprehend.

Given this preoccupation with so varied an assemblage of changes – reaching out from the work done in the fields to the most ethereal products of philosophy and art – it was almost inevitable that thinkers should become somewhat confused as to what were causes, what concomitants, what consequences. They were confronted with an overarching, total pattern of change whose historical origin could be dated, with equal plausibility, to 1789 or 1200; whose prime mover was variously seen as the general advancement in scientific methodology, or specific technological inventions, or even the adoption of a specific social ethic, the 'Protestant ethic' of sixteenth- and seventeenth-century western Europe. Any particular agency singled out proved ultimately to be so completely dependent on every other as to make the search for causes seem in the end both hopeless and irrelevant. What mattered was to grasp the whole complex of functionally interrelated changes involved in the transition to the industrial society; to use this set of structural features as the basis of the comparison with other types of society; and to discern with their help, however schematically, the main outlines of the future industrial society.

There were of course some thinkers, such as Karl Marx, who asserted confidently that they had found the secret of social change:

> Are men free to choose this or that form of society? By no means. Assume a particular state of development in the productive faculties of man and you will get a corresponding form of commerce and consumption. Assume particular degrees of development of production, commerce and consumption and you will have a corresponding form of social constitution, a corresponding organization of the family, of orders or of classes, in a word, a corresponding civil society. Assume a particular civil society and you will get a particular political system, which is only the official expression of civil society.[16]

But such confidence in the role of the productive forces as 'the basis of all man's history' dissolved considerably on further reflection. Where, for instance, was one to put science? As a particular methodology as well as a set of substantive ideas it clearly belonged to the realm of the 'superstructure', the determined expression as opposed to the determining forces (of the 'base'). But just as clearly its part in enhancing the productive powers of society was enormous – so much so that in recent years the development of theoretical science has been seen by many as the primary productive resource of industrial societies. There was no obvious way out of the dilemma, and later Marxists came to concede so much autonomy to the different 'realms' of society that it was difficult to make out where 'social existence' (i.e. the material life) ended and 'consciousness' began. Causation remained locked in an impermeable circle.

Far more typical than this bold attempt is the causal confusion of the following passage. Written in the early 1960s, it comes from a highly influential work of synthesis on the theory of the industrial society, *Industrialism and Industrial Man* by Clark Kerr and his associates:

> Although industrialization follows widely differing patterns in different countries, some characteristics of the industrialization process are common to all. These 'universals' arise from the imperatives intrinsic to the process. They are the pre-requisites and concomitants of industrial evolution. Once under way, the logic of industrialization sets in motion many trends which do more or less violence to the traditional pre-industrial society.[17]

Not surprisingly, the subsequent offering of a cluster of attributes of the industrialization process, jumbled together, lacks all notion of causal priority; and the chief property of the 'logic of industrialization', if logic there is, appears to be its circularity.

Such difficulties are entirely understandable. Nineteenth-century theorists inherited from the eighteenth-century idea of progress a tradition of social thinking that emphasized whole orders and epochs. The *philosophes* were interested in the progress and perfectibility of Man as such, as a single indivisible entity, and as a single unit of observation and study. The actual doings of particular men in particular places at particular times mattered to them only in as much as these contributed the materials for the construction of 'ideal', 'natural' or 'logical' stages in the progress of mankind. This view led to two important characteristics of both the eighteenth- and nineteenth-century theories. One is that, with a few exceptions, they were relatively uninterested in, or casual about, the actual mechanics of change, the transition from one 'natural' order to the next. Since progress was both natural and inevitable, all that had to be postulated was some psychological tendency to progress or betterment in the human mind. Secondly, the philosophic method of 'natural history' made for the rejection of all 'accidentals', all loose or contradictory features in the delineation of the 'ideal' states through which mankind progressed. Both these characteristics had the effect of concentrating attention on the generalized, idealized elements of the social order or social epoch at any one time. Actual empirical societies, situated in historical time, were seen as instances of the general type or species. The fact that they only displayed some of the features of the type, or did so imperfectly or in a disorderly manner, was ignored, in the interests of logical clarity. The concern was with the integrating principle of the type, the ordered interrelating patterns that gave life to the whole and maintained it in being. It was in following a procedure of this kind that the nineteenth-century sociologists could discover beneath the varied surfaces of contemporary European societies the type of 'the industrial society'.

The eighteenth-century *philosophes* could, as we have seen, equably contemplate a good number of stages through which mankind had passed, or would pass. Condorcet thought there were ten. Even Saint-Simon, struck as he was by the novel features of his own time, offered three. But for later nineteenth-century sociologists such generosity to the past was mostly closed off. For them there really could be only one distinction, one movement, that between 'then' and 'now'. The divide between their age and all that had gone before appeared so vast that any further subdivision of the evolutionary sequence seemed trivial. There was their epoch, the epoch of industrialism, and there was the past, the remainder of history, variously conceived. History, by its very propulsion of one part of the world into an era that felt itself uniquely new, had thereby abrogated its authority in the eyes of that part of the world. The French historian Lamartine, writing in the 1840s, gave vivid expression to the predicament of the age, the sense of the lack of any historical precedent to make sense of their times:

> These times are times of chaos; opinions are a scramble; parties are a jumble; the language of new ideas has not been created; nothing is more difficult than to give a good definition of oneself in religion, in philosophy, in politics. One feels, one knows, one lives, and at need one dies for one's cause, but one cannot name it. It is the problem of the time to classify things and men. The world has jumbled its catalogue.[18]

The characteristic nineteenth-century resolution of the question, 'how many stages of social evolution?' was to bundle all previously defined past stages into one, and to contrast it with another, the contemporary stage. In a striking series of polarities the movement from the previous to the present order of society was conceptualized as a succession of two logically and sociologically contrasting states or types of society. Thus Herbert Spencer, echoing Saint-Simon not merely in the terms but in the content of the opposition, traced the movement from 'militant' to 'industrial' society; Ferdinand Tönnies saw it as a movement from 'community' (*Gemeinschaft*) to 'association' (*Gesellschaft*); Sir Henry Maine, from a social order based on 'status' to one based on 'contract'. For Émile Durkheim, the movement was seen essentially in terms of the contrasting principles of social integration, the earlier based on 'mechanical solidarity', the present on 'organic solidarity'. Max Weber saw the distinction chiefly in the differing bases of authority, both political and intellectual, in the change from 'traditional' to 'legal-rational' political forms and modes of thought. Later the American anthropologist Robert Redfield added a further influential polar contrast, in the movement from the 'folk' to the 'urban' society; and yet another dimension of the transformation was stressed by Howard Becker in the contrast between 'sacred' and 'secular' societies.[19]

There were some interesting modifications of this basic schema, although their significance turned out to be less than was thought at the time. Both Comte and Marx, following Saint-Simon, offered a three-stage vision of human history. The former's was a direct borrowing from Saint-Simon: society had passed through the 'theological' and 'metaphysical' stages and was now entering the final scientific or 'positive' stage. Marx in literal terms actually saw six stages: 'primitive', 'slave', 'feudal', 'capitalist', 'socialist', and 'communist' society. But it seems fair to discern behind this a basically tripartite scheme, in which the third stage ('socialism/communism') overcomes and abolishes the alienation of the class-society of the second stage ('slave'/'feudal'/'capitalist'), to restore, at a much higher level, the moral conditions of the first 'primitive' stage.

John Peel makes the illuminating suggestion that whether a

nineteenth-century sociologist adopted a two- or a three-stage scheme depended very much on his ideological posture in relation to his own times. Liberals like Spencer, who were basically convinced of the superiority of their own modern age over all past ages, tended to see the present as simply the polar opposite of the past, with the future being the prolongation of present tendencies and therefore even more unlike the past. Critics of nineteenth-century society, as in their different ways both Comte and Marx were, by contrast saw the present age as transitional to a third final stage, which reverted to the first in certain important respects.[20] Linking the perspective of the social critics was the profoundly important rediscovery, and rehabilitation, of the European Middle Ages, as one of the great 'organic' periods of the past.[21] The virtues of the communal, patriarchal society of the past seemed only too evident to those who were appalled by the egoism, the competitive anarchy, the impersonal relationships of the 'cash nexus' of their own industrial society. Comte's vision of the future was in fact a thinly-veiled medievalism – so thin that contemporaries such as J. S. Mill and T. H. Huxley saw through it immediately. The 'positive polity' would see the re-establishment of shared moral values, of order and hierarchy. Science would replace theology, scientists would replace priests. Marx was never taken in by the medievalist idylls of the nineteenth-century reactionaries, such as Bonald and de Maistre. But he, too, in the future communist society envisaged a set of relationships and attitudes to the world whose expression hitherto was most clearly to be found in feudal and, even more, tribal society: a communalism of things and people, an absence of the division of labour, an aesthetic attitude towards work and the environment.

These differences in the intellectual response to industrialism are of course important, and it is not my intention to exaggerate the uniformity of the sociological account of the 'great transformation'. But it *is* striking the extent to which the early sociologists dwelt on the form and implications of the *one* transition, that taking place in their own lives, even if they recognized a plurality of earlier and future stages. In the case of Comte this was not very difficult, since the era of nineteenth-century industrialism was already 'positive' in principle, and all that was necessary was a certain amount of moral and social tidying-up. Things were not so easy for Marx: the movement from capitalism to communism did represent a qualitative change. And yet it is notorious how vague Marx was about the future communist society, and how casual in outlining the mechanics of the transition to that stage. At the same time he had nothing but the barest generalities to offer on pre-feudal societies. There is nothing in his writings to match in scope or in power the account of the transition from feudalism to capitalism that he gives us in volume one of *Capital.* The conviction remains that the heart of Marx's intellectual legacy will continue to be this superb sociology of the origins, structure, and functioning of capitalist society. He is *the* sociologist of bourgeois industrial society.

For all practical purposes it is not misleading, therefore, to regard the enterprise of nineteenth-century sociology as the anatomy of the distinctive type of modern industrial society. The descriptive and explanatory concepts varied, of course, usually following the various moral evaluations of the new society. The growing division of labour, for instance, which could be regarded by one man as the peak of scientific rationality, could be analysed by another, and damned, as 'alienation'. Nor were all the early sociologists prepared to place the bare fact of industrial technology and industrial organization at the heart of their analyses; although there was not one who did not recognize its novelty and transforming influence. Then, too, they were keenly aware that the changes which they theorized about were as yet restricted to a small part of Europe and the North American continent; and they were not all confident that the same sequences and features that they observed there could be generalized and universalized as symptoms of general evolution, the world over. Many of them did of course do just that; and if not them, then their followers, so that late in his life Marx was driven to admonish a zealous Russian writer 'who feels he absolutely must metamorphose my historical sketch of the genesis of capitalism in Western Europe into an historico-philosophic theory of the general path every people is fated to tread, whatever the historical circumstances in which it finds itself . . .'[22] But against this could be set the studies of Weber on the association between Protestantism and capitalism, emphasizing the distinctive and indeed unique pattern of European development.

What increasingly and in retrospect did seem common to their thought was a concern specifically with *industrial*, set against *non-industrial*, society. The passage of time cast back this generalizing light on their reflections. As North Atlantic industrialization proceeded, joined now by Russia and Japan, the gulf between those societies that had industrialized and those that had not seemed so vast that all other distinctions between them were obliterated. By the same token differences within the industrial world, between the societies of that world, paled into insignificance by comparison with the fact that they were all industrial societies.[23] The nineteenth-century sociologists had, in some degree at least, conceived different patterns and different directions for the modern world. Twentieth-century sociologists, however, were struck by the sameness of the process that apparently resulted from every attempt at modernization – which meant essentially industrialization. The United States and Russia, for instance, had industrialized by very different means, and with very different goals and ideologies. And yet the resulting societies had strikingly uniform features in many important respects. The conviction grew that there was a 'logic' to the process of industrialization, bringing about common basic structural characteristics in all societies that underwent it. Hence the main task of sociology must be to understand and explain that process. As Ernest Gellner has put it, in a powerful statement of this view:

> In the twentieth century, the essence of man is not that he is rational, or a political, or a sinful, or a thinking animal, but that he is an industrial animal. It is not his moral or intellectual or social or aesthetic . . . attributes which make man what he is; his essence resides in his capacity to contribute to, and profit from, industrial society. The emergence of industrial society is the prime concern of sociology.

And he goes on to observe that acknowledgment of this fact is shown 'recently and most characteristically' in the concern of sociologists with 'the notion of *industrial* society, and its antithesis, to the detriment of other classifications, oppositions, and alternatives'.[24]

The nineteenth-century 'oppositions and alternatives' were not abandoned, of course, any more than the more popular and more general ones in later currency, such as 'simple' and 'complex', 'primitive' and 'civilized', 'undeveloped' and 'developed'. They were all simply swept together under the single opposition, 'industrial' and 'non-industrial'. Indeed the analyses of the founding fathers, together with *their* derivations, came to provide the sophisticated core of the twentieth-century sociology of industrialism. Often not specifically acknowledged, *Gemeinschaft* and *Gesellschaft*, status and contract, mechanical and organic solidarity, and all the others, became the heart not just of the analytical but of the emotional contrast between non-industrial and industrial. In the dead prose of a multitude of textbooks on 'industrial sociology' lay buried and congealed the passionate accounts of Marx and Engels on the conditions of the proletariat; Weber's icy and characteristically ambivalent dissection of bureaucracy and bureaucratization; Durkheim's concerned vision of industrial man in the state of *anomie*, impossibly striving after infinitely receding goals.

It is to this sociological image of industrialism, in its details, that I now turn.

3 The Revolution Defined: The Image of Industrialism

From this foul drain the greatest stream of human industry flows out to fertilise the whole world. From this filthy sewer pure gold flows. Here humanity attains its most complete development and its most brutish; here civilization works its miracles, and civilised man is turned back almost into a savage.

Alexis de Tocqueville, on Manchester.
Journeys to England and Ireland (1835).

As a stranger passes through the masses of human beings which have been accumulated round the mills [of the industrial North of England], he cannot contemplate these crowded hives without feelings of anxiety and apprehension amounting almost to dismay. The population is hourly increasing in breadth and strength. It is an aggregate of masses, our conception of which clothe themselves in terms which express something portentous and fearful.

William Cooke Taylor, *Notes of a Tour in the Manufacturing Districts of Lancashire* (1842).

This chapter is devoted to setting out, in some detail, the elements of the contemporary sociological model of industrialism. Since, as I have indicated, those elements derive their force and much of their content from the classic nineteenth-century sociologies in which they originally figured, I have tried as far as possible to present them in the terms and in the language of the original accounts. Any loss of rigour that this procedure involves is enormously compensated for by the stylistic relief that it affords the reader (who needs only to open at random any textbook on industrial sociology to understand what I mean). In the next chapter I shall assess the model of industrialism here presented.

Everyone agrees that while at the centre of industrialization lies a series of economic changes, registered in economic indices, the process always involves a far wider set of social changes. These can be seen variously as the social context, concomitants, and consequences of the economic changes; although as I have said the standard accounts are slippery on just this point. Taken together the economic and non-economic indices add up to, not merely elements in an analytical model of industrialism, but specific long-term predictions about the course of social change. These are obviously enough, in their origins, extrapolations from tendencies visible – or apparently so – in nineteenth-century European society. But as the model of industrialism was plucked from this particular historical matrix, so the predictions came to apply to all societies undergoing industrialization.

So far as the purely economic indices are concerned, there seems to be near unanimity on the central identifying characteristic of industrialization. As E. A. Wrigley puts it, with a wide range of corroborating statements, industrialization 'is said to occur in a given country when real incomes per head begin to rise steadily and without apparent limit'.[1] In an analogy popularized by Walt Rostow, the economy 'takes-off', becomes airborne: all the relevant statistical indices of the economy take a sudden, sharp, almost vertical turn upwards.[2] Associated with this phenomenon are certain core components of the industrial system: major and continuing changes in material technology, so that work is predominantly done by machines rather than by hand, and human labour power is supplemented or replaced by inanimate sources of energy; the marketing of men's labour; the concentration of workers in single enterprises; the existence of a specific social type, the entrepreneur.[3]

Such a list can easily be varied and extended: for instance by emphasizing the condition of rapidly expanding markets, or the accompanying changes in transportation and communication which are entailed by the general extension of the factory system. Moreover, it needs to be remembered that societies – as for instance Denmark and New Zealand – can industrialize through the commercialization and mechanization of agriculture. Agriculture simply becomes another industry, often the largest and most productive, with production carried on under industrial conditions in specialized units of production (farms), and entailing no distinctive rural way of life. Thus even though agriculture may remain an important sector of an industrial economy, because of mechanization the general tendency is for the proportion of the labour force employed in agriculture to drop steadily with industrialization. At the present time, for instance, England, the first industrialized country, has the world's lowest proportion of its work-force employed in agriculture – less than five per cent.[4]

But whatever the different emphases in the various lists of this kind, there is no great degree of controversy on these purely economic attributes of industrialization. They are after all elements in the very definition of industrialism, components which enable us to identify the thing itself. What is far more difficult is to offer a generally agreed list of the non-economic (social, political and cultural) concomitants and effects of industrialization. The following account is drawn mainly from the writings of the nineteenth-century sociologists, supplemented where necessary by other writers of the time and since. It makes no attempt to be complete. Other lists could with equal plausibility be offered. But, so far as can be judged from current sociological work on the subject, this sketch of some of the leading characteristics of industrial society would not be thought unduly eccentric.

1. Urbanism as a Way of Life

'The industrial society is an urban society.'[5] Oddly enough the process of urbanization, which in certain respects might appear as the most obvious accompaniment of industrialization, did not feature very significantly as a *theoretical* element in the classic nineteenth-century accounts of the emergence of industrial society. Marx, for instance, did not make the city an important unit in his analysis of industrialism. What mattered for him was the concentration of workers in large-scale productive enterprises, the new factories, and the new social relations that this gave rise to. He assumed as a matter of course that these factories would be located in towns – towns such as Manchester, of which his friend Engels had given so graphic an account in *The Condition of the Working Class in England*; and in a general way Marx saw the direction of the future as away from the country and towards the towns, away from 'the idiocy of rural life' to the creativity and heterogeneity of urban living. But his theoretical emphasis was on the productive life of man, the social and political forms this took, and he was largely unconcerned with the spatial and ecological features of the environment within which this productive life was played out. As a result the form and shape of the city as an independent determining force in social life received scant recognition in his analysis, a fact which has led to the situation that there hardly exists a Marxist theory of the city at the present time.[6]

The theoretical neglect of the process of urbanization perhaps had something to do with the very obviousness of the widespread movement to the towns in nineteenth-century Europe. Theoretical comment may have appeared superfluous. Take Britain, the country of the first Industrial Revolution. During the first half of the nineteenth century Britain became the world's first urbanized society. In 1760 there were only two cities with a population of over 50,000 (Bristol with some 60,000, London with about 750,000). By the first census of 1801 there were eight (Edinburgh and Glasgow, Manchester, Liverpool, Birmingham and Leeds having been added to the other two). At this time one-fifth of the population lived in cities and towns with 10,000 or more inhabitants (one in every twelve persons was a Londoner). By the time of the census of 1851, with a population that had doubled overall, thirty-eight per cent of the population resided in such towns, and for the first time the census reported an aggregate 'urban' population which exceeded the 'rural' population in size, by one per cent. Britain, the first industrial nation in the history of the world, had also become the first urban nation, and the conviction that there was a necessary connection between these two facts proved irresistible. As industrialization gathered speed in the second half of the nineteenth century, so did urbanization. By the year of Queen Victoria's death, in 1901, the census recorded three-quarters of the population as urbanized, more than half of the population being in cities of 20,000 or more; by contrast, with the exception of Australia, a special case, no other country in the world yet had more than thirty per cent of its population urbanized. Britain alone in 1900 could have been described as a fully urbanized society. The end-point of this astonishingly rapid and explosive development can conveniently be dated to the 1911 census, which classified some eighty per cent of the population as urban. In just over a century Britain had moved from a condition in which one-fifth of its population was urbanized to one in which four-fifths were.[7]

Contemporaries in countries undergoing industrialization at a later date would have been eccentric indeed had they not expected their societies to imitate the basic pattern of English urbanization. Most of this urbanization had to wait until the twentieth century, even in those countries, such as France, Germany, and the United States, whose economies had 'taken-off' into industrialization just beyond the mid-point of the nineteenth century. But the indications were already palpably there by 1900.[8] In any case what seemed to matter was not simply the fact of populations massed in cities, startling as this phenomenon was. This worried administrators and welfare workers; but more analytically-minded observers were more greatly struck by the way in which the city had come to acquire absolute predominance over the life of the society. The pre-industrial city had often been of great commercial, cultural, or political importance. But it had existed encapsulated within, usually parasitic upon, the body of the society as a whole, which in large segments could display attitudes and activities barely touched by urban life. Now in the industrializing societies, whatever the purely quantitative size of the urban sector, the city had emerged from its encapsulated state and come to provide the economic, cultural and political framework of the whole society. Except as quaint retreats for tourists, there was no room for non-urban 'pockets' of social activities. The city had become society itself. The force and appeal of Dickens and Balzac to their contemporaries was precisely that they projected the image of the city – London, Paris – as the representation of the new social system *as a whole*, its dilemmas, costs, and opportunities.[9]

It was this aspect of the matter that most interested the nineteenth-century sociologists. As mentioned earlier, they were loath to give the city, as a socio-spatial unit, any distinctive and independent determining power. But without exception they saw the modern city as the natural arena within which the central tendencies of the age would reveal themselves. The city would show in a highly compressed, visible, and demonstrable form the fundamental relationships and principles of modern industrial society. To that extent the city was the mirror of modern society. It was in the observation of urban life that the new society would be led to the highest degree of self-consciousness and self-knowledge.

Thus the characteristic sociological method of handling the fact of urbanization was to see it as the intensified expression of whatever structural tendency the particular writer had identified as the dominant one of the age. So, the Marxists saw in modern urban life the expression of one of the central aspects of that alienation brought about by capitalist development: the alienation of man from his fellows. This is what particularly struck Engels about London:

> We know well enough that the isolation of the individual – a narrow-minded egotism – is everywhere the fundamental principle in modern society. But nowhere is this selfish egotism so blatantly evident as in the frantic bustle of the great city. The disintegration of society into individuals, each guided by his private principles and each pursuing his own aims has been pushed to its furthest limits in London. Here indeed human society has been split into its component atoms.[10]

Similarly Ferdinand Tönnies, pursuing his contrast between the earlier communal, family-based, 'natural' *Gemeinschaft* society, and the emerging individualized, contractual, 'mechanical' society of the *Gesellchaft*, not surprisingly saw the modern city as typical of *Gesellschaft* in general . . . In the earlier period, family life and home (or household) economy strike the keynote; in the later period, commerce and city life . . . The more general the condition of *Gesellschaft* becomes in the nation or a group of nations, the more this entire 'country' or the entire 'world' begins to resemble one large city . . . The city consists of free persons who stand in contact with each other, exchange with each other and cooperate without any *Gemeinschaft* or will thereto developing among them except as such might develop sporadically or as a leftover from former conditions. On the contrary, these numerous external contacts, contracts, and contractual relations only cover up as many inner hostilities and antagonistic interests.[11]

Something of this contrast persists in the famous essay 'The Metropolis and Mental Life',[12] by Georg Simmel, perhaps the only one of the major nineteenth-century sociologists to take the modern city as the starting-point of his analysis of contemporary life. Simmel's essay, together with a later one heavily indebted to it, Louis Wirth's 'Urbanism as a Way of Life',[13] for a long time served as the main source of the sociological account of the city. Simmel recognized that 'the metropolis has always been the seat of the money economy', and that this in large measure was responsible for the elements of rationality, calculation, and hard-headedness that characteristically informed social relations in the city. But at the same time he was at pains to emphasize the, as it were, *sui generis* features of the modern metropolis: the massing and concentration of the population, the qualitatively different rhythms of life and mental images that made the urban dweller a different species from the countryman:

The psychological basis of the metropolitan type of individuality consists in the *intensification of nervous stimulation* which results from the swift and uninterrupted change of outer and inner stimuli . . . With each crossing of the street, with the tempo and multiplicity of economic, occupational and social life, the city sets up a deep contrast with small town and rural life with reference to the sensory foundations of psychic life.

As a response to this speeded-up tempo, as a defensive mechanism and means of coping with the rush of stimuli, the city-dweller 'reacts with his head instead of his heart': he acquires 'sophistication' and governs his responses by a generalizing 'intellectuality' as opposed to the particularizing tendency of the emotions. Simmel sees the connection between this calculative response and the predominance of a money economy, but stresses the independent force of the special features of metropolitan life itself:

> The conditions of metropolitan life are at once cause and effect of this trait. The relationships and affairs of the typical metropolitan usually are so varied and complex that without the strictest punctuality in promises and services the whole structure would break down into an inextricable chaos. Above all, this necessity is brought about by the aggregation of so many people with such differentiated interests, who must integrate their relations and activities into a highly complex organism ... The technique of metropolitan life is unimaginable without the most punctual integration of all activities and mutual relations into a stable and impersonal time schedule ... Punctuality, calculability, exactness are forced upon life by the complexity and extension of metropolitan existence and are not only connected with its money economy and intellectualistic character.

From these features of metropolitan life Simmel deduces other characteristics of metropolitan man. The intense stimulation of the nervous system produces as a protective reaction the typically urban *blasé* attitude: 'In this phenomenon the nerves find in the refusal to react to their stimulation the last possibility of accommodating to the contents and forms of metropolitan life.' From this same need to protect himself from being overwhelmed by the number and variety of contacts and stimuli springs the equally characteristic urban attitude of reserve. Simmel notes that this not only affords the city-dweller an insulating layer within which he can freely develop his own individuality; it also accounts for the unique isolation to which urban man is subject:

> The reciprocal reserve and indifference and the intellectual life conditions of large circles are never more strongly felt by the individual in their impact upon his independence than in the thickest crowd of the big city. This is because the bodily proximity and narrowness of space makes the mental distance only the more visible. It is obviously only the obverse of this freedom if, under certain circumstances, one

nowhere feels as lonely and lost as in the metropolitan crowd. For here as elsewhere it is by no means necessary that the freedom of man be reflected in his emotional life as comfort.

Finally from the intense specialization and division of labour encountered in the metropolis, with its threat to the development of varied individual personalities, comes, by reactive contrast, an almost excessive emphasis on 'personality', expressed often in superficial but bizarre forms. It is from this desperate need to appear 'different' in an environment that is constantly eroding all fundamental human differences, that there arises the typically urban phenomenon of fads and fashions, 'the specifically metropolitan extravagances of mannerism, caprice and preciousness'.

Nearly all the features of Simmel's analysis of the city appear in Wirth's equally influential 'Urbanism as a Way of Life' of 1938. Wirth in addition drew upon other aspects of the European sociological tradition, especially the contributions of Weber and Durkheim, to round out Simmel's analysis by the addition of certain other, more familiar, features of urbanism. The increasing density brought about by the growth of cities, he argued, itself produces differentiation and specialization of the population, since only in this way can the area support increased numbers. Furthermore the diverse functions performed by the city forces a separation of place of work from place of residence and, in general, the different parts of the city acquire specialized functions, with sociologically distinct populations.

The city consequently tends to resemble a mosaic of social worlds in which the transition from one to another is abrupt. The juxtaposition of divergent personalities and modes of life tend to produce a relativistic perspective and a sense of toleration of differences which may be regarded as prerequisites for rationality and which lead towards the secularization of life.

Furthermore this very heterogeneity of the urban population leads to a breaking down of rigid class and caste boundaries, encouraging social and spatial mobility. The urban dweller ceases to maintain an undivided allegiance to any one social group, 'but acquires membership in widely divergent groups, each of which functions only with reference to a single segment of his personality'. Membership of groups is fluid, turnover rapid. Given such social and physical mobility, wider kinship ties lose their hold and significance, and the neighbourhood ceases to be a meaningful unit of social life. The scene therefore is set for a condition of Durkheimian *anomie*. The social settings that formerly bound the individual most firmly to the social order – especially the family and the community – no longer serve to restrain his appetites or to order his means of satisfying them. The consequence is the fundamental social instability of the urban milieu, an increase, compared with the rural setting, of 'personal disorganization, mental breakdown, suicide, delinquency, crime, corruption, and disorder'.

Wirth's essay is aptly named. In it the city is elevated to the position of primary agent of all that is distinctive in modern industrial society. It is difficult to resist the suspicion that, as with the majority of the earlier sociologists, Wirth is really talking about the city as the *setting* for the new tendencies brought about by industrialization and its associated changes. Too many changes are attributed to the process of urbanization itself to be plausible. But his contribution is of lasting interest for a different reason. It displays in an extreme and exemplary form the sociologists' disposition to treat the city symbolically, as the theatre in which was played out the drama of the industrial society, with its new roles and new identities. In its full portrait of urban man it reveals, perhaps more sharply than any other single piece, the extent to which the sociologists were shaping an elaborate and highly expressive image of the new social order, in which their own fears and hopes were deeply embedded.

The sociological account of urbanization – the obvious enough fact of it and the more ambiguous meaning of it – is interesting for another, more purely historical reason. In synthesizing and systematizing more immediately felt responses to the new type of city, they presented the anatomy of a social formation that was sharply divided from any of its previous manifestations. Many an earlier writer, going well back into classical times, had proclaimed the virtues of country life and decried the vices of the city. But until the Industrial Revolution the tradition of thought which saw the city as the seat *par excellence* of civilization, the repository of the civilized graces and all the progressive elements of social life, remained vigorous and capable of holding off most challenges. With the rise of the industrial city that tradition went heavily on the defensive, and has largely remained there. The revulsion against industrial urbanism, so clear in so much nineteenth-century art and literature, reached a pitch that, far from abating, seems only to have increased with the growth of the twentieth-century 'megalopolis'.

The sociological account was far from single-minded on this. Indeed it was marked by a fundamental ambivalence which was perhaps a fair reflection of the mood of all thinking people in the societies undergoing industrialization. On the one hand the city appeared as a monstrous growth, a permanent threat to the values of civilization to which ironically enough it had given its very name. For all their objectivity, the contributions of Tönnies, Simmel, and Wirth pointed essentially in that direction. On the other hand the conviction remained that were man ever to be fully 'humanized', to realize the potentialities of his species to the fullest extent, only the city could be the arena of this humanization. Such basically was the position of Marx and Durkheim. And, since in this section the antiurbanists have had the predominant say (rightly, since their tradition has been so much more influential), it is fair to conclude with Durkheim's more optimistic conviction that

> great cities are the uncontested homes of progress; it is in them that ideas, fashions, customs, new needs are elaborated and then spread over the rest of the country. When society changes, it is generally after them and in imitation. Temperaments are so mobile that everything that comes from the past is somewhat suspect. On the contrary innovations, whatever they may be, enjoy a prestige there almost equal to the one the customs of ancestors formerly enjoyed. Minds naturally are there oriented to the future. Consequently, life is there transformed with extraordinary rapidity: beliefs, tastes, passions are in perpetual evolution. No ground is more favourable to evolutions of all sorts.[14]

2. 'The Demographic Transition'

Industrialization means population growth. Like urbanization, this feature of industrializing nineteenth-century Europe was too obvious to appear to require much theoretical elaboration. A population explosion seemed to be a clear concomitant of industrialization – although, again, whether population growth itself forced on economic development, or was a consequence of that development, was and remains a matter of dispute. But, whatever time scale we take for purposes of comparison, the facts themselves are hardly in dispute. On the level of world demographic history, the late eighteenth century marks a clear watershed. Roughly up to that time the rate of growth of world population was low, for reasons usually described as Malthusian. In Heckscher's phrase, 'Nature audited her accounts with a red pencil'. Then, from about 1750 onwards, there was a population revolution. Between 1650 and 1850 the annual rate of increase of the world's population doubled, and doubled again by the 1920s. From the 1940s to the 1960s there was another great acceleration: world population grew from about 2·5 thousand millions to 3·2 thousand millions, an increase, in the space of just over twenty years, more than the *total* estimated population of the world in 1800.

More to the point, it was in north-western Europe, the region of the Industrial Revolution, that the demographic revolution began. Hence the unavoidable inference that the two revolutions were intrinsically connected. Once more the facts speak plainly. In the fifty years following 1750 there was a doubling of the growth rate, taking the population of Europe from some 120 million to between 180–190 million. During the nineteenth century there was a further acceleration. The population of Europe was 266 million in 1850, 401 million in 1900, and 468 million in 1913. Expressed in percentages, this meant an increase of about 34 per cent for the second half of the eighteenth century, 43 per cent for the period 1800 to 1850, and 50 per cent for the period 1850 to 1900. Again it was Britain, the first industrial nation, that showed the development in its most concentrated form. With a population of just over 10 million in 1800, Britain had doubled her population by 1850 (20·9 million), and doubled it again by 1910 (40·8 million) – thus moving from a situation in which, in 1800, Britain accounted for 5·8 per cent of the total population of Europe, to one in which she accounted for about 10 per cent of the total population.[15]

During the early part of the twentieth century, population growth in the industrialized parts of the world slackened off, and came almost to a halt. In some industrial countries, such as France, it looked as if the population would actually cease to be self-replacing. Observation of this fact, and reflection on the population history of the industrial countries, led to the formulation of the striking and plausible thesis of the 'demographic transition', or the S-curve theory of the relation between in-industrialization and population growth.[16] The populations of non-industrial societies are relatively stable, it was argued, because in such societies both birth-rates and death-rates are high. This primitive equilibrium is seriously disturbed by the onset of industrialization, which invariably means improvements in medical knowledge and in public health, with a consequent drastic reduction of the death-rate. The birth-rate however remains for the time high and uncontrolled. The result is a rapid increase in population (the vertically-climbing segment of the S-shaped curve). After a time the birth-rate comes into line with the death-rate; it too is lowered. The constraints of urban living, the desire to exploit the expanded opportunities for gaining wealth and achieving social status offered by the new industrial society, all put a premium upon small families. The urban-industrial populations go in for various strategies of birth-control. The curve representing population growth flattens out, and demographic stability is once more achieved.

Nowhere did there seem to be a more spectacular demonstration of the truth of this thesis than in the case of Japan. Here was the only nation outside the European tradition to become industrialized. With such differences of history and culture, the impact of industrialization as an independent causal influence on population history seemed observable in a pure form. And Japan's demographic evolution from the 1870s onwards appears in truth almost a text-book copy of that undergone by north-western Europe half a century earlier. Kingsley Davis demonstrated that if Japan's vital-rate curves were superposed on those of Scandinavia half a century earlier, a remarkably similar, although more rapid, development could be seen. Japan's death-rate fell sharply as industrialization took hold after the First World War; its population grew quickly. Davis says that 'the rate of natural increase during the period from 1900 to 1940 was almost exactly the same as Scandinavia's between 1850 and 1920, averaging 12·1 per 1000 population compared with Scandinavia's 12·3.' Likewise, after a shorter period than in the European case, Japan's birth-rate began to fall, apparently for much the same reasons as weighed with the urban-industrial populations of Europe. Indeed after the Second World War the decline in births exceeded in speed anything comparable in the European experience, amounting to fifty per cent from 1948 to 1960 – as Davis comments, 'perhaps the swiftest drop in reproduction that has ever occurred in an entire nation'. The birth-rate fell so far as to make the Japanese population barely self-replacing. Thus the Japanese case, in the compressed and speeded-up form that typified late developers, seemed to bear out in the most satisfying way the association between industrialization and 'the demographic transition'.[17]

In more recent discussion, reflecting certain aspects of post-Second World War experience, the association has seemed less firm. Partly this was due to the increase in the birth-rate in all industrial societies in the 1950s. The feeling was expressed that perhaps the assumed 'fit' between small families and urban-industrial society was merely temporary and accidental. At a higher level of industrialization, with the era of 'mass consumption', large families once more seemed to be coming back into fashion, spearheaded as usual by the middle classes.

The other troubling fact was observable in the developing societies of the 'Third World'. Here the death-rate was dramatically reduced in the post-war period, largely as a result of the adoption of western medical knowledge and techniques. This was all in accordance with the theory. But even though industrialization was beginning to get a grip on substantial sections of Asia and Latin America, there seemed little sign of the expected reduction of the birth-rate. The result was some of the most gigantic and rapid increases of population known in the history of mankind, with the Malthusian checks removed by virtue of the medicine and economic aid of the developed world.

In the event the theory of the demographic transition has emerged surprisingly unscathed. The post-1950 'baby boom' proved ephemeral. In the late 1970s the industrial societies are almost without exception faced with a static or falling birth-rate, so much so that bare replacement is all that can be expected over the coming decades.[18] Admittedly something of a check to the birth-rate may have been produced by the adverse economic climate of the decade, although this certainly cannot be the whole answer, as the trend was observable earlier than the date by which the sense of a 'crisis' can be said to have seized the imaginations of the populations of the industrial societies. Longer-term factors, such as the changing position of women and their changing aspirations, would probably anyway have brought about the postponement of child-bearing and smaller families that now seem the tendency. In any case, the flattening out of the curve of economic growth is not necessarily something aberrant or accidental in the development of industrial society. It is just as convincing to argue, as we shall be doing later, that this is intrinsic to the industrializing mode.

As far as the Third World is concerned, the judgements of the 1950s now seem premature. One of the reasons why population growth was so slow to stabilize was precisely the slowness of industrialization itself in those societies. The existence of a powerful developed sector of the globe, with its own ambitions and interests, has proved an impediment to serious industrialization which may yet turn out to be insuperable. Moreover, where the pressure of the developed world could to some extent be held off and industrialization proceed, as with communist China from 1949 onwards, the theory of the demographic transition seemed amply vindicated. China in recent years, with a highly successful programme of birth control, seems all set to imitate the earlier demographic pattern of its Asian neighbour Japan.

In sum, the association of industrialization with the demographic transition continues to stand as one of the best-attested phenomena of social development. The contribution of this factor to the image of industrialism is obvious. The pre-industrial 'mob' becomes the 'masses' of the new society. Alarm is voiced at the grave new social and political problems posed by the unprecedented increase in numbers. Fear of the 'dark, impenetrable, subterranean' masses of the industrial population becomes potent.[19] All this was to be expected. But, since it was generally the presence of these vast numbers as members of the new industrial towns, or as potential radicals or revolutionaries, that was the subject of attention, it seems best to consider this feature under the more particularized headings.

3. The Decline of Community

'Modern society acknowledges no neighbour,' wrote Disraeli in *Sybil.* The note was sounded in practically every social tract and treatise written in the nineteenth century. Mostly it was sounded with regret, occasionally with triumph. But, regretfully or triumphantly, and whether it came from nostalgic European conservatives or radical utilitarians and socialists, the decline of the community was one of the most commonly remarked and agreed-upon features of the emerging industrial society. For some, such as Ferdinand Tönnies, this decline became the ordering principle for the entire complex of changes brought about by industrialization. In the movement from the society of the *Gemeinschaft* (community) to that of the *Gesellschaft* (contractual association) Tönnies believed he could trace the emergence of the most distinctive characteristics of modern industrial society.

The contrasts have become familiar through repetition. The heart of *Gemeinschaft* society lay in the small, face-to-face community, whose ultimate solidifying principle was blood relationship, real or assumed.

> The prototype of all unions of *Gemeinschaft* is the family. By birth man enters these relationships: free rational will can determine his remaining within the family, but the very existence of the relationship

itself is not dependent on his full rational will. The three pillars of *Gemeinschaft* – blood, place (land), and mind, or kinship, neighbourhood, and friendship – are all encompassed in the family, but the first of them is the constituting element of it.[20]

Members of *Gemeinschaft* bodies follow collective sentiment, rather than calculating egotistical reason. They are governed by custom, folkways, and religion. The social relations that these give rise to are best expressed in the family, the village, and the town, or the corporative organization of guilds, colleges, churches and religious communities. Intimacy of scale is critical: large increments of numbers or of physical distances would destroy the texture of frequent daily contacts, in different places and for different purposes, that are the hallmark of *Gemeinschaft* life.

Modern *Gesellschaft* society is the opposite of all this. Torn from the body of the organic community, the individual is thrown into large-scale associations to which however he has no right of membership, and to which he is never expected to give more than a part of himself. Social relations are governed by the principles of rationality and calculation – especially the principle of economic rationality. Their typical expression is the contract, arrived at by a process of rational compromise among individuals each pursuing his own interest, and sanctioned by a framework of positive law. The model of *Gesellschaft* organization is the modern business enterprise, towards which all other collectivities aspire. The arena of social action likewise increases in scale. It is now the large city, the centralized nation-state, the world market. Larger numbers of people are more densely gathered together; but the occupation of a common habitat engenders no sense of belonging to a common social entity, owing to the individual, contractual, and instrumental nature of the relationships. Tönnies put as follows the essential distinction between *Gemeinschaft* and *Gesellschaft* forms:

The theory of the *Gesellschaft* deals with the artificial construction of an aggregate of human beings which superficially resembles the *Gemeinschaft* in so far as the individuals live and dwell together peacefully. However, in the *Gemeinschaft* they remain essentially united in spite of all separating factors, whereas in the *Gesellschaft* they are essentially separated in spite of all uniting factors. In the *Gesellschaft*, as contrasted with the *Gemeinschaft*, we find no actions that can be derived from an *a priori* and necessarily existing unity; no actions, therefore, which manifest the will and spirit of the unity even if performed by the individual; no actions which, in so far as they are performed by the individual, take place on behalf of those united with him. In the *Gesellschaft* such actions do not exist. On the contrary, here everybody is by himself and isolated, and there exists a condition of tension against all others.[21]

Tönnies was perhaps exceptional in identifying the decline of community with 'the great transformation' as such. Features he derived from it – urbanization, bureaucratization, the primacy of the economic motive – others were as likely to see as independent causal processes in their own right, themselves responsible for the erosion of communal life. But for almost every writer this aspect of industrialization was uniquely charged with feeling. Try as he might, no one seemed able to give merely a neutral, scientific description of the phenomenon. They were, after all, talking about a loss akin to, indeed almost identical with, the loss of family, and the shock carried a corresponding trauma. The movement seemed irreversible, the loss almost irrecoverable, although some looked forward to the renewal and rediscovery of community in a future order that had overcome the atomizing tendencies of industrialism. For Durkheim, the loss of traditional communal ties was the immediate cause of the present pathological state of *anomie*, in which the individual, lacking the regulation of religion and custom to restrain his needs and appetites, was launched on a boundless and potentially suicidal course of egotistical activities. But in the emerging occupational communities of the industrial order he saw some hope that the individual might once more be securely bound into a form of the collective life. Marx, like Durkheim, was pitiless in the face of nostalgic attempts to restore the communal associations of medieval Europe. He praised the industrial bourgeoisie for having 'torn away from the family its sentimental veil', for 'tearing asunder the motley feudal ties that bound man to his "natural superiors" ', and for 'drowning the most heavenly ecstasies of religious fervour, of chivalrous enthusiasm, of philistine sentimentalism, in the icy waters of egotistical calculation'.[22] But at the same time he could pay his respects to the many-sided activities of the medieval artisan in his guild, and compare it favourably with the impoverished life of the modern factory worker. Moreover, for Marx a crucial aspect of man's alienation under capitalism is his alienation from other men, that is, a sense of belonging to a community. In Marx's vision of the future communist society, community reappears, now made a genuine possibility through the abolition of private property and economic oppression.

Most nineteenth-century thinkers, and their twentieth-century successors, were less sanguine. Community was vanishing, the only hope was to hold on to, and defend, those forms of it with some semblance of life left – above all the family, perhaps also a revitalized Catholic church. But however feeble the hope of stemming the tide of communal dissolution, as a critical concept for commenting on modern industrial society the idea of the organic community was raised to a level of extraordinary power. On the Continent it was unfurled as the defensive standard of conservative social theory, in the writings of such men as Bonald and de Maistre, and as such had great influence on the early sociologists.[23] In England it inspired almost all that was creative in the literary and moral response to industrialism. A whole tradition of cultural criticism was formed on its basis, starting with Edmund Burke, through Coleridge, Carlyle, Ruskin, Morris, down to D. H. Lawrence and F. R. Leavis in this century.[24] Again the stance was mainly defensive, sometimes downright reactionary; but what Lawrence called 'the instinct of community' became the cutting-edge of a superb, subtle critique of what these writers saw as the mechanical, disintegrated, amorphous order of industrialism.

It would in any case have been perverse to expect the continuation of community in anything like the traditional forms. Throughout the industrializing world, forces were at work which were draining the life away from the old pre-industrial communal forms, leaving them in many cases as impotent and lifeless fossils.

The factory encroached on the productive side of the household economy, leaving the home a mere unit of consumption, incapable of sustaining the family out of its own activities. Schools took over much of the educative functions of the village church, thus dividing the effort, and depriving the church of one of its main forms of contact with the local community. Under the ruthless logic of rationalist and utilitarian critiques, the self-governing guilds, trade corporations, and other forms of what Rousseau had denounced as 'partial associations' within the society, were either swept away or submitted to the firm regulation of the state. Above all, the centralized state encroached incessantly on the powers of the autonomous or semi-autonomous bodies governing parish, town, and province. Whatever the future of the industrial societies might be, there seemed little room in them for the close, personal, many-stranded texture of communal life.

4. Specialization and the Division of Labour

All known societies practise some form of the division of labour, if only between the sexes or the generations. It clearly is not a peculiar feature of industrial society. We have only to think of the occupational specialization inherent in the Indian caste system, or the craft specializations of the medieval European towns, to realize how highly developed the division of labour can be in societies that are in no way industrialized. Contemporaries in the industrializing Europe of the nineteenth century were however inclined to think that something new had arrived with industrialism. They may have been prepared to concede that a rudimentary division of labour existed in other kinds of society. But so struck were they by the enormous complexity and interdependence of parts of the new industrial economy, so impressed by the number of new specializations and the speed with which they evolved, that they conceived the change to have been of a qualitative nature, and not merely one of degree. Nevertheless the division of labour that they observed and discussed was fundamentally of the old, non-industrial type. In concentrating so much on this they often failed to notice the distinctively new form of the division of labour that was the creation of industrialism, and were responsible for a confusion of analysis that has persisted to this day.

The division of labour that they commented on was the division of labour *in society*, a social or 'societal' division of labour. It was a division that arose on the basis of new or different needs and functions, necessitating the introduction of new or different structures, roles, and occupations. As before, but with a new intensity, cities and ports became specialized around coal, iron, textiles, or railway construction; new occupations, especially of the professional and technical sort, were added to the old in great profusion. The process was analogous to the growth of individual organisms. Just as, in the development from infancy to adulthood, the individual plant or animal created new specialized organs and structures to meet the changing needs of its own growth, so it was argued the growth of the 'social organism' was a constant process of division, differentiation, and specialization, in adaptive response to the changing needs of its internal and external environment. It was in fact just this biological metaphor – for some it was much more than that – that was seized upon by many nineteenth-century theorists seeking to understand the growing division of labour. In particular it was the organizing principle of two of the most influential accounts, those given by Herbert Spencer and Émile Durkheim.

Both Spencer and Durkheim made it plain that the increasing division of labour was a process of great antiquity and long duration. Indeed for both it had been an inherent, progressive, feature of the growth of society from its very origins. But both also thought that there came a point – and that point had been reached in the industrial society of their day – when the phenomenon achieved such dimension in scope and volume that it introduced a new principle of order into the society. The high degree of the division of labour, and the strict and close interdependence that it entailed, became the very basis of a new social solidarity. Both individuality and mutuality were satisfied, the first by the great variety of occupations now offered, the second by the insufficiency of any one of them to sustain individual or collective life. It was a social order appropriately seen by Durkheim as resting on 'organic solidarity', and contrasted with the 'mechanical solidarity' of less developed societies with a low division of labour, where order was maintained by powerful collective sentiments and harsh punishments. In the order based on organic solidarity there was no need, and no place, for repressive or authoritarian rule. Sentiments of solidarity were created by the natural and necessary dependence of the parts on each other and on the whole.[25]

That industrialization made for much greater differentiation and specialization is obvious and undeniable. But what has to be noticed is that such a process does not necessarily involve the dividing up of the operations of any particular *task*, or act of production. What impressed Spencer and Durkheim was the spectacular growth of new roles and tasks – rather than the splitting and fragmentation of both old and new tasks. It was the latter that was the novel accomplishment of industrialism. It was this, the *detailed* division of labour, rather than simply the division of labour in society at large, that Adam Smith in a famous passage in *The Wealth of Nations* had described and advocated. In his example of the manufacture of pins, he made it clear that the advantages to be gained from the division of labour derived essentially from dividing up the task into simple, easily learned and easily repeated operations, thereby both saving time and opening the way to further mechanization. Pins *could* be made by one man; the skills were by no means too diverse to be mastered by the individual artisan. But by separating out each specific operation involved and assigning each to a separate, detail, worker, 'the important business of making a pin is, in this manner, divided into about eighteen distinct operations, which, in some manufactories, are all performed by distinct hands.' As a result, each worker could be reckoned as producing upwards of 4,800 pins a day where he would have produced only one on his own.[26]

It was this aspect of the division of labour that Marx took as central to the process of capitalist industrialization. The division of labour in society he acknowledged to be an old and well-established principle; the division of labour in the workshop was the really novel and distinctive feature of industrialism. A crucial distinction between the two systems lay in the nature of authority exercised over the worker. The social division of labour implied no more than that independent producers bought and exchanged commodities among themselves, subject to no other authority than the market forces of free competition. The division of labour in the workshop, on the contrary, implied the absolute and despotic authority of the capitalist over the workers, for the commodity is produced only through the combined labour power of the detail workers, whom he alone brings together and co-ordinates in the factory. 'Manufacturing division of labour implies the concentration of the means of production in the hands of the capitalist; the social division of labour implies the dispersion of the means of production among many mutually independent producers of commodities.' Marx pointed to the paradox that

> the very same bourgeois mentality which extols the manufacturing division of labour, the life-long annexation of the worker to a partial operation, and the unconditional subordination of the detail worker to capital . . . denounces just as loudly every kind of deliberate social control and regulation of the social process of production, denounces it as an invasion of the inviolable property rights, liberty and self-determining genius of the individual capitalist. It is characteristic that the inspired apologists of the factory system can find nothing worse to say of any proposal for the general organization of social labour, than that it would transform the whole of society into a factory.

Contrasting this situation with the low manufacturing division of labour in traditional authoritarian societies, which often had an extensive social division of labour, he even thought he had found a general law:

> We may say . . . as a general rule that the less we find authority dominant in the division of labour in the interior of society, the more do we find that the division of labour develops in the workshop, and the more it is subjected to the authority of a single individual. Thus,

authority in the workshop and authority in society, as far as the division of labour is concerned, are in inverse ratio to one another.[27]

Ruskin followed the Marxian rather than the Durkheimian analysis when he commented that 'we have much studied and much perfected, of late, the great civilized invention of the division of labour; only we have given it a false name. It is not, truly speaking, the labour that is divided, but the men ...'[28] The logical extension of this industrial form of the division of labour came at the end of the nineteenth century with Frederick Winslow Taylor and the principles of 'scientific management'. Here, in the decisive separation of a knowledgeable management from a knowledge-less workforce, of conception from execution, of mental from manual labour, was the culmination of a process that had started in the artisan's initial loss of the instruments of independent production, and his enforced enrolment as a detail worker in the factories of the early nineteenth century.

Durkheim was not unalive to this side of the division of labour. He accepted the charge that, in the industrial society of his day, the individual was often 'no longer anything but an inert piece of machinery, only an external force set going which always moves in the same direction and in the same way'.[29] But whereas for Marx this was a normal, indeed inevitable, consequence of the capitalist division of labour, to be remedied only through the abolition of the division of labour itself, Durkheim continued to believe (or hope) that such a condition of individual alienation was simply an abnormal, transitional, form of the division of labour. It was owing to the contemporary condition of the 'forced' division of labour in which, because of sharp inequalities of circumstances, individuals were not playing the parts in the division of labour for which their natural capacities fitted them. True solidarity would only come about when the division of labour was 'spontaneous', that is, when society 'is constituted in such a way that social inequalities exactly express natural inequalities', and that in turn depended on 'absolute equality in the external conditions of the conflict'.[30]

Some might have thought this almost as utopian a hope and a

solution as Marx's expectation of a resolution through a future socialist revolution. But Durkheim, like Marx, believed that the temper of the times was with him, and that the tendencies were all in the direction of greater social justice, and hence a more 'spontaneous' division of labour. Meanwhile he was particularly stern with those who refused to acknowledge that the division of labour was the cardinal principle of modern industrial society, and who opposed to it old-fashioned notions of the universal man:

> We can say that, in higher societies, our duty is not to spread our activity over a large surface, but to concentrate and specialize it. We must contract our horizon, choose a definite task, and immerse ourselves in it completely, instead of trying to make ourselves a sort of creative masterpiece, quite complete, which contains its worth in itself and not in the services that it renders.[31]

It was a judgement with which many of the most thoughtful observers of the nineteenth century agreed. Others may have shared Marx's feeling that the rise of the division of labour in human society was akin to the Fall in Christian theology. But, unlike him, they had lost their faith, and with the onset of industrialization, could see no hope of redemption in a society that seemed bound to push the division of labour to extremes inconceivable in earlier societies.

5. Centralization, Equalization, 'Democratization'

It was no simple historical coincidence that the French and Industrial Revolutions occurred about the same time although in different countries. Both were animated by the same currents of individualism, rationalism, and anti-traditionalism that had been running strongly in western European society for some time. But there was something historically contingent in the way in which, in the aftermath of those revolutions, their characteristics were fused into what increasingly appeared an intrinsic whole. The French Revolution produced the doctrine of modern egalitarian democracy. Now, there was – and is – nothing inherent in industrialism that associates it necessarily with any particular political form. Societies have industrialized under a wide variety of political regimes, ranging from the democratic-constitutional to the élitist-authoritarian. But, owing partly to the coincidence of the two revolutions, partly to the manner in which the earliest societies industrialized, there arose a conviction in the course of the nineteenth century that there was an intrinsic connection between democracy and industrialism.

But not any *particular* species of democracy. This was the essential point. There were indeed some thinkers, mainly in England, who argued that industrialism 'naturally' demanded a system of formal democracy, and would ultimately prove unworkable without it. Most European socialists, too – revealing socialism's inheritance of French revolutionary thought and British political economy – assumed that capitalist industrialization would require formal 'bourgeois democracy' to complement it. But more commonly 'democracy' was interpreted in a far looser sense. 'Democratization' was in fact used by many as a short-hand term to express a phenomenon otherwise described in such phrases as 'the entry of the masses on to the stage of history' or 'the discovery of the people'. We should perhaps say today that what was being referred to was basically the phenomenon of *populism* – and the distortion was not in any case so great, in that the variety of democracy that flourished during the French Revolution was generally more populist than egalitarian.

Hence the argument was rather different than first appears. It ran, not so much that industrialization entailed democratic forms of government, as that industrialization had to be accompanied by the involvement, in some manner, of the mass of the population in the political life of the society. While this assertion made for no definite, positive associations of economy and polity, it certainly did for negative ones. Thus industrialization was incompatible with political systems, such as despotic empires of the Ottoman or Romanov kind, which refused to acknowledge the principle of popular participation or active representation in any form. It was not, however, incompatible with authoritarian regimes such as that of Bismarckian Germany or the French

Second Empire which, while being élitist and dictatorial in practice, enshrined the fact of universal suffrage and the principle of popular sovereignty in their constitutions.

Thus stated, it can be seen that the association of industrialization and 'democracy' (or, which is practically the same thing, the association of industrialization and nationalism) pointed to a larger movement than was, for instance, involved in the extension of the franchise or the triumphs of liberal constitutionalism. One way of summarizing that movement is to speak of 'the nationalization of society'. This phrase not only – and quite accurately – indicates the central association of the emerging industrial order with the developing nation-state:[32] it also suggests the movement of centralization that was taking place in all European societies, breaking down the insulation between the different parts (regions and classes) of society, and tending to a levelling effect in which all individuals became uniformly subject to a centralized state. The obverse of this process was the need to re-integrate the individuals so detached from their traditional moorings – and the most obvious device was through some form of legitimating populist ideology, whether democratic, liberal, or Marxist.

The movement towards centralization and the ideology of populism in their turn squared with the requirements of industrialism. Industrialization from the start, even in England, needed regulation and planning on a scale that could only be performed by a centralized state. (It was perhaps fortunate that England had since the time of the Tudors been politically a highly centralized society – certainly as compared with the Continental states.) Moreover, it required a certain kind of general commitment, a basic ethic of work and discipline, that was hardly compatible with the particularistic loyalties of the traditional political order, and which was best secured by a structure and sentiment of mass mobilization. It was in this sense, therefore, of the massing of the population into a centralized nation-state under a populist ideology, that we must understand the loosely-termed association of industrialism and democracy.

Most nineteenth-century social theorists commented on what seemed a necessary and inevitable increase in scale and centralization with the development of the new industrial order. It was a growth which, typically, they perceived as the off-shoot of, the accompaniment to, the more fundamental principle of change which in their different ways they singled out as transforming the society of their day. Durkheim saw the development of central government as the normal and predictable feature of societies characterized by a vast extension of the division of labour. He regretted the view of contemporary liberals who were inclined 'to regard the present dimensions of the governmental organ as a symptom of social illness'.[33] For Marx, 'nationalization' and centralization were the inevitable consequences of the rise of the industrial bourgeoisie:

> The bourgeoisie keeps more and more doing away with the scattered state of the population, of the means of production, and of property. It has agglomerated population, centralized means of production, and has concentrated property in a few hands. The necessary consequence of this was political centralization. Independent, or but loosely connected provinces, with separate interests, laws, governments and systems of taxation, became lumped together into one nation, with one government, one code of laws, one national class-interest, one frontier and one customs-tariff.[34]

For Durkheim, centralization posed in an acute form the problem of relating the individual to some new social entity with which he could feel solidarity. The occupational community was one of his tentative answers. For Marx, the bourgeoisie's centralizing tendency was but one aspect of the process whereby they dug their own graves. It prepared, indeed pointed, the way to a complete socialization of state, economy, and society. But in neither case did centralization appear as more than an inevitable and natural feature of an industrial order which they were concerned to analyse from a quite different perspective.

The concern with centralization as such, and the associated tendencies towards levelling and the creation of a 'mass society', was characteristically the hallmark of the liberal theorists of the time. Chief among these are Mill, Acton, Burckhardt, and Tocqueville. For these, centralization was not simply an incidental phenomenon of the age, it was one of its central driving forces, offering formidable threats to individual freedom and social diversity. The most thorough and most arresting analysis of this process was given in two works by Alexis de Tocqueville, his *Democracy in America* and *The Ancien Régime and the French Revolution*. In the opening pages of the former he announces:

> In perusing the pages of our history, we shall scarcely meet with a single great event, in the lapse of seven hundred years, which has not turned to the advantage of equality . . .
>
> The gradual development of the equality of conditions is a providential fact, and it possesses all the characteristics of a Divine decree: it is universal, it is durable, it constantly eludes all human interference, and all events as well as all men contribute to its progress.[35]

'Equalization' as a long-term historical tendency always meant for Tocqueville much more than the rise of certain aspirations and ideas, more even than the diminution of economic and political inequality – although of course it encompassed these things. Its force, and its threat, is better conveyed by the word 'levelling', as Tocqueville's works amply illustrate. For what preoccupied him was the fact that the drive towards equality was leading to the obliteration of all distinctions and differences between men, rendering them a uniform mass, common alike in their thoughts and attitudes as in their dependence on an ever more powerful centralized state. In the later work on the French Revolution he attempted to demonstrate how that event was the deposit of the relentless drive towards equality. Its major achievement was to unify and centralize France, and so complete the process started by the French monarchy centuries earlier. But that centralizing movement was only possible because of the appeal to the abstract, universal principle of the equality of all men, thereby making invidious, and defenceless, all distinctions based on class, rank, religion, or region. The upshot was the ending of all regional, religious, or occupational autonomy, and the concentration of all the expropriated powers in the centralized, democratic state, the sole organization that had the authority of the whole people behind it.[36]

In John Stuart Mill Tocqueville found his most thoughtful and eloquent disciple. Powerful though Tocqueville's own writing is, there is no passage in his work that summed up so concisely, and so influentially, the levelling tendencies of the age, as this passage from Mill's essay *On Liberty*:

> The circumstances which surround classes and individuals, and shape their characters, are daily becoming more assimilated. Formerly, different ranks, different neighbourhoods, different trades and professions, lived in what might be called different worlds; at present, to a great degree in the same. Comparatively speaking, they now read the same things, listen to the same things, see the same things, go to the same places, have their hopes and fears directed to the same objects, have the same rights and liberties, and the same means of asserting them. Great as are the differences of position that remain, they are nothing to those which have ceased. And the assimilation is still proceeding. All the political changes of the age promote it, since they all tend to raise the low and to lower the high. Every extension of education promotes it, because education brings people under common influences, and gives them access to the general stock of facts and sentiments. Improvements in the means of communication promote it, by bringing the inhabitants of different places into personal contact, and keeping up a rapid flow of changes of residence between one place and another. The increase of commerce and manufactures promotes it, by diffusing more widely the advantages of easy circumstances, and opening all objects of ambition, even the highest, to general competition, whereby the desire of rising becomes no longer the character of a particular class, but of all classes. A more powerful agency than even all these, in bringing about a general similarity among mankind, is the complete establishment, in this and other free countries, of the ascendancy of public opinion in the State. As the various social eminences which enabled persons entrenched on them to disregard the opinions of the multitude, gradually become levelled; as the very idea of resisting the will of the public, when it is positively known that they have a will, disappears more and more from the minds of practical politicians; there ceases to be any social support for non-conformity – any substantive power in society, which, itself opposed to the ascendancy of numbers, is interested in taking under its protection opinions and tendencies at variance with those of the public.[37]

It is plain that for both Tocqueville and Mill the movement

towards equalization predates the Industrial Revolution by a long time and continues in being irrespective of the industrializing movement. At the same time in the passage quoted above Mill makes it clear that the connection between centralization, uniformity, and industrialization is not an arbitrary one, and that in the historical circumstances of the time the connections were bound to become ever more indissoluble. Jacob Burckhardt had no doubts on the matter: 'Money-making, the main force of present-day culture, postulates the universal State, if only for the sake of communications . . .'[38] Most interesting, because it looks a somewhat unexpected discovery in his own mind, is Tocqueville's finding at the very end of the second volume of *Democracy in America* that

> there exists amongst the modern nations of Europe one great cause, independent of all those which have already been pointed out, which perpetually contributes to extend the agency or to strengthen the prerogative of the supreme power, though it has not been sufficiently attended to: I mean the growth of manufactures, which is fostered by the progress of social equality. Manufactures generally collect a multitude of men on the same spot, amongst whom new and complex relations spring up. These men are exposed by their calling to great and sudden alternations of plenty and want, during which public tranquillity is endangered. It may also happen that these employments sacrifice the health, and even the life, of those who gain by them, or of those who live by them. Thus the manufacturing classes require more regulation, superintendence, and restraint than the other classes of society, and it is natural that the powers of government should increase in the same proportion as those classes . . . As a nation becomes more engaged in manufactures, the want of roads, canals, harbours, and other works of a semi-public nature, which facilitate the acquisition of wealth, is more strongly felt; and as a nation becomes more democratic, private individuals are less able, and the State more able, to execute works of such magnitude. I do not hesitate to assert that the manifest tendency of all governments at the present time is to take upon themselves alone the execution of these undertakings; by which means they daily hold in closer dependence the population which they govern.[39]

In such ways were democracy, centralization, and industrialism linked. And we should remember that this passage was written in 1840, at a time when both democracy and industrialism had scarcely got under way, and when a widely-held expectation, common for the rest of the century, was that industrial society would reduce the functions of the state so greatly that it could practically vanish away.[40]

6. Secularization, Rationalization, Bureaucratization

'Alas! Alas! Religion is vanishing . . . We no longer have either hope or expectation, not even two little pieces of black wood in a cross before which to wring our hands . . . Everything that was is no more. All that will be is not yet.'[41] Alfred de Musset's rather mawkish utterance can be found repeated a hundred times and more during the course of the nineteenth century. Of one thing most people felt certain: the industrial society was a secular society. By this they meant that, on the one hand, there was a progressive decline of institutionalized religion, and of the formal beliefs associated with religious institutions; and, on the other, these beliefs were being increasingly replaced by ones deriving their authority from science and reason, rather than from systems of revealed religion.

For the negative aspect of this view the evidence appeared incontrovertible. Industrial man was not a worshipping man – not, at any rate, of the familiar gods. 'Among the masses there prevails almost universally a total indifference to religion,' commented Engels in *The Condition of the Working Class in England in 1844*. 'In cities and large towns,' wrote Horace Mann, the author of the 1851 Religious Census of Britain, 'it is observable how absolutely insignificant a portion of the congregations is composed of artisans.' Dutiful attenders of Sunday schools in their youth, he noted, on growing up 'soon become as utter strangers to religious ordinances as the people of a heathen country'.[42] The census revealed, to the horror of the Victorian Establishment, that less than twenty-five per cent of the total populations of most of the large cities and industrial towns attended divine service on Sundays. The rural districts did not fare much better, averaging out at a rate of attendance of just over twenty-eight per cent of the rural populations. Methodism was indeed the last organized religion to seize the popular mind; and after 1850 it went into a steep decline.

Moreover, the habit of non-attendance was catching. Towards the end of the century it was clear that the middle classes were staying away as well. Engels again, in a later essay of 1892, noted the change in attitude since the earlier part of the century:

> The introduction and spread of salad-oil (before 1851 known only to the aristocracy) has been accompanied by a fatal spread of Continental scepticism in matters religious, and it has come to this, that agnosticism, though not yet considered 'the thing' quite as much as the Church of England, is yet very nearly on a par, as far as respectability goes, with Baptism, and decidedly ranks above the Salvation Army.[43]

As the historian Ensor puts it: 'Creed sat lightly on the great majority in the upper and middle classes; the Bible lost its hold on them, and the volume of outward religious observance shrank steadily.'[44]

A census of 1902–3 in London showed only two in eleven persons worshipping. The London masses were proverbially heathen; religion undoubtedly did better in the country as a whole. But by the 1960s and 1970s in Britain average Sunday attendance was between ten and fifteen per cent (swollen by Roman Catholics); less than two per cent of the age group twelve to twenty were being confirmed in the Church of England, and only between three and five per cent of the population could be persuaded to attend Communion at Easter or Christmas. The Government's Central Statistical Office gave the data on religion under the heading of 'Leisure', alongside camping and television viewing.[45]

No one of course maintained that simple non-attendance at church equalled secularization. There were even some societies, such as the United States, where for exceptional and largely non-religious reasons church attendance remained high. But non-attendance was nevertheless very important. It was the most visible outward manifestation of the broader trend whereby religious practices, institutions, and thinking came to lose their hold over society as a whole. Typically in industrial society religion becomes a marginal and a minority preoccupation, like a hobby. There remains a decent respect for churchly supervision of the most important *rites de passage*, birth, marriage, death. Church baptisms, weddings, and burials continue to be popular. But Bryan Wilson rightly says of this that 'the church still plays its part in the lives of the many more as a service facility than as an evangelistic agency, more as the provider of occasional and re-assuring ritual than as the disseminator of vital knowledge or the exemplar of moral wisdom.' In matters as important as these the desire is still felt for some touch of the sacred, if only as a form of hopeful insurance:

> The church appears increasingly as some department of a welfare state, which might be corporately supported without personal commitment . . . to be used as and when the individual requires the performance of its services . . . It functions as a service agency providing appropriate ceremonial for prestige and status-enhancement at crucial stages of the life-cycle.[46]

Both at the time and since two main objections were made to the view that industrialization and secularization went hand in hand. The first was historical: the fact that, at the very moment when England was entering on its swiftest phase of industrialization, there should occur what one historian has called 'the greatest revival of religious faith since the middle ages'.[47] The Church of England was temporarily uplifted by the piety and intellectual rigour of the Oxford Movement; sects and denominations proliferated outside; Evangelicalism was part of the reigning ideology of the day.

But the paradox is easily resolved. The parallel can almost be drawn with the behaviour of species in natural evolution, when poised on the edge of extinction: in their decadent phase they give off a glorious explosion of energy, throwing up the most gorgeous and eccentric forms. So with organized religion. The Victorian revival was the prelude to virtual extinction. The emancipation, made possible by industrialism, from the old society and the old religion, led both to an intensification and a purification of religious life, and – not necessarily in the same people – away from it altogether. Harold Perkin aptly remarks that 'the existence of numerous competing sects, which was more characteristic of Britain than any other European country, provided a sequence of stepping stones by which the emancipated individual could make his way from the Church to any position of Christian belief, or at last out into the great desert of unbelief on the other side of the Jordan.'[48] A contemporary neatly made the connection between free-thinking and free trade: 'The same spirit which has produced "free trade" in articles of commerce advocates likewise a free trade in religion.' The eighteenth-century Unitarianism of Priestley and his friends easily led in the nineteenth century to sceptical Utilitarianism and later, to agnostic Positivism. Methodism in its various guises and manifestations provided for the working class the stepping-stones from the Church to Chartism, and later to secular socialism. It was Carlyle who shrewdly remarked in 1838 that theirs was an age 'destitute of faith and yet terrified at scepticism'. Hence the frantic religiosity. But it could be no more than a temporary haven from the slow erosion of the traditional faith. In the end the age found new faiths. But in their secular, rational, cast of thought they marked a deep divide between the industrial society and the religious faiths of every other kind of society.

This last point leads directly on to the second, more serious objection. To the historical argument was added a psychological and sociological one. Responding to the threat of the annihilation of religion the nineteenth century discovered the universality of religion, in the individual mind and in society at large. 'There is,' wrote Durkheim in his *Elementary Forms of the Religious Life*,

> something eternal in religion which is destined to survive all the particular symbols in which religious thought has successively enveloped itself. There can be no society which does not feel the need of upholding and re-affirming at regular intervals the collective sentiments and the collective ideas which make its unity and its personality ... What essential difference is there between an assembly of Christians celebrating the principal dates of the life of Christ, or of Jews remembering the exodus from Egypt or the promulgation of the decalogue, and a

reunion of citizens commemorating the promulgation of a new moral or legal system or some great event in the national life?[49]

On this view there could be no such thing as 'the decline of religion', merely a change in its forms. Religion was functionally necessary to society, the central mechanism of integration of its members and the most important source of its unifying symbols and rituals. While in the earlier part of the century some used this insight to proclaim the eternal necessity of Christianity, later, more radical, exponents of the view were too conscious of the loss of Christianity's hold on the populations of the industrial societies to rest on so untenable a position. Instead they devoted themselves to exploring the new 'secular' religions that were emerging in the age.

This proved a task of no great difficulty. From Burke onwards it became a commonplace to point to the French Revolution's substitution of the Goddess of Reason for the God of Christianity. Then there was Saint-Simon's 'New Christianity', a secular, scientific faith for the new world of industrialism, to replace the obsolete old Christianity of the obsolete old world. This shortly reappeared as Comte's 'religion of humanity', Positivism, aptly characterized by T. H. Huxley as 'Catholicism minus Christianity'. But then, too, Huxley's own scientific humanism had all the hallmarks of traditional evangelical religion, especially when urged on by his own passionate, missionary, advocacy. Once this step had been taken it was easy to discern the essentially religious character of the vast majority of the new ideologies of the century – nationalism, republicanism, socialism, even the ideology of science itself.[50] Later on, and going back to the roots of the whole thing, Carl Becker elegantly mapped out the 'heavenly city' of the eighteenth-century *philosophes*, as they erected the Temple of Reason on the ruins of the temples of traditional Christianity, and transferred the golden age from an unearthly past to a terrestrial future.[51]

Much of this can readily be admitted. The notion of the universality, the functional indispensability, of religion has great force: whether in reference to religion as a psychological thing, in the sense of a special and necessary quality in our attitudes to beliefs and persons; or as a sociological thing, in the sense of society's need for a comprehensive frame of reference which makes sense of its members' relations with each other and with society as a whole. But it is a force that is largely misspent when applied to the argument about secularization and industrialism. For the two arguments are not opposed to each other and are not in fact about the same thing anyway. The 'secularist', if one may use this short-hand term, is not necessarily making statements about the 'essential' nature of religion, whereas the 'religionist' clearly is. Some secularists no doubt think this is what they are doing, in which case they rapidly and rightly find themselves in trouble. But the point is that they need not engage in this kind of debate. It is perfectly possible for the secularist to accept the arguments of a Durkheimian religionist while remaining firmly convinced of the reality and importance of his own position. The critical distinction he wishes to make is not that between, say, 'religion' and 'reason' or 'science', but – to use the religionist's terms – between the 'religion' of industrial society and other kinds of religion. Secularism may very well be said to be a religion. That is immaterial to the present concern. All that is being argued is that industrialization brings with it secular institutions, practices, and beliefs. In what further sense these may also be said to share certain properties in common with traditional religions belongs to another discussion.

So, for instance, Alasdair MacIntyre defines secularization as 'the transition from beliefs and activities and institutions presupposing beliefs of a traditional Christian kind to beliefs and activities and institutions of an atheistic kind'.[52] Peter Berger, on a broader plane, sees secularization as 'a process by which sectors of society and culture are removed from the domination of religious institutions and symbols' and are subordinated instead to the rule of non-churchly institutions and of science 'as an autonomous, thoroughly secular perspective on the world'.[53] Neither MacIntyre nor Berger wish, nor need, to deny that atheistic or scientific beliefs may share certain features with traditional religious beliefs. What they wish to insist upon are the *differences*, especially in terms of practical import.

In theory one might wish to argue that the differences are no greater than, say, those between Christianity and Buddhism. Fortunately this is of academic concern only. For what of course gives these differences their momentous significance is their indissoluble links with the economic and social order of industrialism, and the historical fact of the world-wide triumph of industrialism. People may or may not have been willing to accept science in the abstract, as an interesting alternative ideology or 'world-view'. They were not given the choice. Wherever industrialization took hold, its ultimate tendency was to secularize life, to de-throne and disqualify all other competing religions. In so far as a society accepted industrialism, it had to accept a mode of cognition, science, which had its own exclusive interpretation of the world, its own prescriptions for action within it, and its own, internally self-validating, procedures for testing and confirming the truth of its beliefs. To say that this description fits any and every religion is true but again misses the point: which is that industrialism has undermined and vanquished every social order which it has encountered, and that therefore secularism has triumphed over other religions to an extent and in a manner never accomplished by any previous religion.

Tocqueville caught the birth of this process in his account of the French Revolution, where he saw the revolutionaries' rationalism become 'a kind of new religion in itself – a religion, imperfect it is true, without a God, without a worship, without a future life, but which nevertheless, like Islam, poured forth its soldiers, its apostles, and its martyrs over the face of the earth'.[54] The secularism that was carried by the revolutionary armies was carried even further and more powerfully by the iron ships and cheap manufactured goods of the new industrial society. It is this unprecedented phenomenon of total victory which makes the rise of secularism different in kind from the rise of other religions, and which makes it perverse to deny the real break in continuity of beliefs entailed by industrialization. Whatever the actual quality of the majority's belief in science, or the extent of their knowledge of it, the fact remains that they have available explanations of the world in terms of a system of thought which for all practical purposes has ruled out the explanations of all other systems of thought.

Secularization was, in its turn, a manifestation of an even deeper-lying tendency in industrial society: the drive towards the *rationalization* of all spheres of life. Max Weber, who made the analysis of this process central to his sociology of modern society, made it clear that, as with democratization, it was a tendency that long predated the rise of industrial society. As an attitude and a practice, Weber in fact saw it as a secular distillation of certain features of Protestant Christianity, and therefore dated its origins in sixteenth-century Europe. Moreover, given the fact that perhaps the most significant aspect of rationalization was its transformation of attitudes towards economic life, it had as much claim to be the cause of industrialism as its effect. Nevertheless, by the end of the nineteenth century the origins of rationalization were less important than its contemporary expression. Having helped to give birth to industrialism, it became fused with it and was later carried by it. To become industrialized was to become rationalized, a process affecting every area of society, the most public and the most private, the state and the economy as well as the relations of marriage, family, and personal friendship.

Weber's rationalization is a complex concept, embodying a complex and not altogether coherent historical process. He himself was fond of emphasizing the negative aspects of it, as in his frequent quotation of Schiller's phrase, 'the disenchantment of the world': 'The fate of our times is characterized by rationalization and intellectualization and, above all, by "the disenchantment ment of the world".'[55] Here rationalization referred to the process whereby the world was rid of magic and mysticism, and of the populations of gods, demons, and spirits that had governed its activities in so many systems of belief. This development had matured only in the societies of the Christian religion. Indeed Church, priest and prophet had hurried it on, in their relentless drive towards the bureaucratization of church affairs, their scholastic systematizations of theology, their creations of increasingly monistic cosmologies. In this sense Weber along with several others was led to see Christianity as an *inherently* secularizing and rationalizing religion, producing almost inevitably out of itself its own demise. To this 'disenchantment' early science of course contributed; but then it must be remembered that for many centuries some of the most brilliant natural scientists were clerics, intent, in all sincerity, to demonstrate by their scientific labours the greater grandeur and power of God.

The positive qualities of rationalization can loosely be summed up by saying that it is the embodiment of the method and substance of science in the institutions, practices, and beliefs of the society. Weber was concerned to emphasize the practical bent of such a development and, above all, its reliance on the method of observation and calculation in all activities, even in those of the arts. The prime exemplar of the rational calculating mode was to be found in the economic realm, in the system of modern European capitalism, with its rationally organized labour market of formally free workers, and rational entrepreneurial activities based on exact calculations of profit and loss. The economic substance of the concept is given weight, perhaps too much so, in Julien Freund's definition of rationalization as 'the organization of life through a division and co-ordination of activities on the basis of an exact study of men's relations with each other, with their tools and their environment, for the purpose of achieving greater efficiency and productivity'.[56]

More generally Weber applied the concept to a studied and increasing mastery over the environment, both natural and social, in which the essential tools were those of observation, experiment, measurement, and calculation. The tendency could be observed in all areas of modern culture: in the elaboration of a rational system of laws and formal procedures for handling them; in the rise of a rational system of administration with modern bureaucracy; in painting's achievement of a rational utilization of lines and spatial perspective; in the establishment of a rational system of musical notation, and of rational principles of musical structure in modern counterpoint and harmony.[57]

Weber was careful to point out that rationalization did not by any means necessarily imply that the populations of those societies undergoing it were any more 'reasonable' or knowledgeable individually, as compared with the populations of less rationalized societies. In terms of a better understanding of their environment they might even know less. The primitive man in the bush knows infinitely more about the conditions under which he lives, the tools he uses and the food he consumes. The modern man who takes a street-car or an elevator, suggested Weber, was not likely to know the principles on which those machines worked, nor were the driver or the elevator operator likely to be any more enlightened.

> The increasing intellectualization and rationalization does not, therefore, indicate an increased and general knowledge of the conditions under which one lives. It means something else, namely, the knowledge or belief that if one but wished one *could* learn it at any time. Hence, it means that there are no mysterious incalculable forces that come into play, but rather that one can, in principle, master all things by calculation. This means that the world is disenchanted. One need no longer have recourse to magical means in order to master or implore the spirits, as did the savage, for whom such mysterious powers existed. Technical means and calculations perform the service. This above all is what intellectualization means.[58]

Rationalization, then, here yielded one of its ambivalences. A deeper and more serious ambivalence was revealed in Weber's distinction between 'formal' and 'substantive' rationality. The former refers to the degree to which action is governed by rationally calculable principles, the fitting of the most appropriate and efficient means to a desired end. The latter refers to the degree to which goals and values have been definitely formulated and sorted out according to a rational procedure of ranking, ascription of priorities, realization of contradictory aims and strategies for getting round this, and so forth ('from the standpoint of determinate ethical postulates', was how Weber expressed it, although he believed that the ultimate grounds of ethical choice remained irreducibly arbitrary and 'irrational'). At the abstract level the distinction was just about possible to hold. In historical reality, as Weber knew only too well, the agencies of formal rationality – strictly, the means – had a tendency to invade and undermine the quest for the attainment of substantive rationality.

The dilemma, and the common dénouement, can be illustrated from the fate of classical liberal industrial society. In theory, liberal industrial society was concerned only with the rationalization of means. Ends were seen as diverse and infinite, a matter of individual, private, desires. Hence all the characteristic concepts of liberal economic theory – 'maximization', 'optimization', 'least cost', and so on – related to a concept of rationality that was entirely concentrated on the most efficient means to a given end. In practice, however, things worked out differently. The organization of society, of work, of family life, for the realization of the most efficient means, the most rational way of maximizing output and reducing input – all this inevitably affected and influenced the individual's choices, preferences, and desires. The mobilization of society for the greater and cheaper production of goods had as one of its consequences the production also of a 'consumer mentality', constraining its inhabitants to a passive and unproductive consumption of goods. It had, too, its effect on the whole way in which 'fun' and 'leisure' were perceived, and how the hard-won rewards of economic activity were spent. That is, it affected the ends satisfied by such instrumental activity. The irony was that the rationalized means, which, more than ever before, were supposed to free the individual for the pursuit of more, and more diverse, ends, ended up by enslaving him to their supposedly neutral techniques and technology.[59]

Weber's own nightmare about the 'irrationality' of rationalization was born of the contemplation of the most fateful and formidable agency of formal rationality: *bureaucracy*. In much of his writing, indeed, bureaucratization and rationalization are almost synonymous, so struck was he by the growth of the phenomenon, and so distinctively a western development did it seem:

> No country and no age has ever experienced, in the same sense as the modern Occident, the absolute and complete dependence of its whole existence, of the political, technical, and economic conditions of its life, on a specially trained *organization* of officials. The most

important functions of the everyday life of society have come to be in the hands of technically, commercially, and above all legally trained government officials.[60]

And just as the general process of rationalization, while not initially created by industrialism, was given its greatest impetus by it and later carried by it, so the more specialized deposit of that process, bureaucracy, accompanied the development of industrialism and became functionally indispensable to it. The trained official, said Weber, 'is the pillar of both the modern State and of the economic life of the West'.[61] Bureaucracy had a principled hostility to all 'irrational' considerations of person or place, religion or kinship. It adhered strictly to rationally constituted rules and formal procedures of execution. It submitted to the rationality of scientific expertise. It was consequently the highest expression of the rationalizing tendency in industrial society. Industrial society, in whatever form, capitalist or socialist, needs bureaucracy as much as it needs workers and machines. 'The dependence of the material fate of the masses on the permanently correct functioning of ever more bureaucratically co-ordinated private-capitalist organizations steadily grows, and the very thought of the possibility of eliminating them becomes ever more utopian.' So, too, 'any rational socialism will have to take over and augment' bureaucratic administration.[62]

But Weber's conception of the indispensability of bureaucracy to modern industrial society is accompanied by the perception of its threat to certain key values of the society. This most developed exponent of 'formal rationality' at a certain point complicates the attainment of some of the values of 'substantive rationality'. The technical, means-to-ends, rationality of bureaucracy comes to substitute itself for the goals for which it was instituted. Weber singled out here particularly the threats to individual creativity, personal autonomy, and democracy – all deeply-held values of modern western society. The rationalization of economic life, through the development of modern capitalism, and the unique prominence of economic ends in modern society, had already posed acute problems for the general health of the society and the possibilities of all-round individual development.

The further, intensive, bureaucratization of society also tended to undermine the pursuit of democracy. Weber saw, along with Tocqueville, that democratization had been one of the most favourable bases of bureaucratization, through its attacks on aristocratic and monarchical privilege. But 'democracy inevitably comes into conflict with the bureaucratic tendencies which, by its fight against notable rule, democracy has produced . . . The most decisive thing here – indeed it is rather exclusively so – is the *levelling of the governed* in opposition to the ruling and bureaucratically articulated group, which in its turn may occupy a quite autocratic position, both in fact and in form.'[63] And reflecting, in the long term, on the bureaucratization of ever-larger sectors of social life, Weber was driven to offer a grim vision:

> Together with the machine, the bureaucratic organization is engaged in building the houses of bondage of the future, in which perhaps men will one day be like peasants in the ancient Egyptian State, acquiescent and powerless, while a purely technically good, that is rational, official administration and provision becomes the sole, final value, which sovereignly decides the direction of their affairs.
>
> This passion for bureaucracy is enough to drive one to despair. It is as if in politics . . . we were deliberately to become men who need 'order' and nothing but order, become nervous and cowardly if for one moment this order wavers, and helpless if they are torn away from their total incorporation in it. That the world should know no men but these: it is in such an evolution that we are already caught up, and the great question is, therefore, not how we can promote and hasten it, but what can we oppose to this machinery in order to keep a portion of mankind free from this parcelling-out of the soul, from this supreme mastery of the bureaucratic way of life.[64]

It is perhaps unfair to end this sketch of the image of industrialism on so melancholy a note. Not only does it not, in Weber's own case, do justice to his equally strong conviction of the achievements and advantages of rationalization and bureaucracy; but coming at the end of the whole account, it also has the somewhat unfortunate effect of making that sombre note sound throughout. It has become fashionable in this century, and especially in the last decade or so, to see mainly the dark side of industrialism. The cry of horror uttered by the artists and writers of the early part of the century has been echoed and amplified on a wider scale in the more recent years of noisy, cramped, living and environmental deterioration. The tendency then is to carry that feeling back into the nineteenth century, to read the nineteenth-century social theorists primarily as critics and denunciators of industrialism, and to ransack their writings for corroborative statements conveying the appropriate sentiments of gloom, nostalgia, *angst* and anger.

This is a seriously distorting procedure. The heroic age of sociology was also the heroic age of industrialism. It was almost impossible for the early sociologists not to feel some sense of exhilaration at the novel and sweeping changes taking place in their societies before their very eyes. Marx certainly expressed this sense in the many eloquent passages listing the triumphant achievements of the industrial bourgeoisie, even while he was denouncing that class for its exploitative rule and deploring the dehumanizing effects of industrialism. Moreover his writing is infused with a confidence that industrialism can and will rid itself of the evils of its capitalist form, and that its promise will reach fulfilment in its next, socialist, phase. The note of confidence is even stronger, and with far fewer qualifications and misgivings, in the writings of Saint-Simon, Comte and Spencer, whose sociologies of industrial society were to a large extent also celebrations of it. It is there still with Durkheim, the inheritor of that tradition, who is steadfast in his conviction that the great increase in the division of labour in modern industrial society has been mainly a liberating force; although now, in the late nineteenth century, there is a new concern that the problems of industrialism were deeper and less tractable than had previously been thought. Only with Weber, of all the 'founding fathers' of sociology, does one get the feeling that the doubt has outstripped the confidence, and that Weber faces the modern world with a brave but gloomy countenance; and even here there is no attempt to fudge the accounts, no desire to inhibit the clear expression of the great benefits of a rationalized world.

Of course the doubts, anxieties, and outright hostility were also there from the start: partly in the work of those sociologists we have just mentioned, more characteristically in certain conservative literary circles strongly influenced by Romanticism and the revived medievalism of the nineteenth century. The writings of these critics had considerable influence on the more systematic sociologies of industrialism. In England from the time of Burke onwards there was a strong vein of social criticism expressing deep disenchantment with urban-industrial society, and regretting the loss of the values and mores of rural-agrarian society; although in the best of this writing a sense of the possibilities of industrialism triumphed over sentimental nostalgia. Continental hostility to industrialism (usually and correctly associated with political liberalism) took a deeper, more overtly ideological form – in the writings of militant French Royalist Catholics such as Chateaubriand, de Maistre, and Bonald, and of German Romantic historians and sociologists such as Haller, Savigny, Tönnies and Gierke. These influences had their strongest impact on German social theory and are reflected in the greater ambivalence in the assessment of industrialism of the German sociologists. But even in Germany such anti-industrial sentiments had to contend with the rationalism and confident progressivism of Marxism, which prevented Germany sociology from lapsing into a futile conservatism.

For nineteenth-century sociology, industrialism was, clearly, Janus-headed. Perhaps the most concise expression of these ambivalent sentiments is to be found in Tocqueville's celebrated comment on Manchester following a visit there in 1835. It is quoted at the head of this chapter. In it is summed up the mixture of tremendous hopes and fearful anxieties that fairly reflects the nineteenth-century response to industrialism.

A word, finally, on the constituents of the image of industrialism sketched in this chapter. It is, obviously, a selection of what I consider to be the most important themes in the sociological response to, and definition of, the emerging industrial society. Others, with different interests and purposes from mine, will have wanted to select other themes. But I make no apology for any restrictions contained in my selection. The view suggested there, of the changes entailed by industrialization, involves so sweeping a transformation of the structure, culture, values and beliefs of a society that it is most unlikely that other changes cannot be accommodated under their general rubric. Indeed one of the analytical problems is that each single theme or characteristic usually represented for a particular thinker a more or less *total* characterization of the new society. So it is, for instance, with Tönnies and the decline of the *Gemeinschaft*; Durkheim and the increased division of labour; Weber and rationalization. It is clear from their accounts of these phenomena that almost any one of them could be made to encompass all of the six features that I have chosen to list separately. The justification for doing it in this way is that it makes clearer to a reader today just what were the ingredients that have gone into the common and widely-diffused contemporary image of industrialism. I have not in any way attempted to show the comprehensiveness of the views of any particular thinker. In the development of sociology, certain central insights and inferences about the nature of industrial society were lifted from the general body of thought of the early sociologists, and fused into a 'model' of industrialism. The consequences of this are evident both in scholarly thought and in common opinion. I have wished to show how this may have come about.

A second ambiguity is more serious. Many of the characteristics listed here evidently pre-date the onset of industrialization in Europe. This is true perhaps above all of Weber's theme, rationalization. Their status as an entailment of industrialization may therefore seem absurd. This of course would be true if one were considering the unique case of European – rather, indeed, British – industrialization, and that alone. This is not my purpose. I am merely concerned with the general inferences about the process of industrialization once it had been seen to occur, and some of its long-term tendencies became visible. From this point of view the causes of the Industrial Revolution in Europe are not important. What matters is that, whatever the institutional and intellectual causes, they naturally became embodied in the resulting industrial order, into the industrial system as a whole.

In any case all thinkers emphasized the extent to which all predisposing tendencies were developed and intensified by industrialization. It was the economic core of the system that attracted to it, and then carried, all the social, political, and ideological aspects of industrialism. As far as all other societies but the first were concerned, industrialism was received as a 'package' of institutions, practices and values, which it was as difficult to disentangle analytically as it was practically.[65] As individual items they may have been able to resist any one of them; but insofar as they embarked on the economic transformation involved in industrialization, they seemed constrained to adopt all of them. In historical perspective industrialism and modernity seemed to be the same thing, and it seemed unimportant which aspects of modernity had preceded industrialism in time. To become modern was to go through the process of industrialization, which is to say, to arrive at something like the state of society envisaged in the sociologists' image of industrialism.

4 The Revolution Dissected: Image and Reality

Generally speaking, for the economical development of the bourgeoisie, England is here taken as the typical country; for its political development, France.

Engels, footnote to the 1888 English edition of the *Communist Manifesto*.

Universal History moves in a succession to which the nations are subsidiary.

Lord Acton, letter to contributors to the *Cambridge Modern History* (1897).

The nineteenth-century image of industrialism has great force. I hope in the preceding sections to have indicated my own agreement with much of what it has to tell us about the process of industrialization and the nature of industrial society. It has a depth and comprehensiveness of analysis unequalled in any other period of western social thought, and consequently allows us to understand industrial society, modern society, to a degree impossible for any other type of historical society. It is satisfying by virtue of the sense we have of its penetration to the very core, the moving principles, of the new society. And it was in many ways remarkably accurate in its projection of the main tendencies of that society. As Robert Nisbet says, in the modern world 'we *are* urban, democratic, industrial, bureaucratic, rationalized, large scale, formal, secular, and technological.'[1]

Later sociology acknowledged its debt to the earlier formulations by taking them over wholesale. So struck were sociologists by the power and accuracy of the nineteenth-century anatomy of industrial society that they apparently saw little reason to make any serious modifications. Only, with an eye on the academy and the student, rather than on society and the citizen, their formulations were inevitably drier and more scholastic than those of their nineteenth-century predecessors.

In the reshaping two main directions emerged. One was to distill, as it were, certain more concrete implications from the larger principles enunciated by the earlier theorists, and to structure the investigation of industrial society along those more particularized lines. Thus from Mill and Tocqueville's account of equalization and democratization came the idea of the industrial society as a mobile 'mass society', restless and uprooted, and a concentration on the properties of the twentieth-century 'mass' as compared with the nineteenth-century 'public'.[2] Particularly fertile, too, was the Spencer-Durkheim conception of modern society as the high-point of the process of differentiation and specialization. From this could be derived, at the concrete institutional level, certain major innovations of industrial society: the separation of 'home' from 'work', and of 'work' from 'leisure'; the decline of extended family ties, and the emergence of the elementary or 'nuclear' family as the most appropriate to the conditions of industrial life; the loss of family functions, so that the family was forced to give up its role in the productive process and was reduced to being a unit of consumption only, while its socializing functions were first shared and then increasingly taken over by schools, youth cultures, the mass media, and welfare departments.[3] Weber's account of 'rationalization' was the stimulus to the view that industrialization must lead to the general diffusion of systems of formal education, and to a great growth of professional, scientific, and technical expertise. It would also lead to a class system based on achieved occupation rather than birth or patronage, and a meritocratic system of ranking and rewarding. Or, following Marx and Durkheim on alienation and *anomie*, the emphasis could be placed on the distinctive set of issues and social problems that was placed on the agenda of an industrializing society. There was the problem of recruiting and training the industrial workforce, and the social tensions that had to be 'managed' in disciplining the industrial population to the new rhythms and routines of machines and factory employment. More generally, there was the problem of integrating into the new social order the spatially, occupationally, and socially mobile and uprooted populations set in motion by the forces of industrialism.[4]

The second line followed by twentieth-century sociology moved in the opposite direction. Instead of working downwards, it aspired to generalize, at an even higher level of abstraction, the tendencies singled out by the nineteenth-century sociologists. In these accounts industrialization appeared, for instance, as a three-fold process of 'individualization' (i.e. emancipation from corporative and communal groups), 'abstraction' (i.e. secularization and rationalization), and 'generalization' (i.e. nationalization of interests and loyalties);[5] or as 'specialization', 'differentiation' and 'integration', with or without 'social discontent'.[6] There were many other such schemes. Perhaps the most ambitious, certainly one of the most influential, was that of the American sociologist Talcott Parsons. In origin it was not explicitly or specifically intended to be applied to the process of industrialization. Extending Weber's contrasting principles of 'traditionality' and 'rationality', Parsons sought to show how all social action could be analysed in terms of contrasting pairs of 'pattern variables', that is, variable yet ordered ways of governing ('patterning') action. Generally he found that the pairs could be reduced to four in number, each pertaining to the resolution of certain universal 'dilemmas' of action, and each indicating contrasting choices in the actor's orientation to others and to his environment. These four were: affectivity versus affective neutrality; particularism versus universalism; ascription versus achievement; diffuseness versus specificity. To some extent the meanings are clear from the words themselves, and in any case most of the senses are covered by the better-known antitheses of traditional versus rational, or *Gemeinschaft* versus *Gesellschaft*.[7]

Parsons intended his variables to be analytical tools independent of any historical content whatsoever. But it could hardly escape his disciples how easy it was to bundle the units of the four pairs together so that they added up to very familiar contrasts of types of historical society – 'traditional' and 'modern', 'pre-industrial' and 'industrial'. Rapidly therefore in their work, and often too in Parsons' own, the pattern variables became the basis for the analysis of the transition to industrial society, and of the institutional bases of that society.[8] It was no more than a frank recognition of the nineteenth-century origin of the scheme. But it was unfortunate that this should be one of the major avenues along which the nineteenth-century analysis of industrialism should be carried. The method of distillation of the first line at least had the advantage of directing attention to specific institutional and ideological changes, and so sent the student back to the actual historical experience of particular societies, for confirmation or refutation. With the pattern variables and similar analytical constructs this procedure became unnecessary. Industrialization was simply assumed to be the movement from the left-handed unit of each pair of the pattern variables to the right-handed unit, from particularism to universalism, ascription to achievement, affectivity to affective-neutrality, and diffuseness to specificity. The types of action, abstracted from the historical context that gave them their original meaning, could thus be employed to obviate the need to resort to any history at all.

No nineteenth-century account ever reached such sterile heights. Even in those thinkers – such as Spencer and Durkheim – most hostile to the spirit and matter of history, the writing retained sufficient connection with actual societies at actual times to make their accounts stimulating and suggestive. And in some of the contributions – such as Marx's in the first volume of *Capital*, and Weber's *Protestant Ethic and the Spirit of Capitalism* – the engagement with the materials of history was so rich and so productive as to constitute veritable models of sociological analysis. Sociology (like historical study) lives in the tension between the general and the particular, and on the whole the practitioners of the nineteenth century maintained the tension creatively.

But the dangers were there: implicit in their approach and to some extent in their very enterprise to seize and conceptualize the flow of large-scale historical change.[9] In lesser hands the method could readily became a barren formula, easily learned in academic courses in sociology and as easily imposed on the real world of change, with no more than the most casual investigation of, or reference to, that world. A host of ill-conceived, ill-written, and vastly unproductive books and treatises on 'development' and 'modernization' bear witness to the reality of this danger.[10] I have so far emphasized the positive and creative side of the model of industrialism that the nineteenth-century sociologists bequeathed to their twentieth-century successors. It is time now to say something of the weaknesses and pitfalls that were also part of that inheritance.

1. Modes of Industrialization and Social Change

In three ways the classic model of industrialism left a distorting legacy. It was misleading with respect to the mode of social change; the timing and speed of change; and the directions of change.

Much of all three turned on the first: the adoption of a particularly wide-ranging and comprehensive conception of change as *evolutionary*.[11] I have already, in Chapter Two, discussed the extent to which the early sociologists conceived their task as the description and explanation of the great transformation – industrialization – taking place in the societies of their time. To do this, it seemed evident to them, they had to place the current changes within a framework that gave them a past as well as a future. They had, that is, to give an account both of the mechanisms of change and the directions of change.

In theory there were several ways of handling this. Popular ones in the past had been varieties of Augustine's providentialism, or the device of the social contract. In practice the climate of the times eliminated these traditional solutions, and pointed sociology firmly in an evolutionary and developmental direction. The sciences of the nineteenth century had discovered the genetic, historical, method. In all the sciences there was a universal passion to discover the origins of things, and the principles that had led to their growth and development. Again, in principle such growth could have been seen as random and accidental, exhibiting no order or pattern. Such a view was distasteful to a century that aimed at the discovery of the most fundamental laws of structure and change, being and becoming, in both the natural and the social worlds. The conviction was well-nigh universal that growth was orderly, whether one contemplated the evolution of the universe as a whole or the growth of the minutest individual organism. Given, too, the remoteness of the historical past uncovered by nineteenth-century geology, it seemed plausible to conceive that growth as slow, gradual, and continuous, eschewing all notions of miraculous leaps, sudden mutations, and providential interventions. 'Nature makes no leaps' was an old dictum of the naturalists; and it was a view espoused in relation equally to individual and social development. To an earlier tradition that had drawn the analogy between the organs and functions of the individual organism, and the organs and functions of 'the body politic', was added the historical and developmental perspective of nineteenth-century science. The result, so far as sociology was concerned, was a view of social change as organic change, an orderly process of development or evolution through growth, differentiation, and maturation.[12]

In this conception, change is due essentially to forces intrinsic to the thing changing. Change is constant, cumulative, and coherent. It takes the form of evolution by stages, each stage arising out of the preceding one and, in its turn, being pregnant with the next, and each expressing a 'higher', more developed and more complicated state of the system. The problem of the 'causal mechanics' that moves the system from one stage to the next is resolved by subsuming it under the logic of the evolutionary sequence as a whole. Here the analogy with the growth process of the individual organism was of decisive importance. The stages of development in the life-cycle of any individual organism can be known and predicted with a good deal of accuracy, given a general knowledge of the character of the species to which it belongs. In this sense, at whatever stage of development we contemplate the organism we can reconstruct its past and predict its future. The principle of propulsion taking the organism from one stage to the next is of no special interest here since it can be assumed as a constant. No knowledge of it is required for understanding the present state nor for predicting the future. It becomes a problem only when there is a malfunctioning of the organism, when, in other words, the normal orderly process of growth is disturbed.[13]

Transferred to society, the method therefore allowed the early sociologists to be remarkably casual about the mechanisms of change in their schemes of social evolution. Marx alone paid detailed attention to the problem, in analysing the contradictions in a given mode of production as the dynamic of changes of system. But even for him there was an inevitability to the process of evolution that pointed to the underlying organic model of change – a feature emphasized by his frequent use of organic metaphors in describing change. Given the logic of the whole historical sequence, the contradictions within the different modes of production *had* to work themselves out – and hence lost any independent causal efficacy that they may otherwise have claimed.

With the other major sociologists, concern with this aspect of change was minimal. Often no more was implied than that 'progressive tendency' in mankind that the eighteenth-century *philosophes* of progress had relied on. Spencer offered the general principle of 'the instability of the homogeneous' as the *primum mobile* of social change (and indeed of all change). Thereafter it could simply be assumed as the constant agency moving human society through the various stages from a condition of maximum homogeneity to one of maximum heterogeneity (Spencer here drawing for the details upon the German embryologist von Baer's account of embryonic development as a movement from the homogeneous to the heterogeneous). To account for the great development of the division of labour in modern times, Durkheim suggested as cause a progressive increase in 'material and moral density', a vaguely sketched process of increasing spatial concentration of populations and increasing social relations and exchanges between their members. But Durkheim dwells little on this, and it is clear that his main interest is to trace the *effects* of the increased division of labour on the life of modern society. For the rest, the movement from 'mechanical' to 'organic' solidarity corresponds in most ways to the sort of evolution Spencer described, and with the same organic drives of differentiation and specialization.

As with the mechanics of change, so with its stuff, history. Both were ironed out and subdued by the imposition of the logic of the evolutionary sequence. Once the theorist had characterized the species – Society – by the particular principle which he thought expressed its nature, it only remained for him to segment history in accordance with that principle. But not real history, not the actual chronological sequence of events. History became 'natural history'. What mattered was not to examine the past to demonstrate the actual existence of social forms implied in the particular theoretical perspective – the extended family as compared with the present nuclear form, community as compared with association, and the others. The past had to function as the theatre displaying the progressive logic of the principle. It had to be made to show the principle embodied in its earlier, 'past' forms, proceeding by a logical or 'natural', rather than a historical, process to its contemporary, more developed, forms.

Thus if the particular evolutionary principle singled out was the progress from 'savagery' to 'civilization', the past (including the 'contemporary past' seen in the less developed societies) was ransacked for scraps of illustration that would give the principle a properly historical form, even if it lacked any real historical content. The method was baldly stated by the anthropologist J. F. McLennan: '. . . In the science of history old means not old in chronology but in structure. That is most ancient which lies nearest the beginning of human progress considered as development.'[14] Such a view was bound to mean a casualness, almost an indifference, towards the historical past. And it was a particular irony that the evolutionary method should have got much of its inspiration from the patient and painstaking historical scholarship of nineteenth-century historians. History was invoked as an indispensable part of the evolutionary perspective. But it was invoked in a manner that made it easy at best to abbreviate it, at worst to ignore it.

The weaknesses of this evolutionary conception of change come out strikingly when it is applied to the specific episode that preoccupied the early sociologists: industrialization. To put it simply, on this view becoming industrialized poses no real problems. It has the inevitability of development in natural history. We have seen how the nineteenth-century sociologists tended to compress the multiple stages of the eighteenth-century idea of progress into two polar types, 'then' and 'now', 'pre-industrial' and 'industrial'. The odd thing is that, despite this concentration on the one, overwhelming, episode of transition, they are not much more illuminating on the mechanics of that transition than were their eighteenth-century counterparts. What clearly absorbs their interest is the working out in their society of the principle that for them most significantly characterizes the new industrial society. How that novelty was born, and how it might be diffused beyond its contemporary North Atlantic confines, was something that interested them far less; and largely because the problem was resolved for them even before it was posed.

Here they showed themselves still to be the creatures of the eighteenth-century Enlightenment. They took over the *philosophes*' conception of the essential unity of mankind. It was 'Man' that evolved, or 'Society', conceived of as the community of all mankind. At different times various groups of men had embodied and represented the various stages of that unitary process of evolution: now the Egyptians, now the Greeks, now the Romans, now Christian Europe. At the present time the 'carriers' of man's progressive evolution were the industrial societies of the west. Conceivably there would be other carriers in the future – although most of the nineteenth-century sociologists were convinced that human evolution had reached a culminating point with the rise of scientific, industrial, civilization. At any rate, the question, why industrialism, why the west, was a somewhat idle one. The spirit bloweth where it listeth. The history of mankind was the story of man's growth, in the direction of rationality and freedom.

Why a particular set of societies was selected to represent any particular stage of that growth, and the specific manner in which they represented it, was perhaps a matter of interest to some, such as antiquarians, but could not be a serious concern of philosophic historians and sociologists. The western industrial nations were the current standard-bearers of modernity. The urgent task seemed therefore to explore the nature of this modernity, to show up its novel features, to reveal its problems and difficulties so that its promise should not be left unfulfilled. For unless some new principle arose, which seemed for various reasons unlikely, it was the destiny of the rest of the world to be gradually but inevitably suffused with the principle of industrialism, as the latest and highest expression hitherto of mankind's evolution.

Nothing more neatly illustrates the embrace of the philosophic conception of a single evolving mankind than Engels' innocent footnote to the *Communist Manifesto*, quoted at the head of this chapter: 'Generally speaking, for the economical development of the bourgeoisie, England is here taken as the typical country; for its political development, France.' Engels here constructs and projects forward an ideal bourgeois industrial order, which has absorbed the effects both of the English Industrial Revolution and the French (political) Revolution. It expresses itself with various degrees of strength and clarity in actual historical societies, but it cannot be held to be co-terminous with any one society or any precise tract of historical time. It is in fact like Spencer's industrial society, or Durkheim's society of organic solidarity, a stage of social evolution, which finds embodiment in particular societies but embraces them just as it itself is comprehended by the overall sequence and logic of man's unfolding. Its origins and arrival therefore need no special principle of explanation, any more than its growth and diffusion; none, that is, that is not implied in the principle of evolution itself. Ultimately it is the result of the slow but inevitable growth and maturation of man and society.

There is a grandeur in this conception of change that hides and even compensates for its logical shortcomings. There is also the fact that in its nineteenth-century versions we can to a large extent ignore its influence and concentrate instead on the superb anatomies of industrialism that form the central portion of the sociological legacy. Neither of these compensations, alas, are offered to us in the twentieth-century successions to this tradition of evolutionary thought. The theory of social change, after a period of abeyance, was revived after the Second World War under the stimulus of the anti-colonial movements of the period. The problem arose of how to consider the industrialization and future development of those societies. Superficially the situation seemed analogous to that of nineteenth-century Europe, with the dramatic and rapid creation of new social orders; and the superficial view, unfortunately, prevailed.

With little hesitation, and almost no modification, the evolutionist conceptions of change were imported into the growing field of the sociology of 'development' and 'modernization'. The existence, and the pressure, of the already industrialized parts of the globe were largely ignored, except insofar as they provided the model to which other societies were tending – as well as the 'experts' who would help ease the passage. Abstract models of 'stages of growth' and 'phases of modernization' were constructed by economists and sociologists, and offered as universal models of social development and evolution. It was clear, on inspecting these models, that their elements were derived from the European experience of industrialization; not surprisingly, therefore, they had a certain value as short-hand expressions and typifications of that experience. Transported to the rest of the world these premises became painfully obvious, and the applicability of the models very dubious.

Basically they continued the nineteenth-century tradition of assuming industrialization to be a form of endogenous change, arising naturally out of the preceding state of society and being propelled through the various stages of growth and differentiation until achieving some sort of stable, mature state. The energizing force of this development was often seen as some entelechy called 'the will to be modern', similar in most respects to Turgot's 'innate tendency to progress'.[15] But none of this could for long disguise the fact that the developing 'Third World' was actually in a historically unique situation, differing in fundamental ways from the situation of the societies of nineteenth-century Europe. Its societies lacked Europe's autonomy. They were attempting to industrialize in the shadow and partly under the direction of powerful industrial societies who were very likely, in their own interests, to interfere with the pure logic of the industrializing process. Since that 'logic' was a generalization from Europe's own past, it followed that the mode of industrialization of the new nations could be expected to diverge in many ways from the classic European pattern.

All this is very obvious now, and has been abundantly commented on. But then it seems worth asking, why has this evolutionist view of change, and especially the evolutionist account of industrialization, exerted so apparently irresistible a fascination for social theorists? And here a striking irony appears. The evolutionist account of industrialization was plausible largely because that was the way it seemed to happen in the 'classic' case of industrialization, that of Britain. It was because the British case became, as Engels' remark indicates, the typical model of industrialization for social theory that it was able to give massive support to the older evolutionary conception of change. In other words, the society and the event – the British Industrial Revolution – that had been responsible for one of the most fundamental discontinuities in the whole of human history also became the mainstay of a theory that was concerned precisely to deny radical discontinuities in social evolution.

This impression of the British experience of industrialization was by no means wholly misguided or misinformed. It was of course easy to forget the civil war and subsequent political settlement of the seventeenth century that had been the essential background to that industrialization. But, more than a hundred years on, contemplating a long period of unprecedentedly and enviably peaceful political evolution, contemporaries could be forgiven for remarking on the orderliness and stability of the society that gave birth to industrialism. Certainly as compared with Continental and later cases of industrialization, the British case presented a remarkable picture of organic, endogenous change.

Industrialization seemed to emerge naturally and with no apparent breaks from the social structure and culture of the society. Owing to the exceptional fluidity of the class structure, *all* classes participated in the process. There were no values that militated strongly against involvement in trade and industry. Sons of the English gentry regularly went into commerce. Sections of the aristocracy involved themselves vigorously in the improvement, commercialization, and 'industrialization' of agriculture, and patronized talented mechanics and engineers. There was not even the stigma that in other European societies commonly attached to manual labour and mechanical dexterity. Most of the creators of the first textile machines, for instance, were middle class (John Kay, John Wyatt, Edmund Cartwright, Lewis Paul, Samuel Crompton). It was not discreditable in the eighteenth century for children of good families to be apprenticed out to weavers and joiners.

The working classes themselves would no doubt have had some dissident comments to make on this picture of organic evolution. But what again was impressive to contemporaries, especially on the Continent, was the extent to which working-class protest and reaction in Britain took peaceful and constitutional forms. During the whole crucial period of transition from about 1780 to 1850 there was practically no point at which working-class discontent threatened to become revolutionary. The most dangerous moment for the system came with the struggles over the Reform Bill of 1831. But here too the remarkable thing – as compared with so many Continental states – was the willingness of the aristocratic ruling class to give way, coupled with the fact that the agitation was fed by not a few of the upper and middle classes anyway, anxious for reform so as to avert revolution. Even in the case of the classes that suffered most during industrialization, therefore, what seemed important was the system's maturity, its capacity to contain the disruption and disturbances that must inevitably accompany the movement to an industrial society. It provided a strong confirmation of the Saint-Simonian view that, given the right state of preparedness of the social organism, there were no radical contradictions in the social order of industrialism.

But perhaps the most striking feature of the British case of industrialization was the virtual absence of a political, governmental, element. This squared beautifully with the preconceptions of nineteenth-century sociology. We have already seen in Condorcet and Saint-Simon the extreme hostility to politics in the early sociological tradition, a view of politicians and the state as an artificial excrescence on the social organism. To leave matters to the whims and power struggles of the politicians must necessarily, they thought, do violence to the naturally and gradually developing social forces intrinsic to the society. These must be allowed to express themselves at their own rate and in their own way; political direction 'from outside', usually inexpert and motivated by extraneous considerations, must almost invariably result in an artificial bending and stunting of those forces.

The British Industrial Revolution was a most satisfying demonstration, and vindication, of the correctness of this view. There was an informality and a spontaneity to its development that gave a powerful sense of a whole society in travail, giving birth to a new order through an organic process of seeding, growth, and maturation of the appropriate forces and tendencies. State direction and control was at a minimum – which was as it should be, because had it been otherwise there would have been the suspicion of a forced, unnatural development. Taken with the gradual growth and slow diffusion of the industrial way of life, the British example of industrialization afforded a classic illustration of organic, evolutionary change.

As the original and, in truth, the only example of developed industrialization available to them, the nineteenth-century sociologists were inevitably drawn to the British experience in constructing their theories of industrialism. Marx's account, for instance, of the emergence and development of the capitalist industrial order took the form essentially of reflections on recent English economic history. And what resulted particularly from the sociologists' reflection on that experience was a reinforcement of the evolutionist account of change that they had inherited from the eighteenth-century idea of progress. Industrialization was a process of intrinsic change. It was created, carried and inherited by the classes who formed the most substantial social forces of the time – particularly of course the commercial middle classes, but drawing also on all the sections of the other classes who could see the symptoms of change and did not wish to be swept aside by the inevitable development of the new forces. Its materials, human and physical, were to be found within the developing body of the industrializing society. To seek elsewhere would be to graft on to an unprepared organism alien influences, and so distort the natural course of change. Industrialization, in other words, had to be seen as an effort of the whole society, of one social whole giving birth to another social whole. Extraneous influences, whether of the state or of other societies, had to be regarded as signs of abnormal or pathological growth.

Such a conception left sociology ill-prepared to deal with what actually happened in the later course of world industrialization. Seen from the perspective of the present, a century and a half later, the British case stands out as unique in almost every important respect.[16] It was unique in its gradualness, in its unplanned nature, in its nativeness, and in its privateness. Elsewhere, to a remarkable degree, industrialization came as an import, imposed on the society from on top, or brought in by groups alien or marginal to the prevailing social structure. Moreover, the very fact that Britain had been first in time affected not only the nature of the British experience itself but every subsequent attempt to industrialize. Not only was there the unsurprising feature of British efforts to direct other countries' industrialization in the interests of their own. There was also now an important *knowledgeableness* about the whole process of industrialization, its causes and effects, which tempted every later society to try to bend, thwart, or abridge the 'pure logic' of industrialism. 'One reason why history so rarely repeats itself,' E. H. Carr has said, 'is that the *dramatis personae* at the second performance have prior knowledge of the *dénouement*.' So it was with the course of revolution in the nineteenth century; so, too, with the course of industrialization. All this meant that the further one moved, in time and place, from the British Industrial Revolution of the first half of the nineteenth century, the less convincing it became to hold to an evolutionist view of an organic, 'natural', history of industrialization, arising spontaneously out of the intrinsic development of social forces.

Comparison with Britain's nearest neighbours, in western Europe, where the similarities with the British case might be expected to be greatest, makes this point particularly clear. What strikes one forcibly in considering the industrialization of France and Germany, and even more the lands to the east, is the relative artificiality of the enterprise, the extent to which it went against the grain of the social structure and cultural values of the time. In England, it is fair to say, business was an activity of the whole nation, and not just of the commercial middle class. On the Continent at the same period, commercial values were still scorned and the commercial class looked down upon. The commercial middle class was an oddity, almost an artificial and alien stratum in the midst of the 'natural' orders of monarchy, nobility, Church, and peasantry. This was true of France, truer still of the societies to the east of her. 'Indeed,' David Landes remarks of this period,

> the farther east one goes in Europe, the more the bourgeoisie takes on the appearance of a foreign excrescence on manorial society, a group apart scorned by the nobility and feared or hated by (or unknown to) a peasantry still personally bound to the local *seigneur* . . . Far more than in Britain, continental business enterprise was a class activity, recruiting practitioners from a group limited by custom and law.[17]

The culture of these societies was still hostile to business values. Governments tried, for mercantilist reasons of state power, to stimulate trade and industry, but their efforts were always undermined by the contradictions between these initiatives and their own aristocratic outlook, which shared in the general distaste for businessmen and their activities. '*Geschäfte macht kein Windischgrätz*' was the quip of an Austrian nobleman, neatly expressing the preference for the military over the commercial virtues.

Continental society, then, was unlikely to industrialize by a 'natural' and spontaneous growth. Wealth was pursued, certainly, but more in the spirit of what Weber referred to as 'booty capitalism' than in the rational, calculative spirit of the true capitalist entrepreneur. At the same time Continental governments had to respond to the challenge posed by the British Industrial Revolution. British industrialization upset the entire balance of economic forces in Europe, and so the entire traditional structure of power. If the 'natural classes' of Continental society could not or would not undertake the industrializing effort, then the state must, using whatever means of coercion or persuasion it had at its disposal.

On the Continent 'industrialization was, from the start, a political imperative'.[18] The political element, of low significance in the British case, was central to the Continental experience. It was the state that encouraged the immigration of foreign – mainly British – workers and technicians, that mobilized capital for investment, that underwrote loans, that set up industrial enterprises, that established (well before Britain) schools and institutes of scientific and technical training. It was a state, moreover, that could be called 'bourgeois' only in the loosest possible sense – and mainly in the sense that it was doing the bourgeoisie's work for it, or at the very least stimulating and pushing it into action.

The French Second Empire of Louis Napoleon has rightly often been singled out as a decisive phase of French industrial and financial development, the moment of its 'take-off into self-sustained growth', to use Rostow's well-known terminology.[19] But it has equally often been pointed out that the French bourgeoisie did not vote for Louis Napoleon, preferring instead by a massive margin the republican General Cavaignac. They chafed throughout under the dictatorship of the Second Empire, until it was overthrown by the Prussians and they were at last able to set up their own Third Republic. Similarly German industrialization was launched and sustained by the autocratic Prussian state, later transformed into Bismarck's Reich; and the class that was the principal agent of that development was not the commercial middle class but the Junkers, the pre-capitalist Prussian ruling class who traditionally monopolized the public administration. Such a pattern of what Alexander Gerschenkron calls 'forced industrialization' was indeed almost the commonest mode of Continental industrialization, characterizing, for instance, also Italian industrialization under the energetic direction of the Piedmontese state. Summing up the Continental experience before 1914 Gerschenkron comments:

> There is little doubt that forced industrialization was regarded in Europe before 1914 as being at variance with the dominant value system and was widely rejected as leading to an 'artificial' or 'unsound' growth, these terms having penetrated so deeply into European vocabularies that their metaphorical character was rarely, if ever, perceived. But there is equally no doubt that forced industrialization played an important part in important areas of the continent before World War I.[20]

Later cases of industrialization departed even further from the 'organic' pattern of the British example. Imitating Germany's 'conservative modernization', there was the phenomenon of Japan's spectacular industrialization 'from on top', carried through by a section of the old feudal landowning class under the symbolic leadership of the restored Meiji imperial dynasty, and largely in the face of the indifference and hostility of the conservative merchant class. Starting in the 1880s, the Russian Tsarist state also embarked on a programme of rapid and extensive industrialization, freely employing foreign capital and foreign technical assistance, as well as its more characteristic device of the knout, to bring about a forced development in a society almost wholly lacking in the requisites of a native entrepreneurial class, adequate credit institutions, and a skilled and disciplined workforce.

The void proved too great, and the Tsarist state disappeared into it. But the recommencement of the industrializing effort under the direction of the revolutionary party of Lenin and, even more, Stalin, offered yet another model of industrialization to complement the earlier ones. Industrialization could be accomplished by the revolutionary mass party, based on the peasants and led by a westernized intelligentsia. Since, in the process, the peasantry seemed doomed to disappear or be thoroughly subordinated to a newly-created proletariat, the extrinsic nature of this mode of industrialization could hardly be starker. It was a simple acknowledgement of the non-existence of any social force native to the society which could undertake the development. Such a mode appeared particularly compelling to those peasant societies of the non-western world, such as China and Cuba, who were not prepared to allow industrialization to be carried out by foreign agents with their own interests to further. For those societies which were so willing, or who seemed to have no choice in the matter, as with many countries in Latin America, then this latter option provided still another mode of industrialization: industrialization through the operations of a foreign bourgeoisie working both from their own country and from bases (e.g. branches of multi-national corporations) within the host country.[21]

In contemplating this very rapid historical sketch, and without going any further, we can already identify four separate modes of industrialization. There is firstly the 'organic' evolutionary mode, with a minimum of centralized direction and mobilization, exemplified by the British, the North American, and to some extent the French cases of industrialization. Secondly there is the mode of 'conservative modernization' from above, carried out by elements of the traditional pre-industrial ruling class using the state bureaucratic apparatus, and involving a strong element of state direction and mobilization of people and resources. This is exemplified in part by the French, and almost wholly by the German, Japanese, and pre-1917 Russian cases of industrialization. Thirdly there is the mode of 'revolutionary modernization' from above, carried out by the mass revolutionary party and also involving strong state direction and mobilization, and exemplified in the post-1917 Russian, the Chinese, and the Cuban cases. Fourthly there is the mode of industrialization by formal and informal colonization, carried out by the bourgeoisies of other industrial societies, and exemplified in certain Latin American cases, notably Brazil, parts of South-East Asia, and perhaps also post-1945 Spain. A sub-variety of this last can perhaps also be seen in the comparable case of 'industrialization from outside' where the agent is a foreign state, as in the industrialization of some east European countries after the Second World War.

'The industrial history of Europe appears,' says Gerschenkron, 'not as a series of mere repetitions of the "first" industrialization but as an orderly series of graduated deviations from that industrialization.'[22] The same comment applies just as much if we extend the picture to take in world industrialization. The 'deviations' were indeed not arbitrary. There *is* a certain historical logic to the process, which can be seen at its most general as a series of challenges and responses in different historical circumstances, and within changing contexts of the power relationships between societies.[23] But it is not the 'logic' apparently suggested by the British mode of industrialization, with its conception of a self-contained entity propelling its own growth. The logic of that experience was well-nigh unique; and it was unfortunate for later sociological theories of industrialization that the early sociologists should have been so mesmerized by its power and prestige.

2. Time and Tempo

No less distorting, but in a different way, has been the received account, implicit in the sociological image of industrialism, of the timing and speed of European industrialization. This has been a less obvious aspect of the nineteenth-century legacy, and is less easy to document. Some of the evidence for it comes simply from participation in the contemporary discipline of sociology: in the form of a strong impression carried away from a reading of the current sociological literature on industrialism, and from the common coin of sociological conversation on the most casual as well as the most ceremonial occasions. At the more objective level, there is the evidence of contemporary sociological theories of 'post-industrialism', with their implicit dating of the period and process of industrialism. Both sources reveal in their different ways a serious misconception about when, and how quickly, the industrial society came into being. The consequence has been that contemporary sociology has tended to see the present phase of the industrial societies' history in a distorted light; to see, on the one hand, discontinuities and novelties where there are in fact basic continuities with the past; and, on the other hand, to fail as a result to appreciate what a genuine movement 'beyond industrialism' might entail.

Essentially the error consists in an historical abbreviation and, so to speak, a premature conceptualization, of the movement to an industrial society. In itself this was hardly surprising. The early sociologists were the witnesses to the first wave of industrialization in the world's history. So fundamental a set of changes could not be 'partially' conceived. They had to be grasped as a totality, as the elements of a whole new *system* within which they could be comprehended and described. The requirement was not simply intellectual, but emotional, and also practical. None of the early sociologists felt remote from the changes, or was content merely to describe and dissect. The problems thrown up by the new social order were – or seemed to be – novel both in their character and in their magnitude. Analysis had to be directed to the alleviation or resolution of those problems. To this end, the early sociologists felt compelled to give the new forces of industrialism as definite, comprehensive, and complete a shape and direction as possible. They strove to master them in thought as one means of attempting to master them in practice. Such a drive towards systematization, so urgent a sense to comprehend the past, present, and future of the new order, was bound however to carry the risk of damaging the logic and history of the reality so seized. We have seen something of both the logical and the historical shortcomings with respect to the mode of industrialization. What needs stressing in addition is the extent to which the nineteenth-century model of industrialism, in its intellectual completion, conveyed to its inheritors the notion also of its historical completion.

It is a widespread assumption, certainly among sociologists, occasionally even among historians, that the making of the industrial society was basically a nineteenth-century phenomenon: more or less completed by the mid-century in Britain, rather later in the rest of Europe, but in any case settled and mature by the time of the First World War. (What comes afterwards is therefore 'late' or 'advanced' industrial society, or even 'post-industrial' society). This historical perspective is especially marked in

Marxism, from which, shorn of its political revolutionary content, so much of the modern sociology of industrialism has been distilled. Marxism is particularly fond of the idea of 'the 1848 watershed' in the development of capitalist industrial society, with a preceding 'heroic' period, and a succeeding defensive and increasingly decadent period that culminates in the imperialist scramble of the late nineteenth century and the subsequent World War among the rival imperialist powers.[24] (What comes after *that*, of course, is something of a problem for Marxists – but tends to be labelled the era of 'managerial capitalism', or 'state monopoly capitalism' – in any case, some version of 'late', and imminently departing, capitalism.)

England, as was customary, as the oldest and most developed industrial society, was taken as the exemplary case. But there was a radical foreshortening and compression involved in this assumption. 'It is something of a commonplace,' writes David Landes, 'that the Crystal Palace Exposition of 1851 marked the apogee of Britain's career as "the workshop of the world".'[25] It is consequently something of a shock to realize that, according to the census of that very same year, the workforce of the most advanced industrial society of the time was still heavily concentrated in agriculture and domestic service, with the remainder mostly employed in the old craft industries. If England at this time was an industrial society, it was so mainly in intent, rather than in accomplishment. On almost all the most important features of industrialism, English development was slow and fragmentary, delaying until the very end of the nineteenth century the full working out of the tendencies of the Industrial Revolution.

The factory system was still in its infancy, if by that we understand a system characterized by large mechanized plants, a rational and 'scientific' organization of work, and an extensive use of inanimate sources of power. 'We must remember that the large, many-storeyed mill that awed contemporaries was the exception. Most so-called factories were no more than glorified workshops; a dozen workers or less; one or two jennies, perhaps, or mules; and a carding-machine to prepare the rovings. These early devices were powered by the men and women who worked them . . .'[26] Even in cotton manufacture, by far and away the most advanced sector of industry, almost two-thirds of the units making returns in 1851 employed less than fifty men; while as late as 1858 only about half the workers in the Yorkshire woollen industry worked in factories, and the hosiery industry was still dominated by the system of small master-craftsmen employed, as of a century ago, by capitalist hosiers on a putting-out system. It was indeed one of the unexpected features of early industrialization at first to intensify, rather than supersede, the old 'putting-out' system of the merchant capitalist, the craft-shop, and cottage industry. Putting-out gained, as might be expected, from the decline of household production and handicraft. But it was also strengthened precisely by the growth of the new industries themselves, which made demands for new skills and new products, especially to do with machine building and maintenance, that were for various reasons best satisfied by sub-contracting to the old-style artisanal workshops. Thus 'although factory production meant the end of many [work] shops, it meant the beginning of many more', surviving and indeed thriving in symbiosis with the modern factory.[27]

But even within the factory itself, the organization and technology of work for long carried the marks of the craftsman and artisan tradition. Eric Hobsbawm has remarked on 'the extraordinary neglect of productivity and efficient labour utilization' in much of nineteenth-century industry. That 'rationalization' of work and the workforce which later came to be comprehended by the term 'scientific management', and which was as central to industrial production as the machines themselves, was a surprisingly late development in the nineteenth-century factory. Hobsbawm is inclined to put this down to the spectacular results brought about by early mechanization alone, which blinded employers to the even more spectacular gains which could be had by reorganizing the work process itself. At any rate, he shows how, until well into the 1880s, neither masters nor men seem to have learned fully the rules of the nineteenth-century market economy. Neither side pushed to the limit what market principles theoretically allowed them. Wages, differentials, work-loads, and much of the pace and character of work, were determined largely by customary norms, many of which derived from medieval craft conditions, and which very rarely reflected the true power of either employers or workers under market conditions.[28]

The dependence on customary norms reflected the persistence in the factories of a pattern of work organization deriving basically from the artisan workshop. The work was still predominantly carried out by more or less autonomous teams of skilled and semi-skilled workers, who negotiated their own rates with management, often employed their own men, and generally organized the work to their own taste and convenience. Dobb has pointed out that 'as late as 1870 the immediate employer of many workers was not the large capitalist but the intermediate sub-contractor who was both an employee and in turn a small employer of labour.'[29] In such conditions of work, the 'detailed' division of labour, the splitting-up of the act of production, was necessarily limited, and so also was the further mechanization of tasks. It was not until the coming of systematic 'scientific management' at the turn of the century, symbolized by the organization of the assembly-line, that one could truly say that industrialism had arrived in the factory – and by then the factory was already ceasing to be the main focus of employment for significant sections of the workforce.

If industrialization was slow in working out its tendencies in relation to the division of labour within the factory, there are grounds for saying that it practically *never* fully worked out its tendencies in relation to the division of labour between town and country. Marx had regarded the separation of town and country as the decisive step in the growing division of labour. It was the most profound expression of the basic type of the division of labour, that between mental and manual labour. In industrial society, Marx was quite clear, it was urban life and urban capital that dominated the countryside, transforming it into a specialized branch of production for the benefit of the urban classes. The countryside, commercialized and mechanized, its population reduced to the minimum necessary to man the agricultural machines, was to provide the food to feed the swelling populations of the industrial towns. Economically town and country formed one system, the system of capitalist industrialism. Sociologically, in its values and forms of life, industrial society meant the victory of urbanism over the pre-industrial rural rhythms and patterns of life.[30]

We have seen that, according to the census of 1851, Britain was already an 'urban' society.[31] But what did such merely quantitative expression mean? Certainly not, for a very long time, the prevalence of the distinctively urban styles of thought and behaviour as analysed by Tönnies, Simmel, Wirth, and others. People could be gathered together in relatively concentrated aggregations without casting off many of the features of the older rural community. Urbanization in nineteenth-century England showed this to a remarkable extent. Many cities, particularly of the newer industrial kind in the Midlands and the North, grew through a process of linking up of more or less independent 'industrial colonies', planted either in the countryside or adjacent to existing urban settlements. There were understandable economic and social reasons for this pattern of development. Much of the new industry was actually in the countryside or outside the boundaries of established settlements. Industrialists preferred to have their workforce close to the works, partly for reasons of mutual convenience, partly the better to ensure social control. Whatever the reason, the consequence was that many of the early industrial settlements were both in form and, to a good extent, in substance industrial 'villages', bearing many of the marks of the local rural environment from which they were largely recruited. As with many of the industrial villages in Lancashire, they were independent, self-sufficient communities, showing in the patterns of family life and forms of leisure, for instance, a distinct continuity with earlier rural patterns. The resemblances persisted in the role of the industrialist employer, combining, as with the squire of the past, the characteristic paternalist mix of benevolent benefactor and harsh exploiter. In these ways, as one historian has put it, 'the idiocy of rural life might be rejuvenated and even strengthened in its industrial context.'[32]

Industrial urbanism did not therefore necessarily bring with it the triumph of a distinctive urban style of life. R. E. Pahl rightly comments that 'urbanisation in the nineteenth century is generally thought of as being a matter of huge concentrations of population. The parallel development of industrial de-centralisation must not be overlooked. It created a distinctive form of urbanism'[33] – so distinctive, indeed, that some later commentators were led to wonder whether it deserved the term 'urban' at all. When in the course of time these industrial colonies were linked up or absorbed by larger urban aggregations, they carried with them their self-sufficient 'village' character, reflecting often the particular ethnic group or region – e.g. Ireland – from which they had originated. Many large English towns, right up to the middle of the present century, were indeed shown by a host of sociological studies to be no more than a rather diffuse collection of such villages.[34]

It was this situation that in the early years of this century provoked D. H. Lawrence's famous outburst:

> England has had towns for centuries, but they have never been real towns, only clusters of village streets. Never the real *urbs*. The English character has failed to develop the real *urban* side of a man, the civic side. Siena is a bit of a place, but it is a real city, with citizens intimately connected with the city. Nottingham is a vast place sprawling towards a million, and it is nothing more than an amorphous agglomeration . . . The Englishman still likes to think of himself as a 'cottager' – 'my home, my garden'. But it is puerile. Even the farm labourer today is psychologically a town-bird. The English are town-birds through and through, today, as the inevitable result of their complete industrialization. Yet they don't know how to build a city, how to think of one, or how to live in one. They are all suburban, pseudo-cottagy, and not one of them knows how to be truly urban.[35]

In time the paradox went even further. Just when, particularly after the Second World War, the urban villages were gradually being broken up by projects for urban clearance and renewal, urban dwellers scrambled to get out of the cities: at first intensifying the movement towards the suburbs that went back to the early years of this century, later leaping over even these oases of greenery to seek out homes in the old villages in the countryside.

There was yet another way in which traditional rural influences continued to penetrate into the very heart of industrial urbanism. This had to do with the seasonal pattern of employment of the Victorian workforce. Raphael Samuel has shown how, until the very end of the nineteenth century, large sections of the workforce went 'tramping', following the rhythms of the seasons. As the spring approached, whole families would gradually begin to head out of the towns, to seek employment in the countryside. By the high summer, and especially at harvest times, the movement out of town would become a veritable flood, and many urban industries had to cut back or close down altogether for the peak summer months. With the coming of autumn the drift back to the towns began, deepening in intensity with the onset of winter. Then as spring came round again, workers began once more to stir, and 'the wandering spirit' would again prompt men and women to seek out the green fields and farms of the countryside.[36]

It is difficult to estimate precisely what proportion of the Victorian workforce organized their lives on this cyclical seasonal pattern. But the contemporary evidence leaves us in no doubt as to its central significance for the work routines of Victorian England. As Samuel says, for much of the nineteenth century 'the distinction between the nomadic life and the settled one was by no means hard and fast. Tramping was not the prerogative of the social outcast, as it is today; it was a normal phase in the life of entirely respectable classes of working men ...'[37] Consequently much of that disciplined organization of the workforce which we associate with industrialism was lacking. The concentration of workers in cities and in factories went on apace, it is true; but in an irregular pattern, which meant the constant breaking and re-making of ties with employers and fellow workers, in different parts of the country at different times of the year. This affected not only the power of the employer over his workers, his inability to establish a fully 'rationalized' system of control using the whole span of the year as a single unit of work-time. It also naturally affected the attempts of the early trade unions to organize and discipline their potential members, and to speak with a concerted voice on a given occasion. In the world of 'comers and goers' it was impossible for either employer or trade-union organizer to be certain that they were dealing with workers who had fully acknowledged the system of industrial urbanism.

The change came, but it was slow. By the end of the century there had arrived the mechanization of farming, and the displacement of travelling labourers by regular farm servants. The need, in the more mechanized factories, for a more regularly employed workforce was given practical expression. There was the extension of retail shops into trading areas previously in the hands of itinerant dealers. It was only then that 'the towns began more thoroughly to absorb their extra population, and to wall them in all the year round.'[38]

The same story of the contradictory, uneven, and long drawn-out impact of the Industrial Revolution in England can be told of many of the other concomitants of industrialization noted in the last chapter. Thus while secularization was, as we have seen, a marked tendency throughout the century, it was accompanied by so vast (even though so final) an outburst of religious energy and religious proselytization, that for a long time it made the notion of industrial society as intrinsically secular seem paradoxical and puzzling. Ensor observed that 'no one will ever understand Victorian England who does not appreciate that among highly civilized, in contradistinction to more primitive, countries, it was one of the most religious the world has known.'[39] In many ways the religious sects of Victorian England appear as active carriers of industrialization, rather than as archaic hang-overs and potential obstacles to the process. They were indeed the last formal embodiments of 'the Protestant ethic' that was to a great extent the driving force of the first wave of world industrialization. And they were, it is true, doomed to be extinguished by their own success; just as industrialization was to discover in the course of time that it could develop, and be extended by, non-religious ideologies more directly and more obviously suited to its needs. But these facts were for future experience. To have equated industrialization and secularization was fundamentally a truthful and important insight; but it was misleading to anticipate the consequences too quickly, and to disregard the evidence for the long persistence of religious thought and organization in the first industrial nation.

In a related area there was an equally perplexing phenomenon. Industrialization, it is commonly assumed, promotes, demands, goes hand-in-hand with, a modern secular, scientific and utilitarian outlook. Elites in industrializing countries today count it as imperative to replace their traditional cultural and educational institutions with those carrying the ethos and techniques of modern western science. What then appears quite startling is the extent to which the original act of industrialization, especially in England but also in other parts of Europe, was carried out by groups steeped in the traditional mode of classical humanism – in the study, that is, of the Greek and Latin classics – rather than, as one might expect, the modern mode of the natural sciences. The classics, formally dethroned in the struggle between the 'Ancients' and 'Moderns' at the end of the seventeenth century, nevertheless persisted as a central point of reference and a central element in the upbringing of all the educated classes of Europe throughout the eighteenth and nineteenth centuries. Indeed in the nineteenth century, the century of European industrialization, classical humanism even seems to have strengthened its hold on European culture. 'Never,' says Hugh Trevor-Roper, 'were the Greek and Roman classics so widely read as in that century of boundless materialism and revolutionary science.'[40]

The point is underlined by the degree to which even the most radical, progressive, and utilitarian reformers remained imprisoned within the boundaries of the classics. The most famous case is that of the two Mills. The father, James Mill, the most dedicated prophet of Benthamite utilitarianism in the land, saw to it that his utilitarian son John Stuart Mill should begin to learn Greek at the age of three, and at the age of eight should be competent to teach Latin to his younger sister. Then there was Macaulay, who espoused utilitarian modernity with an outspokenness and a verve that have given his utterances classic status, and who, as a supporter of the foundation of the new utilitarian University of London, declared that the classics should not be taught there. It was this same Macaulay who turned in almost every sentence he wrote to the classics for historical parallels and moral standards.

What was true of the radical reformers was, of course, even truer of the other educated groups in British society. And Trevor-Roper neatly makes the relevant point:

> The domination of the classics over British education in the nineteenth century is, in retrospect, an extraordinary phenomenon. For surely it must strike any historian as odd that an industrial revolution, having triumphed at home, was carried over the whole world by the elite of a society bred up on the literature of a city state and an empire whose slave-owning ruling class regarded industry and commerce as essentially vulgar . . . At the time, this seemed entirely natural. Everything, at the time, seems natural. But in retrospect it is surely a paradox. Modern writers, observing the recent history of China, discover in Confucianism a convenient explanation of the retardation of Chinese society in the nineteenth century. The ceremonious conservatism implicit in Confucianism, they say, was incompatible with modern progress, and was bound to retard it: only when that inhibiting culture had been broken – and it took a revolution to break it – could the great leap forward into modernity be made. The argument sounds very plausible – until we look into our own history and discover that our great leap forward, in Victorian times, took place under a mandarinate which was wedded no less firmly to a culture no less inhibiting: a culture which was accepted not only by the mandarins themselves but by their critics too.[41]

As with formal religion, so with the classics. The long-term tendency did in the end assert itself more visibly. The hold of the classics on education did ultimately slacken and an apparently irreversible decline set in, although not until well into this century. But what again must sober our reflections is an awareness of the slowness of the changes, the enormous capacity for overlap between the old and the new, the paradoxical fact that, here as elsewhere, the old patterns were often strengthened and given a new lease of life by the new and ultimately vanquishing forces.

There is, finally, in the British case, the notable absence of bureaucratization until very late in the course of industrialization; together with the equally delayed achievement of formal democracy. As to the first it is a curious irony that it was Marx, who most obviously of the early sociologists took England as the exemplary case of industrialization, who also most instructively pointed to the oddity of British development with respect to bureaucratization. At the Hague Conference of the First International in 1872, Marx specifically excluded England from the general maxim that the workers would have to conquer political power by force to achieve socialism. He did so on the grounds that England lacked that 'military-bureaucratic machine', the smashing of which, as he put it elsewhere, 'is the preliminary condition for every real people's revolution on the Continent.'[42]

As late as 1886 Engels still felt it necessary to remind English socialists of England's exceptional position on this count, invoking Marx's analysis and declaring that Marx had been 'led to the conclusion that at least in Europe, England is the only country where the inevitable social revolution might be effected entirely by peaceful and legal means.'[43] It was not until 1917 that the Marxists were driven to abandon this view. Lenin, rehearsing the argument that year in *The State and Revolution*, and agreeing with Marx's analysis of 1871–2, had to conclude that 'the restriction made by Marx is no longer valid.' England had joined her Continental neighbours in sinking into 'the all-European filthy, bloody morass of bureaucratic-military institutions'.[44] He was right, of course. The First World War had been particularly instrumental in speeding up the process of bureaucratization which had been for so long delayed in Britain, and whose absence had been noted enviously by many Continental observers. But the history of the Marxist attitude on this subject equally points up the very slow growth in Britain of one of the most basic attributes of industrialism.

As to democratization, it is well known how late was the coming of mass universal suffrage to Britain. True, the association between industrialization and democratization posited in the sociological model of industrialism focuses more on the quality of mass popular involvement in politics than on formal systems of democratic representation. Nevertheless it was generally assumed that the governments of industrializing societies would have to concede universal suffrage to their populations, if only as a means of staving-off a more direct and violent intervention by the masses. On that expectation British political development was slow even by its own very leisurely standards.

A series of Parliamentary Reform Acts during the nineteenth century cautiously opened the door; but even after the Acts of 1867 and 1884 less than thirty per cent of the adult population had the vote. On the eve of the First World War, seventy per cent of the adult population still did not enjoy the franchise; and while the majority of the disfranchised was that half of the adult population who were women, it was also the case that more than forty per cent of adult males were not on the electoral register (and indeed the total number of voters represented only some eighteen per cent of the total population).[45] It was not until the 1918 Reform Act, which almost tripled the electorate (especially by giving women over thirty the vote), that anything like a mass suffrage existed in Britain. In other words, universal suffrage did not come to the oldest industrial society until well into this century. If then the industrial society is the democratic society, we need to remember that this feature of industrialism in Britain had to wait for more than a hundred years after the Declaration of the Rights of Man of the French Revolution. Nothing more clearly illustrates the diffuseness of the patterns of change launched by the 'dual revolution', the (French) political and the (British) industrial, nor the length of time it took for the two aspects to work out their implications in relation to each other.

The British case of industrialization has been treated in some detail because of its significance in the construction of the sociological model of industrialism. Summing up these observations, we may say that, even in the narrow sense, Britain's industrialization did not mature until late into the second half of the nineteenth century, over a hundred years after Watt had invented the steam engine (1769); while many developments associated with industrialization did not come to fruition until our present century. Expand the geographical and historical boundaries, and the general point can be made even more sharply. If the full impact of industrialization in Britain was far later than is generally realized, that on the Continent actually had to wait, for the most part, until well into this century. For instance, not until the last years of the nineteenth century did the urban population exceed the rural in Germany; in France, the even point did not come until after the First World War. Again, as late as 1895 there were more people engaged in agriculture than n industry in Germany; in France, agriculture outnumbered industry until after the Second World War. Moreover at the end of the nineteenth century Continental industry was still usually small in scale, heavily dependent on the putting-out system, widely dispersed throughout the countryside, and involving few concentrations of industrial workers in factory towns.[46]

Sociology has had to pay heavily, in terms of lost opportunities and mistaken directions, for its tendency to abbreviate the history of European industrialization. The very brilliance of the conceptualizations of the early sociologists, in their precocious grasping of the whole system of industrialism, dazzled the eyes of their successors. They took for granted, as accomplished, a system whose principles had been discerned in their most elementary, inchoate, form. What is indeed so astonishing is that the nineteenth-century sociologists were able to see so much, and so clearly. One thinks, for instance, of Saint-Simon announcing the imminence of the industrial society at a time when French society was still struggling with the aristocratic and clerical forces of the *ancien régime*, and when the most obvious representative of French society was the small, conservative, peasant farmer. Or of Tönnies and Simmel, analysing with profound subjective awareness the life of the great metropolises, in a Germany which was still a scatter of small provincial towns and agricultural villages.

The full implications of this position will be seen in a later chapter, when we examine contemporary theories of post-industrialism. Here it is worth noting one consequence, which has been of particular theoretical and practical importance. Marxism, as we have already noted, was especially influential in propounding the scheme of social development that fixed the main periods of European industrialization. As a result there emerged within Marxist analysis, and subsequently well beyond it, a view of the development of class and class conflict that was particularly misleading, and made the job of later analysis far more difficult and confusing than it need have been.

Because of the radical historical compression involved in the Marxist scheme, Marx was inclined to discover and welcome 'the proud, threatening and revolutionary' proletariat well before its arrival on the stage of history. It was indeed a standard claim of both Marx and Engels that, unlike the 'utopian socialists' or the Young Hegelian intellectuals of the 1840s, the theoretical conclusions of 'scientific socialism' – Marxism – 'express, in general terms, actual relations springing from an existing class struggle, from a historical movement going on under our very eyes.'[47] In the writings of the 1840s and 1850s, in particular, they both assumed the existence of a fast-growing and already highly developed urban factory proletariat: a revolutionary class of industrial workers without property in the means of production, a class that was in society but not of it.

Engels, it was thought, had given the definitive account of this developing proletariat in his book *The Condition of the Working Class in England*, published on the Continent in 1845 and immediately hailed by European socialists. The English proletariat was universally thought to be the most sophisticated and advanced; but the French were not far behind, and events suggested that even in Germany the proletariat might be considered strong enough to take on the task of both a bourgeois and a proletarian revolution. In a host of radical movements, Marx and Engels thought they saw the clear signs of the growing consciousness of the European proletariat: in the Chartist movement in Britain in the 1830s and 1840s, described by a modern Marxist, respectfully echoing the received Marxist tradition, as 'the first proletarian movement in history to reach the level of sustained nationwide organization';[48] in the rising of the Lyons silkworkers in 1831, and of the Silesian weavers in 1844; in the insurrection of the Parisian workers in the 'June Days' of the 1848 revolution. To doubters they pointed to the vigorous political debates and political education taking place among the French and English workers in these decades, to 'the untiring propaganda which these proletarians are making, the discussions which they carry on daily among themselves'.[49] 'There is no need,' they jointly wrote in 1845, 'to dwell upon the fact that a large part of the English and French proletariat is already conscious of its historic task.'[50] In the *Communist Manifesto* of three years later they were already sounding the death-knell of the capitalist industrial order (three years, we may remember, before the 1851 census in Britain revealed how barely industrial this advanced industrial society was). The failure of the 1848 revolution everywhere (and its non-occurrence in Britain) did little to dampen their optimism. During the 1850s Marx and Engels were seeing in every shift and dip of the trade-cycle the pre-echoes of the imminent socialist revolution, led by the industrial proletariat.[51] Given this powerful backing from the founders, it is not surprising to hear a present-day Marxist declaring that 'the formative period of scientific socialism was precisely that in which the proletariat of the major European nations raised its coarse and urgent voice.'[52]

This makes for good rhetoric; but it is poor history. The 'coarse and urgent voice' that was raised during this time was not – or not *mainly* – that of the factory proletariat, but of more traditional groups who pre-dated industrialism: artisans, small tradesmen, and small farmers.[53] There really was nowhere, at the time Marx and Engels made their statements and for many decades thereafter, a factory proletariat large enough or sufficiently concentrated to launch a major insurrection, let alone lead the socialist revolution – even supposing it had wanted to. Working-class activity there was in plenty; but for the whole of the first half of the nineteenth century and much of the second, these workers were not 'proletarians' in Marx's sense but groups of workers who can be more accurately called 'pre-industrial' in their skills, work organization, and relation to the means of production. Many of them were self-employed, independent craftsmen who owned their own workshops, or at the very least the tools of their trade, and who generally themselves employed other workers.

In France these groups made the running throughout the radical decades of the 1830s and 1840s – including the 1848 'June Days' – and continued to do so up to and beyond the Paris Commune of 1871. In England, they were the main force behind the Chartist movement, acting in alliance with, and to a good extent under the leadership of, distinctly middle-class radicals; and as late as the 1860s they were the groups which supplied most of the radicals who joined Marx in the founding of the First International Workingmen's Association.[54] It is in fact quite clear, when one examines the kinds of workers Marx was mixing with and championing so enthusiastically in the 1840s, 1850s, and 1860s, that these were the very groups he elsewhere often castigated as 'petit-bourgeois', destined to be swept aside by the inexorable march of industrialization. The 'proletarians' he discovered in the working-class movements of these decades were more likely to be self-employed master bricklayers, cabinet-makers, tailors, printers, carpenters and cobblers,[55] than unskilled factory workers.

None of this should be – or should have been – very surprising, given the actual nature and rate of industrialization in England and the rest of Europe. As Maurice Dobb has said of the English case:

> The survival into the second half of the nineteenth century of the conditions of domestic industry and of the manufactory had an important consequence for industrial life and the industrial population which is too seldom appreciated. It meant that not until the last quarter of the century did the working class begin to assume the homogeneous character of a factory proletariat.[56]

It was only in the 1880s and 1890s, with the growth of the mass 'general labour unions' of unskilled workers, that one saw the kind of scale and the kind of organization of the factory proletariat that had been the premises of Marx's analysis in the middle decades of the century. And by that time Marx was dead (1883).

There was a further irony. Much of the radical and indeed revolutionary activity of the first two-thirds of the century can be accounted for in terms of a *defensive* action against the forces of industrialism. They were the work in the main of men who – as tragically seen in the case that so affected Marx, the rising of the Silesian weavers – did have some small property in the means of production, and who were fighting against those very forces of large-scale industrialism which menaced their mode of existence and threatened to turn them into a proletariat properly so-called. By contrast, when finally a proletariat did come into being, it showed a distinct reluctance to carry out the mission marked out for it. Throughout the European nations revolutionary activity declined in the second half of the nineteenth century, more or less in direct proportion to the growth of the proletariat. The proletariat preferred, or at least was willing to be led in the direction of, the tactics of trade unionism and parliamentary politics to that of mass insurrection and the revolutionary transformation of society. It was in recognizing this that Lenin, by doing some violence to Marxism, was able to bring about a successful revolution. Those western European Marxists who tried to keep closer to the teachings of Marx are still waiting.

In an early article Marx wrote: 'It must be granted that the German proletariat is the *theorist* of the European proletariat, just as the English proletariat is its *economist* and the French proletariat its *politician*.'[57] It was a remark strikingly in keeping with that pronouncement of Engels quoted earlier, and placed at the head of this chapter. In it can be clearly seen the great attractiveness and the great weakness of the sociological conception of industrialism. A particular feature is brilliantly seized and given a general historical and typological significance. At the same time there is a breath-taking casualness as to the actual processes of history, the different modes and rates of development in the different European societies. The 'type' comes to dominate its particular expressions to a degree that threatens to divest it of its usefulness as an organizing principle. Lubasz has rightly said that 'Marx's conception of a revolutionary proletariat is a composite which corresponds to no known historical reality. It conflates certain features of English, of French, and of German history in the late eighteenth and early nineteenth centuries, and fits this abstraction into a quasi-Hegelian schema of social development.'[58] It hardly needs to be said with what force Marx deployed this conception, and how fruitful are the applications to be derived from it. But the particular case examined serves to emphasize the great dangers involved in the procedure, and the distortions entailed when later developments were viewed from the perspective of this condensed and schematized history.

3. The Future of Industrial Society

The sociological model of industrialism contains not simply an account of the mode of industrialization, and of its historical evolution; it also suggests the terminal point of that evolution. It is quite clear that in picking out and highlighting certain features of the industrial societies of their time, the nineteenth-century sociologists felt they were holding up, as in a mirror, the future not just of their own societies but of all societies that underwent industrialization. Even where, as with Marx, it was felt that the new industrial order had not yet reached its final, stable form – that was to be the accomplishment of socialism – it was still considered that the destiny of all societies was to tread the path mapped out by the industrial nations, and to incorporate their institutions and culture as a necessary stage of evolution. As Marx put it in the preface to the first edition of *Capital*: 'The country that is more developed industrially only shows, to the less developed, the image of its own future.'

It was an assumption shared by practically all nineteenth-century social theorists, liberal, positivist, or Marxist.[59] The coming of industrialism was seen to have changed the course of world history. All non-industrial societies in the world were given this option: industrialize, or become an appanage of the industrial nations. The efforts at indigenous industrialization – despite the spectacular case of Japan – proved far more difficult than most nineteenth-century theorists, with their evolutionary assumptions, had expected. The likelier thing, therefore, was that the fate of the non-industrial world was to be drawn willy-nilly into the orbit of the already industrialized world. Industrialization was to come, with varying degrees of cajoling and coercion, from without. But whether internally achieved or externally imposed, the future of the globe was seen as an inexorable process of increasing and intensifying industrialization. And that must mean that, in time, the main features of the industrial order as observed in European industrialization must reappear the world over.

In later academic sociology, the central feature of this assumption came to be formalized as 'the thesis of convergence'.[60] Shorn of the belief that there was necessarily a *world* process of convergence on the industrial type, it argued that, nevertheless, following the 'logic of industrialism', all societies that did embark on industrialization would eventually converge towards one basic form, characterized by a particular set of institutions and values that was alone compatible with a functioning industrial order. Evidence was produced to show that this had happened in the earliest industrializing societies, the countries of western Europe. Indeed the features of the basic type of 'the industrial society' were only too obviously an amalgam of elements selected from the varying historical experiences of industrialization in those societies. In the more recent cases too, it was argued, in North America, Russia, Japan, the same tendency towards uniformity could be observed. Particularly conclusive was thought to be the evidence which purported to show that the United States and the Soviet Union, from vastly different starting points and with deeply opposed political ideologies, were nevertheless moving towards a remarkably similar pattern of industrial organization, occupational structure, education, family life, and general urban style of living.[61]

The thesis accepted that there had been, and would be, different 'roads' to the industrial society, and that different groups in different societies would set the population *en route*. But at the end of each road was fundamentally the same society. A major work of synthesis of the early 1960s, *Industrialism and Industrial Man*, put the view as follows:

> Industrialization transforms an old society or an empty country and creates a new form of society ... Pre-existing conditions will often obscure the underlying processes at work to some degree. But the logic of industrialization prevails eventually, and such similarities as it decrees will penetrate the outermost points of its universal sphere of influence. Each industrialized society is more like every other industrialized society ... than any industrial society is like any pre-industrial society.[62]

The ways in which the industrial societies have developed, and the possible directions of their future development, are matters discussed in the second half of this book. This therefore is not the place for treatment in any detail. But a few general comments may be made, in rounding off this assessment of the sociological model of industrialism.

It certainly is not foolish at the outset to look for some degree of convergence of industrial societies. In recent years a sceptical reaction has taken place against the thesis which sometimes amounts to denying that there are any basic structural similarities at all between societies that have industrialized. (This does not, however, stop those sociologists talking about 'the industrial societies', without their realizing the implied contradiction.) But often the procedure for showing this has meant no more than taking two or three allegedly industrial societies, comparing them on some dimension – such as the ranking of occupations by prestige, or the form of the family – and showing that the societies examined differ sufficiently on that dimension for convergence to be denied: all this without considering how far or for how long the societies compared may have travelled along the path of industrialization, the different points they might be at on the 'trajectory of industrialization', and the danger therefore of thinking that one was comparing like entities.[63]

Basically the problem resolves itself into one of the level of analysis and the time perspective adopted. It all depends, in other words, on what you're interested in. On a sufficiently (but not absurdly) long time-scale, it makes perfectly good sense to see industrialization as making so profound a break with pre-industrial society as to constitute a quite new type of society: one which, considered at this level, makes any variations on the basic type insignificant. A precise analogy can be made here with the Neolithic or Agricultural Revolution which occurred about ten thousand years ago, and which similarly marked off from all others all those societies which initiated or received it. In both cases, the very fact of having a system of settled agriculture or of industry becomes the dominating feature, overshadowing all other differences between the societies that have them. There can then follow from this the derivation of certain 'core' institutions, and certain characteristic problems, which almost by definition and more or less incontrovertibly must accompany the relevant transition.[64]

In the case of industrialization, one list of such core features has been given as follows: 'The factory system of production, a stratification system based on a complex and extensive division of labour and hierarchy of skills, an extensive commercialization of goods and services and their transfer through the market, and an educational system capable of filling the various niches in the occupational and stratification system'; to which is added certain common values, such as the ethic of achievement, and certain institutional mechanisms for responding to and 'managing' the strains and tensions that inevitably accompany so great a transformation of society.[65] The precise elements in this list do not matter; some things could be added, others taken away. What is important is the very widespread acceptance of the view that industrialism does entail the adoption of certain common institutions and values.

It is at this level that it becomes relevant to show, say, that despite the Soviet Union's insistence on being a radically different kind of society from the United States, and *vice versa*, by virtue of the very fact of being or becoming industrial both have converged along certain lines. As one account fairly puts it:

> Historical data would suggest that capitalist societies have developed towards greater political control of their economies and away from a *laissez-faire*, 'free-market' type of system, and that socialist societies

have . . . shown a tendency to move away from absolute centralization and control of all planning resources towards the re-introduction of certain market mechanisms of a limited kind. Perhaps even more important, however, are the ways in which capitalist and socialist societies have become more similar both in their high degree of centralization and bureaucratisation of the economy and of the polity, and in the patterns of conflict which have emerged between bureaucratic interest groups within and among organisations.[66]

No one can say that these developments have not taken place, nor that it is not valuable to point to them; equally, nothing in this account suggests that industrial societies are converging in all or even in the most important respects. But some important kind and degree of convergence is clearly entailed in opting for industrialization.

With regard to the directions of change, the real danger inherent in the received model of industrialism sprang from the features we have already discussed: the evolutionist mode of explanation, and the historical abbreviation of the course of industrialization. The first meant that the future had to be conceived as the evolution of whole social orders, integrated around a single dominating principle. Since the order in question was industrial, it was hardly surprising that industrial technology and industrial organization should have been most commonly singled out as the driving force of this evolution. This, as we have seen, did not matter so much given an adequate time-scale. But it was bound to be misleading when, compounded by the second error, it was used to explain and predict the development of industrial societies over relatively short time-spans – and on this level of analysis, 100 or even 200 years is short-term. As a guide in this kind of exercise, these prevailing assumptions of the model proved dogmatic and mischievous, seeking to put all industrial developments to rest in the same procrustean bed of technological determinism, and arbitrarily terminating them at some point wrongly supposed to mark the end of the western course of industrialization.

Actually the idea of a technologically-determining 'logic of industrialism' was misleading not just as to the character of the later forms of non-western industrialization. It also proved a poor predictor of the future development of western societies themselves, and of the important differences that continued to characterize their political and social structures. Essentially this was owing to its neglect of the differences of culture and historical tradition that provided the context of industrialization in different cases, and which persisted, often with a decisive shaping influence, well into the period of a society's industrialization. In addition it ignored the importance of the timing and mode of industrialization, and the ways in which these might, by a 'feed-back' process of reciprocal and cumulative changes, influence the course of industrialization in a highly 'divergent' direction.[67]

We have said something of the latter already; a few examples, drawn from the development of classes in industrial societies, will serve to illustrate the former point.

In most of the nineteenth-century analyses of industrialism, a firm expectation was that the old ruling class of the landowning aristocracy would lose its influence and power, expecially its political power. The future lay with '*les industriels*', the 'captains of industry', as the 'carriers' of the new industrial order. Saint-Simon had early given powerful expression to this view, and he was followed by Marx, Tocqueville, Carlyle, Spencer, and a host of other thinkers of all political persuasions. Certain struggles and their outcomes in England – over the Reform Act of 1832, the repeal of the Corn Laws in 1846 – were given symbolic significance as stages in the victorious march of the industrial bourgeoisie. And indeed something of the kind did happen in certain parts of Europe, in the Low Countries for instance. But almost everywhere else the striking fact was the long and continued persistence of the aristocratic domination of political life. As Joseph Schumpeter wrote,

> the aristocratic element continued to rule the roost *right to the end of the period of intact and vital capitalism.* No doubt that element – though nowhere so effectively as in England – currently absorbed the brains from other strata that drifted into politics; it made itself the representative of bourgeois interests and fought the battles of the bourgeoisie; it had to surrender its last legal privileges; but with these

qualifications, and for ends no longer its own, it continued to man the political engine, to manage the state, to govern.[68]

Even these qualifications may go too far. In some countries, notably Britain, Germany, and Japan, the landed upper classes were very much more than the 'front men' for the industrial middle class. By taking the lead in industrialization and commercialization, they managed to infuse the style of upper-class life in those societies with so distinctly aristocratic an ethos, containing strong 'pre-industrial' qualities of culture, status, and honour, that they long prevented, in some cases up to the present day, the emergence of a 'pure' type of commercial ruling class. In England the fusion of landed aristocracy and middle class that was the main feature of its industrialization expressed itself in the nineteenth century in the formation of the distinctive type of 'the gentleman', one of whose chief qualities seemed to be a disdain for and concealment of any commercial interest whatsoever. The Marxists were outspoken in their scorn for what seemed to them the timidity and the pusillanimity of the English middle class, which of all middle classes should have had the right and the power to assert itself. As late as 1892 Engels was writing, with his characteristic exasperation at the refusal of English developments to go 'according to plan':

> The English bourgeoisie are, up to the present day, so deeply penetrated by a sense of their social inferiority that they keep up, at their own expense and that of the nation, an ornamental caste of drones to represent the nation worthily at all state functions; and they consider themselves highly honoured whenever one of themselves is found worthy of admission into this select and privileged body, manufactured, after all, by themselves.[69]

Such an attitude of contempt failed to understand the extent to which the evolution of the class structure of industrial society was dominated by the nature of the original manner of industrialization, rather than by some absolute logic of industrialism. In Britain industrialization was carried out by a combination of aristocratic and middle-class enterprise that continued to influence the development of practically every aspect of the society's politics and culture. In Germany and Japan industrialization was launched and supervised even more decisively by the traditional upper classes – in Japan's case, actually against the opposition of the existing merchant class. Throughout the later part of the nineteenth century and well into the twentieth, entry into and acceptance by the upper class of these societies depended upon a learning of many of the ways and attitudes of the traditional land-owning aristocracy. It was in fact not until these ruling classes had been defeated in the Second World War – in Germany's case preceded by the gradual dethronement of the Junker class under Hitler's Fascist regime – that they ceased to exercise a predominant influence on the social structure and values of their societies.

The importance of these facts of the 'pre-history' of industrialization in these countries comes out clearly in a comparison with the industrial society that most obviously produced a commercial ruling class: the United States. For what has struck most observers about this evolution is its dependence on a particular historical fact, the absence of a feudal order and a feudal land-owning class in North America's past. The United States could throw up a 'business aristocracy' – apparently one of the most natural consequences of the logic of industrialism – precisely because there was no other pre-existing, pre-industrial, aristocracy to influence and challenge its emergence. Such a 'logic' might get by in sociology textbooks; but it seems of a most curious kind when its operations are so subject to the peculiar vicissitudes of individual histories over which it has no control or even cognizance.

Similar observations can be made of the working classes of the industrial societies. It was generally expected that even if, despite the Marxist prediction, they did not become revolutionary, the strains of the transition to industrialism would bear most heavily upon them, provoking a radically discontented response. But here again traditional factors made for great differences within the different industrial societies. The French working class, largely schooled by the Jacobin tradition of the French Revolution, assumed radical forms of behaviour from the very beginning of their growth; they expected (and were expected) to be radical, and so were, for the greater part of the nineteenth century. The German working class was soundly educated and led by middle-class socialist theoreticians, and so was also dutifully 'revolutionary'; but at the same time it had absorbed a highly Prussian respect for order and authority, which made it possible for revolutionary declarations to be accompanied by nationalist and decidedly non-revolutionary practice when it suited the leadership to act in this way. The British working class was the biggest puzzle and, to some, disappointment of all. As the initiator of what was widely regarded as the first movement of the industrial working class – Chartism – it was expected that it would become the leader of the European working-class movement. Instead, as it developed its behaviour became, if anything, less radical. Throughout the latter part of the nineteenth century and right up to our own time a large section of it continued to follow 'the politics of deference', eschewing independent class action and preferring to follow the lead of the traditional ruling class, especially the landed gentry. It is an interesting fact that at the present time the proportion – a third – of English workers that consistently supports the Conservative Party is precisely the same as, in the French working class, equally consistently supports the Communist Party. Partly these differences reflect the greater role of the English upper class as compared with the French in the modernization of their countries. More significant, probably, was the absence in the English case of a revolutionary 'rupture' with the past (or at least one too long ago to seem relevant), making it possible to conceive of a peaceful and constitutional pattern of change and integration (which, as we have seen, even Marx admitted as a possibility). In France by contrast the traditional upper class was inevitably identified with the intransigence of the *ancien régime* and treacherous involvements with foreign powers against their own country; at the same time, the great example of the French Revolution of 1789, and repeated occurrences of revolution during the nineteenth century, taught all groups that violent and extremist actions were the more or less normal means of bringing about change.

Parenthetically we might note the peculiarity of the North American case. Here, as has often been pointed out, not only does the working class not follow any of the diverse patterns of the European working classes, it seems to lack definition altogether. Much of this can be explained, as with so much in the development of American social structure, by the vast size of the country and the way in which it was filled up in the expansive westward movement. But there is here also the additional feature that the American working class has been historically constituted by a series of specific ethnic groups – English, Irish, Italian, Puerto Rican, the freed black slaves – and the character of the working class at any one time was determined more by ethnic origin than by any other single factor. This meant above all that the different groups within the working class were not likely to see themselves as sharing a common fate (in which they were quite right) or to make common cause; they were influenced far more by their very diverse pasts than by the dubious prospect of a common future.

It is perhaps especially instructive to note the effect of different cultural and historical traditions on the middle classes of the industrial societies. Here, one would have thought, if anywhere, in the character of that dynamic class most closely identified with the industrialization of society, should be the clearest evidence of convergence. But here too the particular form of industrialization merged with the different values and aspirations of different societies to produce markedly different bourgeoisies. In England the character of the middle class was influenced not just by the close embrace of the landed aristocracy, but by a fundamental tension between its industrial and financial wings that has dogged its fortunes to this very day. The financial and commercial middle class, the merchants and bankers, had been a successful part of the British 'Establishment' long before the coming of industrialization. Their sons and daughters were courted by the more ambitious or the less prosperous members of the aristocracy; for their part, West Indian planters and East Indian merchants set up country houses and modelled their style of life on that of the traditional county squirearchy. By comparison the later industrialists, while rarely from the lowest ranks, were provincial upstarts and parvenus, looked down upon by the old-established mercantile aristocracy. Their bases were usually in the northern industrial towns rather than in the metropolis, to which they rarely came. They kept their provincial accent. So did their sons and daughters, who were likely to be sent to the local non-conformist school but not to university (and if they did go, to the new 'redbrick' provincial universities rather than to the colleges of Oxford and Cambridge). They did not aspire – at least for some time – to gentry status and a gentry style of life: indeed they returned the compliment by disapproving of the idleness and wastefulness of that style.[70] These social tensions were reinforced by economic considerations. The financial barons of the City of London were willing to invest in British industry so long as it paid them. But they had no particular interest in the industry of their own country. They took pride in the fact that their financial services and resources were offered on a world market, of which British industry was simply one part. They did not care very much to what uses their money was put as long as the return was high enough. By the same token they were ruthless in taking their money out of native industry and investing in foreign enterprises when the latter promised higher returns. Such a situation meant that British industry was periodically starved of investment funds – and usually precisely at those moments when it most needed them to catch up with competitors.

To nothing like the same extent did this division mark the character of the French and German bourgeoisies. For in those countries, as with much of the rest of the Continent, the important early stages of industrialization were primarily carried out by the financial institutions of the society, acting under the aegis of the state. Especially significant were banks of the Crédit Mobilier type, pioneered by the Pereire brothers during the French Second Empire. Such banks did not, as in the British case, merely play a passive role as commercial investors. They themselves initiated and supervised the major part of the industrialization effort.[71] They therefore had a direct interest in the continued growth and prosperity of their native industries. As a result, whatever the traditional differences of status between financiers and industrialists, they were united by a structural fusion that made impossible the bouts of suspicion and hostility that periodically divided the English middle class.

But then, similar as they might be in opposition to Britain, the French and German bourgeoisie were at the same time radically different from each other. Once again it was a matter of history and culture. Under the vigorous patronage of the Junker state, the business ethos in the newly united Germany was aggressive and expansionist. The Junkers brought to industry the same conscientiousness and ruthlessness that they had earlier shown in the commercialization of their estates to the east of the Elbe. By contrast French business, as Landes has shown, remained to the middle of the present century conditioned by a specific set of cultural values that enhanced the importance of the independent family firm, as against the big conglomerates and managerially directed corporations favoured by German and American business.

The important thing for the French businessman was the deep social ties between family and firm; and here, as Landes stresses, there was a strong continuity with pre-industrial society. The firm

> is the material basis for the prestige and status of the family, just as the domain was the material foundation of status in an earlier age. The business is not an end in itself, nor is its purpose to be found in any such independent ideal as production or service. It exists by and for the family, and the honour, the reputation, the wealth of the one are the honour, wealth and reputation of the other.[72]

Such a conception excluded, for instance, the competitive urge to growth inherent in the idea of business for business' sake. The overriding concern was family independence, and in tenaciously holding to this purpose the French businessman was often prepared to sacrifice chances of growth and increased profits where this might mean dependence on outside capital. Not profit but social function justified commercial survival and a modest degree of success. This attitude, inherited from the past of the medieval guilds and persisting into the latest period of French industrialization, inevitably imposed a very different, one might almost say 'pre-capitalist', complexion on the evolution of French industry, as compared with its nearest neighbours, Germany and Britain. Characteristically this showed itself in the continued predominance of the small family firm, a dogged conservatism in relation to technical innovation and work organization, and an unwillingness to subscribe to the free-market principles of risk and competition.

Even this brief sketch of the variety of class structures and behaviour in industrial societies should be sufficient to illustrate the truth of Schumpeter's observation that

> social structures, types and attitudes are coins that do not readily melt. Once they are formed they persist, possibly for centuries, and since different structures and types display different degrees of this ability to survive, we almost always find that actual groups and national behaviour more or less departs from what we should expect it to be if we tried to infer it from the dominant forms of the productive process –

that is, from the dominant forms of industrial technology and organization.[73] The exigencies of industrial technology and industrial organization certainly posed characteristic problems to all societies that embarked on the path of industrialization; and in responding to these problems it is hardly surprising if certain uniformities appeared, especially since the very novelty of the situation for most societies, and the speed with which they had to decide, made it tempting to try to imitate the pattern of the older industrial societies. But as with the different modes of industrialization, so with their future working out: there was a diversity to the picture that ought to have warned anyone against inferring a strict logic from it. Such a logic was not merely spurious; later it had a morally inhuman and barbarous aspect to it as well. To take a simple example, it was wrong to treat, as many, especially Marxists, did, German, Italian, and Japanese Fascism as mere local variants in the overall evolution of capitalist industrial society; just as it was wrong to accept the Stalinist terror as a necessary stage on the path to a communist industrial society. No doubt there is some long-term perspective, *sub specie Marxiense aeternitatis*, in which this view is justifiable. But within the reasonable time-span of three or four generations, such differences can mean the difference between life and death for sizeable sections of the populations of industrial societies.

It is an exaggeration, but a pardonable one, to say that, in the sociologists' construction, 'industrialization' as a general and universal pattern of social change was a generalization from the experience of one country – England – at one time – the early nineteenth century – in one industry – cotton textiles – in one town – Manchester. The astonishing thing is the richness of the generalities that can be derived from the study of this process; but inevitably, as a general model, it leaves many significant things out. We are then unduly surprised when, at other times and in other places, different features appear, alien to this basic English pattern.

It is true that there were other elements in the model which could have guarded against this danger. As the last chapter made clear, some of the features associated with industrialism – such as 'rationalization' in the Weberian sense – predate the coming of factories, machines, and industrial workers. In this sense they are prior to the image of industrialism conjured up by Dickens' Coketown and Engels' Manchester – prior to the whole of what nineteenth-century Germans referred to as '*Manchestertum*'.[74] More significantly they were features of industrialism which could justly be stressed even when the age of factories and manufacturing seemed to be coming to an end, and the 'service revolution' was under way. Sociology always possessed an 'esoteric' model, a subsidiary image of industrialism, which gave it a longer and deeper range than that provided by the more popular image.

But sociologists are also people. They are not much more capable of resisting the force of popular imagery and popular associations than other members of society. The Victorian imagery of industrial towns and industrial workers, repeated a hundred times in books, pictures, and songs, could hardly fail to penetrate their vision of industrialism. The more analytical elements of the model were fused with this imagery. For both practical and theoretical reasons it would have been impossible to do otherwise. 'The age of ruins is past. Have you seen Manchester?'[75]

It was particularly important that this fusion was also accomplished at a systematic level in Marxism. Marx shared the view of his friend Engels that Manchester was the symbol of the new industrial order. Machine technology and the manufacturing workers figured heavily in his descriptive and polemical writing. The later sociology of industrialism tended to take the form of a watered-down version of Marx. Hence it seemed a plausible thing to debate the 'end of industrialism', or at least an important phase of it, when '*Manchestertum*' was on the wane. The force of the popular association supported this. In a later chapter we shall be considering these further consequences of succumbing to the power of this image of industrialism.

5 Reculer Pour Mieux Sauter: The Climax of Industrialism

I hate and fear 'science' because of my conviction that, for long to come if not for ever, it will be the remorseless enemy of mankind. I see it destroying all simplicity and gentleness of life, all the beauty of the world; I see it restoring barbarism under a mask of civilization; I see it darkening men's minds and hardening their hearts; I see it bringing a time of vast conflicts, which will pale into insignificance the thousand wars of old, and as likely as not, will whelm all the laborious advances of mankind in blood drenched chaos . . . Oh, the generous hopes and aspirations of forty years ago! Science then was seen as the deliverer, only a few could prophesy its tyranny, could foresee that it would revive the old evils and trample on the promise of its beginning.

George Gissing, *The Private Papers of Henry Rycroft* (1903).

'This here Progress', said Mr. Tom Smallways, 'it keeps on.' 'You'd hardly think it *could* keep on', said Mr. Tom Smallways.

H. G. Wells, *The War in the Air* (1907).

We are suffering, not from the rheumatics of old age, but from the growing pains of over-rapid changes, from the painfulness of re-adjustment between one economic period and another.

John Maynard Keynes, 'Economic Possibilities for our Grandchildren' (1930).

1. A Sense of an Ending

The idea of progress, it was widely held at the time and since, was buried in the mud of Flanders, in the course of the First World

War. The change of intellectual climate was indeed dramatic enough to provide abundant evidence for this belief. The end of the nineteenth century was full of self-congratulatory messages, industrial society basking in the warm sun of its own making. 'Britain as a whole was never more tranquil and happy,' wrote the *Spectator* in the summer of 1882. 'No class is at war with society or the government: there is no disaffection anywhere, the Treasury is full, the accumulations of capital are vast.'[1] Macaulay's mid-century belief, that his was 'the most enlightened generation of the most enlightened people that ever existed', found a confident echo in Bishop Creighton's introduction of 1902 to that monument of the industrial principle of the division of labour, the *Cambridge Modern History*: 'We are bound to assume, as the scientific hypothesis on which history has been written, a progress in human affairs'.[2] In H. G. Wells, the apostle of scientific progress, developing industrial society seemed to have found its most characteristic figure, the Macaulay of his times. In a lecture of 1902 called *The Discovery of the Future* he was declaring that

> in the past century there was more change in the conditions of human life than there had been in the previous thousand years . . . Everything seems pointing to the belief that we are entering upon a progress that will go on with an ever widening and ever more confident stride for ever . . . We are in the beginning of the greatest change that humanity has ever undergone.[3]

As little as five years later, Wells was sounding a vastly more ominous note. The belief in the ultimate triumph of scientific civilization remained. But it was accompanied now by a conviction, amounting almost to an apocalyptic faith, that the industrial nations of the world must first go through a purging fire of war and devastation before coming to their senses and organizing their societies according to rational scientific principles. In a brilliant prophetic novel of 1907, *The War in the Air*, he described a world torn apart by a war waged by the novel means of the airship, a world entering upon a new barbarism, a new Dark Age, from which it would take almost a century to recover. The narrator, writing from the vantage point of a future world state run by scientists, notes 'the hallucination of security', the confident belief that theirs was 'a secure and permanent progressive system', that characterized the pre-war attitudes of the men of the time. He comments:

> The accidental balance on the side of Progress was far slighter and infinitely more complex and delicate in its adjustments than the people of that time suspected . . . They did not realise that this age of relative good fortune was an age of immense but temporary opportunity for their kind. They complacently assumed a necessary progress towards which they had no moral responsibility.

As with Saint-Simon on the French Revolution, but on an infinitely greater and more tragic scale, the industrial world is berated for the lost opportunity to realize its enormous scientific potential in peaceful and creative directions. But probably, concludes the narrator, the disaster was unavoidable, given the complacency of the age. The end, when it came, was swifter than that of any of the great empires of the past:

> Up to the very eve of the War in the Air one sees a spacious spectacle of incessant advance, a world-wide security, enormous areas with highly organized industry and settled populations, gigantic cities spreading gigantically, the seas and oceans dotted with shipping, the land netted with rails and open ways. Then suddenly the German air-fleets sweep across the scene, and we are in the beginning of the end.[4]

Wells, as witness to and survivor of the two World Wars and the dictatorships of the 1930s, saw this very thing happen. With grim satisfaction he was able at successive periods to reprint, with new warning prefaces, his novel of 1907. (The last preface, written in 1941, concluded: 'I told you so. You *damned* fools.') His was a mood shared by many, who however often did not have his faith in science to console them for what they saw as the inauguration of an age of doubt, conflict, and material and moral decline. The First World War was the symbolic event that confirmed a shift in mood and intellectual development that extended well back into the latter part of the nineteenth century. In the thirty or so years preceding the First World War, there occurred a re-orientation in European thought that questioned and dismissed much of the optimism of the previous generation, and went on to undermine systematically the logical, psychological, and historical basis of that optimism.[5] During that period was formed much of the thought that we recognize as characteristic of the twentieth-century mind: cynical, 'realist', disillusioned.

The names alone say most of what needs to be said: Nietzsche, Bergson, Freud; Moore, Russell, Wittgenstein; Michels, Pareto, Sorel; Malinowski and Radcliffe-Brown; Lenin and Trotsky. These last two also suggest the need to include the names of those who were primarily men of action rather than thinkers, men who were coming to maturity in these years. Stalin was born in 1879, Mussolini in 1883, Hitler in 1889, Mao in 1893. Taken together – which, needless to say, for any other purpose than the present one would be absurd – the thought and action of these men amounted to a massive attack on some of the most fundamental assumptions of the nineteenth-century world. As against the premise of reason was uncovered the vast underworld of unreason, in the individual man and in society. Historian and philosopher joined together in undermining the assumption of a progressive and necessary logic of evolution. The equation of material and moral progress was pulled apart. The belief in continuity, cumulation, and 'the inevitability of gradualness' was challenged by a new emphasis on dis-continuity, and the need for active radical intervention to bring about social change. Even in biology, the very paradigm of evolutionist thought, the view of evolution as gradual and continuous was seriously questioned by the rediscovery of Mendelian genetics in 1900, with its emphasis on the importance of mutations, random discontinuous leaps causing hereditable changes in organic structure. In science as well as in society, the evolutionary mode was displaced by the revolutionary mode.

In the narrower perspective of the social sciences, the revulsion against nineteenth-century evolutionism went especially deep. Most influential perhaps were the developments in historical thinking. These took two sharply contrasting forms, both of which however were anti-evolutionary. The first, associated with such figures as Croce and Collingwood, Dilthey and Rickert, radically opposed all attempts to make history a positivist science, with the ambition of discovering general laws akin to the natural sciences. History, it was argued, as opposed to science, was concerned with the unique and non-recurrent. It was also, again in contra-distinction to science, essentially the study of the subjective as against the objective world. The first emphasis, on the unique, is best exemplified in the famous statement in H. A. L. Fisher's Preface to his *A History of Europe*:

> Men wiser and more learned than I have discerned in history a plot, a rhythm, a predetermined pattern. These harmonies are concealed from me. I can see only one emergency following upon another as wave follows upon wave, only one great fact with respect to which, since it is unique, there can be no generalizations, only one safe rule for the historian: that he should recognise in the development of human destinies the play of the contingent and the unforeseen.

The second emphasis, on the subjective, is tersely caught in Collingwood's remark that 'all history is the history of thought': the understanding, in other words, of the subjective meanings, interpretations, and intentions held by individual actors towards events and objects, rather than the establishing of causal connections between supposedly 'objective' facts. Both kinds of emphasis marked a profound hostility to the characteristic nineteenth-century enterprise of discovering universal laws of social evolution.

The second development in historical philosophy had less subtlety or intellectual respectability about it; but it balanced this by an infinitely greater popular appeal and influence. It accepted the possibility of historical laws of social change, but, in opposition to the unilineal forms of evolutionist theory, conceived the patterns of historical change in cyclical form, often on the analogy of the individual life-cycle of birth, maturity, decline and death. It rejected the Enlightenment conception of social evolution as the growth of a single unified humanity, and substituted for this a picture of humanity fragmented into disparate cultures or civilizations, each with its own cyclical pattern of rise and fall.

This of course allowed thinkers to perceive decline and decadence as regularly and as lawfully as they perceived progress in the historical record. Indeed it may well be suspected that the cyclical form in which such theories were couched reflected, rather than promoted, the sense of pessimism and disillusion that already existed, for other reasons. Certainly the most influential of these theories, Oswald Spengler's *Decline of the West*, appeared towards the end of the First World War; and its gloomy prognostications about the future of western civilization chimed in only too well with the tenor of contemporary events, and scarcely needed the validation of a 'scientific' historical law.

Sociology and social anthropology also reacted against evolutionism: the more ferociously since they were also reacting here against their immediate ancestors and progenitors. They readily accepted the criticisms of historians that the evolutionary method when applied to social change was facile, that evolutionist history was simply bad history. The 'universal' stages of development or progress postulated by the method were fictitious, and no substitute for actual historical or empirical investigations and comparisons of cultures. The anthropologists, notably Malinowski and Radcliffe-Brown, were particularly anxious to throw off the mantle of evolutionism. The evolutionists, they said, gave poor or non-existent accounts of the mechanics of change because they had never paid proper attention to what, at any given time, made up a society or culture. 'We cannot,' wrote Radcliffe-Brown, 'successfully embark on the study of how culture changes until we have made at least some progress in determining what culture really is and how it works.'[6] So the emphasis in anthropological and sociological studies moved from an account of the changing forms and conditions of society, to the examination, through field-work and empirical survey, of the interrelationships between social institutions at a given time in particular societies. As a focal point of study, large-scale social change went for some considerable time into abeyance.

These intellectual currents of the pre-First World War period need not all have shaken belief in the idea of progress. Such a belief in any case depended in the end more on a sense of confidence generated by the everyday activities of the real world than on theoretical demonstrations. But the shift in thought pulled away the intellectual underpinning of the belief in progress, and left it nakedly exposed to the vicissitudes of historical events. The attack on the attempt to find laws of social change was especially serious, since any logical validity possessed by the idea of progress turned on the ability to generalize and predict on the basis of such laws.[7] When therefore, to this intellectual onslaught, was added the effect of a particularly brutal and long-drawn-out war, the first major European war for a century, followed by extreme political and economic instability in many industrial societies, it is hardly surprising that the idea of progress received a severe battering. Progress was now seen to be counter-balanced, perhaps overbalanced, by regression and degeneration in all areas of human life. And, in a familiar conjunction, thinking about even the natural world followed a similar pattern, and so lent its great prestige to such convictions. It was perhaps a fitting irony that it was T. H. Huxley, 'Darwin's watch-dog', and one of the most powerful advocates of the idea of progress through science in the 1860s and 1870s, who should towards the end of his life have been grimly stressing that the 'cosmic process' of evolution tended towards death and extinction, unless opposed by a purely human and voluntary 'ethical process'.[8]

2. Recovery and Advance

And yet: the idea of progress survived, and was even after a time powerfully revitalized. Possibly one can argue, as some have, that there was a philosophical necessity about this, that in societies which lacked belief in revealed religion, some secular equivalent had to meet the need of presenting their populations with an image of their future, without which no action whatsoever is possible. But there is also an explanation at a humbler level. The idea of progress survived and was regenerated concomitantly with the survival and regeneration of its 'material base', industrial society itself. From a later perspective, say the mid-1960s, what seemed impressive was not so much the failures and regressions of the 1914–40 period, as the extraordinary resilience of the industrial system, its capacity for persistence and renewal. To the twenty-five years of doubt, dislocation, and pessimism spanning the two World Wars could later be counterposed twenty-five years of confidence, growth and optimism in the affluent era that followed the close of the Second World War. As against the icy scepticism and despair of Huxley's *Brave New World* and Koestler's *Darkness at Noon*, the most extreme manifestations of the epoch of disillusion, the industrial societies of the post-1945 period had rosy scenarios in plenty to offer: although more often in the lifeless prose of economics and sociology texts than in the piercing literary forms of the 'dystopias' of the 1930s.

Actually professions of confidence and a belief in continued progress were plentiful in the earlier period as well, although overshadowed both by events and by more strident voices that seemed better to match the sombreness of those events. Especially on the Left there were those who saw in the very breakdowns and loss of faith of the early twentieth century the symptoms of the imminence of a new order, socialist society. The crisis of confidence certainly affected certain sections of the western European Left which, disillusioned by the unwillingness of the proletariat to perform its historic task of ushering in socialism, either became purely constitutional opposition parties or actually went over to the conservative side. Some of these disillusioned socialists joined up with equally disillusioned liberals to become the proponents of the 'mass society' theory of the 1930s, an extreme pessimistic version of the Tocqueville-Mill concern about the loss of autonomy and diversity consequent upon the democratizing and equalizing tendencies of modern society. Others became even more energetic enemies of their former left-wing comrades, seeing in Hitler's National Socialism or Mussolini's Fascism a more imposing force for the future, and containing sufficient of a residual socialism to strengthen their adherence to those causes.

But the Left also had its victories, to sustain its faith in progress. The socialist risings in western Europe at the end of the First World War all failed; but in eastern Europe, against formidable odds, the Bolshevik regime managed to sustain itself and to inaugurate what was at least in principle a socialist society. For many western European socialists, the Russian Revolution of 1917 stood in the same relation to them as had the French Revolution of 1789 to an earlier generation of radicals in the unregenerate countries outside France. As with revolutionary France, so with the Soviet Union: it stood as a concrete symbol of a new civilization, a model to be imitated and a political force to be drawn upon in the remaining struggles elsewhere. No matter how much uneasiness there might be at the actual developments in the Soviet Union, so long as it existed it suggested the realistic possibility of an alternative to the existing, ailing, organization of industrial society.

By the same token, of course, the Right had even more reason during the inter-war period to feel confident about the future. It was not only active adherents of the Fascist regimes who saw in the states of Hitler and Mussolini the principles of a vigorous new order. Even those who abominated the Fascist technique of rule often felt that it was Fascism, rather than socialism, which had found the way to overcome the conflicts and contradictions of the developed industrial societies. The 1930s saw the flourishing of theories of 'the corporate state' and 'the corporate society', with the argument that developments were increasingly forcing on all industrial societies the need for greater coordination and integration, and that internal social conflicts of the traditional kind could no longer be tolerated by an increasingly complex and interdependent society. A 'social compact' between government, business, and workers was often envisaged in such theories, with Mussolini's Italy offered as the best available example of such a system: although it was freely admitted, both of the theory and of Mussolini's practice, that the state was unquestionably and necessarily the chief weight and executive manager of the compact.

Such theories easily blended with the contemporary theory of 'the managerial revolution', with its view of the accomplished separation of the ownership and the control of property in twentieth-century industrial society, and the consequent rise of the managerial class to effective control over the economy and, increasingly thereby, the polity. It was in many ways characteristic of the time that the most popular version of this theory should be expounded by a man who had been a prominent Trotskyist, James Burnham. In his book *The Managerial Revolution*, written in 1940, Burnham explicitly linked the theory of the managerial revolution to the practice, not simply of the Fascist states, but of all the other contemporary innovators who had espoused some form of active state intervention and state managerialism: such as Roosevelt in the New Deal, and, of course, Stalin. Burnham spoke of the rise of the managers in general, in private as well as public corporations; but it is clear from his book that he saw the main basis of managerial power as the managers' access to and control of the state apparatus. The managers of the state bureaucracy are therefore given a pre-eminent position. It was for this reason that Roosevelt's New Deal administration could be seen as an imperfect version of what Hitler and Stalin were more successfully effecting, and with a clearer presentiment of the future state of things.

Burnham's synthesis was the more influential for this catholic embrace, since it seemed to indicate that there was an irresistible movement, taking a variety of forms the world over, towards the managerial society of the future. It is indeed not fanciful to imagine that the idea of progress could have been revitalized through the theory and practice of managerial corporatism. It seemed to fit so closely the long-term social trends of the industrial societies, and it was so spectacularly exemplified by the most vigorous and successful societies of the time. What prevented this happening may have been no more than the turn of events. We need to remember that the Fascist states did not collapse through their own internal structural weaknesses – they were simply defeated in an international war. Things could very easily have gone the other way (as, for instance, they might have done for Russia in 1917–19). As it was, their defeat and the particular manner of it made it impossible for these particular examples of the corporatist state to symbolize the future social order. The liberal capitalist states triumphed in the Second World War, and took the lead in the recovery and boom of the post-war years. By contrast the surviving corporatist state, Stalin's Russia, devastated by the war, seemed to offer only tyranny without any of the mitigating comforts of affluence. It could certainly serve as a model for imitation by the non-industrial societies of the world, in their efforts at speedy industrialization. But as an image of the future of the developed industrial societies it had no force; on the contrary, all the influences seemed to flow the other way, from the liberal capitalist variety of industrialism.

In the longer-term, however, Burnham may have felt himself vindicated. He backed some of the wrong horses, but he chose the right race. Of all the prophecies of a period unusually rich in prophecies, his turned out to be one of the best. Not in its detailed terms, of course, but in the general direction in which it pointed. For shorn of certain details and some of the ideological trappings, what gradually emerged in the decades following the end of the war, in all the industrial societies, was something not very different from Burnham's managerial state. It was not simply that, as Burnham himself had noted, in meeting the challenge of Fascism, in peace and especially in war, the liberal industrial societies had had to take over many of the features of political organization and administrative centralization of their enemies. There was also the more basic fact that the longer-term tendencies of industrialism had, since the end of the nineteenth century, gradually been propelling the industrial societies along the path of the centralized managerial state.

Recognition of this had, as usual, to wait for some time after the main developments had already occurred. And indeed it was not until the late 1960s and 1970s that theories essentially harking back to Burnham began to be common again in the west. Meanwhile western industrial societies, and to a good extent those of eastern Europe too, found in the post-war period a first point of rest and reflection in the late 1950s. Looking back on that decade some twenty years later, it has increasingly the look of a watershed. It seems to mark the climax of industrialism, both as a social system and as an ideology. Certainly in the consciousness of the time is clearly revealed the view that, after a period of 'unnatural' disturbances, deflections, and retardations, the long-term tendencies of industrialism had re-asserted themselves and reached a point of maturity. It is true that there were many deceptive aspects to this position, particularly in the extent to which the theorists seemed to think that the industrial societies could freeze the flow of history at the date of their theorizing. But in many ways it was also a fair reflection of the actual course of development since the beginning of the century.

The period of disenchantment, starting in the 1880s, was also the period in which some of the most characteristic features of industrialism were given their first clear and systematic expression. In these decades of the late nineteenth and early twentieth centuries were to be found the beginnings of: the systematic application of science to industrial production; mass production and continuous-process technology; the rationalization of work organization and management ('scientific management'), especially around the conveyor-belt and assembly line; the rise of mass 'general labour' unions; the common use of large limited liability companies (instead of the family firm) for the raising of capital; concentration of production and ownership, and control of markets, through cartelization, trusts, and producers' associations; the separation of ownership and control in the large firms, and the rise of managerialism; a marked increase in the degree of state regulation and control of the economy and society; the global expansion of the industrial economy.[9]

These developments, surfacing in such a relatively short space of time, and with such effect, were so striking as to have won them the designation of 'the Second Industrial Revolution'. But this is as much a mistake as the later discovery of a 'post-industrial revolution' in the 1960s. We have already noticed the tendency to predate and anticipate the full achievement of industrialism; and it is this compression that largely gives rise to the need felt to mark off a second epoch of change. In fact what was so visibly manifested in this period were the logical expressions of the currents of rationalization, specialization, and centralization that were the central features of classic industrialism. These took time to work themselves out – indeed they are still doing so. But by the end of the nineteenth century they were seeking and finding an institutional definition hitherto denied them by the persistence of older customary modes of organization and attitudes.

The crescendo of innovations and transformations in this

period can best be seen as 'the consummation of the Industrial Revolution'.[10] The coming of Taylorism or 'scientific management' illustrates this particularly well. As we have seen, employers until the end of the nineteenth century were remarkably casual about the organization of labour, apparently content with the spectacular results achieved by mechanization alone. But sooner or later they were bound to realize that the advance of mechanization would be held back if the organization of work itself lacked the 'rationalization' and science that had gone into machinery. And F. W. Taylor was on hand to help them see this the more readily. As Landes says,

> seen from the hindsight of the mid-twentieth century, scientific management was the natural sequel to the process of mechanization that constituted the heart of the Industrial Revolution: first the substitution of machines and inanimate power for human skills and strength; then the conversion of the operative into an automaton to match and keep pace with his equipment.[11]

Production by the assembly line was, equally, the natural accompaniment to this realization. It eliminated the more or less autonomous teams of skilled workers who dominated the factory till the very end of the century, and whose skill and virtuosity 'were incompatible with the fundamental principle of industrial technology – the substitution of inanimate accuracy and tirelessness for human touch and effort'.[12] What was needed to allow mechanization to proceed to its logical conclusion was the fragmentation of jobs into simple operations capable of being performed by single-purpose machines run by unskilled hands; together with methods of manufacture so precise and regular that assembly becomes routine. In this way the work could be moved to the worker at a pre-determined pace, to be processed and put together by a series of simple, repetitive actions. The increasing simplification of tasks then became a further stimulus to greater mechanization, since it revealed weaknesses in the production process and suggested ways in which relatively simple mechanical substitutions could eliminate to an even greater extent human failings. The logic of the process was clear, and the introduction of the assembly line signalled the full establishment of the principle of the division of labour in the factory. Landes rightly comments that 'the assembly line was far more than just a new technique, a means of obtaining greater output at less cost. In those branches where it took hold it marked the passage from shop, however big and heavily equipped, to factory.'[13] The end-point to which this process tended was equally clear: full automation, the replacement of men by machines that think as well as do. In such a way, and by so clear a logic, were linked the various phases in the long curve of industrialization: from the bare mechanization of the early nineteenth century, through the organization of labour and the assembly line of the late nineteenth century, to the sealed-in, continuous-process mechanical system and excluded human worker of the present time.

Marxist historians, as we noted in the last chapter, have been inclined to see in the period immediately preceding the First World War the clear signs of a social system in decline and dissolution. They point to the international rivalries that led to the First World War, the imperialist scramble, in Africa and the Far East, that symptomatized a deepening economic crisis at home, the rise of labour as an organized political force. But a truer account might instead see these in a wider context as 'the growing pains of a system in a process of germination',[14] whose seeds had been planted in England at the beginning of the century; as the beginning of a new phase of growth of the system, rather than its demise. It would of course be the worst kind of sociological determinism to regard as trivial or, worse, as inevitable and necessary, the wars and economic crises of the first part of the twentieth century; to see these as all concomitants, regrettable but necessary, of the further growth of the industrial system. Change is not so orderly a process. The reverses and regressions were real and immensely costly, materially and culturally; and there was nothing inevitable about them. But nevertheless, looking back from the 1950s, the striking thing was the degree of continuity between the earlier and later period. Cleared of the debris of war and political strife, the economic order that emerged after 1945, now more firmly on a global plane, was recognizably that of the 1890s and 1900s.

Social theory during the first half of the century reflected faithfully this continuity and persistence of system. As compared with the preceding half century, the major characteristic was a negative one: an indifference to theories of large-scale social change. The attack on evolutionism at the turn of the century was one, purely intellectual, reason for turning away from a pre-occupation with change. But probably even more significant was a conviction that in the industrial societies there would not be, for a long time to come, any fundamental change. Even the belief that industrialism had reached its climax before the First World War (rather than after the Second) did not affect the assumption that future developments would consist mainly in the working out of the logic of industrialism, as analysed by the great nineteenth-century sociologists.

Theorizing about large-scale secular change was left, on the whole, to the philosophers of history: Spengler, Sorokin, Toynbee. Only in the United States, experiencing in a belated rush the main force of industrialization and urbanization, was there in the early part of the century a vigorous concern in sociology with problems of the transformation of whole social orders.[15] For the rest, and as far as Europe was concerned, social theory up to the Second World War followed three main directions, all leading off from the nineteenth-century legacy. Following Marx, there was the long debate about the condition of the proletariat, the reasons for its failure to develop a more radical political consciousness, and the significance of the persistence and renewal of the intermediate strata of small traders, farmers, and salaried white-collar employees. In the Mill-Tocqueville tradition, there was a new concern with the forces of centralization and democratization, specifically analysed now under the theory of 'mass society', and related by many theorists to the contemporary rise of Fascist movements. Most importantly of all, there was the line from Weber on rationalization and bureaucratization, leading to the analysis of the new patterns of concentration and control in the state and economy, and to theories of managerialism and corporatism.

Social theory in the west in the 1950s continued this pattern, but in a rosier perspective consonant with a prospering society. These were the halcyon days of industrialism as an ideology. In the social-science view of the industrial societies, there seemed quite simply the belief that all the important structural changes initiated by industrialization had worked themselves out, and had reached a point of maturity and rest. Industrial society appeared to have come of age, to have matured with remarkable fidelity along the main lines outlined by the nineteenth-century sociologists. Even the spectre of the unpleasant shuffle at the end, predicted by Marx in the form of the socialist revolution, had ceased its haunting. The conflicts bred of inequality had largely been resolved, and without the need of recourse to revolution. All the industrial societies, of both east and west, had evolved into rational, 'managed' societies, and in doing so had finally 'got over the hump' of industrialization. No further major institutional changes should be required in the remaining business, to apply the fruits of steady economic growth and a rapidly expanding technology to the clearing up of the marginal pocket of poverty and deprivation. The American sociologist Seymour Martin Lipset stated, in a celebrated passage: '... the fundamental political problems of the industrial revolution have been solved: the workers have achieved industrial and political citizenship; the conservatives have accepted the welfare state; and the democratic left has recognized that an increase in over-all state power carries with it more dangers to freedom than solutions for economic problems.'[16] Similarly at about the same time in Europe Raymond Aron was declaring that 'in a sense it would not be wrong to define the advanced countries as those in which the Left and the Right are no longer opposed to each other on the question of development, because development can take place without any further fundamental changes.'[17]

This view of things led to the characteristic pronouncement of these years, that 'ideology' had come to an end in western industrial societies.[18] There could be no further need, it was argued, for the existence of irreconcilable social philosophies, urging fundamentally opposed strategies of political action. As Aron, again, put it:

> We are more fortunate than previous generations in that we are not forced to make a choice between conservatism and fanaticism [sc. Marxism], i.e. between the defence of the status quo and a kind of blindness that is alternately humanitarian and bloody. We know that modern methods – scientific and technological progress and the rational organization of labour – enable us to achieve the objectives to which liberals and socialists of previous centuries aspired. We know, on the abstract level at least, how to attain them. The advanced countries of the West have or will have the necessary resources to ensure a decent standard of living for everyone . . .[19]

The euphoric mood of the post-war years allowed the pre-war analyses to be picked up again, but with a new gloss on them. Each of the earlier tendencies in social theory was given a new twist, in an analysis that accepted much of the basic factual evidence but saw it in a different light. Thus the proletariat, it was argued, no longer had revolutionary pretensions because it no longer needed them. It had become voluntarily 'incorporated' into the established institutional routines of the society. The vast productivity of modern industrial society had ensured that through a process of bargain, compromise and concession, the working classes had achieved greater gains than they were ever likely to have got through more forceful radical action. These classes were indeed now the mainstay of the 'mixed economy' welfare state, recognizing their interest in its preservation, and impervious to the appeals of disaffected middle-class intellectuals still hankering after the revolutionary millennium.[20]

Similarly, the gloomy atmosphere surrounding the theory of mass society was dispelled by the consideration that, far from atomizing the population and brainwashing individuals into a state of sterile conformity, the centralization of political and cultural institutions had for the first time in the history of the world produced a truly national society. Mass suffrage, mass parties, and the mass media, all meant a far-reaching democratization of the style and substance of political and social life. For the first time ever, leaders and led in modern society shared a common culture. This must in the end make for greater diversity rather than uniformity, since individuals were now freed from narrow parochialisms and inhibiting class cultures, and were all able to play a full part as citizens of the society. Contrariwise, the fear of mass authoritarian movements, common in the analyses both of the Left and the Right in the 1930s, was put down to a cultural class élitism that was shared equally by the conservative critics of mass society and the traditional left-wing intelligentsia of central Europe.[21]

Finally, selected aspects of the pre-war theory of the managerial revolution were taken over and transformed into the cardinal principle of the theory of the liberal welfare state. Burnham's full-blooded managerial society could not be admitted: it was too much tainted by pre-war corporatism and authoritarian ideologies. But Keynes was a more respectable figure, and could be made to serve the same purpose.[22] It was readily accepted that the further evolution of industrial society had forced profound modifications on the old *laissez-faire* conception of the liberal state. The modern industrial state had of necessity to be active and interventionist if there was not to be a repetition of the economic crises and industrial conflicts of the past. All political parties had accepted this. The result was a political system widely described as 'pluralist', supposedly combining some of the qualities of the classic conception of democracy – e.g. universal suffrage – with more novel features such as organized pressure groups, and a managerial welfare state playing the part of 'honest broker' between the competing interests in society.[23] Weber's nightmare was dissipated. Bureaucracy after all turned out to be the friend, not the enemy, of democracy. For did not bureaucratization mean, as Lipset put it, 'a decline of the arbitrary power of those in authority . . . less rather than greater need to conform to superiors . . . a much higher degree of freedom'?[24]

Such complacency was confirmed, rather than contradicted, by developments both in the communist world and in the 'Third World' of newly-independent nations. In both cases it appeared that the western model of industrialism, in its twentieth-century form, was in the process of vanquishing all other competing models, and increasingly standing out as the common future of the whole globe. The heyday of the thesis of 'the end of ideology' was also that of the thesis of 'convergence': especially of the convergence of the industrial societies of west and east. And while it was true that the thesis suggested that western societies would take over some of the characteristics of east European societies, there was no doubt that the flow was expected to be more from the west to the east than the other way round.

Moreover, this was also what seemed to be actually happening. Following Krushchev's denunciation of the Stalinist regime at the Twentieth Soviet Party Congress in 1956, the whole of eastern Europe seemed to be set, willy-nilly, on a course of liberalization that drew the patterns of those societies closer and closer to those of the west. Actually there was a somewhat deceptive aspect to this interpretation: one might easily have said that the flow of influences had worked as strongly in the opposite direction – from east to west – at an earlier time, in the west's conversion to state managerialism. Moreover, the crushing of the Hungarian rising in the same year of Kruschev's speech showed what might happen if the liberal elements tried to force the pace. Nevertheless, the belief plausibly gained ground both in the west and in eastern Europe that the future shape of the industrial society was not likely to be very different from the pattern of 'pluralist industrialism'[25] into which western society had evolved during the course of the century.

These developments in the communist world served to underline the fact that, for the Third World, the future seemed inescapably cast in the mould of western industrialism. We have already noted how, in face of the need to conceptualize the process of development in these societies, social theory reverted to the evolutionism of its nineteenth-century predecessors. The stages of the earlier evolutionists were bundled together into two polar types, 'traditional' and 'modern', 'undeveloped' and 'developed', and the process of development or modernization was conceived as the movement from the first to the second. Nor was there much doubt about the provenance of the model of the ideal-typical modern society. It was the industrialized, urbanized, democratized, bureaucratized and rationalized society seen by the earlier sociologists as the ideal-typical industrial society, and now almost naturally identified with western industrial society of the 1950s.

Again, the identification could not be a simple one. Ideologically, for various obvious reasons, it seemed better to attempt to industrialize under the aegis of some variety of socialism, generally of a populist kind; and this entailed at least formally a certain hostility to western capitalist forms, as well as a higher degree of authoritarianism than was compatible with current western notions of pluralist democracy. But then the west itself had already partly moved in that direction, in its acceptance of a considerable degree of centralized, managerial control. In any case it was assumed that the earlier stages of industrialization would demand greater austerity and centralized management than the later ones; the future itelf, with more industrialization, would bring about the desired relaxation of control. The important point was that that future was conceived essentially on the model of western industrial development; western industrial civilization was its end-point. 'Development,' as J. K. Galbraith announced, 'is the faithful imitation of the developed.'[26]

In this widespread convergence of thought in the 1950s, the idea of progress found its strongest vindication for over half a century. The pessimism of the period 1890–1940 seemed on looking back to be no more than a long-drawn-out interlude: a phase during which the forces of industrialism were struggling to find their appropriate expression, and which they had at last succeeded in doing by the mid-century. Developments were now once more on the right footing; further progress seemed assured; the main outlines of the future were already visible in the existing organization of industrial societies. In a strong affirmation of this belief in the mid-60s, Sidney Pollard thus concluded his book *The Idea of Progress*:

> The wish to catch up with the West is, indeed, not identical with the belief that humanity faces an unending prospect of further progress. But the assumptions on which both are based is so similar, and the dividing line between them is so blurred, that it is difficult to hold to one, yet deny the other. Among the common assumptions are the beliefs that (no matter how divergent their history in earlier ages), the

modern stages are basically identical, and therefore predictable and plannable, for all humanity; that progress along this unilinear path of progress is both 'natural' and desirable; that once certain early steps are correctly taken, the developing societies will continue under their own steam, in inevitable 'self-sustaining' growth, and that growth will inevitably bring in its wake other such desirable developments as greater democracy, more education, and a higher status in the international community, which will promote further growth. Even among the advanced countries, the richer, for example the U.S.A., are taken to mark out the next stage along the route of progress, and for these leaders in turn, it is clear that they are basically on the right road, creating ever greater material wealth, ever greater power over man's environment, ever more assistance for human physical and psychological frailties, and thereby the opportunity, which they cannot but believe will be taken, of ever higher personal fulfilment and achievement. There is similar agreement also to the converse proposition, that without economic growth and the social improvement which it makes possible all hopes of any other progress are doomed from the start.[27]

Pollard leaves us in no doubt as to his own assent to these propositions, which are explicitly couched in the spirit and manner of the Enlightenment idea of progress. It is a measure at once of the great strength of the idea, and of our need for it, that such utterances could still find a representative voice some two hundred years after Turgot had first given definitive expression to them.

6 A Post-Industrial Society?

The traditional sources of identity strength – economic, racial, national, religious, occupational – are all in the process of allying themselves with a new world-image in which the vision of an anticipated future and, in fact, of a future in a permanent state of planning, will take over much of tradition.

Erik Erikson, speaking at the formation of the *Commission on the Year 2000* of the American Academy of Arts and Sciences, 1965–6.

When I am weary or nasty, I sometimes remark that the post-industrial society was a period of two or three years in the mid-sixties, when GNP, social policy programmes, and social research and universities were flourishing. Things have certainly changed.

S. Michael Miller, 'Notes on Neo-Capitalism', *Theory and Society*, Vol. 2, No. 1 (1975).

1. The Rediscovery of the Future

Speaking in 1958, Raymond Aron remarked that 'we are too much obsessed by the twentieth century to spend time in speculating about the twenty-first. Long-range historical predictions have gone out of fashion.'[1] It was a remark perfectly in keeping with the mood of the late 1950s, when the motor of social change seemed to have come to a stop, idling contentedly in happy contemplation of a spreading world-wide felicity. Ten years later a startling change had come about. Long-range forecasting was now all the rage. Institutes of 'futurology' proliferated in all the industrial societies of the world. Governments and learned bodies set up 'think tanks' and commissions to produce reports and 'scenarios' on the future of their societies. There was the French Commissariat du Plan's '1985 Committee'; the Commission on the Year 2000 of the American Academy of Arts and Sciences; the British Social Science Research Council's Committee on the Next Thirty-Three Years (set up in 1967); the European-based *Futuribles* project, directed by Bertrand de Jouvenel, concerned with the commissioning of long-range predictions and projections in every area of society. A stream of books and symposia collections appeared with titles such as *The Year 2000*, *Mankind 2000*, *The World in 1984*, *Life in the Twenty-First Century*, *Future Shock*, *The Sociology of the Future*, even *The Future as an Academic Discipline*.[2] 'We have become oriented towards the future,' declared the American sociologist Daniel Bell, Chairman of the Commission on the Year 2000.[3] 'The future is on the agenda,' was the more portentous pronouncement of futurologist Alvin Toffler.[4]

What brought about this change? Why did social theory in the industrial societies once more seriously engage with problems of large-scale social change, after a half-century of neglect? A number of factors, some remote, some immediate, combined to demand this. The commitment to welfare and planning – especially for economic growth – in all industrial societies forced governments, however reluctantly, to try to see the shape of society some decades ahead, to know what they were planning *for*. It was clear that the span of time over which fundamental policies were formulated and implemented outran the term of most elected administrations; the long-term effects took even longer to work themselves out, and moreover became constraining influences on any future decisions that might be taken. If, as seemed inevitable, the present must exercise some degree of tyranny over the future, the safest course seemed to be to gather together as many disinterested experts as possible, and hope that the forecasts of each in their particular areas would be modified in a realistic direction by mutual inspection and comparison.[5] This procedure at least allowed some expectation that the plans of the present would eventually realize themselves in, and relate to, an environment that had been anticipated, however tentatively and sketchily. It also meant that, knowing something of likely future needs and aspirations, governments could seek to ensure that present decisions did not utterly foreclose the future, that there was sufficient flexibility to allow future generations to alter and perhaps reject the priorities of the present. The contrary danger, of course, was that the planners would plan only for a future which they could control and govern, in which in fact they were the governors. But whatever the dangers, there were clearly urgent governmental needs, springing from long-term political changes, for systematic thinking about the future of industrial society.

There were also more immediate political and ideological reasons for a renewed concern with social change. The 1950s, I have said, marked something of a watershed in the history of industrialism, as a social system and as an ideology. On one side there is the confident expression of a triumphant industrialism, the belief that for the first time in history a particular form of society had resolved the fundamental problems of social survival and growth. On the other side, starting at some point in the 1960s, this belief begins to break up, and industrialism seems to run into separate and often opposed courses. The 'end of ideology' is itself denounced as an ideology, the ideology of a complacent, short-sighted and one-sided materialist society. There is the discovery, or rediscovery, of the dark side of industrialism. So far from having solved its problems, industrial civilization seemed to have raised new ones in a form so acute that its very survival was at stake. The economic benefits of industrialism are seen to be purchased at the cost of increasing 'dis-economies' to the society at large: pollution, crowding, the exhaustion of the natural fossil fuels on which the industrial economy itself depends. The main currents of industrialization – rationalization and bureaucratization – run into an impasse, and increasingly large-scale hierarchical organization seems productive mainly of inefficiency and irrationality. As an issue and as a fact, conflict comes to co-exist with the pragmatic consensus inherited from the 1950s. The official political parties continue to play the politics of consensus. But outside the formal political system a striking opposition, more often ideological than practical, is mounted by diverse groups formerly thought unpolitical: university students, disaffected professionals, 'outcast' groups such as the American blacks. With conflict, ideology revives and thrives; Marxism and anarchism are rediscovered and re-interpreted to fit the conditions of advanced industrial societies.

Many social theorists in the west enthusiastically embraced the radical critique of the dominant patterns of industrialism. Among other reasons, at the ideological level it provided them with intellectual weapons with which to attack their teachers, the previous generation of social theorists, whom they accused of excessive attention to the mechanisms of persistence and stability and a consequent bankruptcy in the face of change and conflict. I shall be examining, in the next chapter, the prospects for a radical alternative to the typical institutions of industrialism. Here I wish to stress the challenge which the radical response threw up to those social theorists who regarded themselves as the intellectual custodians of the whole tradition of progressive industrialism, and so of the established order. The conflicts and critiques of the 1960s could not simply be dismissed as the fabrications of the news-hungry media. There clearly were vast problems still afflicting the social order of industrialism; and they were ill-concealed behind a view that regarded all fundamental social change as essentially accomplished. There had therefore to be a re-thinking of the future directions of the industrial society. Futurology in its many forms was one of the principal responses to this situation. In the face of the manifest disintegration of the system they once saw as 'the good society' of the philosophers' dream, social theorists in this period were busily constructing a new vision, and a new ideology. Often indeed the same men were involved in the process of re-thinking as had been the most prominent exponents of the 'end of ideology' thesis in the 1950s – especially American intellectuals such as Daniel Bell and Herman Kahn. Not surprisingly, therefore, their views of the future were strongly coloured by their more hopeful analyses of the previous decade. Nevertheless the exercise did involve, once more, a commitment to theorizing about long-term social change, with the re-analysis and re-interpretation of the past history of industrialism that this entailed.

A third cause, in retrospect perhaps of less lasting significance, might be mentioned for this renewed interest in social change. The decade that followed the launching of the Russian Sputnik in 1957 was one in which the prestige of science and technology rose to new heights (at the same time as, in a familiar pattern, it was being undermined). Moon shots, Mars probes, and orbiting satellites became the almost commonplace material of world-wide television link-ups, culminating in the first human landing on the moon in 1969. Science fiction saw some of its technological fantasies realized in practice, and retreated into the world of 'inner space', leaving a speculation about outer space to scientists and astronomers. The 'space age' supposedly inaugurated by these developments could hardly fail to give a push to future-directed thinking. More concretely, there was the special prominence accorded to the technologists and men of science, who were widely regarded as the pivotal group of the future. In an influential paean, Sir Charles Snow in his lecture *The Two Cultures and the Scientific Revolution* (1959) contrasted the attitude of the traditional humanists, who seemed to wish that the future did not exist, with that of the scientists 'who have the future in their bones'. In a world in which non-scientists and non-scientific modes of thought were increasingly regarded as marginal, nostalgic hangovers from the feudal age, it was difficult not to resist an impatience with, almost a contempt for, the unscientific past; and to feel that the urgent task was to acknowledge the central role of science in the society of the future, and to plan for its further use and development. The importance of modern science called for futurology – which in turn must be predominantly concerned with the place of science in the society of the future.

I shall not attempt to deal here even cursorily with the whole phenomenon of futurology.[6] What particularly concerns the theme of this book is that part of the new thinking which specifically and systematically addresses itself to the future of the industrial societies. And here what initially reveals itself is a remarkable continuity, convergence, and complementarity in the history of social theory.

We have seen that, when stimulated by the rise of the new post-colonial states after 1945, the theory of social change (in the guise of the 'sociology of development') picked up again the evolutionary form of the nineteenth century. Quite simply, there was no other theory to hand of comparable scope and utility. The attack on evolutionism at the turn of the century discouraged further evolutionary speculation; but the important point is that no serious revision was made of the classic evolutionary conception of change. All that happened was that the topic of social change was put in cold storage for a time. In fact the prevailing functionalist approach of the first half of this century was itself heavily permeated by evolutionist assumptions. It too relied on the organic analogy, emphasizing continuity, interdependence and integration – only now in relation rather to persistence than to change. The approach represented a sort of 'frozen evolutionism', and the basic continuity with earlier evolutionism is readily revealed when one considers that Herbert Spencer had combined a thorough-going evolutionism with a thorough-going functionalism.[7] When the thaw came, therefore, and functionalists turned their attention to problems of large-scale social change, it should have surprised no one to find that they reverted almost without modification to the basic pattern of nineteenth-century evolutionism.[8]

The resurgence of interest in social change did not immediately extend to the societies of the industrial world. Here, as we have seen, the belief prevailed that the developed industrial society of the mid-century represented for some long time to come a firm resting point in the course of evolution. But when events made this view increasingly untenable, and the theory of industrialism was required to include, as in the last century, a view of the past and of the future, it was remarkable how closely the new version mirrored the form of its nineteenth-century predecessor. In this respect futurology – at least that part of it that related to the industrial societies – converged with the main form of development theory, which it also resembled in many other ways.[9] Like development theory, futurology was stimulated into existence by pressing developments in the real world. Like development theory, futurology, in casting around for a suitable conceptualization of large-scale societal change, found only the evolutionary schemes of the past to hand and adopted these for its own purposes.

In doing so, the futurologists have recommenced the characteristic task and pattern of nineteenth-century sociology. Basically their procedure has been very simple. They accept that the nineteenth-century scheme in its strict form will no longer do. 'Industrial Society' as it has been understood hitherto cannot be taken as the fulfilment and final end of social evolution. But all that has to be done is to add another stage to the sequence. The old story is given a new chapter and a different ending – rather as Marx had tried to do, and later James Burnham. But formally the pattern remains the same. The present is once more seen as transitional, as metamorphosis: not now from feudal agrarianism to industrialism, but from the industrial society to 'the post-industrial society'. A transformation is under way which will eventually produce societies as different from the classically conceived industrial societies as those are from the earlier agrarian societies. And just as the social theorists of the last century were forced, in the midst of the transformation, to form as complete and as perfected as possible an image of the industrial society that was in the process of formation, so the theorists of the post-industrial society have felt compelled to project present social tendencies to a future end-point where the shape of a whole new society can be discerned.

It would be foolish to push the parallel too far. There was almost no nineteenth-century thinker who did not feel that his age was experiencing one of the fundamental transformations of humanity. Such unanimity is quite absent at the present. Many thinkers remain sceptical about the notion of a 'post-industrial' revolution comparable in scope and significance to the Industrial

Revolution of the past. But there are enough who do think such a thing is happening for the matter to deserve serious examination. The remainder of this chapter will be devoted to this task. As in the discussion of industrialism in the earlier part of this book, the interest is two-fold: to lay out as fully as possible the 'image' of post-industrialism that is offered us from a diverse range of sources; and to compare and confront this image with the realities of current developments in the industrial societies.

2. The Image of the New Society

Many are the strands, and diverse their provenances, which have converged on the idea of a movement to a post-industrial society. In the west the main proponents of the thesis have been a group of American social scientists, many of whom were prominent in announcing the end of ideology in the 1950s.[10] To these are joined a number of social theorists from western Europe, who have argued for the fact of similar structural changes to the Americans, but who have drawn different implications, often in a radical direction, for the future of industrial society. Their presence, generally under the shadow of the old or the new Marx, belies a commonly-held view that the post-industrial idea is the special preserve of American conservative sociology.[11]

More unexpected has been the concurrence in the east European societies. It is only in recent years that the west has realized what a vast amount of futurological thinking has been going on in eastern Europe: perhaps expressed at its best in the comprehensive report published in 1967 by an interdisciplinary team from the Czechoslovak Academy of Sciences, entitled *Civilization at the Crossroads: Social and Human Implications of the Scientific and Technological Revolution.*[12] The surprising aspect of this thinking is the heavy overlap with the analyses in the west, especially the American ones. The accounts have to be couched in Marxist terms, of course; but east Europeans have quite justifiably argued that futurology has only picked up again the tradition of developmental social theory of which Marx was in any case the supreme practitioner, and they have found no major difficulties in re-interpreting Marxism as a 'futurology'. Moreover they have even been able to decorate their analyses with the complacent reflection that, owing to the existence of a socialist framework, the societies of eastern Europe are politically in a much better position both to receive and to realize to their fullest extent the social and technical changes which are bringing about the post-industrial revolution; whereas in the capitalist societies of the west those changes must necessarily be the source of dis-equilibrium and conflict. But these differences aside, the more remarkable feature of the eastern European accounts has been their very great dependence on the data collected and the analyses conducted by western exponents of the post-industrial idea. There is an extraordinary willingness to accept the idea (first propounded in the west) of a post-industrial transition, provided only that the changes projected be allowed expression within a Marxist framework (theoretically and practically). Given this agreement with western social theory, it might not be misleading to label the post-industrial analysis the 're-convergence thesis', on the analogy of the 'convergence thesis' of the 1950s; and to see in this concurrence of thought a new and more inclusive version of the argument that ideology is at an end in the industrial societies.

The diversity of names for the new society similarly indicates both variety and convergence: variety in the bases from which the changes are viewed, as well as in the singling out of the principal forces promoting the change; convergence on the idea that the industrial societies are entering on a new phase of their evolution, marking a transition as momentous as that which a hundred years ago took European societies from an agrarian to an industrial social order. Thus Amitai Etzioni speaks of 'the post-modern era', George Lichtheim of 'the post-bourgeois society', Herman Kahn of 'post-economic society', Murray Bookchin of 'the post-scarcity society', Kenneth Boulding of 'post-civilized society', Daniel Bell simply of 'the post-industrial society'. Others, putting the point more positively, have spoken of 'the knowledge society' (Peter Drucker), 'the personal service society', (Paul Halmos), 'the service class society' (Ralf Dahrendorf), and 'the technetronic era' (Zbigniew Brzezinski).[13] Taken as a whole, these labels tell us what it is in the past that has now been or is being superseded – e.g. scarcity, the bourgeois order, the predominance of the economic motive; and also what can be expected to be the main principle of the future society – e.g. knowledge, personal services, the electronic technology of computers and tele-communications. Of course none of these theorists necessarily wishes to exclude changes other than the set he has chosen to emphasize; and there is indeed a great deal of overlap in the various accounts. Consequently it is convenient to fall back on Daniel Bell's modest term 'post-industrial' as the most inclusive generic label for the new society, and to specify differences between thinkers where relevant.

As this list of names suggests, the convergence of thought on the post-industrial idea follows upon extended but often disparate investigations into some of the most important aspects of the culture and social structure of modern societies. Analytically and descriptively, the building blocks of the post-industrial idea have been hewn from a very wide range of recent sociological work, much of which cuts across traditional groupings of geography, culture, and ideology. Thus the key idea of 'the knowledge society', which is central to the post-industrial analyses of Daniel Bell and Alain Touraine, can be seen equally informing the very differently cast accounts of a Continental European Marxist such as Jurgen Habermas, the British 'New Left', the American 'New Left', liberal economists and sociologists such as J. K. Galbraith and Clark Kerr, and managerial analysts such as Peter Drucker.[14] All stress the new structural importance of systematic and theoretical knowledge as a crucial 'resource' of present-day industrial society, and the consequent importance of universities, researchers, students, scientific and technical personnel.

Then there is the correspondence of thought which found expression in J. K. Galbraith's influential work of synthesis, *The New Industrial State*, with its argument of the passage of power to the men of 'the technostructure', and the inevitable convergence of socio-technical systems under the demands of advanced technology and the necessity of planning. This kind of economic analysis, putting strongly the case for a 'logic of industrialism', underlies the accounts of practically all post-industrial theorists, and raises in a particularly acute form the role of the technical experts in the future society, and the possibility that they may come to constitute a 'technocracy'.[15]

A further constituent is the idea of a 'post-scarcity economy', which can be found in the writings of socialists such as Herbert Marcuse and Christopher Lasch; technocratic researchers at the Rand Corporation and the Hudson Institute, such as Herman Kahn and Anthony Wiener; and ecologically-minded 'utopian' anarchists such as Murray Bookchin.[16] Here is expressed the belief, widespread since the 1950s, that the vast productivity of the industrial societies has produced a unique historical situation: an era of plenty and abundance, so that for the first time ever the leisure and culture of the few does not depend upon the necessary labour of the many. Radicals such as Marcuse attacked the *use* of that abundance: its grossly unequal distribution, its wasteful employment in continued exploitation at home and military adventurism abroad, the whole irrationality of its use in perpetuating human subjection rather than in the liberation of men made possible for the first time by such economic abundance. But they did not question the basic belief that the industrial societies had solved the oldest problem of them all, that of scarcity and want. Keynes' prediction of the 1930s seemed to have been borne out: the economic problem would be solved within the century. 'This means that the economic problem is not . . . the permanent problem of the human race.'[17]

Closely associated with such views were the more familiar themes embodied in the post-industrial idea: the decline of 'the Protestant ethic' which had underlain the whole industrializing effort of the past centuries, the retreat from the world of work, and the corresponding increase in the importance of 'leisure' and cultural activities. Here a tradition of cultural criticism, as seen for instance in the work of Richard Hoggart, joins up with a good deal of sociological work of the last two decades on attitudes and commitment to work, and was given a further spectacular conjunction in the 'May Events' in Paris 1968, with its strong emphasis on spontaneity, creativity, and 'fun'.[18]

Common to all these approaches is the belief that, going along with abundance, there has been a fundamental shift of values in the industrial world, making much of the discipline and respect for authority which preoccupied their elders seem irrelevant and unnecessarily irksome to the young. In a society in which machines do the necessary work, there is no need for the elaborate structure of attitudes that underpinned the work commitment of the industrial society. Other qualities seem more important: individuality, versatility, autonomy.

Finally one might instance the convergence of thinking around the theme of 'the personal service society'. This includes the widespread observation of a transition to a service economy, but broadens out to insist on the increasing structural importance of social welfare and the 'caring' services, with their associated professional ethic of social responsibility and 'the therapeutic mode'; and which is seen as gradually pervading the whole society. This important constituent of the post-industrial idea is found strongly and optimistically stated in the writings of Paul Halmos, and with an intensifying degree of anxiety and repugnance in the writings of Ivan Illich and Philip Rieff.[19] For the east Europeans, too, the personal service component is destined to move into the centre of the new society.[20]

It would be surprising if all these themes added up to a coherent and consistent account of a new social order in the making: quite apart from the fact that by no means everyone involved in their elaboration would accept the notion of a post-industrial revolution. What seems therefore most useful is to weld them together into the most systematic statement possible, acknowledging the damage done to some in the process, but regarding this as justified for heuristic purposes. Fortunately this task is immensely simplified by the appearance (in 1973) of Daniel Bell's *The Coming of Post-Industrial Society*. Bell has, in any case, special claims on our attention. He is the most frequently quoted exponent of the post-industrial idea, and is generally accepted as the intellectual leader of the post-industrial school. When the French Radical leader Jacques Servan-Schreiber presented a popular version of the idea in his *The American Challenge* in 1967, it was on Bell's account that he drew. As Chairman of the Commission on the Year 2000 (of the American Academy of Arts and Sciences), Bell has frequently and publicly expounded the post-industrial idea, in the United States, Europe, Japan. His book, which is the culmination of more than a decade of public and scholarly presentation of the argument, is by far the most systematic exposition available. More relevantly perhaps for our purposes, it has the special merit of being couched explicitly in terms of the sociological tradition of the theory of industrialism. Bell is specifically concerned to mark off the present epoch from that of the era of industrialism, in which the 'founding fathers' of sociology theorized, and to demand a reshaping of social theory around this fact. I propose therefore to take Bell's account as the general framework for discussion of the post-industrial idea, filling it out or modifying it where suitable with other accounts. This will serve both to present the image of post-industrialism in its most complete form, and also allow a running critical commentary on it based on observations and evidence from other sources.

In summary, Bell's argument goes thus. The industrial societies are entering a new phase of their evolution. This phase, provisionally entitled 'post-industrial', is as different from the 'industrial' as that was from the 'pre-industrial'. The post-industrial society differs from the industrial society principally on the dimensions of economy and social structure. (Politics, as so often in the Saint-Simonian tradition of sociology, is left out of this account: assumed to be either autonomous, or more commonly, brought in as the *deus ex machina* to rescue the theorist from the charge of excessive determinism.) Specifically these are held to be changes in economic activities, such that the post-industrial society is not primarily a goods-producing but a service economy; changes in occupational structure, such that white-collar workers replace blue-collar workers as the single largest category in the labour force, and within the white-collar category there is an increasing predominance of the professional, scientific, and technical groups; and changes in the form of technology, with the older machine technology supplemented by the rise of the new 'intellectual technology'. By this last Bell means essentially management and problem-solving systems making extensive use of the computer, such as information theory, game theory etc., and which allow for rational planning, prediction, monitoring, and self-sustaining technical growth in all areas of the society. Overarching all these changes is what Bell calls the 'axial principle' – 'the energising principle that is the logic for all the others' – of the new society: the centrality of 'theoretical knowledge' as the source of innovation and policy-formation. Bell refers here to a long-term tendency in the industrial societies for 'theory' to take the primacy over 'empiricism'. This is seen, for instance, in the rise to prominence of the science-based industries of this century, or the use of macro-economic theory in the management of the national economy, or computer-based simulation procedures in many areas of decision-making. Theoretical knowledge becomes the 'strategic resource' of the post-industrial society. Its custodians – 'the scientist, the mathematicians, the economists, and the engineers of the new computer technology' – become the key social group, replacing the industrialists and the entrepreneurs of the old industrial society. Its institutions – universities, research organizations, experimental stations – become the 'axial structures' of the new society, superseding the business firm of the industrial society.[21]

Bell's account differs from other versions of the post-industrial thesis mainly on the grounds of greater completeness and certainty; otherwise there is an impressive degree of agreement.[22] Even where apparently there is the strongest divergence, this usually turns out to be a matter not so much of substantive disagreement as of relative optimism or pessimism about these changes, or a somewhat different weighting of factors. Thus for example Alain Touraine's analysis in *The Post-Industrial Society*, which may be fairly taken as representative of the more radical European version, parallels Bell's closely in pointing to the central importance of universities and 'the knowledge class' for the productive and managerial apparatus of the new society (sometimes referred to as 'the programmed society' to make that connection clearer). But whereas Bell sees in this a promise of greater social integration and institutional harmony, Touraine, alarmed by its manipulative potential, foresees a deepening conflict between on the one hand professionals and students upholding the humanist values of a liberal education, and, on the other, their more ambitious peers manning the technocratic apparatus, dedicated to the goal of economic growth.[23] Touraine however nowhere specifies what kind of structural mechanism might drive the educated class to divide against itself; and the impression remains that here, as with similar analyses from the radical camp concerned with the fate of traditional radical values (e.g. Marcuse's), the expectation of conflict is the hope born of a certain desperation. At any rate it does little to affect the basic concurrence of views on the structure of the post-industrial society; other divergences are, if anything, even slighter.

That many of the changes alleged by Bell and others are occurring, and are important, need not be denied. What needs scrutiny is the central claim that all these changes add up to a movement to a new social order, with a new set of problems, a new social framework within which to resolve them, and new social forces contending. There is more at issue here than definitional disputes as to whether or not certain features should be termed 'post-industrial', or at precisely what point a social system ceases to be what it was. The problem is one of the relative significance of the tendencies singled out by the post-industrial theorists. Are they important enough to justify talk of qualitatively new departures in the industrial societies, the creation, as Bell puts it, of a 'new agenda of questions'? Do they imply radical discontinuities in the development of industrial society?

One has to say that one rarely gets a straight answer to these questions from the post-industrial theorists. This is not because they do not raise them – indeed they do so by the very strength of their affirmative assertions. It has rather to do with the nature of the evidence they appeal to in support of their thesis, and their rather innocent manner of handling it. They seem to feel – and Bell is exemplary in this – that the importance of the changes are apparent simply by reference to the statistics that apparently document the changes. Repeatedly the sociological significance of a trend is assumed from its merely quantitative expression in the published records. Thus both the fact and the significance of the transition from a manufacturing to a service economy is inferred from the finding that, in the official returns of most industrial societies, an increasingly large part of the workforce is classified as employed in services. The increasing influence and power of the professional and technical class is assumed from the disproportionately rapid growth of such personnel as recorded in census and man-power returns. The growing centrality of 'theoretical knowledge' is 'proved' by reference to the higher proportions of Gross National Product devoted to higher education, research and development, and the like, in the wealthiest and most successful industrial societies. And so on.

Simply to state the propositions in this way is to question their significance. But more needs to be done if we are to arrive at a realistic assessment of these trends. A closer look at some of the specific assertions of the theory will help towards this end, and will also allow us to suggest any major divergences from the projected trends.

3. The Service Economy

Take first the service economy. Accepting the conventional sectoral division of the economy into primary (mainly agricultural), secondary (mainly manufacturing), and tertiary (services), there is no doubt that, in all the industrial societies, there has been a long-term tendency whereby the majority of the working population has come to be employed in the tertiary, service, sector. Developments, in other words, have borne out a celebrated analysis of Colin Clark's in *The Conditions of Economic Progress* (1940). Clark argued that there was a trajectory along which every industrialized nation would pass, following which, because of sectoral differences in productivity, and the increasing demand for health services, recreation, and the like, as national incomes rose, the greater proportion of the labour force would inevitably move to the service sector. As a category, by virtue of its heterogeneity, the service sector is notoriously difficult to define precisely. But there seems general agreement that it is best thought of as a residual category, comprehending for instance trade, finance, transport, health, recreation, research, education, and government. The United States seems to have been the first country in the world's history to develop a service economy: that is, as Victor Fuchs puts it, at some point in the 1950s it 'became the first nation in which more than half of the employed population was not involved in the production of food, clothing, houses, automobiles, or other tangible goods.'[24] The service sector there already accounts for more than half of the Gross National Product. And by the later 1970s more than sixty per cent of the employed population is expected to be in services. Other industrial societies are moving steadily in the same direction, and some are already there. The United Kingdom, for instance, at some point towards the end of the 1960s also became a service economy.[25]

The evidence at this level is not seriously in dispute. The question is, however, what follows from this move to a service economy? In the first place we must be careful not to see in this development some radically new turn, some unexpected discontinuity with past evolution. As R. M. Hartwell has stressed, 'the structural change involving the continuous growth of the tertiary sector has occurred in both the United States and England from the beginnings of their industrializations.'[26] Moreover the differential rate of expansion of manufacturing and services from the start made it plain that the future lay with services. Thus in the English case, between 1750 and 1850 manufacturing and services both expanded at the expense of agriculture, but the service sector already showed a rather quicker rate than manufacturing both in terms of employment and productivity. Between 1850 and 1900 these trends continued, with service employment increasing much faster than manufacturing but with decreasing productivity: a tendency that has continued up to the present time, so that, as revealed by the 1971 census, a majority of the population is now employed in services (and the difficulties of raising productivity in the service sector is an important contributory cause of inflation). Not unreasonably Hartwell concludes that 'the clear indication is that in 1850 the economy of England was already firmly on the path to being "a service economy".'[27] Whatever significance we wish to attribute to this tendency, therefore, we must initially stress the essential continuity with respect to services in any movement from industrialism to post-industrialism.

Actually the English case here – as elsewhere – complicates what has in fact been the more normal pattern; and one which reveals a more interesting and unexpected evolution than is customarily assumed. The history of occupational trends in England will, at a pinch, support the conventional sequence, primary to secondary to tertiary sectoral predominance, since there was a short period when the industrial employees of the secondary sector did in fact constitute a bare majority of the workforce. Thus 'the industrial society' can superficially at least be equated with the predominance of the industrial worker, just as the 'pre-industrial society' can be equated with the predominance of the agricultural worker, and the 'post-industrial society' with the predominance of the service worker. This then becomes the basis for the neat evolutionary sequence, pre-industrial, industrial, post-industrial.

But the English case was unique in this as in other respects, once more reminding us of the dangers of constructing models on the basis of the English experience of industrialization. In no other case of industrialization did industrial workers come to constitute a majority of the workforce, *at any time in the course of industrialization.* The proportions employed in services and agriculture when combined always outweighed manufacturing. In most countries the industrial 'core' of the economy has stabilized after a time at roughly one third of the workforce. And this percentage has remained remarkably steady throughout the course of this century. The industrial workforce has declined most sharply in the United Kingdom, which in any case had an abnormally high proportion committed to that sector. But in France, Germany, and the United States, the decline has been negligible in the course of this century. By contrast the spectacular and easily most important change has been the rapid decline of agricultural employment, and a correspondingly rapid increase in service employment. For instance, in the United States in 1900 the proportions of the workforce employed in agriculture, industry, and services respectively were 38, 38, and 24 per cent; in 1970 the figures were 4, 35, and 61 per cent. 'The great sectoral transformation of our times,' as Robert Heilbroner rightly says, 'has been not so much a shift from "industry" to "service" as a shift from agricultural to service tasks.'[28]

A consequence of this fact is that one of the important contrasts proposed between the industrial and the post-industrial society stands on very shaky ground. The post-industrial theorists assume that part of the novelty of the post-industrial era is a negative characteristic: a massive emigration from industrial work. This allows the supposition that the populations of post-industrial societies are conscious of new experiences and new needs springing from their new working milieux in the service sector, and can contrast these with the industrial experiences of their parents and grandparents. In fact, however, there is constancy and continuity in the history of the industrial work experience of the industrial societies. The proportion of the population involved in that experience was never a majority – but equally it has remained steady for a considerable amount of time (which is not to say that it cannot change more rapidly in the future). What *has* made for dramatic differences of work experience has been the mass movement from farm employment to service employment; a difference compounded by the fact that this has equally been a movement from the countryside to the city. Much of the politics and culture of the industrial societies during the past half century is indeed incomprehensible without an awareness of this movement, which is still in many countries working itself out.[29] But however one chooses to analyse that set of changes, the emphasis clearly would have to be placed elsewhere than in the contrast between factory and office.

We should note in passing that the reasons commonly given by economists for the growth of services (and implicit in the original formulation of Fisher and Clark) also point to a fundamental continuity rather than discontinuity of evolution. These reasons include: the more rapid growth of final demand for services, caused by the fact that as incomes rise the demand for goods tends to rise less rapidly than the demand for services; the growth of intermediate demand for services by goods-producing industries as a result of increased division of labour; and the much more rapid growth of output per man in industry and agriculture as compared with services, causing the first two sectors to shed labour and the third to be swollen by it. All these causes, and especially the last two, indicate that the change to services must be placed within a much longer-term curve of evolution than the post-industrial theorists seem prepared to contemplate. The dynamic of the change, its location within a systematic pattern of development, is clearly related both temporally and structurally to the original process of formation of 'the industrial society'. Not to investigate that dynamic – and Bell, for instance, certainly does not – is to miss or ignore the major shaping force of life and work in the service economy.

As an illustration of this point, which will be elaborated later, consider that the growth of the service economy owes as much to an active policy of search and intervention on the part of business, as it does to the more passive factors listed above. Beyond a certain level of goods-production, and following a familiar motivation, the 'progressive logic' of rationalization and expansion pushes the business enterprise into the hitherto unfilled sectors of the market – and this means above all services. Hence the growth in the industries of entertainment, recreation, tourism; hence too the rise of private enterprises in education, nurseries, hospitals and nursing homes, and 'therapeutic' institutions of all kinds. This is by no means the whole story of the rise of services; but the systematic link between the secondary and tertiary sectors of the economy is plainly seen in the case of the business corporation that manufactures both television sets and packaged holidays for tourists.

4. White-Collar Work

The mere statement of the passage to a service economy suffices for some post-industrial theorists as indication of the arrival of a new society. Others, sensing that more is needed, have seen in the rise of services a fundamental transformation in the nature of the individual's relation to his work and to his fellows, a reversal of the trends towards alienation and depersonalization in the large corporation of the industrial society. Victor Fuchs, the American economist who has been one of the most prominent analysts of 'the service revolution', puts this view forward in a typically optimistic vein:

> Employees in many service industries are closely related to their work and often render a highly personalized service that offers ample scope for the development and exercise of personal skills . . . The direct confrontation between consumer and worker that occurs frequently in services creates the possibility of a more completely human and satisfying work experience . . . With more and more people becoming engaged in service occupations, the net effect for the labour force as a whole may be in the direction of the personalization of work . . . the line between 'work' and 'leisure' may be difficult to draw . . .[30]

Bell, following Fuchs, concludes that 'the fact that individuals now talk to other individuals, rather than interact with a machine, is the fundamental fact about work in the post-industrial society.'[31] This view is partly based on findings which purport to show that organizations in the service sector are typically small, often non-corporate, and frequently engaged in non-profit operations.[32]

This idealized and happy view of life and work in the service economy regrettably must be seriously qualified. For one thing, it makes very careless use of the contrast of the small-sized, 'personalized' service organization of the post-industrial society *versus* the giant industrial corporation of the industrial society. It is a myth that the industrial societies are or ever were dominated by the large corporation *in terms of the proportion of the workforce employed.* The dominance of the economy by the large corporations is a structural fact and had never turned on the extent to which they absorb a majority of the workforce. Numerous studies and reports have demonstrated the persisting importance of the small manufacturing firm as employer. In the United Kingdom over four-fifths of manufacturing establishments employ less than 200 workers, accounting for nearly one-third of all manufacturing employees; 97 per cent of manufacturing establishments employ less than 500 workers, accounting for over half of the total manufacturing labour force.[33] The 'typical' manufacturing firm is no less small than the typical service organization.

Moreover, the service sector shows the same tendency towards throwing up a small number of large-scale concentrations as in manufacturing. In the United States the top fifty banks account for a third of all banking employment; the top fifty insurance companies for almost half the employment in that field. In Britain, enterprises employing 500 people or more absorbed thirty per cent of the non-manufacturing labour force in the mid-1960s; and the Censuses of Production show a marked trend towards concentration both of employment and of output.[34] The future of the tertiary sector in this respect seems likely to be remarkably similar to the present of the secondary sector: marked by a 'centre' made up of a small number of very large and powerful units, and a 'periphery' of a very large number of small units, significant in terms of employment but relatively marginal in terms of output, investment, and innovation.

But the more important question turns on the nature and quality of work in the service sector. Here an initial distortion has to be guarded against in the common identification of the 'service revolution' with the 'white-collar revolution'.[35] The identification then allows one to speak, at a somewhat idyllic distance, of all service work as 'characterized by trim surroundings, neat dress or prestigious uniform, constant exposure to a "clientele", coffee breaks, telephone calls',[36] culminating, no doubt, in promotion to the Board of Directors or marriage to the boss. Such an account reflects an apparently inescapable tendency on the part of writers on the service economy to take as the general pattern of work the conditions in the most attractive and prestigious parts of the service sector. The image of service work that is conjured up is taken from the world of the mass media and the advertising agencies, the luxury hotels and international airports, the small professional agencies and consultancies. In this glossy world, whose image is of course strenuously promoted by the very service organizations of which it is the idealized reflection, it is difficult not to think of the typical service worker as the glamorous air hostess, hotel receptionist, or personal secretary.

Even were this an acceptable account of the generality of white-collar work, which it manifestly is not, it doubles the distortion by suppressing the fact of the existence of a considerable body of manual workers in the service sector. It is misleading to equate, in a simple way, the move to a service economy with the explosive growth of white-collar work. The average garage mechanic or night-cleaner does not wear a white collar. Indeed, in a rather unexpected way manual work in this century has been kept up largely through the expansion of the service sector, while in a parallel development manufacturing has been expanding its white-collar workforce while shedding its manual workers through continuing mechanization. Moreover the conditions of manual work in the service sector – in areas such as catering, cleaning, maintenance, transportation – are often more unpleasant, dirty or dangerous than in the manufacturing sector. Where it is not actually sweated labour it is very often sweaty labour. We must remember, too, that service-type occupations are spread across both manufacturing and service concerns. This is obvious when we consider cleaning and maintenance, and other forms of manual work; but there is also the important point that a good part of the expansion of white-collar service workers has come in the growth of the marketing, managerial, and clerical departments of manufacturing concerns, as part of the process of continuing rationalization of the business enterprise. In both the United States and Britain, something like a third of all employees in manufacturing are white-collar workers.[37] The location of such workers in these enterprises, which cannot be held to share the same lofty, non-profit, concerns ascribed to many service industries, must further caution us against accepting too rosy a picture of the working conditions of service workers.

It is true that white-collar workers make up the bulk of service workers, and that in all industrial societies they are on their way to becoming the largest single category of workers in the workforce. No other industrial society has yet reached the position of the United States, where in 1956 the white-collar workers surpassed blue-collar workers for the first time, and by 1968 were assessed as forming 4·67 per cent of the total workforce, compared with the blue-collar share of 36·3 per cent. But the signs are clearly pointing in that direction for the other industrial societies – in the United Kingdom, for instance, white-collar workers made up 38·3 per cent of the workforce in 1966, and by the 1971 census seem to have almost reached the American figure.[38]

For the theorists of post-industrialism, the white-collar revolution marks one of the fundamental, most obvious, discontinuities with the industrial society of the past. Its occurrence, for Bell, decisively refutes Marx's projection of

> the industrial worker as the symbol of the proletariat. For the paradoxical fact is that as one goes along the trajectory of industrialization – the replacement of men by machines – one comes logically to the erosion of the industrial worker himself. In fact, by the end of the century the proportion of factory workers in the labour force may be as small as the proportion of farmers today; indeed the entire area of blue-collar work may have diminished so greatly that the term will lose its sociological meaning as new categories, more appropriate to the divisions of the new labour force, are established.[39]

Similarly George Lichtheim, contrasting the present 'post-bourgeois' society with the bourgeois society of the industrial era, argues that 'there cannot be a bourgeoisie without a proletariat, and if the one is fading out, so is the other, and for the same reason: Modern industrial society does not require either for its operations.'[40]

The vast and still continuing increase in the number of white-collar workers is certainly one of the most arresting phenomena of the recent history of the industrial societies; and there can be no doubt that it will affect the culture and consciousness of those societies, although in ways that are by no means yet clear or agreed upon.[41] What does seem clear, however, is that for the great majority of white-collar workers, the work environment, work activities, and work relationships will be remote indeed from the humanized, personalized, and self-fulfilling pattern envisaged in the post-industrial scenario. Once again, as with the service sector in general, there is a tendency to glamorize white-collar work by drawing selectively on some of its more attractive but quite unrepresentative areas. As Harry Braverman has commented, 'the white-collar category tends to get its occupational flavour from the engineers, managers, and professors at the top of the hierarchy, while its impressive numerical masses are supplied by the millions of clerical workers, in much the same way as the stars of an opera company occupy the front of the stage while the spear carriers provide the massive chorus.'[42] Put another way, any assessment of the general quality of work in the white-collar world must start from the fact that the vast majority of white-collar workers are clerks: mostly female, and mostly involved in routine, unskilled duties.[43]

A certain amount of optimism even about the lowly clerical grades is sometimes generated by recalling the conditions of the nineteenth-century clerk, in something of his Dickensian form. The nineteenth-century male clerk, close to his employer, having an overall comprehension of the office, affecting gentlemanly ways, could reasonably expect to rise through the bank, office or store, often through marriage to his employer's daughter. Such, alas, is not likely to be the fate of his generally low-skilled, generally low-paid, generally female, twentieth-century successor. Taylorism, the principles of 'scientific management', having conquered the factory has moved into shop and office. Shop and office have been 'industrialized': that is to say, they have been subjected to the same processes of increasing rationalization, routinization, division of labour, and mechanization, as had the factory in an earlier period. Following the logic of the 'economies of scale', units have increased in size and centralization, thereby increasing the impersonality of the enterprise and dividing, segregating, and fragmenting the workforce. Far from working in cosy intimacy with her boss, the average typist, filing clerk, or secretary these days is likely to find herself one among a large 'pool' of similar female white-collar employees, under the beady eye of a secretarial supervisor, and in a large office often remote from those occupied by managers and executives. A secretary is not very likely to end up marrying her boss if she hardly ever sees him.

Not only the character of the labour force but that of the tasks themselves has been affected by continuing rationalization and mechanization, exactly as with level of work skills and craft autonomy in the case of the factory worker. Mechanization in the shop and office divides and fragments the operations previously performed by one person, and hands them in ever-simplifying forms to a series of minimally-trained employees. Tasks are routine and repetitive, often in association with machines that embody the skill, intelligence, and information previously expected of the human being. The routing procedures of large offices serve the same pacing function as the assembly line of large factories, giving rise to the same mechanical and drone-like quality of labour. Key services which are replicated in different parts of an organization are brought together and centralized, eliminating further the diversity of tasks performed by individual employees. The flexibility of work-time possible in the unmechanized office is abolished almost altogether by the introduction of automated equipment which demands constant and regular 'feeding' and monitoring. This also creates the need for more intensified supervisory procedures, thereby introducing an even more factory-like atmosphere into the social life of the office. On present trends the computerized office of the future will resemble the automated factory in most important respects: a few highly trained systems analysts and programmers at the top, segregated in almost every conceivable way from the mass of 'proletarianized' office workers at the bottom. These are likely to be mostly key-punch operators, a job that 'can be learned in a matter of a week or two', and carries almost no prospects of promotion or the opportunities to learn new skills.[44]

We should note too the gradual disappearance of another aspect of white-collar work often thought to enhance its attractiveness when compared with most manual work: the possibility and the likelihood of frequent face-to-face contact with customers, clients, and members of the public in general. Here again the worker is increasingly being displaced by the forces of rationalization: by self-service counters in supermarkets and department stores, cash-dispensing machines in banks, teaching machines in schools, laboratory testing equipment in clinics and hospitals, self-service restaurants and petrol-stations. Such a decline in personalized service means a loss of status for the white-collar employee, as well as isolation from the more agreeable centres of consumer and customer activity. Both losses are compounded by a further movement: the increasing tendency towards geographical separation between the executive offices in the town centres, and the more routine clerical offices in the off-centre, lower-rent districts, often near warehouses or industry. Setting-off at different times, diverging on the way, factory and office at the end are united in a common space and a common condition.[45]

5. Professionalization

The rise of the service economy, therefore, and the expansion of white-collar work, cannot by themselves be taken as the hallmark of a new social order. Indeed, as far as the conditions and quality of work are concerned, the evidence clearly shows that work in the service sector is on the whole less skilled, lower paid, less unionized, and less secure, than in manufacturing. It is disproportionately characterized by large numbers of weakly organized or uncommitted women workers, older workers, and part-timers.[46] To find in this economic sector, and these social groups, the principle of a new society is startling. The typical service worker has every reason to feel that he (or mostly, she) is living in a work environment which has been invaded and conditioned by the same structural tendencies as have long been at work in the industrial societies.

The recourse of the post-industrial theorists, faced with all this, is to put great stress on certain specialized tendencies within the growth of services and white-collar occupations. The 'tertiary sector', it is argued, must be more carefully dissected if the full significance of its growth is to be grasped. When closely examined, trends of such distinctiveness reveal themselves that it might be better to introduce new sectoral categories, the 'quaternary' and even the 'quinary' sectors, and to mark these off from a more narrowly defined tertiary sector. The tertiary sector is restricted to the area of classic services, common enough in the capital cities of pre-industrial societies: commerce, financial services, administrative departments. The quaternary (sometimes subdivided to include a 'quinary' sector) includes most of the more recent service activities and occupations: in science, research, development, education and culture, health services and social welfare, leisure and recreation. And what the evidence shows, say Bell and co., is that the expansion in the tertiary sector is a preliminary phase to the more novel and fundamental expansion of the quaternary sector. It is in the growth of the professional, technical, and scientific groups that the essential underlying movement to post-industrialism must be discerned. In the post-industrial society, says Bell, 'the central person is the professional, for he alone is equipped, by his education and training, to provide the kinds of skill which are increasingly demanded.'[47] Paul Halmos similarly declares:

> The total professional complement of society, vastly increased in number and influence, is now in the process of slowly re-newing society itself . . . The process of professionalisation is the widest single avenue along which moral change in our Western industrial communities is being guided today, and will be guided during the coming decades.[48]

None of these thinkers denies that, in sheer numerical terms, the mass of fairly low-skilled, routine, employees of the old tertiary sector still predominates in current industrial societies. But the evidence from a number of societies suggests that this may well be a transitional phenomenon, leading eventually to the settled predominance of the quaternary employees. The further development of science and technology, expressed in greater mechanization and rationalization, will eliminate the need for large numbers of routine white-collar workers. Indeed, according to the old law of 'the privilege of backwardness' it may be possible for the phase of routine white-collar expansion to be severely abbreviated or truncated, using the already existing organization and technology of 'leader' societies. It has been noted that the curve of the explosive expansion of routine service workers in the United States is already flattening out, under the impact of better use of management systems and cybernation; while in Sweden, for instance, commerce, finance and clerical occupations account for a much smaller proportion of the overall service sector than in the United States, and a relatively larger share is taken by welfare, health, education, and cultural services.[49]

In a striking calculation, Bell establishes that out of the 20 million *male* white-collar workers in the United States in 1970 (almost 42 per cent of the male labour force), almost 14 million were 'managerial, professional, or technical'; further, that the rate of growth of professional and technical employment has been twice that for the labour force as a whole, and that a particular group, the scientists and engineers, has been growing at three times the average rate. On present trends, it is claimed, by 1980 the professional and technical employees will constitute the second largest occupational group in the United States, surpassed only by the clerical workers, and by the end of the century they will form the largest group.[50] For Britain, similarly, Professor Sayers Bain notes the 'extraordinary increase in the number of scientific and technical employees' since the beginning of the century. 'Although the total number of such workers is relatively small, they are increasing more rapidly than any other component of the white-collar labour force' (e.g. scientists and engineers increased by 894 per cent between 1921 and 1966). A projection by the Cambridge economist V. H. Woodward suggests that by 1981 the British position will be very similar to the American. He calculates that by then the professional and managerial groups will make up over one-fifth of the workforce. This would make them the second largest occupational category, following only the 'clerical, sales and service' workers.[51]

Galbraith generalizes from these trends to project forward a new image of the overall occupational structure of the industrial societies in the coming decades. He notes that during the years from 1947 to 1965, 'the number of professional and technical workers, the category most characteristic of the technostructure, approximately doubled. No other group has increased so rapidly.' The rise of 'the scientific and educational estate' is traced directly to the new manpower needs of the industrial system, and especially of its creative heart, the 'technostructure': the organization of the planning and technical specialists who constitute 'the guiding intelligence – the brain – of the modern business enterprise'. The rapid growth of the educated and specialist groups is transforming the shape of the occupational hierarchy from that of a squat pyramid, with a wide base of unskilled and unqualified manpower, to that of

> a tall urn. It widens out below the top to reflect the need of the technostructure for administrative, co-ordinating and planning talent, for scientists and engineers, for sales executives, salesmen, those learned in the other arts of persuasion, and for those who programme and command the computers. It widens further to reflect the need for white-collar talent. And it curves in sharply towards the base to reflect the more limited demand for those who are qualified only for muscular and repetitive tasks and who are readily replaced by machines.[52]

The growth of the professional and technical groups is indeed impressive; and one can only wonder why it has not been reflected more directly in the day-to-day activities and ethics of the society. Might it be that the 'professional' or 'scientist' is not what we have long taken him to be? What in fact is a professional or technical employee? Ironically Bell himself observes, *à propos* the status-striving of engineers, that 'they complain that the word engineer is now used to describe everyone from a salesman (a "systems engineer" at I.B.M.) to a garbage collector (a "sanitary engineer", in the Chicago euphemism).'[53] It is clear that Bell does not see the relevance of this remark to his own procedure of argument, which is also that of many of the other proponents of the post-industrial thesis. Drawing as he does on the official statistics of occupational censuses, Bell does not trouble to ask what real degree of professional expertise, technical training, or education, might be involved in the increasingly common practice of assigning 'professional' or 'technical' status to a very diverse range of occupations. He seems scarcely aware of the motives of status, power and economic interest that impel occupational groups – especially some of the newer ones in the service sector – to designate themselves professions and to seek recognition as such in the official classifications. As Harold Wilensky has said, 'in a culture permeated by the idea of professionalism but little touched by its substance, many occupations will be tempted to try everything at once or anything opportunity and expedience dictate [to secure professional standing]. The "professionalization" of labour, management, and commerce is largely of this kind.'[54]

The sociological sleight of hand involved in this procedure is the more difficult to discern because both employers and employees, management and unions, have an interest in the transformation of the humble artisan or routine service worker into a technician, engineer, manager, or artist. Re-labelling or re-grading suits the employees, naturally, because it allows them to claim higher pay and status for the same or even less skilled work. It suits the employers because it is an easy way of keeping good labour relations, as well as a handy exercise in public relations, satisfying outside bodies such as governments and researchers that mechanization is actually increasing skill and educational levels in the workforce (and possibly, as a bonus, qualifying the relevant industry for extra grants, tax remissions, etc., for increasing the number of its educated and highly-trained workers).

We joke about the familiar examples: the barber turned 'tonsorial artist', the plumber transformed into 'the heating engineer', aspiring professionals among salesmen, estate agents, public relations and personnel men (the latter often think of themselves as specialists in 'human relations'). But insofar as these groups scrape some kind of official recognition, this is the stuff which makes up the argument, commonly met with, that society is becoming thoroughly 'professionalized'. At a higher level there are the claims of what have been called the 'semi-professions', with reference particularly to employees in education, social work, and the health services. Indeed an important part of the post-industrial case rests on the rapid expansion of these areas, with an assumed increase in the society at large of the traditional attributes of the professional: specialized skills, work autonomy, and the service ideal.

These assumptions have to be looked at sceptically. The clear evidence is that the vast bulk of expansion in these fields has been at their lower ends, on almost any indicator we care to choose – qualifications, autonomy, pay. The growth is dominated by school teachers, nursing staff, junior and relatively unqualified social workers, and ancillary technical staff of various kinds.[55] Their conditions of work have little in common with that of the traditional professional, and indeed shade off readily into the sphere of routine white-collar work (with which they also share the common feature of a predominance of female workers, with corresponding loss of pay, status, autonomy). Above all the 'semi-professionals' cannot escape their attribution as dependent employees of public bureaucracies. These bureaucracies not only keep firm control over the levers of power, and general conditions of work; they also force upon their workers, willy-nilly, the role of policeman and regulatory supervisor, turning them into the 'other ranks' of the welfare state, manning at the lowest but most crucial levels the multifarious agencies of social control.[56] Such groups are therefore in many cases prevented from taking the initiative, in terms of a new social ethic of social welfare and social responsibility, which their putative role as the professionals of the post-industrial society enjoins upon them. Since they also have on the whole the minimal level of professional qualifications, they cannot be said to be contributing much in the direction of 'the primacy of theoretical knowledge' either.

These aspirants from below form, as it were, the upward push in the movement creating the impression of an increasing professionalization of society. But at the same time, from the top, there is a parallel movement in the opposite direction. Just as other groups are striving for professional conditions of work and status, the traditional professional groups are losing their distinctiveness in precisely the terms that other groups are making their claims. The idea that professionals are immune to the currents of bureaucratization and 'rationalization' that have afflicted other kinds of workers is a curious one, though often held;[57] but it is, in any case, increasingly remote from the life and work of many professional and technical groups. Large numbers of professional workers have lost their traditional autonomy and become the employees of private or public bureaucracies, with all that that implies by way of a hierarchical command system, specialization, and extensive division of labour. Furthermore, as with manual and routine white-collar work, mechanization, especially through the use of computerized systems, has led to the fragmentation of tasks, the diminution of skills, and the tying of the professional worker to the tempo and mode of the machine. Lastly, and predictably from the foregoing tendencies, have come 'job evaluation' for professionals, and the attempt to enforce new forms of employee accountability.[58]

Mike Cooley, research officer of the British Amalgamated Union of Engineering Workers, has drawn together some vivid examples of the process as it has affected various professional and technical groups. Thus in a major exercise of 'scientific management' by Rolls-Royce in 1971, the company sought to impose on the design staff at its Bristol plant the following conditions: 'The acceptance of shift work in order to exploit high capital equipment, the acceptance of work measurement techniques, the division of work into basic elements, and the setting of time for these elements, such time to be compared with actual performance.' Overall, and particularly with the introduction of computer-aided design, design staff have suffered a severe fragmentation of tasks and narrowing of skills:

> The draughtsman of the 1930s in Britain was the centre of design. He could design the component, stress it, specify the materials to be used, define the method of lubrication, and write the test specs. With the increasing complexity of technology, each of these has now been fragmented into narrow specialised areas. The draughtsman draws, the stressmen carry out the calculations, the metallurgist specifies the materials, the tribologist decides upon the means of lubrication.

Nor has the élite of the design profession, the architect, been neglected:

For him there has been specifically produced a software package known (appropriately) as HARNESS. The concept behind this system is that the design of buildings can be systematized to such an extent that each building is regarded as a communication route. Stored within the computer system are a number of pre-determined architectural elements which can be disposed around the communication route on a Visual Display Unit to produce different building configurations. Only these pre-determined elements may be used and the architect is reduced to operating a sophisticated 'Lego' set. His creativity is limited to choosing how the elements will be disposed rather than considering in a panoramic way the types and forms of elements which might be used.[59]

And what of the scientist, whose own activities lie behind so much of this process of rationalization and routinization? Science has, in its turn, been 'scientized'. The F. W. Taylor of science was Carl Duisberg, who, some ninety years ago, as research director at Bayer, submitted research work to the same division of labour as production work. Since then the industrialization of research has become a well-nigh universal trend. André Gorz describes the situation as follows:

As industry found that science could be a force of production, the production of scientific knowledge has been submitted to the same hierarchical division of labour and fragmentation of tasks as the production of any other commodity. The subordination of the laboratory technician or anonymous researcher to his or her boss, and of the latter to the head of the research department, is not very different, in most cases, from the subordination of the assembly-line worker to his foreman, and of the foreman to the production engineer, etc. The industrialization of research has been responsible for the extreme specialization and fragmentation of scientific work. The process and the scope of research have thereby become as opaque as the process of production, and the scientist has in most cases become a mere technician performing routine and repetitive work. This situation has opened the way for the increasing military uses of scientific work and the latter, in turn, has led to further hierarchization and specialization of research jobs. Science is not only militarized as regards its uses and orientations; military discipline has invaded the research centres themselves as it has the factories and administrations.[60]

To these long-term pressures on professional workers must be added more recent ones which further reveal the current weaknesses and dependence of these workers. There has been, in all the industrial societies, endemic unemployment among professionals, spectacularly so in the United States as a result of cutbacks in spending on defence and space exploration. While the latter might appear a local and temporary feature, it is more significant for illustrating the great dependence of so much of the educated workforce on large-scale bureaucracies over which they have virtually no control. The precariousness of their market position weakens their ability to resist a widespread and intensified movement on the part of employers (including government) to impose strict accountability measures, and to increase output. Since the measure of the latter is peculiarly difficult in the case of much professional work, the tendency has been for administrators to select what is clearly quantifiable (e.g. staff–student ratios) and to press for increased productivity along these dimensions, to the exclusion of other considerations. Professional output is thereby 'rationalized' in its classic industrial form, i.e. made subject to quantifiable calculations of input and output, to the displacement of qualitative criteria. The result of this whole process of declining status and deteriorating work conditions of professionals has been plain to see in recent years: an unprecedented number of strikes among professional workers of all kinds, and a move towards unionization and collective bargaining.[61]

6. The Role of Knowledge

The rise in the number of professional and technical employees may, therefore, suggest far-reaching changes in society that are largely illusory. In particular, there are serious grounds for doubting that 'the knowledge classes', in their current conditions of existence, are capable of exercising that controlling initiative, and supplying that special ethic of service and welfare, that the post-industrial thesis requires of them.

These professional groups are of course singled out for a

special destiny primarily because they are the men of expertise and knowledge; and knowledge is, allegedly, the 'axial principle' of the post-industrial society. Indeed in most of the accounts the new, pivotal, significance of the knowledge class is not so much demonstrated through the actual activities and influence of that class, as inferred and assumed from a more fundamental tendency established on rather different grounds. This is the tendency identified by Bell as the rise to primacy of 'theory' over 'empiricism', and the consequent 'centrality of *theoretical* knowledge' in present-day industrial societies. It is through the application of systematic and codified knowledge (both of the natural and of the social sciences) that modern societies now grow and evolve; and by a natural extension, it is the men of knowledge who must guide and control that evolution.

The growing importance of 'theoretical knowledge' is illustrated by Bell in the changing relations of science and technology: an important example since, says Bell, 'the roots of post-industrial society lie in the inexorable influence of science on productive methods'.[62] It is generally agreed that the great inventions and industries of the nineteenth century – such as steel, steam engine, electric light, telephone, automobile – were the work of inspired and talented tinkerers, many of whom were indifferent to the fundamental scientific laws which underlay their inventions. Science and technology progressed along different paths, and at different rates, the former usually lagging well behind the latter.[63] From about the end of the nineteenth century a closer relation between the two began to appear, with science increasingly governing the nature and pace of technological innovation. The outstanding and most frequently quoted example is that of the chemical industry, where many of the inventions were based on 'pure science' knowledge of the properties of macro-molecules, which were 'manipulated' to achieve the planned production of new materials. This development is seen as characteristic of the modern, post-industrial type of industry. It reveals, declares Radovan Richta's Czech team, 'a law of higher priority' in the evolution of the productive forces: 'the precedence of science over technology, and of technology over industry'.[64]

It is the application of this law at an intensifying rate, according to the post-industrial theorists, that has been responsible for most of the novel and characteristic accomplishments of the industrial societies of this century. It is the fusion of science with industry that has been the motor of the vast increases of productivity, since these increases have largely come through technological innovation, and theoretical science is the matrix of technical innovation these days. Moreover this development, seen at its most striking in the realm of production, has been extended into every important area of the life of society. This century has seen the application of codified knowledge in business management, public administration, and the national economy.

Macro-economic theory has given the state the intellectual tools to plan and manage economic growth in an orderly way, thereby avoiding the social strains and conflicts that had often in the past put a stop to growth. The new 'intellectual technology' based on the computer – linear programming, systems analysis, game theory, etc. – allows for the possibility of large-scale 'controlled experiments' in social life, allowing us to plot realistically 'alternative futures' for ourselves, and thereby greatly increasing the control that society has over its future. Society, instead of as in the past responding as it could to environmental pressures over which it had little control, becomes an 'active society', capable of initiating and controlling the major directions of its future.[65] 'Industrial society,' states Bell, 'is the co-ordination of machines and men for the production of goods. Post-industrial society is organized around knowledge, for the purpose of social control and the directing of innovating and change.'[66]

Unquestionably, the new role ascribed to knowledge is the culminating and convergent point for all post-industrial theorists, linking thinkers of both east and west, Right and Left. And following from this, there is also the common perception of the unprecedented importance of 'the knowledge factory', the university. Thus Peter Drucker writes:

While the *Grosstadt* [the nineteenth-century industrial city] was founded on the industrial worker, the megalopolis [of post-industrial society] is founded on, and organized around, the knowledge worker, with information as its foremost output as well as its foremost need. The college campus rather than the factory chimney is likely to be the distinctive feature of the megalopolis, the college student rather than the 'proletarian' its central political fact.[67]

For the theorists of the 'New Left', the new importance of knowledge to industrial society provides the primary explanation for the phenomenon of the university, rather than the factory, in recent years becoming the cockpit of social conflict. So Touraine argues that

if it is true that knowledge and technical progress are the motors of the new society, as the accumulation of capital was the motor of the preceding society, does not the university then occupy the same place as the great capitalist enterprise formerly did? Thus is not the student movement, in principle at least, of the same importance as the labour movement of the past? . . . From the moment that knowledge becomes an essential force of production, the organization of teaching and research also becomes a problem of general policy and the choices made in this area can no longer be governed by respect for traditions or by strictly technical demands.[68]

Similarly the Marxist theoretician Ernest Mandel writes that 'what the student revolt represents on a much broader social and historic scale is the colossal transformation of the productive forces which Marx foresaw in his *Grundrisse*: the re-integration of intellectual labour into productive labour, men's intellectual capacities becoming the prime productive force in society.'[69] Few of the 'New Left' theorists are prepared to ditch the workers altogether, to argue along with Bell 'that the "labour issue" *qua* labour is no longer central', and that economic class conflict based on the workplace is a dying issue, to be replaced by 'communal conflicts' over such matters as health, education, the environment, and so forth.[70] But Touraine goes a considerable way in this direction in sharply reducing the importance of industrial conflict:

Increasingly, the workers' interests are particular interests. Unionism is a historical reality inseparable from private enterprise. Because this private enterprise is no longer at the heart of decision-making [increasingly the province of government alone], unionism is no longer at the heart of the movement for social transformation. These remarks indicate the distance that separates labour unionism from the student movement.[71]

Clearly, if this central importance of knowledge to the industrial societies can be established, it would alter substantially the themes both of industrial society and of sociology itself. What kind of evidence is offered to sustain these large claims? Much of it is familiar and, at one level, irreproachable. At its simplest, and often most fatuous, it consists in the wide-eyed telling of the story of the quantitative growth of science and scientists: for instance, Alvin Toffler's '90 per cent of all the scientists who ever lived are now alive', and Derek Price's demonstration of the exponential growth in the number of scientific journals and papers since 1750.[72] No doubt, we are living in the middle of a dizzying and unprecedented explosion of scientific knowledge; but this kind of evidence tells us nothing about the uses to which it is put, or whether indeed it has any use at all, or has had any profound effect on the life of society. Equally unrevealing, as it stands, is the familiar account of the rapid expansion of education since 1945, and especially the growth in numbers in higher education, and of those possessing postgraduate qualifications such as the Ph.D.[73] The existence of unprecedentedly large numbers of people who have been through school and college is truly a fundamental fact about present-day industrial society, fraught with implications of very diverse kinds; but it is naive simply to equate an increase in formal education with an increase in the contribution of knowledge to social life.

More impressive are the calculations which purport to show the steadily growing role of knowledge in promoting economic growth. The work of two economists, Solow and Denison, has been particularly influential in the argument that, since a relatively early date in this century, the contribution to productivity of increased labour or (unchanged) capital inputs has been declining relative to that of increments of education and training of the workforce, or improved technology (applied knowledge).[74]

In other words, 'knowledge-power' has taken over from 'labour-power' as the motor of economic growth. Most economists readily admit the enormous difficulties involved in trying to 'operationalize' knowledge-related inputs. Nevertheless there must be some force in the conclusion of the generally sceptical Robert Heilbroner that 'there is little doubt that statistical examination of growth patterns among industrialized nations shows a steadily increasing importance of "knowledge-related" inputs, and a corresponding decline in increases in brute "labour power" or sheer quantities of unchanged capital (e.g. the addition of more railway tracks).'[75]

Lastly there is the evidence which for most of the post-industrial theorists is held to be the most significant indicator of all: the increasing share of the Gross National Product devoted to the production and distribution of knowledge, particularly in the critical sphere of 'research and development' (R. & D.). It is by appeal to this sort of evidence that these theorists have come to speak of the 'institutionalization' of scientific discovery and application, with the consequent assumption that industrial societies are now on a course of self-sustaining and controlled economic growth. Given also the intellectual tools available for monitoring and managing the society as a whole, the stage seems set for the realization of the cybernetician's dream: a social organism with a seemingly infinite capacity for orderly growth and development, able to manipulate or adjust itself to every demand of its internal and external environment. It is the scientific utopia, the 'heavenly city', of the Enlightenment *philosophes*, at last achieving earthly and historical embodiment.[76]

In a celebrated exercise, Fritz Machlup calculated that in 1958 the United States devoted 29 per cent of its G.N.P. to knowledge, nearly half of this on education alone, and about 8 per cent of it on R. & D.[77] This astonishingly high and much-quoted figure was probably more important for directing interest to the new significance of 'knowledge production' than in establishing, at one fell swoop, the claims of the post-industrial theorists. Using stricter criteria of what constitutes knowledge, Bell shows that in 1965 the United States spent more than 9 per cent of its G.N.P.

on R. & D. and education, 3·4 per cent going on R. & D. alone; and that by 1969 more than 7 per cent of G.N.P. was going on education (compared with 3·4 per cent in 1949). No other country yet matches these figures (e.g. the United Kingdom, second only to the United States, in 1964 spent 2·3 per cent of G.N.P. on R. & D.); but an O.E.C.D. report pronounced the American figure of over 3 per cent of G.N.P. as 'a symbol for other countries which now regard this as a target to be reached'. At any rate, it is the strikingly large and historically unprecedented amount of national wealth devoted to the stimulation, production and dissemination of knowledge that for Bell is the conclusive evidence. Present-day industrial society is better described as 'a knowledge society', he asserts, in the double sense that 'the sources of innovation are increasingly derivative from research and development' and that 'the weight of the society ... is increasingly in the knowledge field'.[78]

So many thinkers, and not simply those associated with the post-industrial theory, have been impressed by statistics of this sort that we are clearly dealing with a phenomenon that is far from negligible. But again we have to ask if the evidence can bear the significance, the interpretation, that the post-industrial theorists lay on it. The simple figures themselves conceal some curious features. Machlup, for instance, includes in his definition of knowledge such things as stationery, office supplies, musical instruments, and typewriters. The growth in the volume and use of such things is no doubt important, but it is not in any obvious way related to the increase in theoretical knowledge that Bell emphasizes. Or take the U.S. Government's figures for R. & D. expenditure: sceptical students on examining them closely have noted how, particularly in the later years, they are inflated by the growing tendency to include routine testing or marketing procedures within the category of 'research'. As an example, J. M. Blair computes that on a realistic assessment the actual amount spent on research in new industrial products in the U.S. in 1966 was not, as the official figures have it, 20 billion dollars but *one* billion.[79] Exactly as in the case of 'professionalization', the inflation of figures in the knowledge industry is clearly a widespread phenomenon, and for the same mixture of political, economic, and prestige motives.

Secondly, there is considerable doubt as to the importance of institutionalized science and research in stimulating the technical and economic developments of this century. A classic study of 1958 by Jewkes and his colleagues showed that a majority of seventy major twentieth-century inventions were made outside the R. & D. departments of large firms: by private inventors, small firms, and individual researchers in universities.[80] The conclusions that Jewkes naturally drew from the study have been the subject of much dispute ever since; but more recent work has tended to support his verdict.[81] Moreover it has become quite clear that 'pure' or 'basic' research – a central component of Bell's 'theoretical knowledge' – forms only a tiny fraction of the overall R. &. D. effort in all industrial countries. For instance, of the more than 3 per cent of G.N.P. spent on R. & D. in the United States, something like 68 per cent is spent on the development of existing knowledge, 22 per cent on applied research, and only 10 per cent on basic research.[82] And while it is true that professionalized R. & D. has been very important in the process of innovation (i.e. putting inventions into commercial development and production), even here the bulk of the effort is concentrated on the exploitation of existing knowledge of products and processes: 'there is firm empirical evidence that most professional industrial R. & D. is concentrated on product and process improvement and on new "generations" of established products.'[83]

Thus there must be serious questioning of the significance of 'theoretical knowledge' – not, obviously, knowledge as such – to technological innovation and growth: a point further underlined by the finding that 'unqualified' scientific workers continue to be of as great importance in invention and innovation as graduate scientists.[84] It appears that, as in the past, market forces and political goals ('need-pull') are far more important in determining the nature and rate of technological innovation than the ideas and inventions springing from pure research ('idea-push'). Post-war Japan demonstrates this conclusively: with one of the lowest levels of R. & D. expenditure of all industrial nations, it has had the highest economic growth rate in the post-war period.[85] Indeed a wide-ranging study by S. R. Williams shows that generally there is no correlation between R. & D. expenditure and economic growth rates.[86] Rightly Langrish and his colleagues have commented on this finding: 'If this applies to figures for total R. & D., most of which is accounted for by applied and development work, then one would expect even less correlation between basic research and economic growth. It is difficult to believe that much national economic benefit arises from the knowledge output of a nation's own basic research.'[87]

Thirdly, and at a more general level, there is the complacent assumption of the post-industrial theorists that more money spent on education and research, and larger numbers involved in them, *ipso facto* means a better-educated, more self-conscious and more 'knowledgeable' society. There are various reasons, some of which will be considered later, why all industrial societies have gone in for a massive expansion of formal education. Some of these are remote from educational purposes at all, and it is still an open question whether more and more inclusive systems of formal education also entail a more educated population. At any rate there is reason enough to heed Robert Heilbroner's warning that

> it would be hasty to jump from the fact of a higher stock of embodied education to the conclusion that the stock of 'knowledge' of the society has increased *pari passu*. For along with the increased training undergone by the labour force has come an increase in the compartmentalization and specialization of its skills, best exemplified by comparing the wide-ranging capabilities of the farmer with the much more narrowly defined work capabilities of the office-clerk.

The average citizen of present-day industrial society no doubt knows more of the world, in the sense of having more abstract knowledge of it, than his counterpart of an earlier age. The mass media have seen to that. But below that abstract level the gain may be very much less. For instance,

> within that very important branch of social knowledge concerned with the operation of the socio-economic mechanism, what seems to mark

the education-intensive post-industrial society is a marked *decrease* in the ability of the individual to perform work outside his trained speciality – witness our helplessness in the face of a broken utensil, vehicle, electrical system, or plumbing fixture, compared with the versatility of the farmer (or industrial artisan), proverbially jack of all trades, even if master of none.[88]

Heilbroner's critical gloss on the concept of a 'knowledge society' is obviously of fundamental importance, suggesting a way of reading the post-industrial trends that would lead to a very different assessment from that of Bell and co. In the next chapter I shall be considering various aspects of this possible re-reading. Here what needs to be emphasized is the crudeness of an analysis that can judge the extent of knowledge in a society by an arithmetical addition of books, papers, students, teachers, and money spent on research.

Finally the post-industrial theorists show an extraordinary naivety as to the whole shaping context of the world of 'theoretical knowledge'. For instance, on Bell's own admission the enormous growth in R. & D. expenditure in the United States was almost entirely owing to the initiative and funding of the Federal Government, who in 1965 were providing over 64 per cent of all R. & D. spending. What is more significant, however, is that throughout the decades of the 1950s and 1960s more than 80 per cent of all Federal R. & D. was connected with what Bell, following the bureaucrats, calls 'the external challenge': that is to say, mainly war – the fighting of it, preparation for it, and defence against it ('atomic, space, and defence' objectives, in the O.E.C.D. classification of R. & D. expenditure). If we take non-Federal spending into account as well, we find that 'the external challenge' motivated more than 60 per cent of *all* R. & D. expenditure in the United States – and this is probably a considerable underestimate, as a large part of privately financed industrial R. & D. is also connected with 'defence', although it is not categorized as such. By contrast, the U.S. spent less than 10 per cent of its R. & D. budget on the O.E.C.D.'s category 'welfare and miscellaneous' (including health and 'non-directed' basic research) – an indifference to these aspects of social development that was fully matched in those other countries – the United Kingdom, France, Sweden – which also devoted the largest part of their R. & D. budgets to objectives connected with 'the external challenge'.[89]

Bell notes this phenomenon but astonishingly fails to draw the obvious inference from it. An explanation for the rapid growth of knowledge institutions and the knowledge classes offers itself in the shape of Cold War politics. The science-based 'welfare' state can be rapidly reclassified as the science-based 'warfare' state, and with greater respect for the actual history of the last fifty years.[90] Such an account would by no means deny the significance of the trends discussed by Bell; but it would suggest a social purpose and intention behind the 'post-industrial' developments that would seriously question the idea of a movement to a new kind of social order. Political interests, political values, and political goals urge themselves upon us for scrutiny, with more than a suggestion that some very familiar strivings and fears would reveal themselves. Bell however, having raised the spectre, passes by on the other side. His postulate of 'the autonomy of the political realm' allows him to concentrate on social structural changes without further considering the political purposes that might be the causes of those changes. For him the bare facts of the rise of the professional and scientific groups presage an entire switch in the premises of the social order. The ethos of the new scientific estate is professionalism, not profit. Its professional concern is general welfare. The old industrial society, dominated by the business élite, followed an 'economizing' mode, concerned with the most rational allocation of resources consistent with the goal of the maximization of private profit. The post-industrial society, increasingly influenced by the scientific and professional ethos, will follow a 'sociologizing' mode, concerned with non-market communal planning in the direction of maximum general welfare.[91]

It is an attractive idea, but needs to be argued in the face of much contrary evidence. The uses to which much 'theoretical knowledge' and many 'theoretical' persons have been put strongly imply an overall social purpose which is only too clearly a continuation of the ethos of 'that stubborn bitch', the industrial society (whether market or state capitalist). Much of the growth to which knowledge has contributed has only a dubious relevance to general welfare. There are the familiar examples of the atomic bomb, other weapons of the biological and chemical kind, space exploration, and large-scale capital-intensive technology with its propensity to pollute the environment and exhaust the earth's supply of fossil fuels. Then there is the ingenious and expensive gadgetry of the mass consumer industry, with its built-in principle of 'planned obsolescence' and marginal technical improvements (the ceaseless concern of the R. & D. departments). Less familiar, perhaps, are the uses and purposes of much basic research in medicine, where the general welfare content might be expected to be higher than in other sciences. But medical research seems equally skewed in the direction of particular groups with the power to pay and persuade – attending, for instance, far more closely to the diseases that afflict middle-aged members of the middle classes than to the occupational health hazards of many working-class jobs.[92] And finally one hardly needs to add that ninety-nine per cent of the knowledge effort of the industrial societies is devoted to the problems of the developed world, considered as a self-contained entity, a 'post-industrial enclave'.[93] The realization that a concern for welfare might involve a consideration of the future of the globe as a whole, conceived as an interdependent system, seems yet remote from the preoccupations of the post-industrial scientific élites.

7. Persistence and Change

For all the qualifications one might make, the industrial society was a genuine novelty, marking a radical break with previous history. The same cannot be said of 'the post-industrial society' – not, at least, in the version we have been examining. At whatever level we consider the concept, we are constantly reminded of some of the main themes of industrialism and the industrial society. The 'agenda of questions' for post-industrial society seems remarkably like that for the industrial society. Beneath the post-industrial gloss, old, scarred, problems rear their heads: alienation and control in the workplaces of the service economy; scrutiny and supervision of the operations of private and public bureaucracies, especially as they come to be meshed in with technical and scientific expertise. Framing all these is the problem of the dominant constraining and shaping force of contemporary industrial societies: competitive struggles for profit and power between private corporations and between nation states, in an environment in which such rivalries have a tendency to become expansionist and global. Faced with such an agenda of questions it is difficult not to conclude that the politics of the post-industrial society will be essentially the politics of the industrial society – only, as it were, writ large. Were Marx or Tocqueville, Weber or Durkheim, to return today what might give them cause for despondency would not be the insufficiency of their original analysis, but its continuing relevance. The surprise might be that the tendencies they observed had been of such long duration – coupled, in some of their cases, with a sorrowful reflection that they had been unduly optimistic about the capacity of industrial society to initiate radically new patterns of social development.

Why then the widely-expressed feeling that a new society is emerging? We have already seen something of the immediate pressures, and the immediate ideological context, in response to which the post-industrial idea was formulated. But at a deeper level there is also the heritage of the sociological tradition itself, as we have examined it in the earlier part of this book. In particular there is the conviction, prominent in all the post-industrial theorizing, that industrialism matured and reached its peak at a very early point in this century, and that therefore many of the developments characteristic of the century, especially those of the post-1945 period, must plausibly be interpreted as the heralds of a new social order. Here is reflected not merely the radical foreshortening of the history of industrialism discussed earlier, but also the dependence on an over-literal impression of what constituted the substance of industrialism. The importance of the English experience of industrialization, and the influence of the

English literary and moralist tradition fashioned in response to it, comes through especially strongly in this connection. Ultimately it is from Dickens, Carlyle, and Mrs Gaskell – refracted through Marx and Engels – that the post-industrial theorists take their picture of industrialism as an affair basically of factories, the factory proletariat, and factory towns.[94] Since there have manifestly been changes in the prominence of these features, it appears necessary to find a new ordering principle for the newer or previously less noticed phenomena, such as services, automation, and the white-collar bureaucracies.

Far from being departures from the main tendencies of industrialism, however, these developments only too clearly fall within them. The post-industrial theory assumes that the structural features of the new society mark actual discontinuities with the patterns of the old industrial society: novel and to a large extent unexpected directions in the nature of economic activities, the quality of work, the shape of the occupational structure, the future of class conflict, and so on. The theory postulates a 'system break' in the transition to post-industrialism. Such a break is largely illusory. What are projected as novel patterns of development turn out on examination to be massive *continuities* within the basic system of the developing industrial society. Essentially, and insofar as they are actually occurring, the trends singled out by the post-industrial theorists are extrapolations, intensifications, and clarifications of tendencies which were apparent from the very birth of industrialism.

We have already seen how the rise of the service economy was implicit in the very origins of the industrial economy. We have noted, too, the extent to which the work and organization of the white-collar service bureaucracies have been stamped by the continuing processes of mechanization, rationalization, and specialization which were the very defining characteristics of industrialization. What needs emphasizing in addition is the long-standing nature of many of the developments thought to be peculiarly of our century. Just as sociologists have tended to predate and anticipate many of the central features of industrialism, so, in a contrary direction, there were certain positive features of the developing industrial society that were also hidden by the stereotyped image of industrialism. As a result, when these manifested themselves in a more palpable way at a later date they could be hailed as the signs of a new society.

So, for instance, sociologists are surprised, as they should not be, to discover that the white-collar revolution was already under way by the mid-nineteenth century. This reflected partly the growing importance of banks and credit institutions to industrial development, and the rise of the joint-stock company with its decisive separation of ownership from control and its extensive requirement for managerial, clerical and administrative personnel. The growth of this 'new middle class' was extensive enough to make a somewhat disconcerted Marx pay particular attention to it in the third volume of *Capital*, and to try – with considerable success – to fit into his account of the development of capitalism the rise of the vast 'labour of superintendence' which had grown up with the new commercial and credit institutions.[95] We should remember, too, that Pitman's shorthand had been taught to students since the 1830s, and the typewriter had arrived from America by 1880, so that by the end of the century the shorthand-typist, the most representative figure of the white-collar revolution, was already an established social type in Europe.

Then there was, already in the mid-nineteenth century, the rapid growth of new professions and the modernization of the old. A class structure defined primarily in terms of property ownership was already being complicated by the claims of professional qualifications and bureaucratic office – a position that in essentials remains today.[96] The growth of bureaucracy, in its turn, was intimately connected with the increasing elaboration of the machinery of planning and regulation – both public and private – a feature that had from the beginning marked the process of industrialization in all Continental states. And there is the clear indication of the growing awareness of the importance of 'theoretical knowledge' to nineteenth-century industrial society, as seen in the rise of the German chemical industry.[97]

Finally there is the historical continuity which has perhaps the deepest roots of all: the internationalization and 'globalization' of the industrial system. One important reason why the post-industrial thesis has an initial plausibility is that it seems to reflect some of the most palpable and readily observable facts of contemporary life in the advanced societies – such as, for instance, the decline of heavy manufacturing industry, especially of the environmentally most polluting kind. It is here that the illusion may be of the most cruel, in the long run at least. For the impression of post-industrialism can be created in the developed societies largely owing to the intensified internationalization of economic activity since the end of the last century, seen especially in the rise to prominence of the multi-national corporation. The economic division of labour within the industrial society has now largely been replaced by a division of labour on a global scale, expressed in a certain systematic relation between the industrial societies and the industrializing or non-industrial regions of the world. It is a relation, needless to say, in which the richer and more powerful countries derive most of the benefits and keep fairly tight control. Thus the 'clean' tertiary sectors of the international economy predominate in the cities of the wealthy industrial societies while the 'dirty' secondary manufacturing industries, on which the tertiary sector depends, are sited elsewhere, in the societies of the Third World or the less developed industrial countries, such as Spain. The 'secondary' cities of Taiwan and Singapore permit the existence of the 'tertiary' cities of Europe and North America (just as, at an earlier time, the peasant hinterland supported the largely tertiary activities of the pre-industrial city). The organization of the multinational corporation spans both; but its headquarters and most of its support staff are to be found in the latter. Hence their 'post-industrial' gloss and glamour. It is only when the bauxite workers of Jamaica or the tin-miners of Bolivia strike or threaten to take over their industry that the reality of a single unified world economic system becomes evident.

These, briefly, are some of the sociological continuities with the main pattern of industrialism. The intellectual continuities are plainer to see, if we recall the earlier themes of this book. In comparing the sketch of the post-industrial society with that of the industrial society outlined earlier, it becomes clear that the industrial and the 'post-industrial' society are linked, not simply by the persistence of particular trends in social and economic life, but by the most general and abstract principles governing their development. At the most basic analytical level there is a continuity of theme which was first given expression in the nineteenth-century sociological account of industrialism. The charge of political conservatism sometimes flung at the heads of the post-industrialists is not nearly so accurate as a charge of intellectual conservatism.

Remotely there is Saint-Simon, who ought truly to be hailed as the prophet not just of industrialism but also of post-industrialism. It was he, the first thinker to grasp comprehensively the emergence of the new industrial society, who in a prescient vision announced the imminent rule of the scientists, industrialists, and artists. His account of the supersession of politicians and politics in favour of expert administration is uncannily close to Bell's sketch of the post-industrial society. The society of science, based on the science of society, was slow in realizing itself in the nineteenth century: but if Bell and his co-thinkers are right, it is well on the way to doing so in the twentieth. At any rate Saint-Simon would have good reason to be satisfied that the analysis – and prescription – that he offered of nineteenth-century industrial society should make so plausible a showing for twentieth-century post-industrial society.

Proximately and most immediately important there is Weber. Almost every feature of Bell's post-industrial society can be seen as an extension and a distillation of Weber's account of the relentless process of 'rationalization' in western industrial societies. Particularly this is evident in the functional importance Bell ascribes to bureaucracy, especially the public forms, and the gradual elimination of market forces. More generally there is the assumption of the spread of scientific rationality, not simply in the sense that 'technical reason' guides the approach to particular problems, but as an all-pervading ethos of the post-industrial society. Important, too, is Weber's influence in focusing on the problematic relation between the amateur politician and the scientific expert, owing to the 'functional indispensability' and hence increasing strategic power of the latter. Most post-industrial theorists are loath to abandon the notion of the autonomy of the political realm, and Bell in particular hangs on to it with all his might. But the whole weight of his argument goes against this, above all his insistence on the importance of theoretical knowledge and its practitioners.[98]

This perhaps most clearly demonstrates the intellectual continuities: for in both the Saint-Simonian and the Weberian accounts, the centrality of knowledge, especially scientific knowledge, stands out. It is particularly interesting to observe that Raymond Aron, a leading proponent of the idea of 'the industrial society', explicitly defines it in terms of scientific knowledge and its applications, emphasizing the Saint-Simonian roots of the concept and thereby eliminating the necessity for a further phase of industrialism specifically conceptualized around scientific knowledge.[99] And Anthony Giddens makes the same point well when he says that 'it is a myth that industrial man was made by the machine; from its first origins industrialism is the application of calculative rationality to the productive order. In this sense, modern technology is not "post-industrial" at all, but is the fruition of the principle of accelerating technical growth built into industrialism as such.'[100]

We should finally, in this recital of the intellectual antecedents of the post-industrial idea, mention James Burnham and the managerial and corporatist theories of the inter-war period. Many of these were repudiated not so much for their supposed inaccuracies as that they appeared to confer some degree of intellectual respectability on the Fascist regimes of the 1930s. Forty years on this seems less troublesome an issue; or perhaps contemporary theorists have simply suppressed the memory of these earlier theories. At any rate, acknowledged or unacknowledged, the ghost of Burnham hovers visibly over the post-industrial idea. His projection of the rise in all industrial societies of a commanding managerial and technical élite differs from the post-industrial theorists mainly in its greater explicitness and boldness, rather than in any essential respect. Certainly he would have felt entirely at home with 'the technostructure' that is the determining force of Galbraith's new industrial state, or the knowledge élite of Bell's post-industrial society – not to mention the 'corporatist state' that has, once more, been seen as the future of industrial societies.[101]

These intellectual predecessors are attended to not in order to score points off the post-industrial theorists – who in any case are often prepared to acknowledge them. The issue is a more fundamental one, as is shown in the very fact that the post-industrial theorists do not seem to realize the significance of acknowledging these intellectual mentors. They do not apparently see that to be drawing so heavily and so centrally on the classic analyses of industrialism makes it highly implausible that they can be describing the transition to a new order of society. In what can the novelty of that order consist, if the society continues to be dominated by the persistence of the central and, so to speak, defining process of classic industrialism? Yet it is quite evident that Bell and most of the post-industrial theorists are announcing what they see as a profound discontinuity in historical development – a radical change in the dynamic of economic and technological growth, in the principle of social structure, and in the values and priorities of industrial societies.

Everything that we have been considering in this chapter argues against this view. When the post-industrial thesis is broken down into specific assertions, examination dissolves it into the more familiar story of *plus ça change, plus c'est la même chose*; or, the same, only more so. We should in any case have been led to expect something like this from the discussion on the timing and tempo of industrialization in Chapter Four. For it was apparent there that by the end of the nineteenth century the major tendencies of industrialism still had to work themselves out, and that a good part of the history of the twentieth century was likely to be taken up with their more complete realization. To contemplate a movement to 'post-industrialism' therefore entails 'killing off' the order of industrialism just at the point in time at which, on past rates, it should be reaching its culmination, rather than its decrepitude. Of course history is not as regular and orderly as this. Compressed and accelerated developments do occur, as much as retardations and digressions. But simply on the face of it, it is in the highest degree improbable that changes *of the same revolutionary order* could be transforming the industrial societies so soon after the fundamental and long-drawn-out rupture with the feudal, agrarian and peasant societies from which they emerged. The nineteenth century, it is generally agreed, is largely taken up with the story of the struggle, supersession, and in part fusion of the pre-industrial and the industrial orders. But we should remember that even in our own century some of its most striking episodes have involved what might fairly be called the clash of pre-industrial and industrial forces: as in the fall of the absolutist empires of Central Europe, or Hitler's 'bourgeois revolution' in Germany.[102] It is not, of course, impossible that feudal echoes and post-industrial portents should be present in the same set of societies at the same time; but such a co-existence should warn us against a too ready acceptance of claims of radical discontinuities with industrialism, rather than, as seems more plausible, the working out of incipient or suppressed tendencies.

This is not, at the same time, an argument for simply saying: Let us return to our Marx, Weber, and Durkheim. We do no service to those thinkers to ignore the changes that have taken place in the half-century and more since they wrote. Indeed the post-industrial theorists are, in one sense, less interesting precisely because they remain so much the prisoners of the classic analyses of industrialism. They seem incapable of conceiving what a genuine movement *beyond* industrialism would entail. Edward Shils, commenting on what he calls 'the generously stimulating tyranny of our classics', has aptly said that

> one of our great difficulties is that we cannot imagine anything beyond variations on the theme set by the great figures of nineteenth and twentieth century sociology. The fact that the conception of 'post-industrial society' is an amalgam of what Saint-Simon, Comte, de Tocqueville and Weber furnished to our imagination is evidence that we are confined to an ambiguously defined circle which is more impermeable than it ought to be.[103]

In the end, post-industrial theorizing might seem important more for what it promises than for what it performs; more for re-opening certain questions to do with social change, than for supplying much help in answering them. At the very least post-industrial thinking marks a welcome revival of concern with large-scale change in the industrial societies, following a long period in which change as a major preoccupation seems to have been banished from the theorizing about industrial society, to be relegated to the domain of 'the developing world'. Even the Marxists, going against the spirit of Marx, seemed constrained to treat all twentieth-century developments within a framework constructed too literally out of the features of nineteenth-century European industrialization. Post-industrial theorizing can certainly claim as one of its accomplishments that it has directed us back to one of the central tenets of the formative period of sociology, that the study of being and becoming are indissolubly linked.

There is a more immediate and more relevant gain. The resurgence of thinking about social change forces us to make certain necessary discriminations in examining the structures of contemporary industrial societies. For whether theories of post-industrialism take the form of constructing scenarios for the year 2000, or focus more modestly on what are held to be the observable and emergent properties of the new society, they force us to ask: Are *these* the significant features, the significant tendencies, that can bear the weight of extrapolation into the future? And if not these, are there any others which appear to be more pregnant with future possibilities? Whatever our final assessment of the post-industrial idea, one of its unquestionable merits is the way it makes us review and take stock of the whole history of industrialization and industrialism. It is especially valuable in directing our attention to the relatively unfamiliar, hidden, and now dramatically accelerating tendencies that form the 'undergrowth' of classic industrialism: features – such as the growth of services and white-collar occupations – which we ought perhaps to have been more aware of but which have been obscured by the received stereotypes of the industrial society. And in opening up this ground, it allows the possibility of fresh interpretations of some of these less familiar developments, and some suggestion of the ways in which, taken in conjunction with other tendencies, they might become the springboard for new departures in the evolution of industrial societies. This is the concern of the next chapter.

7 Continuities and Discontinuities in Social Development

We are now ... confronted with a revulsion from bureaucratic organization, with a growing perception of the dominant institutional forms of society as hostile and threatening instead of appropriate, inevitable and progressive. There is, in this sense of social processes over-reaching themselves, a parallel between our situation and that which was experienced just after the 'Great Transformation' of the Industrial and French Revolutions.

Tom Burns, 'On the Rationale of the Corporate System' (1974).

It might be said that it is the ideal of the employer to have production without employees, and the ideal of the employee to have income without work. The question is: Can the pursuit of these two ideals, undertaken with the marvellous ingenuity of modern science and technology, lead to anything but total alienation and final breakdown?

E. F. Schumacher, 'Survival of the Fitter', *Listener*, 1 May 1975.

Under No Circumstances should any attempt be made to service this module. In the event of failure please return it to us for replacement.

Notice inside Roberts' Portable Radio.

A Map of the World that does not include Utopia is not worth even glancing at.

Oscar Wilde, 'The Soul of Man Under Socialism' (1891).

Summing up at the end of a British Sociological Association conference on the development of industrial societies, T. H. Marshall remarked that 'one cannot assume, and ought not to expect, that any theoretical or conceptual apparatus that fits the analysis of industrialization will be equally appropriate for the study of the further development of societies already industrialized.'[1] No one will of course be surprised if the future is one of futher industrialization, the enlargement and intensification of the processes launched by the Industrial Revolution of the nineteenth century. That, as we have seen, is indeed the major assumption of the post-industrial theory, for all its claims to the contrary. The post-industrial vision of the future might more accurately be re-named 'hyper-industrialism', since what it essentially projects are further instalments of industrialism. Whatever else it might contain, the post-industrial society clearly continues the industrializing drive towards greater scale, centralization, bureaucratization, specialization, and rationalization.

What however of the alternative possibility: that the future of industrialism will be radically discontinuous with its past? What grounds are there for believing that the future of industrial society will not be the past 'writ large', but marked by a qualitative change of direction? In this chapter I want to examine these possibilities, not simply as the desired hopes of certain kinds of radical thinkers, but as the likely outcomes of particular pressures and tendencies which are confronting the industrial societies with a fundamental choice about their future.

1. The Service Society Revisited

As a first step, it is an interesting and instructive exercise to 'play back', as it were, the social trends focused on by the post-industrial theorists. The post-industrial scenario is basically an optimistic one, whatever the personal *angst* of its particular proponents. It sees in the extension of science, the application of ever more sophisticated and complex technology, and the growth of services, the indications of an increasingly prosperous, civilized, and knowledgeable society. It is a society capable – thanks to scientific knowledge and scientific management – of more or less continuous material growth, which in turn makes possible the realization of a service society, suffused with an ethos of social responsibility, social welfare, and the service ideal.

But how much reality and how much sleight of hand is there in such an interpretation? Consider the common use of a society's Gross National Product as the primary index of its prosperity. The sense of progress generated by a fixation on its growth turns out to be largely illusory. G.N.P. is a misleading index not simply in terms of more rounded notions of progress but even within its own terms of economic welfare. G.N.P. measures the total volume of goods and services bought and sold on the market. But this total can be swollen in curious ways. If, for instance, a productive activity which causes pollution, spoliation, or ill-health – e.g. chemical plants, motor cars, noisy aeroplanes – leads to further economic activity to remedy the damage – e.g. purifying processes, medical services – then the resulting chain of activities appears as a double contribution to national wealth, since both kinds of activities count as additions to the total volume of goods and services in the national economy.

This is clearly an insane way of calculating increments of welfare; and while insanity of this kind does not necessarily drive a society to self-destruction, pointing it up does put a different gloss on that hyper-industrialism or 'super-industrialism' (Toffler) so euphorically anticipated by contemporary futurologists. For, given the pronounced growth in services in this century, it could mean that much of the increase in national wealth in the industrial societies amounted to no more than vast increases in pollution, environmental destruction, and personal suffering, with the consequent expenditure on fresh capital and labour to repair, maintain and renovate the physical, social and psychological fabric of the society. Building high-rise, high-density blocks of flats gives people homes to live in. To that extent it is a real contribution to welfare. But not only are such blocks of flats actually more expensive to build than an equivalent amount of housing at lower density; by virtue of their scale and lay-out they are extremely costly to repair and service; and they give rise to endemic problems of vandalism, social control, alienation and social isolation – the social costs or 'external diseconomies' of the economists. To make the costs of treating and remedying these problems an actual *addition* to total economic well-being is like shooting a man and then claiming to benefit him by treating his wounds. Ivan Illich makes exactly this point in connection with the illusion of medical progress created by growing medical expenditure. As he says, 'medical bills measure the health of a patient in the same way that G.N.P. measures the wealth of a nation. Both add on the same scale the market value of benefits and the defensive expenditures which become necessary to offset the unwanted side effects of their production.'[2]

We might think this an apt symbol of an exploitative and predatory industrialism, which ends up creating its wealth by a process of self-laceration. At any rate it should caution us against a too ready acceptance of the view that increasing instalments of industrialism mean increasing prosperity or welfare. It is frequently argued that while industrialism may be unpleasant in many ways, it justifies itself in the end by producing the goods, and ever more of them. This now seems an elaborate deception, a mystifying mirage, and makes a poor case for an extension of industrialism into the future. If increases in economic welfare mean mainly the more and more intensive laundering of each other's dirty washing, we might reasonably begin to fear for the very survival of the clothes.

The illusion of greater welfare is fostered by a further quirk of social accounting. The growth of services in this century is rightly seen as one of the most distinctive features of recent economic history. But does it represent a real increase in *service*? A. C. Pigou long ago pointed to the problem by observing that if a widowed vicar paid his housekeeper a weekly wage, this was an addition to the national income; if he married her, it became a subtraction.[3] The visibility of the 'service revolution' of this century has tended to conceal the fact that what has mainly happened has been a vast transfer of services from the home (and the neighbourhood), where being unpaid they were not counted as 'productive', to the market, where they have generated much employment and many monetary transactions. Thus work done at home, such as cooking, cleaning, educating, tending and caring, has moved into the market as the restaurant industry, the laundry industry, public and private systems of education, health, and social welfare.[4] Since in the latter case market transactions are usually involved, and since this is what G.N.P. measures, the movement suggests a vast increase in the national production of goods and services. This obviously has meaning only within the very narrow, capitalist, definition of what constitutes 'productive' activity. By any other realistic definition the change from home to market (or state) may mean very little in the way of either the quantity or the quality of services. Undoubtedly the movement has had enormous consequences in other directions, especially in the rise of female employment, and the extension of state activity. But again we must be careful to recognize the spurious aspects of this growth in employment and welfare, and to see that our societies are not necessarily the richer, or more comfortable, or more civilized for it.

It is of course not just the market but the state that has taken over most of the service functions of the home and neighbourhood. In all industrial societies, even those formally suspicious of 'the welfare state', this fact has become so prominent in the decades since the Second World War[5] that we must see in it a further clue to the interpretation of the trends towards a service society.

Conventionally many reasons are given for the growth in the distinctively modern 'quaternary' service sector, in the health, educational, and welfare services. There is the liberal strand of humanitarianism coming from the eighteenth-century Enlightenment. From the same source comes the utilitarian concern with efficiency, and its environmentalist philosophy with the demand for a healthier, better-housed, and better-educated population. Undoubtedly, too, there has been involved in the growth of services a display of 'conspicuous consumption' on the part of the wealthy societies of the world, to others less fortunate. But perhaps the most persistent, and ultimately the most important, factor has been the need for other agencies to take over the comprehensive role of the family. With increasing industrialization, there has come the break-up of long-standing residential communities, the separation of kin, and a growing disposition for all adult members of the family to go out to work. The scope and functions of the family have narrowed sharply by comparison with its pre-industrial past. The need now was for some other set of institutions to perform the function, not only of formal education and training, but of all the other tasks of socialization and social control which had been central to the family. Someone else had to watch over the young with both parents out at work, to keep them off the streets of the large cities, and to put them somewhere where they could be conveniently and safely managed, and prepared for the roles and occupations which in some cases they might see fit to reject. Increasingly the state stepped in to carry out these tasks.

In all this, the expanding educational system was of pivotal significance; and a brief look at its development brings out clearly the breadth of social function that it has been expected to fulfil. From the very start it is made clear that the scope of the system is to go well beyond the narrow confines of education and instruction, to encompass a whole range of socializing, moralizing, and regulating tasks previously performed by the family, community, and, of course, the Church. As early as 1770 William Temple proposed that children from the age of four should be removed from the home for a large part of the day, dividing their time between workshop and school. The reason he gave for advocating this course has an engaging frankness about it: 'There is considerable use in their being, somehow or other, constantly employed at least twelve hours a day, whether they earn their living or not; for by these means, we hope that the rising generation will be so habituated to constant employment that it would at length prove agreeable and entertaining to them . . .'[6] Exactly one hundred years later, referring to the Education Act of 1870 that had made elementary education compulsory, Her Majesty's Inspector for Schools in London put a similar point with equal frankness: 'If it were not for her 500 elementary schools London would be overrun by a horde of young savages.'[7] As Landes says about the Act, 'whatever the ostensible aims of compulsory elementary education, its essential function . . . was not to instruct. Rather it was to discipline a growing mass of disaffected proletarians and integrate them into British society. Its object was to civilize the barbarians.'[8] The Ragged School Union made this explicit in 1884: 'The proletariat may strangle us unless we teach it the same virtues that have elevated the other classes of society.'[9] Something of the same concern perhaps underlies Robert Lowe's famous remark of 1870, following his strenuous opposition to the 1867 Reform Bill, that 'we must educate our masters'. Since it was obvious that the masses would never actually rule, they had to be 'educated' into making the appropriate choice of people and issues at the ballot-box, thereby ensuring that they would not develop fanciful ideas of their own.

The battle between schools, truancy officers, police, and the 'street arabs' and 'bare-footed ragamuffins' who refused to be schooled continued for some time after the passing of the Act. It had largely been won by the schools by the end of the century. But the battle was clearly not simply about education. The educational consequences of the 1870 Act are nearly always exaggerated. Most English people could read and write, most indeed went to school, well before the Act made it compulsory.[10] The social consequences however were enormous. As Samuel says, 'it was the School Board Attendance Officer, rather than the Factory Acts, which brought an end to child labour . . . A family producing unit which had survived the competition of factory industry did not survive the compulsory education under the School Board.'[11] It is common to rejoice in these changes but, as Samuel stresses, 'it should be clear if one chooses to do so that one is discussing the progress not of education but of moral engineering and of social policing'.[12] By the end of the century parents, children, and society at large had accepted formal schooling, not simply as the best or most practical, but as the exclusive, means of education. All progressive thinking supported this view. The stage was set for the massive expansion of the education system that has been witnessed in this century in every industrial society.

In 1965, for the first time ever in Britain, education overtook defence in its share of public expenditure. It became, for a time, the single largest spender of public money. Its share of public spending doubled between 1920 and 1940 and almost tripled between 1940 and 1970. By the late 1960s social-security expenditure had overtaken education as the foremost claimant on public funds, but education has remained in second place. In 1973–4 it accounted for 13·2 per cent of total public expenditure (as compared with 17·6 for social security). It claims between 6 and 7 per cent of Gross National Product; this is expected to rise to 8 per cent by the 1980s. It continues to extend its hold at both ends of the age-range from childhood to adulthood. The percentage of seventeen-year-olds in full-time education doubled from 2 per cent to 4 per cent between 1902 and 1938; by 1962 it was 15 per cent, by 1972 it was 21 per cent; it is expected to rise to 35 per cent by 1985. Since 1970 almost 15 per cent of the age group has gone on to some form of full-time higher education; estimates of future trends have varied more than normally widely, but most anticipate between 25 and 30 per cent of the age group to be undergoing higher education by the mid-1980s. At the lower end, in the age group two to four, there has been an increase in the proportion schooled from less than 10 per cent in 1961 to over 20 per cent by 1975; and the official projection is for over 30 per cent by 1985.[13]

This pattern can readily be generalized for all other industrial societies. As usual, the United States has moved faster and further. The share of (the much larger) G.N.P. taken by education more than doubled between 1949 to 1969, from 3·4 per cent to 7·5 per cent. The U.S. also schools a much greater proportion of the relevant age groups. By the early 1960s over 75 per cent of seventeen-year-olds were graduating from high school; by the end of the 1960s more than 50 per cent – a 'historic norm' – of eighteen- to nineteen-year-olds were entering higher education. As the historian T. C. Cochran has said, 'the United States of 1970 represented, for the first time in history, a nation in which a majority of its younger citizens had from 14 to 19 years of formal education.'[14] Even at the most elevated end of the educational system the figures are startling: in 1966 over 6 per cent of twenty-five-year-olds received master's and professional degrees, and 0·6 per cent received Ph.D.s. J. S. Coleman pointedly remarks that 'the fraction of the age group earning Ph.D.s in 1966 is a little less than the fraction of the age group earning high school diplomas a hundred years earlier.'[15]

But educational expansion in this century is clearly much more than a matter of increasing student numbers. That is in some ways the tip of the iceberg, the visible expression of a vast industry, one of the largest in all contemporary industrial societies. As the American Council of Economic Advisers somewhat indelicately put it in 1967, 'outlays for education have been rising by 10½ per cent a year for the last decade, making it one of the major U.S. growth industries.'[16] Not only is education in the United States second only to defence as a spender of public money, it absorbs an increasing proportion of the civilian workforce. In 1965 public educational employment accounted for about 5·5 per cent of all civilian employment in the U.S. The rate of growth is even more impressive. In the fifteen years from 1950 to 1965, total employment in the U.S. increased by about 21 per cent; public educational employment however grew by 130 per cent, the increase in the latter accounting for about one out of every six new jobs created in the U.S. economy during that period.[17] Teachers of course made up a good part of that growth: in the 1970 U.S. census they appeared as the single largest group in the category 'professional and technical persons', comprising indeed a quarter of all such persons.[18] But a significant part of the expansion is also due to the development of a range of ancillary administrative and welfare functions within the educational system. In addition to the growth of the non-academic administrators, there has been growth in careers guidance, student counselling, and teacher-linked social work of various kinds. If to all these direct employees of the educational system we now add the clients – the students – we arrive at the remarkable and widely quoted figure of 30 per cent of the population of the United States engaged full-time as students, teachers, or administrators, in the educational system.[19]

The educational establishment in Britain is not quite so spectacularly large, but is nonetheless impressive. In 1974 there were nearly a million and a half educational employees (teaching and non-teaching staff), which means that they constitute 6 per cent of the total workforce of the country, and more than 50 per cent of all local authority employment. Moreover, as in the United States, the growth of non-teaching staff is as dramatic as the growth in the number of teachers themselves. In the British educational system teachers and non-teachers are almost exactly equal in number: over 700,000 of each.[20]

What is this vast educational complex for? The conventional answer, while making some vague gesture in the direction of 'education for citizenship', usually comes down to the need for a more highly trained and better informed population to maintain and improve economic performance. In a worldwide competitive economic environment, it is argued, with an increasingly complex and sophisticated technology, it is the nation with the best quality – that is, best educated – 'human capital' that will thrive. The launching of the Russian Sputnik in 1957 and the attendant successes of the Soviet scientific establishment were seen as the direct result of superior Soviet education. It stimulated a frenzy of educational expansion in the United States, especially at the higher end of the system. A number of elegant and powerful economic analyses, associated particularly with the names of Denison, Schultz, and Solow, lent their considerable weight to an aroused public opinion, and created almost a professional orthodoxy around the view that, as Schultz put it, 'improvements in the quality of human resources are one of the major sources of economic growth.'[21] A central assumption of the argument, more or less unquestioned, was the equation of more years of formal education with a more educated, more skilled, more informed population.

No doubt the growth of the educational system may be sufficiently explained by the fact that many politicians and administrators believe these arguments, whether or not they turn out to have any substance. But one suspects that this is not quite the case, and that many policy-makers have other grounds for promoting educational growth. The outline of English developments has already suggested this; in addition there is now a good deal of evidence that casts doubt on the orthodox view, and which can hardly have come as a surprise to public officials, or private employers.

There are firstly the isolated findings which, taken together, suggest that whatever other functions the schools are serving, the provision of academic skills is one they perform very inefficiently. Basic skills in literacy and numeracy seem actually to be falling in the populations of the industrial societies. In Britain, a survey of sixteen-year-old school-leavers in Liverpool revealed an average reading age of nine. Another survey, of employment agencies specifically concerned with school-leavers, found widespread complaints from the agencies of school-leavers barely literate and scarcely able to fill in application forms correctly.[22] The University Grants Committee, in its 1974–5 Report, pointed to the disturbing number of students who were entering universities without the basic skills and information needed to pursue their courses, and suggested that universities may have to lengthen their courses to teach basic academic skills. The Committee's chairman, Sir Frederick Dainton, commenting particularly on the decline in mathematical ability, declared that 'universities are increasingly going to have to go into remedial work in these fields.' The evidence – which was supported by similar findings from the United States – was no more encouraging in the field of languages, the arts, and the social sciences.[23] Perhaps the most spectacular and expensive demonstration of the schools' inability to educate efficiently has been the failure of 'Operation Headstart' in the United States, an ambitious scheme designed to use the schools to compensate for the deprived family backgrounds of many young children.[24]

The most important finding however concerns the relationship between education and job performance. Here, if anywhere, is supposed to be the pay-off for those long and costly years in schools and universities; here is where the hard-headed economist and the starry-eyed educationalist can at least reach a minimum point of agreement on the value of education. But there is little support for the orthodox view in the most thorough-going report on the issue, Ivar Berg's *Education and Jobs* – which he sub-titles *The Great Training Robbery*.[25] Berg's report, covering the work of manual as well as professional and technical workers, systematically demolishes the case that improved job performance results from higher educational attainments. He summarizes his findings, which include his own research, thus: 'A search of the considerable literature on productivity, absenteeism and turnover yielded little concrete evidence of a positive relationship between workers' educational achievements and their performance records in many work settings . . .'[26] By contrast, the American Federal Aviation Administration, for example, employing people in a variety of demanding managerial and technical occupations, and having to make do with its own training programmes, seemed not to suffer in any way from having a majority of its higher-grade employees with no academic training beyond high school (i.e., secondary school). Berg concludes generally that 'to argue that well-educated people will automatically boost efficiency, improve organizations, and so on may be to misunderstand in a fundamental way the nature of American education, which functions to an important, indeed depressing, extent as a licensing agency.'[27] Higher educational qualifications will undoubtedly enable their holder to get better jobs than those not so qualified; but this seems as much a matter of faith, or prejudice, on the part of employers, as of demonstrated capability.

Actually there is a growing amount of evidence that this faith has by now been severely shaken, and that employers are perfectly well aware of what they are doing. They have become – or perhaps more accurately, remained – sceptical of the performance value of education, but have found it difficult to resist the gain in 'public relations' and in their general 'image' that has come from employing the more highly-qualified applicants. In a situation of mass education the level of educational qualifications becomes a handy screening device. It is a calculation in which there appears to be a familiar mixture of cynicism and social prejudice. Thus an American study of job vacancies in Monroe County, New York State, found that the educational requirements for given kinds of jobs varied with the different stages of the academic year, being relatively high at the end of semesters and lower at other points in the year. In other words, higher qualifications for the *same* jobs were required when there could be expected to be a fresh supply of more highly-qualified candidates, than at other times in the year when the labour market was not so generously endowed. Not unreasonably the study concluded that 'employers may have tailored their requirements to match the qualifications of the new supply of labour.'[28]

Further evidence as to the real degree of employers' scepticism about the contribution of education to job performance is found in the striking fact that in the United States the educational level of both the employed and the unemployed population is now roughly equal. Previously the unemployed were nearly always also the less educated, reflecting the faith both of society in general and the employer in particular in the higher educational requirements of modern industrial and bureaucratic occupations. Gradually the message has sunk in that employees with a longer period of formal education might from the employers' point of view be more of a liability than an asset; and the hiring policies of many firms seem to have undergone a corresponding change. A report of the U.S. Bureau of Labor Statistics summed up the situation as follows:

> In the past, jobholders had more education than did jobseekers – in 1959, for example, the median education of the employed was 12·0 years, while that of the unemployed was only 9·9 years. Since then, the average education of unemployed workers has risen so that by 1971 the difference between the median education of employed and unemployed workers, 12·4 and 12·2 years respectively, is no longer statistically significant.[29]

If occupational requirements are not the main reason for educational expansion, and if this fact is increasingly being acknowledged, what other functions might the system be serving? One that is steadily becoming manifest is its critical role in relation to employment, or rather, unemployment. If education is not much of a preparation for employment, it seems to be a good deal better at helping people to avoid it. The educational system affects employment in two ways. On the one hand, as we have seen, it is itself one of the largest direct employers of labour – not just of teachers, but of administrators, technicians, clerks and secretaries, catering workers, cleaners, porters, drivers, maintenance and construction workers, gardeners and groundsmen. (This leaves out of course the massive indirect employment effects created by the existence of the school system – in services provided for the students and employees in the locality, in publishing and printing, and so on.) But equally important is the educational system's function in absorbing, as students, in increasing quantities and for increasing lengths of time, large numbers of potentially productive young workers who would otherwise be competing for jobs in the market. In other words, the educational system has become an important agency in controlling unemployment and absorbing surplus manpower. In a statement pointedly reminding the Government of this fact, Ralf Dahrendorf, the Director of the London School of Economics, remarks: 'I wonder whether those who are considering cuts in educational expenditure should not make a careful comparison of the marginal (and the social) cost of the next 100,000 unemployed with that of the next 100,000 students.'[30] At the very least, as one commentator has said, it is less insulting to the recipients for the state to pay for their continued studies in schools and universities than to dole out unemployment pay.

It is a role that has become of great significance with the end of the post-war boom and the period of full employment. Writing of the situation in the United States, Harry Braverman declares that 'the postponement of school leaving to an average age of eighteen has become indispensable for keeping unemployment within reasonable bounds.'[31] John and Margaret Rowntree have made some interesting calculations that underline this point. Arguing that the function of much employment in the armed forces is of the same surplus-absorbing kind, they show that in the United States in the mid 1960s 'about 50 per cent of all young men between the ages of 18 and 25 were either in school or in the armed forces'; and that to return to the 1950 enrolment-enlistment *proportions* of young people employed in the military or engaged in school – that is, to let the additional youths out on the labour market – would have increased the 1965 unemployment figures by three and a half times.[32]

This is not an entirely new phenomenon, although it is novel in its extent. During the Depression many American states passed legislation restricting the participation of youth in the labour force, thus hoping to reduce unemployment by eliminating a section of the population from the job market. A direct consequence of this, which was both anticipated and intended, was a prolongation of schooling for many young people. As Berg puts it, 'in a bizarre manifestation of Parkinson's Law, education expanded to fill the time of many youths whose social roles had been re-designed by the several state legislatures.'[33] After the Second World War – which satisfactorily dealt with the problem of the unemployed – there was once more the fear that the return of the demobilized men would create mass unemployment. A part response was the veterans' educational subsidy ('the G.I. Bill') which allowed for a sharp increase in educational enrolment as well as direct subsidies to educational institutions. But it is only with the recent mass expansion of higher education in all the industrial societies, in a situation where there is great pressure on industry to mechanize and rationalize, that the connection between the educational and the labour market systems has become palpable. In California, for instance, it has been observed that enrolment in higher educational institutions varies directly with the fluctuations of the labour market; while in Britain a tendency for student numbers to slacken off in the early 1970s seems to have been checked and reversed by increasing difficulties in finding employment.[34]

Keeping young people off the labour market then appears to be one latent function and dynamic of the educational system. Keeping them off the streets, and attached to their allotted tasks, seems to be another, perhaps in the end more important. The recognition of this function occurs at some point, usually near the beginning, in the evolution of the educational systems of practically every industrial society. We have already seen this in the British case. It is not of course simply a matter of literally keeping young people off the streets: although we should not underestimate this very direct function in the earlier period when the fear of city mobs was still a potent memory, nor indeed in much more recent times when periods of high unemployment have aroused anxieties about groups of unemployed youth roaming the streets. More significant however is the need felt to inculcate discipline and obedience, to prepare young people for the occupational and social roles that they will be expected to fill, and to ensure that their aspirations do not get out of hand. Both tasks – of physical and moral surveillance and supervision – had previously been carried out by the family, closely supported by the church and the élites of the local community, and confirmed by early employment in domestic service or the apprenticeship system of the guilds. As these agencies declined in influence or were diverted to other purposes, the schools were developed as the central instruments of social control.

The early schools were quite evidently direct replications and extensions of the family and church. The learning of knowledge and cognitive skills was firmly subordinated to instruction in moral prescriptions and character development. Catechism and learning by rote were the standard devices. While the schools were mainly elementary and concerned with the saving of souls of the great urban unwashed, no great sophistication was thought necessary in the form of social control. Later evolution to mass secondary education, and the inclusion of young people of other classes, complicated the picture. There was the need now not simply to socialize the young into general modes of conformity, but to select out the able and to accommodate the rejected to their future positions in society. The latter concern, from the point of view of social control, was overwhelmingly the more important, and the schools were adapted accordingly. It was in this context that there developed the elaborate schemes of curriculum reform, new forms of teaching and classroom organization, and courses preparing the less able children 'for life' (the more able, of course, were prepared for university). A. H. Halsey has described the change in the eduction of the unselected as one 'from gentling the masses to taming the individual'.[35]

It is a change reflected not simply in curriculum and classroom, but in the wide variety of ancillary agencies and institutions that have increasingly come to be linked to the school, and which suggest the most likely pattern of future social control. Student counselling, for instance, has long been known in American schools; and studies indicate that it functions not simply as a moral welfare or careers guidance service but as a significant determinant of pupils' sense of their current identities and abilities, and hence of their future occupational roles.[36] In Britain a newly professionalized Youth Service is now formally treated as part of the education system. Careers guidance services, counsellors and teacher-social workers are creating institutionalized links with social welfare, probation, child care and child guidance services, ensuring, as one researcher has said, that 'individual cases of deviance are detected and treated at an early age'.[37] The entire net of the modern welfare state seems intent on cocooning the school pupil so that there is the least possibility of any serious failure of socialization and social control.

A recent statement of the position in the United States seems not too melodramatic or inaccurate on account, and not so far removed from the situation in the other industrial societies:

> In the interest of working parents . . . and in the interest of social stability and the orderly management of an increasingly rootless urban population, the schools have developed into immense teen-sitting organizations, their functions having less and less to do with imparting to the young those things that society thinks they must learn . . . It is difficult to imagine United States society without its immense 'educational' structure, and in fact, as has been seen in recent years, the closing of even a single segment of the schools for a period of weeks is enough to create a social crisis in the city in which this happens. The schools, as caretakers of children and young people, are indispensable for family functioning, community stability, and social order in general . . . In a word, there is no longer any place for the young in this society other than school. Serving to fill a vacuum, schools have themselves become that vacuum, increasingly emptied of content and reduced to little more than their own form.[38]

Education is the exemplary case. In considering the original cause of its growth, the form of its expansion, and the functions it has been called upon to perform, we can see the underlying dynamic of the growth of the service sector as a whole, and of many of the other 'post-industrial' trends. These reveal themselves as novelties not so much of substance as of form. It is impossible to give quantitative indices for the earlier perod, when education, welfare, and much household service, were informal, 'hidden', services contained in the general performance of family and community tasks. It is therefore easy to claim spectacular increases in these services when they enter the public realm of market and state expenditure and employment, and their growth can be graphically demonstrated in the rising curves of welfare provision and numbers of service employees. But really all that this allows us to say is that there has been a change in the form in which services are offered, from the family to the market or the state, and *probably* an increase in scale and comprehensiveness – by how much is anybody's guess. Certainly it is a much more difficult matter to argue that there has been a qualitative change – either in the ordinary sense of a better quality of service, or in the more specialized sense that the institutionalized provision of service marks a fundamental change in the line of social development. In any case, as we shall see in the next section, there is much evidence accumulating that the intensive and extensive growth of institutionalized services may have reached a critical point, where further expansion will be highly problematic.

2. The Relevance of Utopianism

It is of course one thing to question the novelty of what is allegedly most modern and progressive, and to qualify the optimism that so often accompanies the assertions. It is quite another to argue that things both can be and may be different in the industrial societies of the future. It is this possibility that I want to consider now.

The radical thinker Ivan Illich has advanced the interesting idea that the history of industrialism be considered as marked by two watersheds.[39] In the first phase, leading to the first watershed, science is applied to a range of traditional problems –

scarcity, disease, etc. – which it resolves with unprecedented efficiency, bringing about the widespread provision of goods and services previously available only to the very few, the rich or powerful. In the second phase, leading to the second watershed, the manifest success of the first phase becomes the basis for a further expansion and increased legitimation which actually reverses the progressive tendencies of the earlier phase. Growth and expansion now continues largely for the benefit of the élites who initiated and supervised the first phase, and who are now in command of the society – 'self-certifying professional élites', Illich designates them. (In the terminology of Arnold Toynbee's philosophy of history, we might say that the 'creative élites' become the 'dominant élites'.) The population at large finds that its commitment to the system brings in diminishing returns.

A number of the major institutions of industrial society are now seen by Illich as having moved over their second watershed. 'Schools are losing their claims to be effective tools to provide education; cars have ceased to be effective tools for mass transportation; the assembly line has ceased to be an acceptable mode of production.'[40] The answer is seen in the development of a contrary mode which Illich calls 'convivial' production, and which is based on the design and use of simple tools, renewable resources, personal skills, small-scale operations, and the 'deprofessionalized' provision of services such as health, education, and transportation.[41]

This may seem familiar utopian stuff. What gives it a concreteness and a foothold in contemporary reality are various indications that industrialism is in a state of genuine crisis, and that consequently certain varieties of utopian thought, new or traditional, might now have a relevance previously denied them by the powerful currents of a developing and triumphant industrialism. Something of this kind is in any case suggested by the revival of utopian social theory that began in the 1960s in the industrial societies of the west. From the hindsight of the somewhat leaner decade of the 1970s, some of that utopianism can no doubt seem little more than the fanciful posturing of a generation which, for the first time in history, had had no experience in their societies of brute material want, and for whom the politics of consumption eclipsed that of production. Ideological allegiances, moreoever, were no guide to sobriety here. As we have seen, the 'post-industrial' idea can itself be regarded as a 'utopianism of the Right' – of the modern technocratic Right – with its assumption of a society that had moved beyond the politics and problems of material scarcity. More characteristically, the Left too produced some unconvincing utopianism, especially that variety which thought that 'alienation' could be overcome by withdrawing into 'liberated' enclaves within the cities, or by emigrating to the remoter rural spots, there to practise the free life on an idealized pre-industrial pattern of natural farm produce and a simple technology. What they often forgot, as Peter Harper points out, is that 'many devices which are approved as being simple and small-scale at the point of *use* require massive scale at the point of *manufacture*', and that many of the basic components making up the 'simple technology' of windmills, water turbines, solar panels, and the like, still had to be produced by factory workers in distinctly alienating industrial environments.[42]

But it is too glib to see the whole of the utopian response in this light, as the ideological reflex of a glossy, consumer-oriented decade. The problems identified and the values celebrated outlive the particular moment that may have driven them into public consciousness. Environmental deterioration, overcrowding, the depletion of resources, the costs of large-scale organization and rapid economic growth, all remain issues which must concern the industrial societies over the coming decades. Of continuing relevance too is the rediscovery of 'the quality of life' as a criterion of value that takes into account imprecise but significant factors not adequately tapped by the economic and social indicators of the industrial and welfare bureaucracies. Nor can the élites of the society afford to ignore the renewed concern with human scale ('small is beautiful'), human control, and personal satisfaction as irreducible requirements of any system of industrial and political organization.[43]

These are admittedly all concerns which typically reflected the preoccupations of a generation confronted for the first time ever with a society of high mass consumption. There is a danger therefore in seeing them as 'luxury' concerns, the kinds of things that a wealthy population can afford to be worried about; and to be somewhat impatient of them at a time when more traditional problems of wealth production are once more to the fore, and when relatively slow rates of economic growth and anxiety about scarce raw materials and energy resources have uncomfortably reminded the industrial societies that the problems of production have by no means been solved. But it would be a fatal error to suppose that the utopian critique matters less now. Indeed paradoxically it has become more important. Industrialism is currently being faced with certain fundamental dilemmas and choices about its future development, and only by attending to the sorts of issues raised in that critique does there seem much hope of finding an acceptable way forward.

It is not too portentous to put the matter as follows. There has been a fundamental contradiction in the manner of development of the major industrial societies over the past two centuries. In a pattern familiar from the history of past civilizations, the dynamic tendencies almost universally acknowledged as progressive have carried an undertow of regressive features, which finally break the surface and threaten to hurl the tide of progress back to the the dissolving deep. In the earlier stages of development, two forward steps produce, in a dialectical motion, one step back; in the later stages, the dialectic loses its progressive character and each further step forward is punished by two in the contrary direction. This reversal of fortune is not of course due to any basic change in the form or direction of development; on the contrary it is the consequence of the indefinite expansion and intensification of those tendencies, which may increasingly be seen to have outlived their usefulness.

As we saw in Chapter Three, industrialization entailed the drive towards ever greater scale, centralization, mechanization, specialization, and bureaucratization – in a word, 'rationalization'. The triumphs of industrialism were premissed on the degree to which these tendencies prevailed. But precisely to that very degree there was correspondingly involved a progressive decline in the skills, competence, autonomy, and responsibility of the bulk of the population in the industrial societies. Knowledge and skills have gone into machines and the professionalized service institutions; authority and autonomy into the hierarchical and bureaucratic structures of large-scale organization. The individual worker, in conjunction with the sophisticated technology and complex organization of industrialism, can produce fabulous wealth; by himself, with his own tools and skills, he can barely keep himself alive. As Marx put it in the classic analysis of his *1844 Manuscripts*, in the social order of (capitalist) industrialism 'the more the worker produces, the more he diminishes himself.'[44]

This appears so obvious a consequence of the 'logic of industrialism' that it is remarkable to find a widespread assertion of quite the contrary view. As we saw in the last chapter, much census data records an actual rise in the levels of skill and training in the population at large. The 'unskilled manual worker', in particular, in all industrial societies is a vanishing phenomenon. Partly this is accounted for by the separation of men from machines altogether, and their conversion into service employees with a supposedly richer working life. But partly also it is due to one of the commoner ideological features of industrial society, whereby social processes are disguised by formal acts of reclassification and re-labelling. Thus censuses in all industrial countries show a massive increase in this century of 'semi-skilled' over 'unskilled' workers. But this, it turns out, has nothing to do with an investigation of actual levels of skill or competence in the workforce. The increase of skill is made possible by the simple device of classifying as 'semi-skilled' *all* workers merely associated, in whatever capacity and with whatever actual skill, with machines: though they may be no more than watchers, tenders, or feeders of these machines, requiring levels of skill that can be acquired in a matter of hours or days. Given the continuing mechanization of factory, store, and office, an 'upgrading' of the workforce follows automatically.

But, as Harry Braverman says, 'it is only in the world of census statistics, and not in terms of direct assessment, that an assembly line worker is presumed to have greater skill than a fisherman or oysterman, the forklift operator greater skill than the gardener or groundskeeper, the machine feeder greater skill than the longshoreman, the parking lot attendant greater skill than the lumberman or raftsman.'[45] We have observed already the same sleight of hand at work in theories of the increasing 'professionalization' of society, and of a more 'knowledgeable' population in general. The common feature throughout is an assertion or assumption of greater skill, training, or education, coupled with a striking indifference to what actually takes place in the course of training, or precisely what skills are involved in allegedly 'skilled' or 'professional' occupations. On inspection, the training frequently turns out to be a formality, the skill nugatory.

This wholesale 'de-skilling' of the population would probably have found its retribution in any case at some point in the future. What has brought this somewhat sooner than might have been expected is the wider context within which the process of de-skilling took place. The industrialization of the west was from the start a global process – a fact clearly enough recognized by the nineteenth-century sociologists but insufficiently reflected on so far as the long-term implications went. Western societies industrialized by incorporating ever-increasing fractions of the world into their own rationalized economic system. The world was parcelled up into specialized and differentiated regions, strategic 'resource areas' for the benefit of the industrial countries. So long as these areas remained passive and politically weak, the industrial societies could pursue the logic of the rationalizing mode with scant regard to the long-term consequences. Hence in particular the progressive shifts towards increasingly 'high', capital-intensive, large-scale technology. All orthodox economic theory supported and urged on this development, which indeed in an apparently stable world context made good economic sense. The resulting problem of the loss of human control and comprehension in the workplace was noted, but generally regarded either as the regrettable price of economic progress, or as a temporary, transitional phase towards a society of full automation, abundance, and leisure. Less noticed and certainly hardly discussed was the dependence of this pattern of technological development on continuing supplies of cheap energy and cheap raw materials. The idea of the finitude of the fossil fuels, of their ultimate exhaustibility, was remote indeed from the minds of all but a handful of ecologically-minded anarchists.

The high point of this type of development can in retrospect be seen to fall in the boom period which followed the Second World War. It is clear now the extent to which the virtually continuous economic growth in the industrial countries was subsidized, and probably made possible, by abundant supplies of a peculiarly cheap and accessible energy resource: oil, especially from the Middle East. Geoffrey Barraclough has emphasized how novel a phenomenon is this dependence of industrial society on oil and oil products. Basically it is a post-1945 development. In 1925 oil contributed only 14 per cent to America's energy needs, for instance, and much less elsewhere. Even in 1950 solid fuels accounted for approximately two-thirds of energy consumption in America. It was only after that that the spectacular change took place, reversing the ratio so that by 1970 petroleum and natural gas supplied more than 60 per cent of the much greater total. One consequence was a dramatic change in the balance of home-based and imported fuels. Between 1960 and 1970 the dependence on fuel imports of the European Community grew from 30 per cent to over 60 per cent, and that of the United Kingdom, from 25 per cent to 44 per cent.[46] The easy availability of oil affected all other major developments in the economy. The coal industry was run down. Supposedly obsolete forms of passenger and freight transport such as the railways were severely cut back; the car was king. The utilities switched massively to oil. Technological innovation was either slowed down or skewed as the industrial societies basked in the great oil lake.

That high point can now also be seen as a turning point (it may yet turn out to be a terminal point). In the winter of 1973 the oil-producing countries quadrupled the price of oil. In the ensuing consternation it was often made to appear that the problems of the industrial societies were the direct outcome of these short-term political manoeuvrings by the Arab oil cartel. Nothing could be further from the truth. As Barraclough says, 'what we are experiencing is not a short-term emergency but a last desperate attempt by industrial society . . . to climb out of a crisis of its own making.'[47] The action of the Arabs was historically significant not so much for its immediate impact on the economies of the industrial societies as for its dramatic highlighting of the long-term nature of the crisis. Ultimately the crisis was created by a mode of development that had come to depend on energy sources which have long been known to be limited and of a relatively fixed term, and whose cheapness was premissed on the continuing political weakness of the non-industrial world. The Arabs' action announced that this political passivity was now at an end; and it was of course a declaration aimed not simply at the industrial world, but at all the societies of the 'Third World' whose supplies of raw materials had kept the industrial system going. The French Prime Minister Giscard d'Estaing spoke truly when he said of the crisis that 'what we are witnessing is the revenge on Europe for the nineteenth century';[48] and he was referring to the nemesis brought on not simply by colonial exploitation, but by a particularly savage and one-sided exploitation of nature itself.

The industrial societies are being forced into a re-adjustment for which they are psychologically and structurally extremely unprepared. Henceforward they have to expect some tough 'trade-union' bargaining, individually and collectively, from the Third World. They have to contemplate a future – at least in the medium term – of much higher prices for the raw materials and energy resources to which they have geared their technologies. This will mean that they will probably be less wealthy. It also means that in order to stop standards of living dropping too far, they will need to be very careful and imaginative in the husbanding of the resources that they have, or can still afford to buy. More fundamentally, and in the longer term, it involves the search for other, renewable, sources of energy, and the designing of technologies appropriate to them.

It is in this general historical context that the loss of general skills and competence is seen at its most damaging. The industrial system of plentiful consumer goods and expensive professionalized services is under severe strain. It can no longer support itself, in its traditional form, at reasonable cost. So far as the social services are concerned, the evidence is beginning to accumulate that the even point may have been reached in many industrial societies, and that the volume of expenditure necessary to maintain the welfare services is leading to an actual and absolute drop in the material standard of living. In Britain, for instance, between 1963 and 1974 deductions from paypackets in the form of income tax and social-security contributions increased so much that the average living standard, in terms of what actually can be bought in the shops, rose only 1·6 per cent per annum, and since 1973 has begun to fall. The male worker on average earnings now suffers deductions of nearly 30 per cent from his paypacket, the payment for the 'social wage'.[49] Much of the militant trade-union action of the last decade has indeed been defensive – the attempt not so much constantly to increase the standard of living as to increase money wages to offset higher prices and higher taxation.

Moreover while it could be argued for much of the time that the higher 'social wage' was adequate compensation for smaller net monetary wages, this argument is beginning to wear increasingly thin. Compared to most other European societies, British workers give up a greater proportion of their paypackets to support welfare services, yet there is no evidence that health, education, or social-security services are any better in Britain than in those other societies.[50] The suspicion must be, therefore, that what is operating here is Illich's 'second threshold', or the law of diminishing returns, or, more straightforwardly, Parkinson's Law of the indefinite multiplication of staff and bureaucratic tasks. Beyond a certain stage welfare expenditure has a tendency to increase irrespective of the extent or quality of service offered; and this is now, in conjunction with other economic difficulties, imposing great strain on the economy of the welfare state.

The most important of the industrial society's resources – as of any kind of society – are its human ones: whether of human skills, imagination, effort, commitment or sacrifice. It is these resources however that have been most impoverished and stunted in the course of industrial development. In the current situation, and for a good time to come, what is needed is a population that, as private individuals and groups, should once more be able to rely upon itself for the repairing and maintenance of much of the physical structure of the society; for the invention of tools and appliances that are modest and flexible in the use of resources, and relatively easy to service without complicated and specialized equipment; even, perhaps, for the growing of a certain proportion of its own food. Above all there is the need that people should come to depend much more upon themselves, their families, and their community, for the provision of many services to do with general health and welfare, at present supplied by professionalized private and public bodies. But the industrial bureaucracies have expropriated the individual craftsman of his skill. The service bureaucracies have dispossessed the population both of the knowledge and of the confidence to attend to many of their health and welfare problems.

We have already considered some examples of 'de-skilling' in the case of professional workers. What has to be emphasized is how deep this tendency has gone, how pervasive at all levels of working and non-work life, and how crippling a legacy it has now become. It was not so very long ago that the average male, without special training or equipment, could service his own car, or make minor repairs to his radio or television set. But technological 'progress' makes this less and less easy. Specialization and miniaturization of components, made especially possible with the invention of the transistor, mean that 'the works' are increasingly sealed in and inaccessible to general-purpose tools or general mechanical knowledge. To service a car with confidence now requires elaborate ranges of specialized tools and gauges, plus large-scale equipment for testing and monitoring the performance of parts. Threatening notices on the back of television sets warn the customer under no circumstance to tamper with the works at the back, but to summon the technician for all faults. The result is an endless, frustrating, and costly series of visits for minor faults which previously could have been remedied without danger by most householders. Nor is the diminished competence of the private consumer counterbalanced by an increase of skill on the part of the technician who arrives to do the 'repairs'. All the skill that he needs is the ability to follow a colour-coded chart which allows him to remove and replace some overall component, the structure and functioning of which he can be, and usually is, totally ignorant. The damaged components are then repaired in a centralized and well-equipped workshop by a few highly-trained electronicists. In other words, the dividing line between conception and execution of tasks, between brain and hand, continues its relentless way up the technical hierarchy, de-skilling the many and elevating the few. Eliminated practically altogether is the non-specialist consumer.

What has been said about cars and television sets applies equally of course to a wide range of consumer goods – toasters, heating irons, vacuum cleaners, and the like. Here too as in the other examples we also encounter the marked phenomenon of professional self-interest (or hubris) which leads the garage or the appliance manufacturer to urge private individuals to 'leave technical matters to the technicians', always to bring their cars to the garage for service, or always to send their appliances back to the manufacturer for repair. Ultimately what may be of greatest significance is not so much the disuse of actual skills and knowledge in the population at large as the wholesale demoralization and apathy caused by the process. The habit of dependence, once it has taken hold, is seductive and long-lasting. The pride in workmanship, the old instinct of self-help and self-maintenance, long repressed and undermined by the ideology of professionalism, do not easily respond when the situation once more calls upon them.

Nowhere is this lack of confidence of more consequence than in the field of medicine and welfare. Time was when mothers happily had their babies at home, attended by the local midwife. Families kept medicine chests to deal with minor injuries and ailments; a certain rough store of medical knowledge, part folklore, part science, was drawn on to diagnose and remedy these without the need of calling in medical specialists. Advice, often from older relatives, was sought and taken in the rearing and educating of children, but there was not the anxious dependence on the doctor, schoolteacher, or child-care specialist. Much of the care of the elderly and the mentally disturbed took place within the family or local community.

Clearly in all this there were many instances of suffering and neglect, caused by ignorance or indifference. But then it must be remembered that the remedying of this would also often have been easier in the more public, visible, and extended structures of kin and community. The changed position today neither means that welfare is necessarily better taken care of, nor that failures of the system are more readily noticed or dealt with. Now mothers are made to feel guilty and neglectful if they wish to have their babies at home; and the occupation of midwife is a virtually disappearing one. The result is enormous pressure on hospital beds, with long periods of waiting for pregnant women and almost dangerously short periods of stay in hospital for the birth of the child. Similarly the medical profession has managed to indoctrinate most parents with a deep distrust of homely remedies, and a corresponding inclination to seek out the doctor for every pain and ache, most of which the doctor can do absolutely nothing about. The medicine chest, with its array of bandages, potions, and pills, vanishes from the home. The result is a factory-like situation in the general practitioner's surgery, with the numerous patients the victims of brusque and casual treatment, and the harassed G.P.s in their turn looking enviously (though mistakenly) at the hospital doctors. More seriously there is the pattern of escalating dependence on medical services which has been termed 'iatrogenesis' – doctor-induced illness – and which comes from the overwillingness to prescribe drugs, as well as a mystifying professional jargon and complex of medical rituals which further threaten the patient and keep him supine, thus prolonging the illness.[51] Again, when family and community care of the aged and the mentally ill is replaced by institutionalized care in homes and hospitals, we get the familiar and disturbing pattern of segregation of these groups from the rest of society. This compounds the difficulties of the mentally ill, leading to institutionalized dependence and a more or less permanent adaptation to the 'sick role'; while for the elderly it removes the dignity and health-enhancing activity of playing a productive role in the life of the society, especially in relation to the rearing of the young.

We have already noted the enormous expense of the institutionalized system of social services – currently in Britain running at about twenty per cent of the Gross National Product, if we include only the public health, education, and social-security and welfare services.[52] What needs to be raised as the more important issue is the wisdom of extending a system which may turn out to be too costly not only in financial terms but in terms of social and moral effect: that is to say, in precisely the terms by which the system justifies its great expense. Two recently publicized cases in England raise this issue in an acute form. In 1973 there occurred the death of a young girl, Maria Colwell, as a result of parental neglect and maltreatment. Two and a half years later a sixteen-month-old baby, Steven Meurs, died in similar circumstances. The situation of both children had been well known to a variety of social workers and social-work agencies. Accusation and counter-accusation flew across the indignant nation in the ensuing debate about the state of the social services. To the charges of individual incompetence and bureaucratic inefficiency the social workers pleaded severe understaffing and intolerable case-loads. The changes currently taking place in social-work practice were a further fruitful source of dispute about the responsibility for these tragic deaths. The Government had acted on the Seebohm Committee's Report of 1968 recommending greater integration of the social services and the replacement of the specialist worker by the generic social worker. Those who supported the report argued that these two cases showed that the reforms had not yet gone far enough, and that integration needed to be speeded up to prevent other needy individuals slipping through the welfare net. Their opponents retorted that on the contrary the cases proved that the reforms had gone only too far, and that the gain in professional status achieved by promoting the better-qualified generalist had been more than offset by the loss of critical specialized skills in such areas as child care.

All these disputes are beside the point. The real issue is the institutionalization of caring, and the extent to which cases such as Maria Colwell's or Steven Meurs' are remediable features of the system or symptoms of its inherent limits. In very principle it would seem that such cases are bound to crop up repeatedly. The goal of drawing the mesh of the welfare net so tight that almost no one can slip through is a Fabian's pipe-dream, and any thoughtful person's nightmare. It is in the nature of large-scale bureaucratic institutions to make and compound these errors. As *The Times* said in its editorial on the Meurs case, 'a bureaucracy, however liberal its organization and humane its intentions, cannot reproduce the sensitivity and the flexibility of the individual's response to social distress.'[53] When care was the informal personalized concern of families and the local community, there could be grave deficiencies in the quality of service, but it was very difficult for cases actually to be overlooked and ignored. Both 'clients' and 'social workers' were part of the same community, living twenty-four hours a day in close proximity with one another. Helping those in need was part of the daily round of life, incorporated in all the other daily activities, not a separate professionalized activity. The professionalized social worker, however personally concerned in the case, generally has his or her own life to lead, usually in a part of the region remote from the homes of the majority of the clients. However much time he puts in he is bound to miss crucial aspects of the case, either in the behaviour of the client or in other people's responses to him. Moreover it is vain to hope that the situation will be made any better by increasing the number of social workers or the number of agencies involved in the case.[54] The problem is one of professionalized and bureaucratized social service as such. Each new worker, each new agency, multiplies the problems of the last. Eventually as the number of workers and agencies piles up one reaches the familiar situation where the bulk of workers are involved in clearing up the personal and administrative problems created by each other's involvement in the case.

3. Dilemmas and Alternatives

The general problem has been stated so far to be one where the situation of the industrial societies calls for reserves of personal skill, personal independence, and a personalized ethic of social welfare, and where such reserves are lacking because of the tendency of industrialism to subvert them. Industrial society finds it difficult to convert to the 'convivial' mode because of its very success in supplanting earlier and alternative patterns in favour of its own rationalizing and bureaucratizing mode. The question that can further be posed is what signs of reaction there might be to this situation. What forms of consciousness or action exist that might indicate both an awareness of the current dilemma, and some preparedness to attempt a resolution, in however incomplete and inconclusive a fashion?

Let us consider first some of the responses to what is perhaps the central institutional feature of industrialism: the large-scale, hierarchical, centralized and bureaucratized organization. The development of this agency has always been seen – pessimistically or approvingly – as the inevitable and indeed characteristic expression of the currents of industrialism. Weber, we will remember, saw bureaucratic organization as 'always from a formal point of view the most rational type. For the needs of mass administration today it is completely indispensable. The choice is only that between bureaucracy and dilettantism'.[55] Echoing him seventy years later, Michel Crozier also stresses the indispensability of the large organization to modern life:

> The large corporation . . . seems to be a uniquely powerful instrument for carrying on economic activity. This organizational construct has gradually come to embody collective rationality for all industrial and post-industrial societies. Whatever its shortcomings, its basic pattern of functioning cannot be questioned within the present socio-economic framework.[56]

To these general arguments about the rationality of the large-scale organization have been added more specific economic claims about 'the economies of scale', involving the specialization of men and machines, the spreading of costs, capital economies of various kinds, and the ability to plan on a long-term basis.[57] As with many of the other tendencies of industrialism, the post-1945 period saw a galloping acceleration of organizational size and complexity, in pursuit of the twin goals of economy and efficiency. The intellectual rationale of the movement was contained in the widely-accepted theory of managerialism. Every function was managerial: town-planning was 'urban management', headmastering was 'school management', crucially economics and politics were about managing the economy and society. The 1960s in Britain saw the triumph of managerialism in government and industry. A whole series of Government commissions and reports – the Plowden Report on public expenditure (1961), the Robbins Report on higher education (1963), the Fulton Report on the Civil Service (1968), the Seebohm Report on local authority social services (1968), the Maud Report on local government (1969), the Baines Report on local government management structure (1972) – all urged a greater degree of 'rationalization', that is, integration and centralization, on their respective areas of investigation. Key concerns were 'the integration of functions', large-scale and long-term planning, greater central control over all relevant areas, and greater attention to managerial functions.[58] In industry the same tendencies were observable at work in the 'merger-mania' of the late 1960s, spurred on by the Government's own Industrial Reorganization Corporation. Between 1961–68 mergers reduced the number of manufacturing companies in Britain by one-third. In 1960 100 companies owned 22 per cent of industrial assets; by 1973 56 per cent of British industry was owned by 87 firms.[59]

The failure of British industry to improve its performance, indeed its tendency to drop further behind its other industrial competitors, despite all this 'rationalization', might in itself cause one to reflect on the inadequacies of the faith in the large-scale hierarchical organization, whether private or public. In any case much other evidence exists to cast doubt on traditional arguments about the economies of scale, and the like. Increasingly organizations are showing their 'other face' of dis-economies and dysfunctions. Beyond a certain size and a certain degree of centralization of institutions, the advantages gained up to that point seem to be outweighed by the losses incurred as a result of the endemic problems of large-scale organization.

Part of the reason why this has not been so evident, at least until quite recently, is that we have accepted at face value the official accounts of the reasons for managerialism and mergerism. These are all, we are told, to do with greater efficiency and economy. When these processes then do not produce the results expected of them, the blame can be put not on the 'rationalized' organization itself but on extraneous forces – the 'gnomes of Zurich', the Arab oil sheikhs, etc. But a closer investigation of the reasons for the growth in size and centralization point to goals which have little to do with efficiency or economy, at least in the usual sense of those terms. Newbould's study of the industrial mergers of the 1960s concluded that, while the declared aim was industrial efficiency, the real object was to create, maintain, or reinforce market dominance, and to shut out competitors.[60] No doubt some may argue that the pursuit of a monopoly situation leads ultimately to greater efficiency, and greater benefit to the community; but it has to be said that on past evidence monopolies benefit mainly monopolists, and then only in the short term, as rising waste and inefficiency strangle the enterprise.

Newbould's findings are strengthened by more general considerations of the internal life of large-scale organizations. All relevant studies stress the extent to which that life is dominated by internal *political* criteria, rather than, as conventionally held, the economic ones of efficiency and maximization of output (of goods or services). Hobbes, not Marshall, would seem to be the better guide to understanding the modern corporation. At every level in the hierarchy there appears a competitive struggle for power and control, with consequent disregard for the ideal rational functioning of the organization as a whole. Tom Burns has drawn attention to one particularly serious 'dysfunction' occurring in present conditions. He points out that senior management today feels peculiarly threatened and vulnerable in the face of rapid technical changes and new computerized management techniques. Senior managers sense that they can be outflanked by the superior technical knowledge and greater adaptability of the more recently trained junior managers. In seeking to assert their greater power and prestige, senior managers therefore have recourse to other less controvertible aspects of their position, such as control over the machinery of promotion and career development, and over the flow of information within the organization. This last is of crucial importance:

> Communication control becomes both the basis and the overt expression of power within the corporate system ... By even tighter control over the flow of information, [senior managers] can reinforce the divisions inherent in the increasingly specialized nature of the information used, and ensure that decision-making processes at lower levels which might conceivably be analytical conflicts are in fact political, and so have to be referred up to the point at which the people at the top become the 'experts' who alone are able to treat bargaining and political conflict as if they were analytical.[61]

What is described of course is a situation in which *no one*, at any level of the hierarchy, has sufficient information or capability to make rational decisions. Those at the top can act, but don't know; those at the bottom know (to a limited degree) but can't act. Burns elaborates this further as follows. At progressively lower levels of the organization, the quality of information becomes more specific, more adequate, more appropriate, and more valid. At the same time, by the hierarchical and specialized nature of the organization, this information is limited in kind and degree, requiring the coordination of other pieces of information and expertise in the organization for decision-making. This coordination is achieved at the higher levels of the hierarchy, which to that extent possess the more adequate range of information. But that information, as it moves up, is processed in such a way as to make it seriously inadequate on several dimensions. All lower-level deliberations, as Burns notes, in the progressive move to the top have to undergo 'a perpetual translation of information bearing on choice and decision into an homologous language (money). All decisions emerge as decisions concerning monetary expenditure for current and future activities.'[62] This translation means a fundamental 'homogenization' of knowledge, which renders it dangerously unspecific. Moreoever, given the hierarchic nature of the system, the information has to be *reduced* as it travels up; and the 'increasing limitation of channel capacity' as decisions move upwards requires a further process of *filtering*. Hence decisions have to be reached 'on the basis of homogenized, limited, filtered, and distorted knowledge provided from within the hierarchic order below to the decision-makers'; 'uncertainty increases at each rising level of the decision-making hierarchy'; and 'it follows that the whole decision-making system operates on the basis of increasingly distorted as well as minimal information.'[63]

This has no doubt been true of all large-scale organizations at any time in history. But it becomes particularly weakening in a situation where bureaucratic conflicts take the form they do because of the loss of technical competence on the part of those at the top, and the consequent removal of the arena of conflict to the sphere of internal politics and careerism. Senior managers, through a perfectly rational impulse of self-interest, are forced to rely more and more on mechanisms of control – careers and communication – which both enhance the preoccupation of all employees with careerism, and undermine the ability of the organization as a whole to discharge its manifest tasks. There is a sense, therefore, as Burns says, 'in which the very increase in the rate of overall technological change produces its own tendency towards organizational ossification, and hastens the obsolescence which so many writers have suggested is characteristic of big corporations.' And he notes the historical irony in this: 'It is as if bureaucracy, the chosen instrument of *Zweckrationalität*, action determined by rational choice and the rational use of resources, in the context of the market society and the rationale of possessive individualism, were being sabotaged, or eroded, or stifled by the very characteristic of rational self-interest which brought it into being.'[64]

That this 'rationality' – economistic and calculative – embodied in large-scale organization could produce an equal degree of irrationality, as a necessary consequence of its principle of action, was something already foreseen and feared by Weber. But he considered this to be something the modern world would have to live with; and in his more optimistic moments thought that the disadvantages were small when compared with the immense gain in power and efficacy conferred by modern bureaucracy. Were he to return today he might not be so sure that the price is worth paying. Internally and externally to the organization, the pile-up of dis-amenities in terms of economic and social costs, environmental destruction, personal frustration, and individual powerlessness and alienation, all seem to suggest that the balance sheet needs to be inspected more critically.

Externally the effects of large-scale organization – and its natural handmaid large-scale technology – have most spectacularly shown up as the 'hidden costs' or 'external dis-economies' of continuous economic growth. Ultimately the most serious of these dis-economies, as we have already noted, is the one-sided dependence on and exploitation of limited fossil fuels as the basic energy source. 'The modern industrial system, with all its intellectual sophistication, consumes the very basis on which it has been erected.'[65] A dis-economy that, on present trends, will lead to industrial breakdown and probably social chaos is, apart from being absurdly misnamed, an offsetting cost against which any alleged 'economy' is virtually unthinkable. As the *Ecologist* put it starkly at the very outset of its 'Blueprint for Survival': 'The principal defect of the industrial way of life with its ethos of expansion is that it is not sustainable.'[66]

All calculations as to the date by which, on present rates of usage, the fossil fuels will run out are of course contentious, as well as somewhat unreal. But very real is the nature and direction of the trend. This shows, firstly, the enormous dependence of the industrial system on fossil fuels as compared with renewable sources of energy (such as water, wind, sun). The latter currently contribute less than four per cent to the world total of energy use; and to increase this contribution to eighty to ninety per cent involves a reorganization and transformation of the industrial system of truly revolutionary proportions. So far there are negligible signs that the industrial societies are prepared to contemplate such a reorganization. We continue, as Schumacher says, to treat the most basic capital of the industrial system as income. The simple fact is that 'fossil fuels are not made by men; they cannot be recycled. Once they are gone they are gone forever.'[67] The other aspect of this trend is the great acceleration in recent years in the exploitation and use of the fossil fuels:

> In comparison with what is going on now and what has been going on, progressively, during the last quarter of a century, all the industrial activities of mankind up to, and including, World War II are as nothing. The next four or five years are likely to see more industrial production, taking the world as a whole, than all of mankind accomplished up to 1945.[68]

Taken together these two features of current energy use allow us to say with a good deal of certainty that fossil fuels will be exhausted within a realistically foreseeable future. The age of hydrocarbons is drawing to a close, and we are doing remarkably little about adapting ourselves to any alternative system of energy use. For instance, in Britain the Government proposes spending 320 times as much money in 1976–7 on research and development into coal and nuclear energy as on solar energy research.[69]

The exhaustion of fossil fuels is only the most spectacular of several disasters that can follow from the logic of the 'economies of scale'. All too often that 'logic' turns out to be a Panglossian version of the misguided philosophy of putting all your eggs in one basket. Thus one has the spectacle in recent years of large industrial complexes, employing thousands of people, becoming almost entirely dependent on a single product – a large supersonic aeroplane, a high-powered engine, a range of motor cars. When the social environment changes, as it has a habit of doing, and people seem no longer to be quite so keen on fast planes or multiple car ownership, whole sectors of the economy are convulsed. Desperate international consultations take place, huge subsidies are poured out, and patently uneconomic products, such as Concorde, turned out to avoid the social consequences of putting an end to what are clearly wasteful ventures. The centralizing and agglomerating tendency of industrial evolution indeed runs directly counter to the lesson taught by Darwin's account of the evolutionary process as a whole: that the condition of survival and progress is diversity; and if the price of this is a certain degree of waste and inefficiency, this seems preferable to certain extinction.

Curiously, the proponents of large-scale organization and technology often justify its 'incidental' social costs by arguing that it has enormously increased and widened choice, and hence led to much greater diversity in the lives of the industrial populations. On examination this usually turns out to involve a peculiarly narrow concept of choice. As Edward Mishan observes, the apologists of growth 'have failed to observe that as the carpet of "increased choice" is being unrolled before us by the foot, it is simultaneously being rolled up behind us by the yard'.[70] Increased choice in certain things there certainly has been. We can now clean our teeth with an electric toothbrush, as well as with a wide range of the more conventional hand-powered brushes. The range of cars, cosmetics, hi-fi radios and gramophones, toasters, mixers and a multitude of other household gadgets, continues to expand. We can take our holidays almost anywhere on the face of the earth, and probably soon above and beneath it. But on the other hand 'for many decades now private firms have, without giving it a thought, polluted the air we breathe, poisoned lakes and rivers with their effluence, and produced gadgets that have destroyed the quiet of millions of families . . .'[71] In the area of choice that selects quietness over noise, smallness over largeness, slowness over speed, local over metropolitan, public over private means of transportation, individualized over standardized products, skilled craft work over mechanized mass production, rural over urban pursuits, home-based over mass forms of entertainment, clean air and water over polluted skies and seas – in these areas it is clear that the range of choice has been diminishing very sharply. No doubt a precise balance sheet showing gains and losses in choice and diversity would be very hard to draw up. Nevertheless it would be as well to be aware that while we concentrate on the marvellous variety of consumer objects produced by the ingenuity of modern technology, we tend to forget the real loss of choice in substantial regions of our work, leisure, and family lives.

It is conventional to balance these 'external dis-economies' against the alleged great economies achieved internally by the large industrial organization, and the presumed increase in efficiency and capability. We have already found good cause to be sceptical of this claim. Even on the narrow issue of economic efficiency, students of large organizations have concluded generally that the gains in one area are usually offset by losses in another, so that – except for this one – no firm generalizations can be made concerning the economies of scale.[72] Writing in the 1950s, for instance, S. R. Dennison found in his review of British industry that 'over a wide range of industry the productive efficiency of small units was at least equal to, and in some cases surpassed that of the industrial giants.'[73]

Indeed not much more than common sense is required to see where the sources of internal dis-economies may lie in the large organization. Communication is frequently delayed or distorted, leading to duplication and the pursuit of contradictory aims by different departments. Decisions are taken at levels and in areas remote from those of their intended application. Errors of a relatively minor kind, magnified on such a scale, become major disasters. A project once started – Concorde again comes to mind – can involve a commitment of men and money in such proportions that escalating costs and a subsequent realization of the uneconomic nature of the project is not enough to halt it. On this scale paradoxically it becomes too costly to pack up. (Macbeth recognized the dilemma: 'I am in blood/Stepp'd in so far that, should I wade no more/Returning were as tedious as go o'er.') At every level and in a hundred different ways, the rationality of 'scientific management' has its hidden costs to the organization. The large department store decides to replace its individual sales assistants at separate counters by centralized pay desks, thereby cutting down on staff. This means that not only does the standard of service drop perceptibly – customers cannot find things, or things of the right size or quantity, get frustrated and give up, hence fewer sales; the store also finds that it is beginning to lose significant amounts in thefts, at the now unsupervised counters. At a medium-sized Marks & Spencer store in Canterbury, for instance, the management has calculated that it loses £20 an hour in thefts, or about £200 a day. No doubt the management covers its losses well enough in higher prices for those customers who do pay; but as a 'rational' form of business administration this seems a decidedly curious way of doing things.

In the end perhaps the most severe and intractable 'dis-economy' confronting the large organization is the constant difficulty of keeping the commitment of its own employees. This is not by any means a new problem, of course, although there are signs in recent years that it is becoming more serious and, in particular, that it is spreading to groups previously regarded as the most loyal and committed of the organization's employees. As far as the lower levels of the workforce are concerned – the traditional industrial workers and their newer counterparts, the routine clerical and service workers – the drudgery and monotony of their work in the large mechanized factory, office, or store has always provoked resentment and indifference, whether taking the form of a resigned fatalism or a more bitter and explosive hostility. 'Why does he work?' wrote Engels impassionedly of the industrial worker in his *Condition of the Working Class in England in 1844*:

> From love of work? From a natural impulse? Not at all. He works for money, for a thing which has nothing whatsoever to do with the work itself. He works because he must. If only because his hours of labour are so long and so dismally monotonous, the worker must surely detest his job after the first few weeks, assuming that he possesses a spark of humanity. The division of labour has multiplied the brutalising effects of forced labour. In most branches of industry the worker's activity is reduced to some paltry, purely mechanical manipulation, repeated minute after minute, unchanged year after year.[74]

Marx in the very same year was reflecting on the consequences of what sociologists were later to call this 'instrumental' attitude to work. 'The worker feels himself at home only during his leisure time, whereas at work he feels homeless. His work is not the satisfaction of a need, but only a means for satisfying other needs.

Its alien character is clearly shown by the fact that as soon as there is no physical or other compulsion it is avoided like the plague.'[75] And later observers have with a wealth of concrete detail confirmed this picture of an alienated and bored workforce. 'The guys yell "hurrah" whenever the line breaks down . . . You can hear it all over the plant'; 'You don't achieve anything here. A robot could do it. The line here is made for morons. It doesn't need any thought. They tell you that. "We don't pay you for thinking," they say. Everyone comes to realise that they're not doing a worthwhile job. They're just on the line. For the money.'[76] To these comments of British and American car workers on the assembly line we can add the reaction of the clerical worker of the factory-office who feels his work to be so pointless as well as monotonous that he can think of effacing himself altogether from the work process: 'if the system were better, clerical work would not be necessary . . .'[77]

But the consolations of leisure, as Marx seems to suggest? Unfortunately these have not been forthcoming in either the quantity or quality hoped for. For apart from the fact that there is a good deal of evidence that boring and repetitive work produces boring and repetitive leisure, thus rather undermining the notion of a fair bargain of forced labour for creative leisure,[78] there is also the clear evidence that work time has not declined by anything as much as was confidently predicted by almost all nineteenth-century thinkers. The official or 'standard' working week has fallen considerably, it is true. From being about 60 hours or more a week in the 1840s (in England – rather more in the United States and on the European continent) it has dropped to 40 hours today in most of the industrial countries.[79] But the actual number of hours worked still remains high, and appears to have changed remarkably little over the past forty years. In Britain the average number of hours worked in the late 1930s was between 45 and 47 a week; in the late 1970s it is still between 45 and 47.[80] Moreover this average conceals significant variations. In one survey of 1971 over a quarter of a million workers in Britain were found to be working more than 70 hours a week.[81] In the United States the number of people working more than

48 hours a week rose from 13 per cent of the workforce in 1948 to 20 per cent in 1965; while the number of people who are 'moonlighting' (holding more than one job) has doubled since 1950.[82]

The most significant trend however is in the longer hours worked by the professional and managerial groups. A 60–70 hour week was not uncommon among the British managers studied by the Pahls.[83] Willmott and Young found that the average working week of a group of managers and professionals in the London area was 48 hours (57 including travelling time), and that among these several were working more than 60 hours a week.[84] In the United States Heckscher and de Grazia found managers working a 62-hour week (including business travel);[85] and more than half of Wilenksy's middle-class group of professionals and executives in Detroit were putting in 45 hours or more a week, with a sizeable minority working at least 60 hours a week.[86] The importance of these findings derives from the great growth, in all industrial societies, of the professional and managerial groups – projected to be the second largest occupational category in the workforce in both Britain and the United States by the 1980s.[87] Whatever the intrinsic quality of the work these people will be doing – and our previous chapter suggested that it was not likely to be very rewarding – it seems at least clear that the 'leisured society' is an ever-receding goal, and that in terms of sheer time work will continue to be a central part of most people's lives in the coming decades.[88]

Not that this persisting eagerness to work has much to do with the old curse laid upon Adam, at least not as that has traditionally been interpreted. It is not, in other words, a matter of necessity in the strict sense. What the pattern shows is that leisure has been bartered for more income. The good life, defined in terms of material possessions, beckons seductively, but always at one further step removed, so that extra hours of work have to be put in to get the money to procure the accoutrements of the good life. As a result commonly it is not the male breadwinner but his children and non-working wife who appear to be the main beneficiaries of this toil. But even his earnings, with large stretches of overtime and perhaps a second job, increasingly seem not to be enough. Wives go out to work in growing numbers – between 40 and 50 per cent in Britain and the United States – to add to the household earnings. Thus paradoxically but not surprisingly, as the demands of the good life grow, more people are spending more time at work and have correspondingly less time to spend on enjoying the good life. The old utilitarian bargain, the 'pain' of work exchanged for the 'pleasure' of leisure, really does turn out to be fraudulent. The gratification of the pleasures have to be indefinitely deferred in the endless and painful pursuit of them.

We know that there were those such as Marx who argued that the industrial workers would not forever tolerate such conditions of work and leisure. Their very shared tribulations would produce a common revolutionary consciousness which would lead them to overthrow the economic system that condemned them to so degraded an existence. This has not happened so far in the industrial countries, and there are good grounds for doubting that it will happen in the future.[89] But there are many gradations of dissatisfaction, and the expression of it. Throughout the period since the Industrial Revolution workers have expressed their resentment against the industrial system in a number of ways: from simple machine-breaking, through strikes and sabotage, to rapid labour turnover, absenteeism, slow-downs, and diverse forms of non-cooperation through collective informal control over the pace and organization of work. Owners and managers have always accepted this as the additional 'hidden' cost of the enormous wealth produced by the rationalized technology and work organization of the industrial system. While regretting these costs they have generally considered them negligible by comparison with the gains, and in any case have usually passed them on to their customers in the form of higher prices for goods and services. But here too there are limits. The question that once more arises is whether this situation has now changed significantly. From various quarters there appear the signs that worker resentment is increasing, and that management can no longer afford to regard this 'internal dis-economy' in so complacent a light.

Consider these indications. In Britain 'voluntary absenteeism' is estimated to have caused the loss of between 200 and 300 million working days per year, which is at least thirty times more than have been lost by strikes. In the mining industry absenteeism is the major managerial problem: up to 20 per cent of the workforce may be absent on a given day. In Italy, one in seven workers doesn't turn up for work on a given day; in the car industry the figure is higher. In the Swedish car industry three in ten workers are absent daily in many sections. Absenteeism in the United States is also at its highest in the car industry: for the industry as a whole the absentee rate doubled in the second half of the 1960s. At the General Motors' plants, 5 per cent of workers are absent without explanation every day; on some days, notably Fridays and Mondays, the figure moves up to 10 per cent. At Chrysler's, a daily average absentee rate of 6 per cent was reported in 1971. Turnover rates have also been of serious concern in most industrial countries. In Sweden's car factories a third of the labour force turns over each year – 50 per cent at Volvo's. At Chrysler's in Detroit, the turnover rate in 1971 was almost 30 per cent; at Ford's, it was 25 per cent in 1970. Overall in the American car industry the turnover rate doubled in the second half of the 1960s.[90]

The changing pattern of strikes, especially since 1945, gives further evidence of an increasing restlessness about the quality of working life and the nature of the job itself. What is revealed is a move away from a concern with wages *per se* to concern with wider aspects of the work environment. Analysing the trends in strikes in Britain between 1911 and 1947, Knowles concluded that 'strikes on "basic" questions [wages and hours of work] have declined in relative importance, and strikes on "frictional" issues [work organization, rules, discipline, etc.] have correspondingly increased . . . It is significant that wage-increase strikes in particular have shown a very marked decline.' McCarthy, continuing the analysis up to 1957, confirmed this view: 'It is clear . . . that this trend has continued.' Turner interprets the trend as follows:

In the twenty years of high employment from 1940 the proportion of strikes about 'wage questions *other than* demands for increases', and (particularly) about 'working arrangements, rules and discipline' rose remarkably: from one-third of all stoppages to three-quarters . . . One could say that these disputes all involve attempts to submit managerial discretion and authority to agreed – or, failing that, customary – rules: alternatively, that they reflect an implicit pressure for more democracy and individual rights in industry.[91]

A spectacular American example of this trend comes from a much-publicized strike in 1972 at General Motors' plant at Lordstown, Ohio. The management's proud boast was that this was the most advanced plant of its kind in the world, the fastest and most automated production line, turning out 100 Vegas an hour, 20 hours a day. Workers had 36 seconds to complete work on each car and get ready for the next. The workers' response was a four-month battle with the management over the pace of the assembly line. Absenteeism settled at 6 per cent. There was sabotage: showrooms full of torn wires, ripped seat covers, broken gear levers, and dented panels. The struggle culminated in a bitter three-week strike, in which the workers moved from their demand to ease the pace of the assembly line to a demand for a re-organization of the very method of assembly-line production; that is, they wanted cars made differently.[92]

Absenteeism, turnover, restrictions of output, and the like, are the familiar and much studied signs of discontent. Less studied and commented upon, but in some ways more significant, is industrial sabotage, that 'dark, invincible, terrible Damocles sword that hangs over the head of the master class', as a French enthusiast put it early in this century. It can occasionally play a part in a rational strategy of confrontation; but more frequently it seems simply the most basic gesture of distancing and defiance, in a hated situation about which the worker feels he can do nothing. From management's point of view it should count as the evidence that is most worrying. Its 'irrationality' contains its greatest threat. Precisely because the worker does not expect to change anything, he is prepared to resort to sabotage as the easiest and potentially most damaging form of action in the long unending war of attrition with management.

Here are some examples gathered by two English researchers:

> They had to throw away half a mile of Blackpool rock last year, for, instead of the customary motif running through its length, it carried the terse injunction 'Fuck Off' . . . In the Christmas rush in a Knightsbridge store, the machine which shuttled change backwards and forwards suddenly ground to a halt. A frustrated salesman had demobilized it by ramming a cream bun down its gullet . . . In our researches we have been told by Woolworth's sales girls how they clank half a dozen buttons on the till simultaneously to win a few minutes' rest from 'ringing up'. Railwaymen have described how they block lines with trucks to delay shunting operations a few hours. Materials are hidden in factories, conveyor belts jammed with sticks, cogs stopped with wire and ropes, lorries 'accidentally' backed into ditches.[93]

'They make the decisions, we couldn't care less,' said a steelworker, describing how he and his mates allowed steel slabs that were perceived by them to be too cold for rolling nevertheless to go through the roller, according to the routine of the plant. 'When the slab comes up I've seen them break rolls valued at £800–£900 . . .'[94] And an example from the American car factory. On the one hand the car workers admired their product as the culturally approved symbol of freedom. On the other hand, because of the conditions of work under which they made it,

> it is hated and despised – so much so that if your new car smells bad it may be due to a banana peel crammed down its gullet and sealed up thereafter, so much so that if your dealer can't locate the rattle in your new car you might ask him to open up the welds on one of those tail fins and vacuum out the nuts and bolts thrown in by workers sabotaging their own product.[9]

We have been concentrating, as is traditional, on the dissatisfaction of the manufacturing worker. But some of the examples above indicate how similar are the feelings of workers in the mechanized and bureaucratized offices and shops, as indeed we should expect from the tendencies in white-collar work discussed in the last chapter. Perhaps it will suffice to note the comment in the report *Work in America*, prepared in 1973 for the U.S. Secretary of Health, Education, and Welfare:

> . . . the Survey of Working Conditions found much of the greatest work dissatisfaction in the country among the young, well-educated workers who were in low-paying, dull, routine, and fractionated clerical positions. Other signs of discontent among this group include turnover rates as high as 30 per cent annually and a 46 per cent increase in white-collar union membership between 1958 and 1968 . . . These changing attitudes . . . may be affecting the productivity of these workers: a survey conducted by a group of management consultants of a cross section of office employees found that they were producing at only 55 per cent of their potential [sic!]. Among the reasons cited for this was boredom with repetitive jobs.[96]

It is quite impossible for managers, workers, or social scientists to establish with any degree of precision the costs to the organization of these various actions and reactions among employees. Few would in any case consider these to be so high as to make the system insupportable; moreover, it is very difficult to know whether the organization has more of these hidden costs to absorb now than in the past. But that they *are* costly, and maybe mightily so, seems undoubted: think of the cost of constantly re-training even relatively unskilled workers in a situation where the annual turnover is over thirty per cent. At any rate there are some significant indications that management at least now considers these costs too uncomfortable a burden to bear, and have been looking for ways to reduce them. They have apparently taken to heart the findings of the social scientists on the boredom and frustration of much contemporary work. In recent years both public and private management have been publicly and sometimes avidly espousing schemes of work re-organization which go under the banner of 'job enrichment'. The French Government has created a post of Minister of Job Enrichment. The British Government's Department of Employment published a report on job enrichment entitled *On the Quality of Working Life*, and set up a steering party in 1973, with members from both the employers' and trade-union organizations, to see how the ideas contained in the report could be put into practice. Most far-reaching of all were the schemes actually implemented in their factories by Saab and Volvo in Sweden; Philips at Eindhoven in Holland; Fiat and Olivetti in Italy. Less ambitious but equally illustrative of the same tendency was the experimental re-design of jobs at I.C.I. in England, and a number of firms in the United States, such as I.B.M., American Telephone & Telegraph, Texas Instruments.[97]

The aim in most schemes of job enrichment is to give each worker, or small groups of workers, responsibility for a clearly identifiable sub-assembly, whole product, or task. This larger piece of work involves more difficult, hence more involving, tasks, as well as a greater variety of simpler ones. The work cycle is lengthened and made more 'challenging'. The worker has greater flexibility in organizing his own work. He is often made responsible for the quality of his output, which means that he can be given 'feedback' on his performance and try to improve it.

As an example, here is Mary Weir's account of the schemes which Volvo introduced at many of their old-established plants in the early 1970s:

In response to a high rate of turnover and increasing difficulty in recruiting new employees, Volvo embarked on an ambitious programme to increase their employees' motivation and job satisfaction, by giving them greater responsibility, and involving them in decisions affecting their work, as well as improving the physical surroundings. An important part of improving the jobs at Volvo was the creation of small work groups which are responsible for the assembly of a complete section of the vehicle, such as the truck cab or the brakes and wheels. The size of each work group varies between three and twelve members, depending on the particular tasks involved. The group's tasks are allocated a few days in advance and the group members are responsible for organizing production, dividing the work between themselves and controlling the overall work pattern. The group elects a leader who becomes the spokesman for the group, to liaise with the foreman. A monthly meeting is held, consisting of the spokesman, some other members of the group, the production engineer and the foreman, to discuss questions about work patterns, equipment and tools as well as problems which have arisen, and general information. *Job rotation* has been introduced in many areas so that an individual may do several different work tasks, from assembly work up to inspection, and this introduces some variety into the jobs; a training programme has been introduced to give people the necessary additional skills. Some *job enlargement* schemes have also been used in Volvo, where the number of tasks completed by each operator is increased, to lengthen the cycle time of the task performed.[98]

More radical still was Volvo's construction of an entirely new plant at Kalmar in 1974 which carried the work group concept further, and abolished the traditional assembly line altogether. Robert Taylor, who visited the plant after two years of operation, felt that 'what Volvo is doing means a frontal attack on the doctrine of scientific management that has dominated capitalist methods of production since the early part of this century.' He described the work organization as follows:

> Volvo has escaped from the inflexible flow-line method of assembly by introducing trolleys on rubber wheels run on batteries . . . which carry each car individually round the plant being assembled. Each trolley (six by two metres in size) is controlled by a central computer sending messages along the floor, which is kept entirely free of any fixed installations. The trolleys operate on both floors of Kalmar plant. Above, the body is put together; below, the chassis, engine, and gearbox are assembled. They are married near the end of the process. At Kalmar, Volvo has broken down assembly work into twenty different functions. They are performed by teams of 15 to 20 workers doing each one. 'They are the size of a football team plus reserves', a manager told me. The workers work along the outer walls of the plant, which is shaped into four hectagons. As they assemble they can look out through long, high windows at the surrounding (nondescript) countryside. The trolleys move around quietly from one team to another. Their flexibility enables workers either to stand on them to assemble cars as they move along, or – what is now more popular – to dock each trolley in a siding while the team as a whole works on the car in a 20–25 minute stint before passing it on to the next team round the corner. [Compare the 36-second work span of General Motors' Lordstown plant.] . . . Each team has its own entrance to the plant as well as its own locker room, sauna, toilet, shower and coffee room with fitted carpets and a fridge. Noise levels are very low in the plant at around 65 decibels, so workers can talk together as they work or listen to gramophone records which they can bring from home. Each team can pace the work so that it can enjoy an extra five minutes or so every hour in a coffee break . . . The teams are not organized in any hierarchy, though

each of them does have an instructor to help the uninitiated. Production technicians and foremen are responsible for two to three team areas apiece. But there are no more than a handful of managers among the 440-strong labour force . . .[99]

Management have on the whole good reason to feel that many of these schemes have fulfilled their objectives. Volvo's turnover rate at Kalmar is 16 per cent, compared with 50 per cent in many plants before changes were introduced. Absenteeism is down. Saab too, following the introduction of group assembly, cut absenteeism and drastically lowered the turnover rate. In the British mining industry, absenteeism was more than halved when the National Coal Board introduced group working at one colliery. Productivity increased by nearly 20 per cent. At Texas Instruments in the United States, the quarterly turnover of cleaning attendants fell from 100 per cent to under 10 per cent, as a result of 'job enrichment'. Productivity – 'the cleaning achievement' – was raised from 65 per cent to 85 per cent. American Telephone & Telegraph cut employee turnover in ten of their companies by 27 per cent, and eliminated a substantial number of jobs, mainly through job enlargement and the granting of greater employee autonomy. In many of these cases, moreover, the costs of the projects, including additional capital investment, and expenditure on directing, staffing, and monitoring them, were more than covered in net savings to the company concerned.[100] N. A. B. Wilson thus summarized his review of the evidence for the Department of Employment's *On the Quality of Working Life*:

. . . the examples already available demonstrate convincingly that it is usually possible to increase job satisfaction for most (though seldom all) members of a workforce, increase their learning, versatility and potential, greatly reduce absences (and in certain cases, formal grievances), while increasing (or at least conserving) the productivity and feasibility of the enterprise . . . Modern work systems [it is clear] can be devised to meet the needs of a competitive economy while at the same time affording a range of jobs which are at the least comparatively satisfying and progressive for most of the people available to do them.[101]

This in one sense is precisely what left-wing critics of job enrichment fear. For them, the whole movement is subversive, and calculatedly so, of worker militancy. It is replete with the dangers of 'false consciousness'. They rightly point out that the changes leave the essential levers of planning and control in managerial hands. The purposes of the plant, what is produced, the terms of sale, all remain managerial prerogatives. Workers are conned into a sense of participation and partnership, and may forget that the basic conflict of interests between men and managers is unchanged. The goal of the organization is still the same: maximization of profit, or output, and nothing that fundamentally interferes with this goal can be permitted, however desirable in terms of industrial relations. On this view, then, job enrichment is no more than the latest phase of the 'soft sell', 'human relations' approach to the problems of the large-scale organization.[102] As Braverman puts it, the reforms

> represent a style of management rather than a genuine change in the position of the worker. They are characterized by a studied pretence of worker 'participation', a gracious liberality in allowing the worker to adjust a machine, replace a light bulb, move from one fractional job to another, and to have the illusion of making decisions by choosing among fixed and limited alternatives designed by a management which deliberately leaves insignificant matters open to choice.[103]

Certainly the 'enrichment' provided by these schemes seems paltry when set besides Marx's vision of a humanized and diversified totality of work and leisure, when 'I might do one thing today and another tomorrow, hunt in the morning, fish in the afternoon, rear cattle in the evening, criticize after dinner, just as I have a mind, without ever becoming hunter, fisherman, shepherd or critic.'[104] Nor do I offer them as instances of resolutions of the problems of worker commitment in large organizations. Their significance is otherwise, at least so far as the present discussion is concerned. It lies in their being symptomatic, at the highest levels of the industrial system, of the realization of the costly and wasteful nature of the large organization. The remedies offered may be minor, and largely illusory; but out of their symbolic admission, their concession that current conditions of work are unfit for human beings, may come the pressure for a more radical restructuring of technology and work organization.

Management may be able to stave off serious disaffection among 'the workers' by schemes such as the above. It will find it much harder to deal with the discontent that has, perhaps more alarmingly, revealed itself among its own ranks. This, again, is not an entirely new thing. The chartered accountant who gives up his career to become a lighthouse keeper; the bank manager who retires early to cultivate a few acres of farmland; the civil servant who becomes a country milk-delivery man: these are all familiar examples of one traditional Gauguinesque response to the pressures of middle-class occupations, the element that forms the emotional staple of much of Somerset Maugham's stories about middle-class life. So it is not the quality of response that is novel. It is the indications – admittedly fragmentary and impressionistic for the most part – that now many more middle-class managers, executives, and professionals are finding the frustrations of their working life unbearable, and are expressing this in a variety of ways hostile to the large organization.

We have already had reason, in the last chapter, to note the main causes of this increased resentment. Middle-class occupations have been subjected to the same processes of rationalization, fragmentation, specialization, mechanization, and bureaucratization as have lower-level occupations. Many occupations which traditionally enjoyed the professional's autonomy – lawyers, doctors, architects – find themselves increasingly in large bureaucratized organizations where they become in effect managerial, but where the freedom to manoeuvre is severely curtailed. Computerized managerial systems and the new information technology can routinize tasks once done in conference and committee by men skilled in human relations and the workings of the organizational machinery. They can allow the top to control the middle, as scientific management in the past allowed supervisors to control the workers. The men who applied Taylor to the workers are now themselves Taylorized. Moreover, the organization's involvement with its environment has widened and complicated in ways which nearly all work against the authority of middle-level managers and professionals. The industrial manager of the nationalized or internationalized corporation finds himself at the centre of a field of forces which includes the manual unions, his own Board of Directors, the state, overseas owners or shareholders, and consumer and environmentalist groups. He finds himself bypassed in many negotiations between the trade unions and top management, and between the corporation and the state. At the same time, managers and professionals are finding that they have to work longer hours to cope with the increased bureaucratic work-load laid upon them. They take home briefcases stuffed with paper that they have not had time to work over at the office. Family and leisure time correspondingly suffer.

Already in the late 1950s David Riesman was noting 'a loss of appetite for work . . . among the more highly-educated and the well-to-do'. He put this down to changes in the nature of professional and organizational life which made these traditionally highly committed workers no longer expect the same interest or involvement in their work: 'they have given up the notion that the work itself can be exciting.'[105] Since then there have been signs of a persisting alienation and a significant degree of rejection of the middle-class career. Many university graduates in both the United States and Europe have shown a marked disinclination to commit themselves to the traditional career patterns of their parents, and more than a decade after graduation are still recorded by their University Careers Offices as 'holding themselves ready for employment' – i.e., as unemployed (which does not of course mean that they may not be working very productively on their own account as itinerant or intermittent casual workers). British managers have been shown to be increasingly drawn to the spheres of private family and leisure life, and to be reluctant to extend their working hours as seems necessary. They do not use their leisure time to further their careers, and seem prepared to take increased leisure and early retirement in preference to higher income and promotion.[106] As one industrial manager put it: 'I know if I earned more I wouldn't work harder. I'd go and live in the country.'[107] Middle-class employees, going against the traditional stereotype of an ambitious, careerist, mobile group, seem now less prepared to change jobs or to move house for career reasons.[108]

In a more striking movement, a number of professionals in recent years have 'dropped-out' altogether, at least in the sense of having deviated from their conventional career patterns and withdrawn from their career organizations. This has applied to doctors, architects, lawyers, teachers, social workers, and media workers. Some have simply withdrawn, as casual 'free-lancers', aspiring novelists, social-security clients, or cultivators of small allotments in the country. Others, more interestingly, have gone into or set up alternative, parallel, agencies and practices, using their skills and experiences in a manner which they consider more truly in accordance with the principles of their professional vocation. One recent student of these movements has commented that 'most professions now have a radical or revolutionary movement within them whose aim is to radicalize or revolutionize the profession to which it belongs.'[109] In Britain for example these tendencies have expressed themselves in the setting up of neighbourhood law centres, to give free legal advice and support to poor and uneducated people, and which are staffed full-time or part-time by ex-career barristers and solicitors; in the movement of scientific professionals into various ecological and environmentalist groups, such as Friends of the Earth, or the radicalized British Society for Social Responsibility in Science; and in the radical Case Con movement within the social-work profession (not to mention the many practices engaged in by social workers which are implicitly or explicitly in defiance of their statutory employers).[110]

Once more, it would be wrong to see these movements among middle-class workers as much more than merely reactive, or symptomatic. They suggest, in many ways and with different voices, a preparedness for change, but they do not themselves add up to a mass movement capable of bringing about fundamental social change. Nevertheless there is no mistaking here as with the less skilled workers the mood of discontent, even if the overt expression of it is as yet restricted to an active minority.

And what gives this reaction a possibly greater significance than that of other workers is that these middle-class professionals and managers are the very workers who have been hailed, by Bell and others, as the 'new class' of the post-industrial society. It is their expertise, ethic, loyalty and commitment that is seen as crucial to the functioning of the service bureaucracies of the new society. If they come to proclaim, in substantial numbers, '*ohne mich*', it is hard to see how this highly complex, technical and bureaucratized society could continue to perform without crippling deficiencies.

The mood that has found its main practical expression in a reaction against the life of large-scale organizations has chimed in with another, even more generalized and even more difficult to pin down and delineate. This is the disillusion with the fruits of continuous economic growth, with its natural agent, large-scale technology, and, at the most abstract level, with the very mode of cognition of industrial society, science itself. There seems, in other words, to be a reaction against industrialism at its most pervasive and compelling level of operation, that of ideology. The evidence for this probably does not convince the really hard-headed social scientist who wants it in bulk quantities, preferably in precise numbers and proportions. But for those who are prepared to experience their society through a variety of senses and sources, there can scarcely be much doubt that over the last decade and a half technological civilization has seen its ideological underpinning seriously weakened. Science, both as practical accomplishment (technology) and as a form of understanding of the world, has found itself under attack.[111] At the crudest level there has been the Luddite response, with its cry 'Abolish the machines! Back to the land! To each his five acres and a cow!' At the most sophisticated analytical level has come a questioning of the mode of scientific understanding as privileged and superior to all others, and a suggestion that its narrowness of comprehension is ultimately the fatal cause of the growing problems of industrial civilization.[112] Certainly it would be impossible to say that such an awareness or sentiment has spread widely through the population at large. It has, not surprisingly, affected mainly the middle class, and particularly the intellectuals and professionals. But these are after all the ideologues of industrial society. A basic change in the orientation even of a minority of them can on past experience be highly significant of a more general re-direction of society.

As it happens there *is* a certain amount of evidence of the conventional kind for the view that the ideology of science has weakened its hold on the industrial societies. In a world-wide survey on 'images of the year 2000' held by the various populations, a team headed by Johan Galtung found a marked 'science pessimism' in the technologically most advanced societies (and a corresponding degree of optimism among the less developed). The populations of the advanced societies, having experienced a strong dose of science and technology, seem decidedly unconvinced that their problems can be solved by the 'technological fix,' that is, by more of the same. The researchers linked this negative attitude to science to a wider pessimism about the future which they found in the industrial societies, and which they termed (not entirely seriously) 'development fatigue'. As they put it: '. . . the people living in the most developed countries where technology and economy are concerned do not seem to feel that they are at the threshold, at the beginning of a new, great era. On the contrary, they rather seem to reflect a feeling of being at the end of something, of moving into a corner, without seeing any clear escape.'[113]

At a more modest level, there is the evidence of the persisting flight from science and technology subjects in the schools and universities of the industrial societies. In Britain not only is it true that the science and technology faculties are half-empty, but it seems that even science graduates are somewhat loath to practise their skills once learned, and are to be found in considerable numbers re-training to become public administrators or social workers.[114]

But in some ways the most convincing, as well as the most gratifying, evidence is of a purely symbolic kind. It comes in the recognition, the recantation almost, by some of the most fervent advocates of industrialism that they need to qualify in a serious way their earlier accounts. The future of industrialism, they now admit, may well be discontinuous with its past. It is no longer possible to envisage the future simply as the past writ large. Daniel Bell, for instance, has become increasingly preoccupied with what he calls the 'antinomian' and hedonistic currents in the culture of late industrialism: anti-rational and subjectivist tendencies in both the popular and 'high' culture which cut across the rationalizing and bureaucratizing mode of the economy and social structure, and which threaten the efficient functioning and perhaps the very survival of the post-industrial society.[115] Even more interesting is the 'Postscript' which is now added by the authors of *Industrialism and Industrial Man*, that classic summation of the triumphant industrialism of the late 1950s. They now feel the need to give a central place to a tendency which they had earlier, under the term 'the new bohemianism', relegated to the marginal realm of play. Since *Industrialism and Industrial Man* is, in a sense, where we first came in, it makes a fitting conclusion to this section to quote their new observations at some length:

> A decade ago we called attention to the 'new bohemianism' as one of the major factors potentially affecting the 'road ahead' to pluralistic industrialism. In the intervening decade, the 'cultural revolution', with its 'counter-culture', has spread rapidly. Related to it has been the attack on the 'consumptionist society' with its emphasis on material goods, and on the 'one-dimensional man' ruled by technology and those who manage technology. Bohemian attitudes have spread and deepened significantly. We thought we saw Bohemianism as a largely off-the-job phenomenon. Now it seems to be penetrating some jobs in society, particularly white-collar jobs, causing a more casual attitude towards performance. Furthermore, some persons refuse employment altogether in favour of a way of life separated as far as possible from the discipline of industrialism . . . The old distrust of technology and of revulsion against the machine has taken on a new emphasis as the new Luddites reject the industrial system the way the old Luddites rejected the individual machine . . .
>
> Underneath this humanist reaction . . . lies a central problem in industrialism: a society requires more discipline to go along with the greater interdependence that the new technology brings, but the more highly educated labour force wants more freedom for spontaneous

individual action within the work environment, as well as outside it. Thus technological society might carry the 'seeds of its own destruction' – not in class versus class, but in the discipline that the technology requires versus the spontaneity of the labour force that it helps to create. Some of the requirements of the new society run into conflict with the new man it spawns.[116]

In this chapter and the last, we have considered two possible lines of development for the future of the industrial societies. The first basically extends the pattern of the past, the second disturbs it. It is an unprofitable exercise to attempt to predict the outcome of the clash of these two tendencies. The future remains unknown and unknowable, otherwise it isn't the future. But it might be helpful to state the two possibilities more starkly.

Industrialism may – as I believe – be driving itself, and the societies subject to it, into an impasse. The fossils of numerous civilizations bear eloquent testimony against any view which holds this to be an improbable direction for society to take. Indeed if we were to take our guidance from history we would have every reason to expect the massive and settled routines of classic industrialism to negate the more recent, more fragmentary, opposing currents. In the short run, at least, they clearly have the predominant economic, political, and cultural power; and in history as in politics it is usually the short run that counts.

Against this, one could argue that at least the alternatives have been posed; and they have been posed in a contemporary situation which daily and in a hundred manifest ways points up the relevance both of the critique of industrialism and of the alternatives proposed. Critics of industrialism there have always been since its very origins at the beginning of the nineteenth century. But however passionate the criticism, it has always had the problem that, to the majority of the population, the benefits of industrialism seemed to outweigh the costs. Set against the material scarcity of the past, above all, the industrial mode promised to lift societies above a material level virtually unchanged since the norm was established by the Neolithic Revolution over six thousand years ago.

It is this situation which has now changed. At the objective level, industrialism has run into the ground. For two centuries it has developed its institutions and technology on the basis of more or less unchanging expectations as to both the material resources and the political configuration of the world. Both these promises are now clearly revealed as shaky, and a most precarious basis on which to confront the future. The need now, as a matter of sheer survival, is to restructure those institutions and technologies to meet the new situation; though this simple way of putting it has to suppress the recognition of the truly formidable problems involved in this readjustment.

Some hope that this can be achieved in time comes from the subjective expression of dissatisfaction and dissent. For the first time in the history of industrialism a significant number of people of all classes are beginning to show signs that, on balance, they do not feel that the benefits of industrialism now outweigh the costs. Both as workers in the industrial and clerical bureaucracies, and as the consumers, clients, claimants and victims of those same bureaucracies, they are in their daily lives experiencing a sense of deep frustration with the routines to which they are subjected. In diverse ways, especially over the past fifteen years, they have given vent to some of that frustration, and have attempted to reconstruct and to take control of small, localized, aspects of their lives. This is hardly revolutionary, either in intention or in effect. But as large-scale institutions continue to become more frustrating, costly, inefficient and brutal; as services deteriorate, and taxation and public spending grow to meet the ever-increasing need of 'patching up' the material and moral environment; so we might hope and expect these small seeds to grow.

8 Progress and Industrialism

Progress is crab-like.

Jean-Paul Sartre.

1. Past, Present, and Future: The Dialectic of Progress

With the idea of progress we started, and with some reflections on its vicissitudes we should end.

There seems little doubt that the curve of its development, as we have glanced at it over the two centuries of its history, has been one of declining conviction. The appeal was strongest at the beginning, in the period of the eighteenth-century Enlightenment. Reason then was the agency of progress, and the application of reason seemed capable of solving everything that was humanly solvable. With the Industrial Revolution, which in at least one of its guises was an expression of this rationalizing impulse, progress was linked to the diffusion of the more complex idea and system of industrialism. Belief in progress remained confident, as is clear in the accounts of Saint-Simon and his many disciples. But already the first fruits of industrialism, and the spontaneous cry of outrage which they evoked, had produced a vigorous counter-reaction against the ideology of progress, and especially its dominant agency, industrialism. In this movement were raised the powerful voices of Burke and Cobbett, Coleridge and Chateaubriand.

The triumphant march of industrialism during the rest of the nineteenth century largely stilled these protesting tones. Even Marx, who produced the most monumental moral indictment of the system, dismissed opposition to it as puerile and nostalgic.

Instead he looked ahead to its more developed phases to bring about the resolution of the terrible contradictions that were producing such inhumanity and unhappiness. Less subtle and more popular were the euphoric celebrations of the system by Macaulay and Spencer. Their advocacy, and that of a host of lesser writers, ensured that for most of the century progress and industrialism were synonymous.

A fundamental and sustained questioning of this equation first occurred at the end of the nineteenth century, in the period immediately before the First World War. There was an unresolved ambivalence in the treatment of industrialism in the sophisticated accounts of Weber, Durkheim, Tönnies and Simmel – drawing as often as not for their moral as well as analytical force on the early nineteenth-century critics of industrialism. The attacks of artists and philosophers, noticeable from the mid-century, became increasingly savage, amounting sometimes to a wholesale rejection of industrialism. Industrialism was seen as destructive not just of valued institutions, but of the very possibility of art and culture. Anti-rational, anti-industrial ideologies of racism, aestheticism, and mysticism proliferated.

The mood of pessimism persisted into the interwar period, but was increasingly qualified by a renewed confidence in the power of scientific knowledge and technical expertise to solve the problems of industrial society. Even the destructiveness of the Second World War failed to shake this basic conviction. With the seemingly continuous economic boom of the post-war period, and the world-wide eagerness to embrace industrialism, industrialism and progress were in the 1950s reunited at a level almost as high as a century before. The idea of a 'post-industrial' society of abundance and leisure began to be elaborated, and to be accepted.

First to be stripped away in the 1960s was the illusion that progress through industrialism took place on all fronts. The seamy underside of pollution and environmental destruction was increasingly displayed to the societies which had advanced furthest. Then in the late '60s and early '70s came the realization that even material prosperity was not secure. The galloping demands of large-scale organization and capital-intensive technology, as more and more of the world industrialized, brought the threat of the exhaustion of the basic energy resources on which the whole industrial system depended. A critical vulnerability to the pressures of the non-industrial world was revealed. For the first time ever in the history of industrialism a terminal point of development could be clearly perceived. The remaining years of the century seemed likely to be marked by a decisive slowing down of economic growth, involving a succession of economic recessions, high levels of unemployment, and a general deterioration in the standards and conditions of living. In the second half of the 1970s, it is impossible to find among any of the populations of the industrial societies a confident belief that further progress can mean further industrial development.

This might seem a sad end to the Saint-Simonian dream. 'Where shall we find ideas which can provide the necessary and organic social bond? In the idea of industry; only there shall we find our safety and the end of the revolution.'[1] Thus did Saint-Simon hope that the new system of industrialism might harness and develop all the energies that had been burgeoning in European societies since the late Middle Ages. And it seems fair to say that something of this hope was realized. Despite some severe internal conflicts, and some even more severe external ones, industrialism succeeded in raising the material standard of living of the population as a whole to historically unprecedented heights. The consequence of this was that ultimately there was virtually no group interested in looking beyond the confines of the system that had produced such material abundance. A degree of social integration was achieved that, once more, seems historically unique. Revolution, which had haunted the minds of most European statesmen for the first half of the nineteenth century, had ceased its haunting by the end. For all practical purposes it disappeared from the agenda of European societies. In the twentieth century there has hardly been a moment when revolution seemed possible, or even desired by any significant section of the population of the industrial societies.[2]

But social integration, or 'consensus', has not really turned out to be the problem in the end. The chief concern has become the future of the industrial mode as such. Here the Saint-Simonian inheritance is of doubtful value. Indeed one might say that that very tradition constitutes the core of the problem. For although Saint-Simon could not be expected to see all the consequences of his system, the centralizing and rationalizing features of industrialism – the cause of the present discontents – are contained only too clearly in the many sketches he gave of the model industrial society. So the revolutionary prophet of the early nineteenth century, of the heroic age of industrialism, now becomes the graven idol of the decadent epoch. He is the revered deity of 'the religion of the engineers' (whether they know it or not), of the managers, technocrats, and bureaucrats who hope to replace the 'government of men' by the 'administration of things' largely through the conversion of men into things.

But while the substance of the Saint-Simonian legacy may not be of much help in the 'hyper-industrial' phase of industrial civilization, something of the general form of his thinking suggests some more relevant considerations. One of the most original and arresting aspects of Saint-Simon's thought was its rejection of the dominant philosophical individualism and atomism of the time. (The continuing influence of the ideologies of utilitarianism and *laissez-faire* during the course of the nineteenth century only shows how 'advanced' was Saint-Simon's thought in this respect.) In searching for the principle of the new industrial order, Saint-Simon looked back over the individualistic currents of his own time to the structure of sentiment and social organization – and even of thought – of the European Middle Ages. He was not alone in this. A number of other thinkers of the time, mainly conservatives such as Burke, Bonald, and de Maistre, were counterposing to what they regarded as the anarchic tendencies of the day the ordered, custom-based communal institutions of feudal Europe. Saint-Simon's distinctiveness lay in that, unlike them, he was not using the Middle Ages in a battle of the past against the present, but in a struggle for a new future state against a disorderly present. The congruence which, on an idealized view, the Middle Ages presented in the relations between family ties, economic activities, and religious beliefs, seemed perfectly fitted as the model for a new society struggling to be born, in which the main threat to survival seemed the incompatibility between the dominant individualistic outlook and the highly socialized nature of the new economic organization. The future industrial order, as Saint-Simon conceived it, then turned out to be a synthesis of an older order which had in most respects been superseded, together with what he regarded as the most dynamic elements of the society of his time.

Progress in this account appears as a crab-like movement: one step back, two steps forward. (Although, as with crabs, there is no guarantee that the forward steps will not be annulled by rapid movements in a backward direction.) Quite apart from considerations of any particular concrete situation, there is a general plausibility about this conception. This is shown partly by its popularity: while clearly visible in Saint-Simon, it achieved much greater influence as the 'dialectical progression' of Hegel and Marx. Basically it recognizes that novel and creative developments almost never arise from the further exploitation of existing practices. So it is in nature, and so it is in society. The attitudes and institutions that dominate a society at any particular time are the result of a successful adaptation, in conditions of more or less severe competition, to the current internal and external environment. But the current or contemporary equals the merely temporary. The environment inevitably changes, if only as a result of the effects of the continuing adaptation of the successful pattern. When this happens, the currently dominant mode is the least capable of adapting to the new situation, having perfected itself, and exhausted itself, in adapting to the old. In this situation it often happens that practices which have been ignored, or which have been left 'on the shelf', or which have flourished in the interstices of the dominant institutional order, come as it were from behind to provide the impetus to a new and more successful initiative. So, for instance, the ancient organization of the city-states in Italy was able to come forward to provide the dynamic for the regeneration of European society, following the collapse of the overcentralized and overbureaucratized Roman Empire.[3]

The industrial societies, I have been arguing, also seem to have reached a point of overadaptedness to an environment which is swiftly changing. The dominant ideology and institutions of the industrial mode can only offer more of the same, which in these circumstances is like administering larger doses of poison to an already sick organism. Now it might seem somewhat arbitrary to resort to a Saint-Simonian procedure in considering the present crisis; and so it would be if we were to be too slavish. But there does seem to be a real and valuable sense in which the way out of the present dilemma of the industrial societies may be to pick up aspects of their pre-industrial past and fuse them with some of the most advanced elements of the present. At any rate, from a number of different quarters there are indications of various kinds that it is not unreasonable to be looking in this direction.

Some confirmation that the search itself is not merely fanciful comes from a widely-expressed conviction that the present era is at an end – whether or not the past might represent a new beginning. For some indeed this ending shows itself particularly in the *irrelevance* of the past to the resolution of the present predicament. It is not, Ernest Gellner says, 'that all of the past is abrogated, but that none of it is authoritative'.[4] Others have taken this further. Adopting the sometimes mindless slogan 'the future is on the agenda', certain thinkers in the recent futurological movement have expressed the view that not only is the past no longer any guide to modern societies but that they must increasingly allow themselves to be directed by their conceptions or 'images' of the future.[5] The varieties of post-industrial theory belong here, although as we have seen the novelties they point to are conspicuous chiefly by their slightness. Others still, rather differently and with more plausibility, have emphasized the changed context of action of men and nations in the twentieth as opposed to the nineteenth century, and have argued for the fact of a fundamental break in the historical continuity of the two. We are, says Geoffrey Barraclough, living in the age of 'contemporary history', which differs from the Europe-centred era of 'modern history' with respect to such crucial matters as the place of Europe in the world context, the emergence of the United States and the Soviet Union as 'super-powers', the breakdown of old imperialisms and the rise of the coloured peoples to nationhood, and the coming of thermonuclear power.[6]

These views alert us to the possibility of discontinuities but say very little about the character of future directions. A second perspective comes a little nearer to the point at issue. This takes the form of the suggestion that our familiarity with industrialism has blinded us to the character of its most important phase, and so of its nature in general. We need to recognize, these writers urge, that what we generally regard as the era of 'classic industrialism' – the hundred years or so which followed the English Industrial Revolution – was in many ways an exceptional, almost aberrant, period. This should make us aware that there is something qualitatively different about the industrialism of the second half of the twentieth century, and direct us to conduct our analyses accordingly. One of the earliest and most interesting suggestions of this kind was made by Joseph Schumpeter in the 1940s. He asks us to consider the era of capitalist industrialism – essentially the nineteenth-century European experience of industrialism – as a residual phase of transition between feudalism and socialism. He does not mean this in Marx's sense, that capitalism is a social order which succeeds feudalism and precedes socialism. For Schumpeter does not see 'classic industrialism' as ever having been a full social order at all. He literally wants to suggest that capitalist industrialism is a hybrid, a temporary period during which the forces and structures of European feudalism were gradually being overcome. But 'in breaking down the pre-capitalist framework of society, capitalism broke not only barriers that impeded its progress but also flying buttresses that prevented its collapse.'[7] When the process was more or less completed, not only had feudalism gone, but capitalism also. Seen in this light, capitalism appears as 'the last stage of the decomposition' of feudalism. What is left at the end of this process is an administered, centralized, and planned society which Schumpeter called socialism, and which he regarded as a different species from the nineteenth-century hybrid which preceded it.

This view of the exotic nature of the formative period of industrialism has come to seem increasingly attractive, as new features alien to that period appear, or older ones reappear. So for instance George Steiner notes a widespread current alertness to, and anxiety about, violence and disorder. But, he observes, 'when we lament safeties, courtesies, legalities now eroded, what we are in fact referring to is the *belle époque* of middle class hegemony, notably in Western Europe, from about the 1830s to the Second World War.' He cautions us against drawing topical comparisons on the basis of this 'nagging sense of paradise lost'. For

> far from being the historical rule, the stabilities, the general absence of violence, the law-abidingness, the sanctity of property and contract, the spaciousness of work and play which we associate, erroneously or not, with the epoch from Waterloo to the economic and social crises of the 1930s, were an exception, a rare and fragile *entente* between ruler and ruled . . . So far as Western history goes, the long peace of the nineteenth century begins to look like a very special providence.[8]

Then there is Ernest Gellner – again – reminding us that when we engage in contemporary debates about the 'free market' *versus* the planned (i.e. politicized) economy, we are posing an opposition that is historically and sociologically unreal, and which is based on an illusion fostered by a too schematic view of nineteenth-century European history.[9] For it is wrong to see these two principles as equals, sociological 'universals'. The sociological norm across time and place is overwhelmingly 'politics in command'. It is the 'free-market' principle that is the anomaly; and the fact that this is not immediately apparent is due to a historical accident which placed the 'free market' at the centre of the original process of European industrialization. In the era of 'classical capitalism' (argues Gellner) there took place a separation of the economic and political realms that was 'highly eccentric, historically and sociologically speaking', and which gave rise to the unprecedented and erroneous belief in a 'natural' economy based on the operations of the untrammelled market. It was a separation that took place in circumstances which were historically highly specific, depending mainly on the existence of a state which for various reasons had neither the inclination nor the need to interfere with the economy. 'So the miracle occurred – a society in which, for once, wealth was mightier than the sword.'[10] These historical circumstances have now changed; the customary norm has reasserted itself; politics once more dominate economics. Whatever we wish to do about this situation, it is clearly wise to recognize that it is the normal one.

The perspective of these three writers is revealing in two ways. It makes firstly the necessary point that, however we assess the present condition of the industrial societies, we would be ill-advised to cast our reflections in the categories appropriate to the developing industrial society of the nineteenth century. Secondly it emphasizes the *openness* of the options available to the industrial societies at the present time. It warns us against relying on the schematization of history that so often serves sociology as a short-hand for historical knowledge, and which leads us to expect social orders or epochs to succeed each other in orderly progression – as 'feudalism', 'capitalism', 'socialism', and so forth. If there was indeed something peculiar and exceptional about nineteenth-century industrial society, then we should not expect to discern any future state of that society by a simple extrapolation of trends, or by conjecturing some sort of 'natural' or determined evolutionary supersession. The relationship between the past and the future of industrial society is likely to be far more disjunctive than is implied in either of these modes of procedure.

Gellner's argument goes so far as to suggest that it may well be the *pre*-industrial past of European societies that will turn out to be the better guide to the future. He hardly sees this as a hopeful sign; but the interesting thing is that he regards this sort of historical recurrence as a distinct possibility. Others have also at various times been driven to draw parallels between some of the more striking twentieth-century developments and certain characteristic features of pre-industrial Europe. It is important to stress that by no means all of these parallels are comfortable. And before we try to rescue the more desirable aspects of that past, it might be as well to begin with the less welcome returning visitors.

The most important of these is already hailed by Gellner. It shows itself in the development of a 'corporatist' economy and society which recalls no other period more strongly than that of the mercantilist era of the sixteenth and seventeenth centuries – the age, so far as England is concerned, of the Tudors and Stuarts. In mercantilist theory and to a good extent in practice, the state legitimized, chartered, and protected corporations – often conferring monopoly privileges upon them – in return for co-operation in political ventures, and a certain degree of 'social responsibility' in relation mainly to consumers. So, in the present, commentators are observing the growing institutionalization of a system of politico-economic organization which some have been disposed to label 'neo-mercantilist' or 'neo-guild', as well as more simply 'corporatist'. Its main features are remarkably similar to the mercantilist system. It is characterized by the absence of the 'free play' of market forces. Firms and organizations, including trade-union organizations, are 'co-opted' or 'incorporated' into a unified system supervised on behalf of the community by the state. The state takes over much of the responsibility for finance and investment. It guarantees survival through loans, subsidies, written-off debts, and a generally protectionist strategy, on nationalist grounds. In return for this security and share in national decision-making, the state demands of employers that they develop an ethic of 'social responsibility', both in the sense that they become sensitive to consumer and environmentalist demands, and that they respond to the needs of their employees to be consulted about the firm's activities and to be satisfied in their work. Equally in return for rights of consultation and participation at national level, the state requires of the trade unions that they cooperate in current governmental policy and, crucially, see to it that their members do so as well.[11]

It is interesting to recall that it was precisely this aspect of pre-industrial social organization that attracted Saint-Simon and his great disciple, Emile Durkheim. In looking to an end to the social anarchy that prevailed in the early industrial period, both hoped that some sort of guild-like system of corporations would provide that involvement and attachment to society that seemed to be lacking in the principles and practice of the existing liberal *laissez-faire* system. Both were contemptuous of political and economic competition alike, seeing it as wasteful and destructive to self and society. The ultimate political model for both was a parliament based on 'functional' representation, an 'industrial parliament' in which the main constituents would be 'associations of producers'. Here too trends seem to be going their way.[12]

The irony is that this very feature of the past that Saint-Simon and Durkheim brought in to save the industrial system in the long run manifests itself as part of the crisis of that system. In a sense they can hardly be blamed for not anticipating this, and anyway it is fair to say that for various reasons they would probably both heartily dislike the emerging corporatist system. The fact is that the guild system, even in its late mercantilist form, remained embedded in a society that contained a multitude of countervailing forces against the centralizing and autocratic principles implicit in it. For all practical purposes, given the prevailing levels of technology and communications, it was a pluralist, decentralized, minimally-governed society. The state controlled from the centre so far as it could, but that was not very far. Only with the democratic and industrial revolutions of the nineteenth century could state power so extend as to make corporatism a potentially totalitarian system. Few nineteenth-century thinkers – the exceptions of Tocqueville and Weber come to mind – had the remotest conception of the qualitative change that might be involved in the degree of bureaucratization and centralization which this century has experienced, largely as the result of the two World Wars. To that extent Saint-Simon and Durkheim cannot be blamed for the fate of their system.

These mitigating remarks probably apply less to certain other related developments in which the twentieth century echoes the sixteenth, and about which Saint-Simon at least was inexcusably casual. These have to do with the more overtly political and constitutional changes that have taken place since the end of the last century. In 1929 the then Lord Chief Justice of England, Lord Hewart, traced the decline of Parliament and the courts in face of the growing power of the executive branch of the state. He put this down partly to the unification of the executive and the legislature brought about by the growth of the mass political parties with their extra-parliamentary organization; and partly to the spread of 'administrative law', overriding Common Law, as a result of the extension of bureaucratic rule. He called his book *The New Despotism*; and saw the closest parallels to his own times in the age of the Star Chamber and 'Tudor despotism'.[13] The comparison is well merited, excepting only the common tendency to overestimate the power of earlier 'despotic' monarchs. For king, read prime minister or president; for royal prerogative, read the ministerial and bureaucratic discretion contained in statutory Instruments and Orders, not to mention the powers of prime minister or president in 'states of emergency' which they themselves are judged the most fitting to declare. Indeed no royal Henry (Tudor) or Charles (Stuart) possessed anything like the executive power of royal Harold (Wilson) or Edward (Heath).

In a third area, that of social movements, there seems an interesting case of historical reversion. Pre-industrial social movements in Europe typically related to the sphere of consumption, not of production. The commonest form of such a movement was the bread riot in town and country, sparked off by abnormally high prices. An important feature was the frequent and intense involvement of women – for obvious reasons. Little effort was directed at changing or even seriously affecting the system of production and distribution that might be responsible for the periodic fluctuations in the price of food. The Industrial Revolution opened an era of intense conflict at the workplace, where even if the system was unchallenged it was in the heart of the sphere of production that issues were raised and fought out. The hours worked, the level of wages, the conditions of work became the staple of these conflicts.

These issues continue to generate conflict, of course, just as price rises in the nineteenth century still often occasioned movements of protest. But in the last twenty-five years the conflicts in the realm of production have been significantly accompanied, and in some degree replaced, by renewed conflicts in the sphere of consumption – once more, significantly involving women as major actors. This development has closely mirrored the change of emphasis in the economy from the production of capital goods to consumer goods, and from the production of goods to the production of services. Both enhance consumerism as a way of life, and act to direct the consciousness and interest of the population away from problems of production to problems of consumption. So we have had the rise of the consumer movement itself, and of movements generally remote from the world of work and centred on the spheres of leisure, consumption, welfare, and family life. It has proved in many respects more possible to stimulate into action students in their schools and universities, housewives in their homes and neighbourhoods, clients, consumers, and claimants in relation to transport, recreation and welfare services, than workers in their factories and offices. The pendulum has not swung right back, and there are reasons for thinking that conflicts over production may intensify in the future. But the widespread revival of concern with issues of private, domestic, and community life, where all members of the family or community have asserted a collective interest, is yet one more instance of a bridge between the pre-industrial and the post-industrial worlds.

It is also in a sense a bridge between the less desirable and the more desirable features of the dialectical movement we have been describing. The first two developments may be considered – as Gellner's and Steiner's remarks suggest – almost as reversions to a historic norm. Except when occasionally lucky or inspired, the civilized world seems resigned to authoritarian and centralized control, whether of the old-fashioned autocratic kind or the more modern totalitarian variety. In that sense, these developments may be said to have cosmic sanction. But there are certain other developments, perhaps still best described as future possibilities ('*futuribles*' has been Bertrand de Jouvenel's term) which have not that natural momentum, and which indeed will probably require strong conscious political direction if they are to be more than merely marginal. These too arise from some significant tendencies and pressures in developed industrial societies; and they similarly contain an element of reversion, having in many ways stronger affinities with the basic pattern of pre-industrial than of industrial societies. But whereas the trends already considered on the whole graft easily on to the body of industrial society, and at a higher level can even be seen as basic continuities,[14] these reversions would amount to a substantial change of direction and may not be comfortably accommodated to existing patterns.

2. The Past in the Future

A small historical footnote may serve as an introduction to these further speculations. As far back as 1917 an English Guild Socialist, Arthur Penty, coined the term 'post-industrial' to describe a future state of society which in essential respects reversed the dominant tendencies of the existing industrial society. In the place of an increasingly large-scale bureaucratized society, Penty – a follower of William Morris and John Ruskin – called for a move to a 'post-industrial' society based on decentralized units, and a re-fusion of work, leisure, and family life around the small artisanal workshop. Daniel Bell, who quotes Penty's book in his own work on the post-industrial society,[15] clearly finds the whole idea very quaint and absurdly utopian. Utopian it may be, in the sense of hoping for a total reversion of the tendencies of the time. But if Marx is right in cautioning us that 'it is not enough that thought tend towards reality, reality itself must tend towards thought', then there exist sufficient indications in reality at the present time to think that Penty's vision is not wholly absurd. A post-industrial society in which the influence of William Morris, Guild Socialist, balances that of William Morris, motor-car magnate (the later Lord Nuffield), seems not only highly desirable but a distinct possibility.

We can start with the family. In different ways a number of

trends have converged to restore to the family something of the function and even the form of the pre-industrial family. Young and Willmott, in their study of contemporary family life in the London Metropolitan region, draw attention to some interesting parallels between what they call the Stage I, pre-industrial, family, and the Stage III, present-day, 'symmetrical' family.[16] The most important of these, in their eyes, is the restoration of the family to the centre of the individual's attention and interest, and as the focus of his main commitment. This was hardly possible in the period of the Stage II family – roughly the hundred years following the Industrial Revolution – when the abrupt separation of workplace and home, and the extensive demands of the worklife on the man, fragmented and impoverished family life and reduced it to little more than a vestigial appendage of the factory system. Now, with fewer children, shorter working hours, the conveniences of the 'miniaturized' technology of domestic appliances and the private car, wives can go out to work, husbands can spend more time at home, and tasks are increasingly shared. Something of the pre-industrial unity of joint and complementary roles, in work and at home, is re-created in the 'symmetrical' family.

The family, far from losing its importance as many of its traditional tasks – production, education, and so forth – are taken over by specialized institutions, actually gains in significance as the only remaining institution capable of giving a sense of identity and belonging in a world of shifting impersonal ties and contractual relationships. As against the tendencies towards specificity, instrumentality, impersonality, and ephemerality in the roles people play in the wider society, the family stresses diffuse obligations, a wider conception of tasks beyond the purely calculative, emotional and expressive relationships, and lasting loyalty and commitment. As Young and Willmott put it, in accounting for the resurgence of the family,

> its advantages offset some of the disadvantages of the sort of society that technology has created. People who are not much valued by their employers, and are paid a wage that shows it, can still be valued at home, their bad and good qualities combining to make up a whole

personality, in the round: not a machinist or a park-keeper, a solicitor or a sociologist, but a person. Whether or not leisure activities are a compensation to people who do not fulfil themselves in their work, the family certainly is. As a multi-purpose institution (although not to anything like the same extent the all-purpose one of Stage I) it can provide some sense of wholeness and permanence to set against the more restricted and transitory roles imposed by the specialized institutions which have flourished outside the home. The upshot is that, as the disadvantages of the new industrial and impersonal society have become more pronounced, so has the family become more prized for its power to counteract them.[17]

They even go so far as to suggest that

as far as religion goes, the family itself may have become more than any other social institution an object of devotion, the beneficiary of a kind of western Confucianism which reveres the descendants more than the ancestors, but like Confucianism also manages without a god, let alone a purely male god. The smaller has become more sacred, the larger less. If once it was the transfer of obligations from family to wider community that was stressed, more recently the trend has been in the opposite direction.[18]

This worship, it is clear, is not a matter of sentimentality but of the performance of essential functions. The paradox is that as the family has come to be stripped of many of its traditional tasks – a process widely regarded as progressive by most thinkers of the nineteenth century and since – it has had new ones heaped upon it. The family has come to be surrounded by a host of other institutions, advising, giving, cajoling, remedying, threatening. But far from having taken the pressure off the family these have in fact increased it in many difficult ways. With so many necessary points of contact with their environment – schools, welfare agencies, doctors, hospitals, tax offices, and so on – families have to be small archives of information and expertise to cope successfully with the welter of institutional demands made upon them. And these demands come alongside a parallel process which has been making it more difficult for family members to live near each other, to help and support each other, and at the same time abolishing or diminishing the significance of the informal sources of information and advice once available in neighbourhood and community. No wonder that, faced with these pressures, individuals have felt driven to rely more than ever before on the natural sense of obligation and commitment to help of family members.

Young and Willmott recognize certain counter-trends that challenge the renewed importance of the family. Of these, the most serious seems to be the disproportionate amount of time spent on or at work by managers and professionals. This means less time and energy, and also less interest, for family matters. Given the expected growth in the number of managerial and professional workers, given also the fact that women are increasingly likely to be found among them, the suggestion may well arise that the family in the future may once more be eclipsed by work concerns, this time perhaps for both spouses.

One rejoinder to this has already been offered. If it is simply a matter of increasing time, and not satisfaction, in work, the professional workforce may simply vote with its feet and refuse the work commitment demanded of it. In these circumstances the family is likely to remain even more important as a refuge and a point of identification. But there are in any case other possibilities compatible with increased work involvement which maintain the family's centrality. Many of these have to do with variations on, and divergences from, the prevailing norms in the arrangement of work and leisure time. Women in part-time work, for instance, have often said how well such a pattern has enabled them to combine the demands of the home with outside commitments. Similarly, though to a somewhat lesser extent, men working shifts have sometimes found that not only is there less stress involved in such things as travelling, but that they have more opportunities for sharing activities with their wives and children. Since both these patterns of work are on the increase,[19] we might expect them to offset to some extent the intensified demands of the workplace.

Even more interesting possibilities are revealed in the many experiments now taking place with flexible working hours and other variations on the standard units of work time. In principle, although not yet very much in practice, these suggest a questioning of traditional assumptions not just about the working day, week, or year, but of the whole of working life, and of the relation between work time and free time in general. Already in all the industrial societies many firms have introduced schemes of flexible working hours, a compressed working week (the four-day, forty-hour week being currently most favoured), and, most widely, staggered working hours.[20] Significantly, in one study of the effects of flexible working hours, employees reported the most important benefit to be the ability to 'strike a better balance between work and private life'.[21] And once one goes beyond traditional patterns of working hours to this extent, more ambitious schemes of dividing up work and leisure time suggest themselves. Young and Willmott found among their respondents a greater enthusiasm for leisure when there was the possibility of compressing the working year, with longer annual holidays, and even the working life, with something like 'sabbaticals' being offered.[22] It was not, in other words, a matter simply of demanding less hours of work – this was not often thought possible or even desirable – but of a much greater flexibility in the individual organization of work and leisure.

'Man has refashioned the use of space. He has left the use of time unchanged.'[23] All these methods of varying the working routine of men and women challenge the tyranny of the clock, that temporally-phased mass work discipline which from the very start was rightly regarded as the crucial underpinning of the industrial system, and which at the same time did most to undermine the family system.[24] They make it at least plausible to contemplate keeping family commitment and activities going without a sacrifice of working life. But most far-reaching of all would be changes in work organization and technology which would move towards the re-creation of a home- or locality-based economy. This would rescue a central aspect of the essential economic basis of the pre-industrial family system. Perhaps an inescapable air of fantasy must surround proposals of this kind. But once again certain tendencies and possibilities in existing knowledge and organization point towards the real feasibility of such an aim.

Thus, speaking of the effects of automation on industry, Langdon Goodman rightly comments that

> automation can be a force either for concentration or dispersion. There is a tendency today for automation to develop along with larger and larger production units, but this may only be a phase through which the present technological advance is passing . . . Automation, being a large employer of plant and a relatively small employer of labour, allows plants to be taken away from large centres of population.

If this tendency were permitted to develop, he envisages a truly radical change of direction:

> Rural factories, clean, small, concentrated units will be dotted about the countryside. The effects of this may be far-reaching. The Industrial Revolution caused a separation of large numbers of people from the land and concentrated them in the towns. The result has been a certain standardization of personality, ignorance of nature, and lack of imaginative power. Now we may soon see some factory-workers moving back into the country and becoming part of a rural community.[25]

Computers in particular hold out the strongest potential for the de-centralization and domestication of work, especially white-collar work. In this they are even more promising than the telephone, whose de-centralizing possibilities have still barely been touched. Working with a computer essentially involves a communication channel, connecting the computer terminal with the computer itself. There is consequently no need for a worker in a computerized office to do anything physically in some central location. He can obtain the information or instructions he needs from the computer store on the wire – the existing telephone transmission system will do – and send his own contribution back by the same channel. In practice then he can perfectly well work at home for at any rate a great proportion of the time. 'The Post Office,' suggest Young and Willmott, 'could be more and more the modern version of the putter-out' of the pre-factory system.[26] It is admittedly a somewhat breathtaking step to move from this to the assertion of Martin and Norman, the authors of *The Computerized Society*, that 'we may see a return to cottage industry, with the spinning wheel replaced by the computer terminal.'[27] Technology operates in no such self-determining vacuum. But it seems quite fair to argue, as they do, that the computer is the most powerful instrument of dispersal and devolution since the invention of cheap printing. Potentially every aspect of education, work, politics, domestic tasks, and leisure can be affected by it. Contemplating such a situation, embracing the home and work tasks of both men and women, Young and Willmott comment: 'If the four jobs could be done more fully in one place a new version of the domestic system could spring up as a more leisurely or at least a more intimate form of industry than its large-scale counterpart, with family intruding on work more than work on family.'[28]

While work could become more domestic, in a parallel movement there is the possibility of domestic service itself once more becoming acceptable and attractive work. This could have the effect of further freeing both parents for the pursuit of their work careers, whether within or without the home; and at the same time attracting to the home as 'family' members people from outside, much as the craftsman's household of the seventeenth century contained many such people as domestics or apprentices 'living-in' as members of the family. As C. H. Waddington has pointed out, 'it is one of the paradoxes of history that the trend of employment away from productive secondary industry into tertiary service work has been accompanied by a reduction in the status of domestic service.'[29] But there are signs that the paradox is being resolved. Already in the pre-nursery schools we have examples of skilled and acceptable domestic service – if not actually carried out in the home. The existence of highly mechanized domestic appliances and simplified power tools makes it possible to envisage the development of a whole range of domestic professions, taking in everything from cooking, cleaning, decorating and repairing, to many aspects of child-rearing, education, and recreation. The growth of such domestic workers, especially among young people, has already been noted in Sweden and the United States.

The prospect held out is of individuals or groups performing such services becoming 'attached' – not necessarily living-in – to particular houses, or a small group of them in a particular community, and becoming personally acquainted with family members as well as perhaps participating in a wider range of family or community activities. Something of this pattern is already observable, in a minor way, in the phenomenon of the student or 'au pair' girl who lives with the family, offering some domestic service in return for lodging, and who subsequently for all practical purposes actually joins and becomes a member of the family on a long-term basis.[30] We need also to note that the stigma of personal dependence, which has made many women in this century choose less well-paid and in many ways less agreeable work in shops and factories in preference to domestic service, seems now to many younger people less of a burden as well as less of a threat. To many, domestic service of this kind may seem more fulfilling and rewarding than life at the middle levels of the large-scale bureaucracies – not to mention on the dole.

A further building-up of the resources of the household – of people and projects – could come with a more literal extension of the family. Most industrial societies have looked with regret and despair on their inability to engage and to make use of the experience and energy of their old people – 'old', that is, at the retiring age of sixty or sixty-five, with something like ten to fifteen years of life remaining. Most of these people are condemned to a futile and mind-destroying existence in lonely isolated rooms or old peoples' homes. At the same time young married couples become housebound and 'privatized' with the arrival of young children, a process especially hard on the wife who may be attempting to pursue her own career. There seems no reason why these two groups should not be mutually supporting, and to their mutual benefit. Houses and estates could be so built as to make it possible for older relatives to rejoin their married children and their families at some stage after retirement. This need not necessarily mean living together in the very same house – perhaps an extension of it, perhaps a nearby dwelling. Older working-class families often show this extended family pattern. The newer working and middle classes have tended to develop more isolated nuclear families; but the changing aspirations of women as well as harder economic circumstances may make them come to regret such an organization and to take steps to do something about it. There is, after all, no shortage of services which elderly kin could offer in return for residential or other kinds of support. R. E. Pahl thus foresees a situation where 'the advantage of having elderly, but spry, kin in the immediate locality may discourage geographical mobility within the middle class and may encourage the extension of existing owner-occupied houses to include a grandparents' annexe.'[31] So that here too, as with the inclusion of professional domestic workers, we could see in the very structure of the family establishment a partial return to the 'extended' household – not necessarily extended *family* – of the pre-industrial system.

It is not difficult, especially in a country like Britain, to get emotional assent to proposals of this kind. The call for a return to a locality-based system integrating work, leisure, and family life (with its inevitable political concomitant of decentralized government), strikes warm chords in a society which has always celebrated the small against the large, the concrete against the general, locality and diversity against centrality and uniformity.[32] The motto 'small is beautiful' I have found to gain enthusiastic acceptance from groups as diverse as university students, head-masters, business executives, senior military officers, civil servants, trade unionists, and housewives. Distinguished visitors to this country have in recent years been led to protest at the national mood of breast-beating, and to argue that the features of traditional British society which are widely seen here as obstructive and stagnant are in fact its strength in the coming years. In a letter to *The Times* in October 1976 Professor Robert Socolow, the American physicist, expressed this view spiritedly:

> It seems likely to this visitor that the world's developed countries will be emulating Britain within a decade or less. The limits of nature's resources and the limits to our own cleverness in protecting ourselves from our own mischief put severe constraints on the level of activity any developed society will freely choose. As these limits are faced more and more squarely, the developed countries will acknowledge the vigour attained by a mature society that cherishes the past, cares for

its physical surroundings, socializes in pubs, and changes houses reluctantly . . . There is much wisdom embodied in your people's silent scepticism about participating in the current round of industrialization . . . When the next round of industrialization – which will emphasize durability, quality, and community-level systems – arrives, you will more quickly recognize how well matched its demands are to your national strengths.[33]

This is pleasant and flattering to the national pride. But is it also complacent and misleading? Is it possible, not only to maintain the characteristics of traditional British society that have stood out against the dominant currents of industrialism, but to reinforce and augment them? Does, for instance, the hope of a return to smaller units of production based on a skill-intensive technology run so directly counter to the main pressures of the existing industrial system that it must appear forlorn and futile? There are, and have been in the past, powerful voices proclaiming the technical impossibility of reverting to non-hierarchical, small-scale production – without, that is, sacrificing all the benefits of industrialism. Thus Friedrich Engels in 1894:

> If man, by dint of his knowledge and inventive genius, has subdued the forces of nature, the latter avenge themselves upon him by subjecting him, in so far as he employs them, to a veritable despotism independent of all social organization. Wanting to abolish authority in large-scale industry is tantamount to wanting to abolish industry itself, to destroy the power loom in order to return to the spinning wheel.[34]

Robert Heilbroner points to another and related kind of difficulty when he says that 'the machine has stamped the modern mind with notions of efficiency that go very deep, and that will not, I think, lose their force unless future societies shed not only capitalist but industrial assumptions.'[35]

No one will doubt the force of these remarks, or think that the deflection or re-direction of industrial routines will be anything but extremely difficult. But settled habits of thought make it more difficult than it really need be. The problem is as much one of being aware of alternative possibilities as of seeing the difficulties of realizing them in practice. Conventional accounts of crucial episodes in the past, especially, need to be re-examined, since so much of 'common sense' is faulty or biased historical memory. So it is important for the general argument that, in this particular example, we can at least say quite clearly that the evidence does not bear out Engels and those many others who have insisted on the need for large-scale hierarchical organization. The argument from technical necessity turns out to be based on very slender foundations when the origins of the factory system are re-examined. No one recognized this better than Engels' friend and collaborator Karl Marx, when he wrote:

> The accumulation and concentration of instruments and workers preceded the development of the division of labour inside the workshop. Manufacture consisted much more in the bringing together of many workers and many crafts in one place, in one room under the command of one capital, than in the analysis of labour and the adaptation of a special worker to a very simple task.[36]

Essentially the same point, of the non-technical reasons for the early factory system, comes out in Marx's observation that 'in England, strikes have regularly given rise to the invention and application of new machines. Machines were, it may be said, the weapon employed by the capitalists to quell the revolt of specialized labour.'[37]

In making these points, which he did explicitly to combat the views of those who saw the new factory system as a necessity to accommodate a new industrial technology, Marx drew heavily on Andrew Ure's *Philosophy of Manufactures* (1835). Marx emphasized what Ure brought out very plainly: that the factory system, with its centralization of men and machines, and its principle of hierarchy of organization, *preceded* the invention of most of the new machinery, as well as the extensive division of labour that developed only under the suggestion of the new mechanical inventions. So what was the primary achievement of the factory system? What was the original impulse behind it? Ure pointed to this in commenting on the real achievement of Richard Arkwright. This lay not so much in that commonly attributed to him, the invention of the water frame in spinning – Lewis Paul and several others had made a similar invention many years before. It lay in the fact that, perhaps for the first time ever, Arkwright managed to achieve mass work discipline by bringing all operations together in the factory. 'The main difficulty [faced by Arkwright],' Ure says,

did not, to my apprehension, lie so much in the invention of a proper self-acting mechanism for drawing out and twisting cotton into a continuous thread, as in . . . training human beings to renounce their desultory habits of work, and to identify themselves with the unvarying regularity of the complex automaton. To devise and administer a successful code of factory discipline, suited to the necessities of factory diligence, was the Herculean enterprise, the noble achievement of Arkwright.[38]

Later research bears out this interpretation of the factory system. Steven Marglin points out, for instance, that 'factory spinning took hold in the woollen industry as well as in cotton.' Its success in the wool trade could only have been for reasons of organization, because 'the technology of wool-spinning for many years after the factory made its appearance was the same in factory as in cottage; in both the "spinning jenny" was the basic machine well into the nineteenth century.'[39] Similarly in weaving: 'Long before the power loom became practicable, handloom weavers were brought together into workshops to weave by the same techniques that were employed in cottage industry . . . There is no evidence that the handloom in the capitalist's factory was any different from the one in the weaver's house.'[40] From these and similar examples he concludes that 'the key to the success of the factory, as well as its inspiration, was the substitution of capitalists' for workers' control of the production process; discipline and supervision could and did reduce costs without being technologically superior.'[41]

Of course, as Marx also recognized,[42] once the factory system was established for these kinds of reasons, technological innovation and work organization eventually and inevitably followed its contours and demands. Helped in England by a patent system which favoured inventions for factory rather than small-scale domestic use, the stream of inventions which previously favoured domestic as much as factory production was increasingly diverted exclusively towards factory application. In time this made the factory superior to the domestic unit, but only because the latter was neglected as a field of inventiveness and innovation. As Marglin says:

> It is important to emphasize that the discipline and supervision afforded by the factory system had nothing to do with efficiency, at least as this term is used by economists. Disciplining the work force meant a larger output in return for a greater input of labour, not more output for the same input . . . The factory system was not technologically superior to the putting-out system; at least not until technological change was channeled exclusively into this mould.[43]

The lesson is easy enough to draw. If, in so important an area, the conventional arguments about efficiency and technical necessity turn out to be so suspect, why not in many other areas? As a parallel to the process discussed here, the contemporary example of alternative sources of energy for industrial application immediately springs to mind. Here too people argue about the difficulty and expensiveness of switching to wind, water, or solar energy. But a good part of the difficulty consists in our unwillingness to see them as proper alternatives at all, and, above all, in our reluctance to devote a reasonable amount of money and talent to investigating their possibilities. As with the early factory system, power and money dictate the continuation of routines already established, for whatever original reason.

'Nothing that has not yet been done, can be done, except by means that have not yet been tried.' So said Francis Bacon.[44] The future remains open, infinitely variable even though infinitely limited by persistencies from the past. (Infinite collections contain one another, as Russell showed.) It so happens that all we can know are such persistencies from the past. The future itself, strictly speaking, remains unknown and unknowable. When we attempt to predict the future, on the basis of current trends, we are attempting to dominate the future by the past. A prediction that turns out to be true represents the triumph of continuity over change.

The practice of this procedure of thought is inevitable, and indeed generally there is nothing wrong with it. A future that does not involve continuities from the past is literally inconceivable and so there is nothing to be said or thought about it. But we can and should try to ensure that the domination of the past over the future is limited, not absolute. The future needs space for novelty, for inventiveness. The problems it inherits from the past cannot properly be solved by remedies conceived and executed in the principal terms of that past. Technological 'fixing' can clear up some of the problems created by technology, but it invariably creates others which cannot be so cleared up. So with all problems. They come trailing the conventional wisdom of the very time and circumstances that gave rise to them, and which therefore constitutes precisely part of the problem. Inventing the future, allowing it its own freedom to find new solutions, cannot involve perpetuating the hold of the dead hand of the past.

The problem with so much 'futurology' in the past decade has been just this attempt to close off the future. The future is conceived as a bigger, better, more efficient version of the present. Logically there is no reason why this should not turn out to be correct. In practice it will almost certainly be disastrous to confront the future with this vision and this expectation. The nature of the problems facing developed industrial societies – and so now the whole world – demands responses that have not been part of their central tradition of thought and practice. Partly we shall need to rescue practices and ideas which have been overwhelmed by industrialism, or which have persisted as marginal or subterranean currents. We will also need, no doubt, to invent new ones altogether, or at least a new synthesis of past and present practices. But we cannot allow, nor need we, the future to be the past writ large. If the passage from the industrial to the post-industrial society ever occurs it must live up to the promise of its name. The post-industrial society must contain a principle and a direction very different from that of the industrial, just as the latter distinguished itself radically from its pre-industrial forms. To express this as a hope and a requirement is very much in the spirit of the Saint-Simonian tradition. As the great theorist of that earlier momentous transition, Saint-Simon would surely have blessed this enterprise, even though it meant the eclipse of his own system.

Notes and References

1 New Worlds

1. J. B. Bury, *The Idea of Progress* (Macmillan, 1923).
2. Frank E. Manuel, *The Prophets of Paris* (Harper Torchbooks edn, New York, 1965).
3. ibid., p. 6.
4. As, for instance, in Herbert Spencer's famous assertion: 'Progress . . . is not an accident, but a necessity.' Spencer, *Social Statics* (John Chapman, London, 1851), p. 65.
5. Quoted Manuel, *Prophets of Paris*, p. 21.
6. For the quotations in this paragraph, see K. Kumar (ed.), *Revolution: The Theory and Practice of a European Idea* (Weidenfeld & Nicolson, 1971), p. 18.
7. See especially Hannah Arendt, *On Revolution* (Faber & Faber, 1963), Ch. 1.
8. Manuel, *Prophets of Paris*, p. 60.
9. ibid., p. 61.
10. Auguste Comte, *Plan des Travaux Scientifiques Nécessaires Pour Réorganiser la Société* (1822), Appendix to the *Système de Politique Positive* (Paris, 1929), IV, pp. 94–5.
11. Manuel, *Prophets of Paris*, p. 96.
12. Émile Durkheim, *Socialism* (trans. Charlotte Sattler, Collier Books, New York, 1962), p. 143. First given as lectures 1895–6.
13. George Lichtheim, *The Origins of Socialism* (Weidenfeld & Nicolson, 1969), p. 40. For the ferment of ideas during this period, centring around the concept of 'industrialism', and of the Saint-Simonian contribution to it, see also Shirley M. Gruner, *Economic Materialism and Social Moralism* (Mouton, The Hague, 1973).
14. Quoted Frank E. Manuel, *The New World of Henri Saint-Simon* (University of Notre Dame Press, Indiana, 1963), p. 191.
15. Quoted Sidney Pollard, *The Idea of Progress: History and Society* (Penguin Books, 1971), p. 109.

16. Quoted Manuel, *The New World of Henri Saint-Simon*, p. 221.
17. Quoted Pollard, *The Idea of Progress*, p. 110.
18. Quoted Durkheim, *Socialism*, p. 158.
19. Quoted ibid., p. 176.
20. Saint-Simon, 'On Social Organization', in *Social Organization, The Science of Man, and Other Writings* (trans. and ed. Felix Markham, Harper Torchbooks edn, New York, 1964), pp. 78–9.
21. This was particularly emphasized by Saint-Simon's greatest disciple, Durkheim, who wrote of his master:

    A definite social crisis had stirred his thought, and it was entirely to solve it that all his efforts were bent. His entire system, consequently, has a practical – not a remote – objective which he hastens to attain, and he has science do nothing but approach this goal. Therefore, although he was the first to have a really clear conception of what sociology had to be and its necessity, strictly speaking he did not create a sociology. He didn't use the method, whose principles he had so firmly stated, to discover the laws of evolution – social and general – but in order to answer the very special question – of entirely immediate interest – which can be formulated as follows: what is the social system required by the condition of European societies on the morrow of the Revolution? [Durkheim, *Socialism*, p. 146.]

22. There is an excellent account of the influence of the École Polytechnique in F. A. Hayek, *The Counter-Revolution of Science* (The Free Press of Glencoe, New York, 1955), pp. 105 ff.
23. Markham, Introduction to *Social Organization, etc.*, p. xli.
24. Hayek, *The Counter-Revolution of Science*, p. 165. For the importance of the Pereires brothers and the model of the Crédit Mobilier in the industrialization of Continental Europe (and beyond), see also A. Gerschenkron, *Economic Backwardness in Historical Perspective* (Harvard University Press, Cambridge, Mass., 1962), pp. 12ff., 22ff. Gerschenkron comments (p. 24):

    That Saint-Simon's stress upon the role to be played by the banks in economic development revealed a truly amazing – and altogether 'unutopian' – insight into the problems of that development is as true as the fact that Saint-Simonian ideas most decisively influenced the course of economic events inside and outside France.

25. Markham, op. cit., Introduction, p. xliv. And cf. the remark of the distinguished contemporary French economist, François Perroux: 'We have all become more or less Saint-Simonians', quoted S. Lukes, 'Saint-Simon', in T. Raison (ed.), *The Founding Fathers of Social Science* (Penguin Books, 1969), p. 27.

26. See the very interesting table of influences in Ghita Ionescu, 'Saint-Simon and the Politics of Industrial Societies', *Government and Opposition*, Vol. 8, No. 1, Winter 1973, p. 46.
27. Quoted Durkheim, *Socialism*, pp. 173–4.
28. Durkheim, *Socialism*, p. 177.
29. ibid., pp. 180–81.
30. Quoted Hayek, *The Counter-Revolution of Science*, p. 127.
31. Quoted Durkheim, *Socialism*, p. 192.
32. For a good account of the 'sublimation of politics' in nineteenth- and twentieth-century social thought, see Sheldon S. Wolin, *Politics and Vision* (Allen & Unwin, 1961), pp. 352ff.

2 The Great Transformation

1. See Anna Bezanson, 'The Early Use of the Term "Industrial Revolution" ', *Quarterly Journal of Economics*, Vol. XXXVI, 1921–2, pp. 343–49.
2. E. J. Hobsbawm, *The Age of Revolution 1789–1848* (The New American Library, New York, 1964), p. 46.
3. Carlo Cipolla (ed.), Introduction to *The Industrial Revolution* (Collins/Fontana, 1973), p. 7.
4. For a discussion with some well-chosen illustrations, see Francis D. Klingender, *Art and the Industrial Revolution* (Paladin Books, 1972. First published in 1947).
5. For the literary and cultural responses to industrialization in England, see R. Williams, *Culture and Society 1780–1950* (Penguin Books, 1963).
6. R. Williams, *The English Novel from Dickens to Lawrence* (Chatto & Windus, 1970), p. 11. See also idem., *The Country and the City* (Chatto & Windus, 1973).
7. It is interesting that as late as 1961 Lewis Mumford could still use 'Coketown' in this generic sense in his discussion of industrial cities. See *The City in History* (Penguin Books, 1966), Ch. 15: 'Palaeotechnic Paradise: Coketown', and the comment (p. 509): 'In a greater or lesser degree, every city in the Western World was stamped with the archetypal characteristics of Coketown.'
8. Thomas Carlyle, 'Signs of the Times' (1829), in A. Shelston (ed.), *Thomas Carlyle: Selected Writings* (Penguin Books, 1971), pp. 65, 67.
9. Williams, *Culture and Society*, p. 108.
10. V. I. Lenin, 'Frederick Engels', in H. Pollitt (ed.), *Lenin on Britain* (Martin Lawrence, 1934), p. 18.

11. W. O. Henderson and W. H. Chaloner, Introduction to their translation of F. Engels, *The Condition of the Working Class in England* (Basil Blackwell, 1958; first published in German in 1845), *passim*. For an interesting treatment of the book precisely as a kind of imaginative literature, see Steven Marcus, *Engels, Manchester and the Working Class* (Vintage Books, New York, 1974).
12. 'The way in which Engels handled his material falls well below generally-accepted standards of scholarship', is how Henderson and Chaloner severely put it: op. cit., Introduction, p. xx. For a different assessment of Engels' status as a historian, see E. J. Hobsbawm, 'History and the "Dark Satanic Mills"', in his *Labouring Men: Studies in the History of Labour* (Weidenfeld & Nicolson, 1964), pp. 105–119.
13. Cf. R. Bendix's remark that 'Western modernization has been accompanied throughout by a particular intellectual construction of that experience, prompted by moral or reforming impulses often presented in the guise of scientific generalizations': 'Tradition and Modernity Re-considered', *Comparative Studies in Society and History*, Vol. XI, 1967, p. 313.
14. P. Abrams, 'The Sense of the Past and the Origins of Sociology', *Past and Present*, No. 55, May 1972, p. 22.
15. There is a particularly good treatment of the brilliant school of social theorists in post-1815 France, who seem to have been the first to analyse systematically the idea of a 'general crisis', in Shirley M. Gruner, *Economic Materialism and Social Moralism* (Mouton, The Hague, 1973), pp. 87ff.
16. K. Marx, letter to P. V. Annenkov (1846) in K. Marx and F. Engels, *Selected Correspondence* (Foreign Languages Publishing House, Moscow, 1953), p. 40.
17. Clark Kerr, John T. Dunlop, Frederick Harbison, C. A. Myers, *Industrialism and Industrial Man* (Penguin Books, 2nd edn, 1973), p. 42.
18. Quoted Abrams, 'The Sense of the Past and the Origins of Sociology', p. 22. And cf. the similar sentiments of John Stuart Mill:

> Scarcely any one, in the more educated classes, seems to have any opinions, or to place any real faith in those which he professes to have . . . It requires in these times much more intellect to marshal so much greater a stock of ideas and observations. This has not yet been done, or has been done only by very few: and hence the multitude of thoughts only breeds increase of uncertainty. Those who should be the guides of the rest, see too many sides to every question. They hear so much said,

or find that so much can be said, about everything, that they feel no assurance of the truth of anything. [Quoted Walter E. Houghton, *The Victorian Frame of Mind 1830–1870* (Yale University Press, New Haven, 1957), p. 13.]

19. For these typologies see, in order: Herbert Spencer, *The Principles of Sociology*, 3 Vols., 1876–97; F. Tönnies, *Community and Society* (*Gemeinschaft und Gesellschaft*), 1887; Sir Henry Maine, *Ancient Law*, 1861; E. Durkheim, *The Division of Labour in Society*, 1893; M. Weber, *The Theory of Social and Economic Organization*, 1925; R. Redfield, 'The Folk Society', *American Journal of Sociology*, Vol. LII, No. 4, 1947, pp. 293–308; H. Becker, 'Sacred and Secular Societies', *Social Forces*, Vol. 28, No. 4, 1950, pp. 361–76.
20. J. D. Y. Peel, *Herbert Spencer: The Evolution of a Sociologist* (Heinemann, 1971), pp. 198–200.
21. In which rehabilitation Saint-Simon was of course a key figure. For the significance of the new evaluation of the Middle Ages for nineteenth-century sociology, see R. Nisbet, *The Sociological Tradition* (Heinemann, 1967), *passim* – although I think he overstresses his case.
22. K. Marx, letter to the editors of the Russian journal *Otechestvenniye Zapiski* (1877), in S. Avineri (ed.), *Karl Marx on Colonialism and Modernization* (Doubleday & Co., New York, 1969), p. 469.
23. cf. this comment from Clark Kerr *et al.*, op. cit., p. 56: 'Every industrialized society is more like every other industrialized society – however great the differences between them – than any industrial society is like any pre-industrial society.'
24. E. Gellner, *Thought and Change* (Weidenfeld & Nicolson, 1964), pp. 35, 49. And cf. the similar attitude of T. Burns: 'Industry is the characteristic institution of modern advanced societies. So much so, indeed, that the old distinction between "civilized" and "primitive", "literate" and "pre-literate" societies is nowadays preserved and given relevance in the terms "industrial" and "non industrial" . . .' Introduction to T. Burns (ed.), *Industrial Man* (Penguin Books, 1969), p. 7.

3 The Revolution Defined: The Image of Industrialism

1. E. A. Wrigley, 'The Process of Modernization and the Industrial Revolution in England', *The Journal of Interdisciplinary History*, Vol. III, No. 2, Autumn 1972, p. 226.
2. See W. W. Rostow, *The Stages of Economic Growth* (Cambridge University Press, 1960).
3. For such a list, see, e.g., Introduction to Tom Burns (ed.), *Industrial Man* (Penguin Books, 1969), p. 7.
4. For international comparisons see Table 2 in Clark Kerr *et al.*, *Industrialism and Industrial Man* (Penguin Books, 1973; first published in 1960), p. 50.
5. ibid., p. 49. For the argument that industrialization and urbanization are strongly and positively correlated, see also S. Kuznets, 'Consumption, Industrialization, and Urbanization', in Bert F. Hoselitz and Wilbert E. Moore (eds.), *Industrialization and Society* (UNESCO, Mouton, 1966), pp. 99–115; and N. Ginsburg 'The City and Modernization', in M. Weiner (ed.), *Modernization: The Dynamics of Growth* (Basic Books, New York, 1966), pp. 122–37.
6. Although one is clearly now on the way. See, e.g., David Harvey, *Social Justice and the City* (Edward Arnold, 1973); and C. G. Pickvance (ed.), *Urban Sociology: Critical Essays* (Tavistock Publications, 1976).
7. For these figures, see J. Steven Watson, *The Reign of George III 1760–1815* (Oxford University Press, 1960), pp. 13, 517–18; H. J. Dyos, *Urbanity and Suburbanity* (Leicester University Press, 1973), pp. 10–11; Eric E. Lampard, 'The Urbanizing World', in H. J. Dyos and M. Wolff (eds.), *The Victorian City: Images and Realities* (2 Vols., Routledge & Kegan Paul, 1973), Vol. I, pp. 3–57.
8. In 1801 there were 21 cities in Europe with a population of more than 100,000; by 1901 there were 147, accounting for at least a tenth of Europe's population: Asa Briggs, *Victorian Cities* (Penguin Books, 1968), p. 85.
9. For some valuable reflections on this theme, especially as applied to Dickens, see Raymond Williams, *The Country and the City* (Chatto & Windus, 1973), pp. 142ff. It is a point also repeatedly stressed in Briggs, *Victorian Cities*.
10. F. Engels, *The Condition of the Working Class in England* (trans. and eds. W. O. Henderson and W. H. Chaloner, Basil Blackwell, 1958), p. 31.

11. Ferdinand Tönnies, *Community and Society* (*Gemeinschaft und Gesellschaft*) (trans. and ed. Charles P. Loomis, Harper & Row, New York, 1963; original German publication 1887), pp. 227, 232. And cf. the following interesting passage:

> The village and town [of the *Gemeinschaft*] have in common the principle of social organization in space, instead of the principle of time which predominates through the generations of the family, the tribe, and the people. Because it descends from common ancestors, the family has invisible metaphysical roots, as if they were hidden in the earth. The living individuals in the family are connected with each other by the sequence of past and future generations. But in village and town it is the physical, real soil, the permanent location, the visible land, which create the strongest ties and relations. During the period of the *Gemeinschaft* the younger principle of space remains bound to the older principle of time. In the period of *Gesellschaft* they become disconnected, and from this disconnection results the city. It is the exaggeration of the principle of space in its urban form. In this exaggeration the urban form becomes sharply contrasted with the rural form of the same principle, for the village remains essentially and almost necessarily bound to both principles. In this sense the whole continual development may be considered as a process of increasing urbanization ... That is, from a certain point on, the towns by their influence and importance achieve, in the nation; predominance over the rural organization. In consequence country and village must use more of their own productive forces for the support and furtherance of the urban areas than they can spare for purposes of reproduction. Therefore, the rural organization is doomed to dissolution, which in consequence leads later on to a decay of its organs and functions. [ibid., pp. 232–3.]

12. Georg Simmel, 'The Metropolis and Mental Life', in *The Sociology of Georg Simmel* (trans. and ed. Kurt H. Wolff, The Free Press, New York, 1950), pp. 409–24. Simmel's essay first appeared, in German, in 1902–3.
13. Louis Wirth, 'Urbanism as a Way of Life', *American Journal of Sociology*, Vol. XLIV, July 1938.
14. Emile Durkheim, *The Division of Labour in Society* (trans. George Simpson, The Free Press, New York, 1933; first published in French in 1893), p. 296. And cf. this spirited defence of the industrial city from Joseph Cowen, the northern politician and editor of the influential *Newcastle Chronicle*:

> The gathering of men into crowds [he wrote in 1877] has some drawbacks, yet the concentration of citizens, like the concentration of

soldiers, is a source of strength. The ancient boroughs were the arks and shrines of freedom. Today, behind the dull roar of our machinery, the bellowing of our blast furnaces, the panting of the locomotives and the gentle ticking of the electric telegraph . . . we can hear the songs of children who are fed and clad, and the acclaim of a world made free by these agencies. When people declaim in doleful numbers against the noise and dirt of the busy centres of population, they should remember the liberty we enjoy as a consequence of the mental activity and enterprise which have been generated by the contact of mind with mind brought together in great towns. [Quoted Briggs, *Victorian Cities*, p. 67.]

15. Population figures in this section are from A. Armengaud, 'Population in Europe 1700–1914', in Carlo Cipolla (ed.), *The Industrial Revolution* (Collins/Fontana, 1973), pp. 22–76; and Kingsley Davis, 'Population', in Garrett Hardin (ed.), *Science, Conflict, and Society*, Readings from *Scientific American* (W. H. Freeman & Co., San Francisco, n.d.), pp. 101–110.
16. There is a clear statement of the thesis in Davis, 'Population'. For a critical discussion of the argument see H. J. Habakkuk, *Population Growth and Economic Development since 1750* (Leicester University Press, 1971).
17. For the Japanese case, with comparisons, see Davis, 'Population', pp. 105–7.
18. For European projections, see the report *Post-War Demographic Trends in Europe and the Outlook until the Year 2000*, prepared by The United Nations Economic Commission for Europe, July 1975. The report (which is summarized in *The Times*, 8 July 1975) predicts zero population growth in Europe by the turn of the century. For Britain, figures showing a similar trend were published by the Office of Population Censuses and Surveys in 1976. See *The Times*, 3 August 1976.
19. For some representative reactions in early Victorian England, see Walter E. Houghton, *The Victorian Frame of Mind 1830–1870* (Yale University Press, New Haven, 1957), pp. 54–58.
20. Tönnies, *Community and Society*, p. 192.
21. ibid., pp. 64–5.
22. Karl Marx and Friedrich Engels, *Manifesto of the Communist Party*, in Marx and Engels, *Selected Works in Two Volumes* (Foreign Languages Publishing House, Moscow, 1962), Vol. 1, pp. 36–7.
23. For the importance of conservative thought on the early sociolo-

gists, see Leon Bramson, *The Political Context of Sociology* (Princeton University Press, Princeton, 1961); and, especially, Robert A. Nisbet, *The Sociological Tradition* (Heinemann, 1967). Nisbet indeed asserts that 'the most fundamental and far-reaching of sociology's unit ideas is community. The re-discovery of community is unquestionably the most distinctive development in nineteenth century social thought . . .' (p. 47).

24. The outstanding treatment, if not indeed definition, of this tradition, is Raymond Williams, *Culture and Society 1780–1950* (Penguin Books, 1961).

25. On all this, see Durkheim, *The Division of Labour in Society*. Spencer's similar account focused on the process of evolution from 'homogeneity' to 'heterogeneity', the last expressing a condition or state having both the qualities of high individualism as well as high interdependence – and so very similar to Durkheim's concept of 'organic solidarity'. But characteristically Spencer, unlike Durkheim, saw the process in cosmic, and not merely human or social, terms. Cf. this early (1857) statement on the law of progress:

> We believe we have shown beyond question, that that which the German physiologists have found to be the law of organic development, is the law of all development. The advance from the simple to the complex, through a process of successive differentiations, is seen alike in the earliest changes of the Universe to which we can reason our way back; and in the earliest changes which we can inductively establish; it is seen in the geologic and climatic evolution of the Earth, and of every single organism on its surface; it is seen in the evolution of Humanity, whether contemplated in the civilized individual, or in the aggregation of races; it is seen in the evolution of Society in respect alike of its political, its religious, and its economical organization; and it is seen in the evolution of all those endless concrete and abstract products of human activity which constitute the environment of our daily life. From the remotest past which science can fathom, up to the novelties of yesterday, that in which Progress essentially consists, is the transformation of the homogeneous into the heterogeneous. [Spencer, 'Progress: Its Law and Causes', in *Essays, Scientific, Political and Speculative* (3 Vols., Williams & Norgate, London and Edinburgh, 1891), Vol. 1. p. 35.]

26. Adam Smith, *The Wealth of Nations* (2 Vols., Everyman edn, Dent & Sons, 1910), Vol. 1, p. 5.

27. Karl Marx, *Capital* (trans. Eden and Cedar Paul in 2 Vols.,

Everyman edn, J. M. Dent & Sons, 1930), Vol. 1, pp. 374–7. See also Marx, *The Poverty of Philosophy* (International Publishers, New York, 1963), pp. 135–6.

The confusion between the two forms of the division of labour is common in contemporary sociology. See, e.g., the following assertion by Wilbert Moore:

> Social differentiation and division of labour are universal attributes of human society. Contrary to the view persisting into the recent past that primitive man lives in completely homogeneous and amorphous groups, modern knowledge of primitive and peasant communities reveals more complexity and specialization . . . modern specialization cannot therefore be contrasted with an assumed society or period having no division of labour. The difference is one of degree and not of kind. [Moore, 'The Attributes of an Industrial Order' in S. Nosow and W. H. Form (eds.), *Man, Work and Society*, (Atherton, New York, 1962), pp. 92–3.]

28. Ruskin, quoted R. Williams, *Culture and Society 1780–1950*, p. 147.
29. Durkheim, *The Division of Labour in Society*, p. 371.
30. ibid., p. 377.
31. ibid., p. 401.
32. For a powerful statement of this view, see Ernest Gellner, *Thought and Change* (Weidenfeld & Nicolson, 1964), Ch. 2.
33. Durkheim, *Division of Labour in Society*, pp. 221–2.
34. Marx and Engels, *Manifesto of the Communist Party*, p. 38.
35. Alexis de Tocqueville, *Democracy in America* (2 Vols., trans. Henry Reeve, Schocken Books, New York, 1961; first published in French 1835–40), Vol. 1, pp. lxx–lxxi.
36. Tocqueville comments that the ideal society of the eighteenth-century *philosophes* and of the French Revolution inspired by them was one 'in which all was simple, uniform, coherent, equitable, and rational in the full sense of the term'. *The Ancien Régime and the French Revolution* (trans. Stuart Gilbert, Collins/Fontana, 1966; first published in French in 1865), p. 167.
37. J. S. Mill, 'On Liberty' (1859), *The Essential Works of John Stuart Mill* (ed. Max Lerner, Bantam Books, New York, 1961), pp. 320–21.
38. Jacob Burckhardt, *Reflections on History* (trans. M. D. Hottinger, Allen & Unwin, 1943; given as lectures 1868–71, first published as a collection in 1906), p. 116.
39. Tocqueville, *Democracy in America*, Vol. 2, pp. 370–72.

40. It is sometimes said – e.g., by Nisbet, *The Sociological Tradition*, pp. 200ff. – that as opposed to this image of the industrial society as mass and atomized – the image presented by Mill, Tocqueville, and Burckhardt – there was counterposed the Marxist image of industrial society as communal, in the sense of a society divided into highly cohesive class communities. This seems to me to misunderstand Marx's account of capitalist industrial society. Marx is very conscious that, with industrialism, a historical threshold has been crossed. There is no sense in which the class society of the bourgeois epoch is anything like the pre-industrial society of estates, ranks, and orders. Industrialism has reduced class to the most naked and explicit criterion of economic interest – and it has done so in the full glare of a national, centralized society, in which individuals are massed together, always conscious of each other's lives, always conscious of respective gains and losses. Not only is this true of relations between the classes, between bourgeoisie and proletariat. It is also true of the relations between individuals of the same class, who in the social order of industrialism are *normally*, and for most of the time, in an intense competitive relationship with each other. Marx makes this clear when he says that 'The separate individuals form a class only insofar as they have to carry on a common battle against another class; otherwise they are on hostile terms with each other as competitors' (*The German Ideology*, Pt I: Feuerbach). Elsewhere, (*Capital*, vol. 3) he speaks of the 'infinite distinctions of interest and position which the social division of labour created *among* workers as *among* capitalists and landowners' (my italics). The inference here must be that it is only as class conflict reaches a certain point, and forces individuals into a realization of their common class interest, that any real sense of communal consciousness develops in industrial society at all; and that point may very well not be reached until very late in the developent of industrial society (for a non-Marxist, it may not of course be reached at all).

Now this is very remote indeed from the genuinely communal groupings of pre-industrial society, one of whose premises was a necessary *insulation* between social groups, so that consciousness of each other's doings and aspirations was limited. Marx by contrast is much closer to Mill and Tocqueville than Nisbet supposes – his bourgeois industrial society is one in which all the old religious, geographical and even occupational barriers have come down, and 'has left remaining no other nexus between man and man than callous "cash payment"' (*Manifesto of the Communist Party*). This was the *terrible simplification* brought about by industrialization.

41. Alfred de Musset, quoted Lewis Coser, *Men of Ideas* (The Free Press, New York, 1965), p. 101.
42. Quoted J. F. C. Harrison, *The Early Victorians 1832–51* (Panther Books, 1973), p. 151. For details of the Census of 1851, see G. Kitson Clark, *The Making of Victorian England* (Methuen, 1962), pp. 148–9.
43. F. Engels, 'Special Introduction' (1892) to the English edition of 'Socialism: Utopian and Scientific', in Marx-Engels, *Selected Works in 2 Vols.* (Foreign Languages Publishing House, Moscow, n.d.), Vol. 2, p. 99.
44. R. C. K. Ensor, *England 1870–1914* (Oxford University Press, 1936), p. 526. For the religious censuses of this period, bearing out this point, see pp. 308–9. See also Henry Pelling, 'Popular Attitudes to Religion' in his *Popular Politics and Society in Late Victorian Britain* (Macmillan, 1968), pp. 19–36, for evidence of the further decline of working-class support for religion.
45. For the contemporary data, see Geoffrey Gorer, *Exploring English Character* (The Cresset Press, 1955), pp. 237–77; Bryan Wilson, *Religion in Secular Society* (Penguin Books, 1969), pp. 21–39; and *Social Trends*, annually from 1970 (H.M.S.O.).
46. Wilson, *Religion in Secular Society*, pp. 34–5, 38.
47. Harold Perkin, *The Making of English Society 1780–1880* (Routledge & Kegan Paul, 1969), p. 203.
48. Perkin, *The Making of English Society*, p. 203.
49. Durkheim, *The Elementary Forms of the Religious Life* (trans. J. W. Swain, Allen & Unwin, 1915; first published in French 1912), p. 427.
50. For some powerful contemporary accounts of the religious character of the French Revolution, see the extracts in K. Kumar (ed.), *Revolution: The Theory and Practice of a European Idea* (Weidenfeld & Nicolson, 1971), pp. 111–15. Engels himself drew the parallel between Christianity and Socialism as social movements in his 1895 Preface to Marx's *The Class Struggles in France 1848–50*.
51. Carl Becker, *The Heavenly City of the Eighteenth Century Philosophers* (Yale University Press, New Haven, 1932).
52. Alasdair MacIntyre, *Secularization and Moral Change* (Oxford University Press, 1967), pp. 7–8.

53. Peter L. Berger, *The Social Reality of Religion* (Faber & Faber, 1969), p. 107. For a further discussion, see Peter G. Forster, 'Secularization in the English Context: Some Conceptual and Empirical Problems', *Sociological Review*, Vol. 20, May 1972, pp. 153–68.
54. Tocqueville, in Kumar (ed.), *Revolution*, p. 115.
55. Max Weber, 'Science as a Vocation', in H. Gerth and C. Wright Mills, *From Max Weber: Essays in Sociology* (Routledge & Kegan Paul, 1948), p. 155.
56. Julien Freund, *The Sociology of Max Weber* (Allen Lane The Penguin Press, 1968), p. 18.
57. Weber's clearest statement on the all-embracing movement towards rationalization in western society is to be found in his Introduction to his *The Protestant Ethic and the Spirit of Capitalism* (trans. T. Parsons, Unwin Books, 1930; first published in 1904–5 in German).
58. Weber, 'Science as a Vocation', p. 139.
59. Although the example is not his, the line of argument here is close to Herbert Marcuse's critique of Weber, 'Industrialization and Capitalism in the work of Max Weber', *New Left Review*, 30, March–April 1965, pp. 3–17.
60. Weber, *The Protestant Ethic*, p. 16.
61. ibid., p. 16.
62. Weber, 'Bureaucracy', in Gerth and Mills, *From Max Weber*, p. 229.
63. ibid., p. 226.
64. Weber, quoted Marcuse, 'Industrialization and Capitalism . . .', p. 15; and in Nisbet, *The Sociological Tradition*, p. 299.
65. For the idea of modernity as a 'package', see Peter L. Berger, Brigitte Berger, and Hansfried Kellner, *The Homeless Mind* (Penguin Books, 1974).

4 The Revolution Dissected: Image and Reality

1. Robert Nisbet, *The Sociological Tradition* (Heinemann, 1967), p. 317.
2. Of a large literature it is perhaps sufficient to cite A. Kornharser, *The Politics of Mass Society* (The Free Press, Glencoe, 1959), who refers extensively to contemporary theories of mass society.
3. For representative examples of such a list of 'concomitants of industrialization', see Joseph A. Kahl, 'Some Social Concomitants

of Industrialization and Urbanization', in William A. Faunce (ed.), *Readings in Industrial Sociology* (Appleton-Century-Crofts, New York, 1967), pp. 28–67; H. Wilensky and C. N. Lebeaux, *Industrial Society and Social Welfare* (2nd edn, The Free Press, New York, 1965), Chs. 3–5. An influential study of the family that draws especially on this tradition is N. Smelser, *Social Change in the Industrial Revolution* (Routledge & Kegan Paul, 1959). Durkheim himself was impressed not only by the specialization of functions outside the family but within it as well:

> The history of the family, from its very origins, is only an uninterrupted movement of dissociation in the course of which diverse functions, at first undivided and confounded one with another, have been little by little separated, constituted apart, apportioned among the relatives according to age, sex, relations of dependence, in a way to make each of them a special functionary of domestic society. [*The Division of Labour in Society* (trans. George Simpson, The Free Press, New York, 1933), p. 123.]

4. For examples of general accounts focusing on these characteristic problems, see E. Lampard, 'The Social Impact of the Industrial Revolution', in Melvin Kranzberg and Caroll W. Pursell (eds.), *Technology in Western Civilization* (Madison, Wisconsin, 1967), pp. 302–21; Wolfram Fischer, 'Social Tensions at Early Stages of Industrialization', *Comparative Studies in Society and History*, Vol. 9, 1966–7, pp. 64–83; N. Smelser, 'Mechanisms of Change and Adjustment to Change', in Bert F. Hoselitz and Wilbert E. Moore (eds.), *Industrialization and Society* (UNESCO-Mouton, The Hague, 1966), pp. 32–54.
5. Nisbet, *The Sociological Tradition*, pp. 42–4.
6. See, e.g., Faunce and Form, 'The Nature of Industrial Society', in William A. Faunce and William H. Form (eds.), *Comparative Perspectives on Industrial Society* (Little, Brown & Company, Boston, 1969), pp. 1–18.
7. For a clear and helpful explanation of Parsons' pattern variables, and their relation to the typologies of Tönnies, Weber, and others, see the Introduction by Charles Loomis and John McKinney to Loomis' translation of Tönnies' *Community and Society* (Harper & Row, New York, 1963), pp. 1–29.
8. See, e.g., Talcott Parsons, 'Some Principal Characteristics of Industrial Societies', in Cyril E. Black (ed.), *The Transformation of Russian Society* (Harvard University Press, Cambridge, Mass.,

1960), pp. 13–42; and cf. also E. A. Wrigley, 'The Process of Modernization and the Industrial Revolution in England', *The Journal of Interdisciplinary History*, Vol. 111, No. 2, Autumn 1972, pp. 225–59, who uses Parsons' pattern variables as the basis of his concept of modernization, but argues interestingly that this is only contingently related to industrialization.

9. For some valuable critical reflections on nineteenth-century sociology's use (or abuse) of history, see Philip Abrams, 'The Sense of the Past and the Origins of Sociology', *Past and Present*, No. 55, May 1972, pp. 18–32; and Ian Weinberg, 'The Problem of the Convergence of Industrial Societies: a Critical Look at the State of a Theory', *Comparative Studies in Society and History*, Vol. 11, No. 1, Jan. 1969, pp. 1–15.
10. For an effective critical review of such literature, see H. Bernstein, 'Modernization Theory and the Sociological Study of Development', *Journal of Development Studies*, Vol. 7, No. 2., 1971, pp. 141–160.
11. There are now some excellent critiques of this aspect of nineteenth-century sociology. See Karl Popper, *The Poverty of Historicism* (Routledge & Kegan Paul, 1957); Kenneth Bock, 'Evolution, Function, and Change', *American Sociological Review*, Vol. 28, No. 2., 1963, pp. 229–37: E. Gellner, *Thought and Change* (Weidenfeld & Nicolson, 1964), Ch. 1; R. Nisbet, *Social Change and History: Aspects of the Western Theory of Development* (Oxford University Press, 1969).
12. It should hardly need pointing out these days (but unfortunately still does) how little this conception was related, and how little owing, to the Darwinian concept of evolution, which it preceded not just by decades but by centuries. See especially Kenneth Bock, 'Darwin and Social Theory', *Philosophy of Science*, Vol. 22., No. 2, 1955, pp. 123–34; and J. W. Burrow, *Evolution and Society* (Cambridge University Press, 1966).
13. This, of course, precisely *was* Darwin's problem, and why he offered the 'causal mechanics' of natural selection. It is a measure of just how different are the interests, preoccupations, and explanatory devices of Darwinian evolution compared with the common forms of nineteenth-century evolutionism (which T. H. Huxley rightly described as 'the oldest of all philosophies').
14. Quoted P. Abrams, 'The Sense of the Past and the Origins of Sociology', p. 28.
15. For some influential examples of this approach in contemporary

theories of modernization, see W. W. Rostow, *The Stages of Economic Growth* (Cambridge University Press, 1960); Almond's Introduction to G. Almond and J. S. Coleman (eds.), *The Politics of the Developing Areas* (Princeton University Press, Princeton, 1960); D. Lerner, *The Passing of Traditional Society* (The Free Press, New York, 1958). For criticisms of this approach, see note 10, above.

16. cf. Reinhard Bendix:

> It was indeed a unique constellation of circumstances which gave new emphasis to the old view that social change is internal to the society changing, that social change originates in the division of labour, and that, consequently, government or the state are products of the social structure. It may be suggested that this intellectual perspective unduly generalizes from a very limited phase of the English experience. [Bendix, 'Tradition and Modernity Reconsidered', *Comparative Studies in History and Society*, Vol. XI, 1966–7, p. 325.]

The special nature of the English case of industrialization is also emphasized in the excellent discussion by H. J. Habakkuk, 'The Historical Experience on the Basic Conditions of Economic Progress', in S. N. Eisenstadt (ed.), *Comparative Perspectives on Social Change* (Little, Brown & Company, Boston, 1968), pp. 29–45. See also H. Freudenberger and F. Redlich, 'The Industrial Development of Europe: Reality, Symbols Images', *Kyklos*, Vol. XVII, 1964, pp. 372–401. The authors show the misleading inferences drawn by such theorists as Marx and Sombart concerning the stages of industrial development, from their excessive attention to the experience of the English textile industry.

Perhaps the nearest thing to the British experience was the case of North American industrialization in the late nineteenth century. But even here the form of industrialization, and especially the response to it, was complicated by the presence of groups of very diverse ethnic origin (not to mention, of course, the legacy of black slavery), as well as the phenomenon of the moving frontier.

17. David Landes, *The Unbound Prometheus: Technical Change and Industrial Development in Western Europe from 1750 to the Present* (Cambridge University Press, 1969), p. 129.
18. ibid., p. 139.
19. See W. W. Rostow, *The Stages of Economic Growth*, *passim*.
20. Alexander Gerschenkron, 'The Typology of Industrial Development as a Tool of Analysis', in his *Continuity in History and Other Essays* (The Belknap Press, Cambridge, Mass., 1968), p. 83.

21. For a stimulating discussion of the various 'routes to modernity', see especially Barrington Moore, Jr, *The Social Origins of Dictatorship and Democracy* (Allen Lane The Penguin Press, 1967). See also Alain Touraine, 'An Introduction to the Study of Social Classes in a Dependent Society', Paper presented to the Annual Meeting of the British Sociological Association, University of Kent at Canterbury, March 1975.
22. Gerschenkron, 'Reflections on the Concept of "Prerequisites" of Modern Industrialization', in his *Economic Backwardness in Historical Perspective* (Harvard University Press, Cambridge, Mass., 1962), p. 44.
23. The structured differences in the mode of industrialization caused by varying degrees of "backwardness" are illuminatingly discussed in Gerschenkron, 'Economic Backwardness in Historical Perspective', pp. 5–30 of the book of the same name (see note 22). A famous earlier generalization of this type, still very fruitful, was Trotsky's 'Law of Combined and Uneven Development', in the first part of his *History of the Russian Revolution* (1929).
24. Such a periodization has been especially influential through the writings of the Hungarian Marxist theoretician Georg Lukacs. See, e.g., his *Studies in European Realism* (Grosset & Dunlap, New York, 1964).
25. Landes, *The Unbound Prometheus*, p. 124.
26. ibid., p. 65.
27. ibid., p. 118. For the long persistence, and co-existence, of the putting-out system, see also Maurice Dobb, *Studies in the Development of Capitalism* (rev. edn, Routledge & Kegan Paul, 1963), pp. 263–5.
28. Eric Hobsbawm, 'Custom, Wages, and Work Load', in his *Labouring Men: Studies in the History of Labour* (Weidenfeld & Nicolson, 1964), pp. 344–70.
29. Dobb, *Studies in the Development of Capitalism*, p. 266. See also Landes, op. cit., pp. 305–7.
30. For Marx's account of the growing subordination of the countryside to the towns, see especially *The German Ideology* (International Publishers, New York, 1947), pp. 43–58. There is a careful discussion, along Marxist lines, in J. Merrington, 'Town and Country in the Transition to Capitalism', *New Left Review*, No. 93, Sept.–Oct. 1975, pp. 71–92.
31. It is worth pointing out here, however, that this increase in the numbers living in towns was not at the expense of the countryside.

Far from draining the population from the countryside to towns, the 'industrialization' of agriculture actually increased the demand for farm labour: from 1750 to 1830, Britain's agricultural counties doubled their population. See J. D. Chambers, 'Enclosure and the Labour supply in the Industrial Revolution', *Economic History Review*, 2nd Series V, 1953, pp. 318–43.

32. J. D. Marshall, quoted R. E. Pahl, *Patterns of Urban Life* (Longman, 1970), p. 21. Scott and Tilly indicate a further interesting aspect of rural to urban continuity in the pattern of women's work in the nineteenth century. As they show, there was nothing particularly new in the employment of women outside the home – it was a common feature of rural and peasant life. Thus whether we consider employment as factory workers or as domestic servants, what we are seeing is a pattern whereby 'traditional families, operating on long-held values, sent their daughters to take advantage of increased opportunities generated by industrialization and urbanization.' See Joan W. Scott and Louise A. Tilly, 'Women's Work and the Family in Nineteenth Century Europe', *Comparative Studies in Society and History*, Vol. 17, No. 1., 1975, p. 42.
33. Pahl, op. cit., p. 21. In this account of the pattern of English urbanization I have drawn directly on Pahl's discussion.
34. For useful surveys of such studies, see Viola Klein, *Samples from English Culture* (2 Vols., Routledge & Kegan Paul, 1965); and R. Frankenberg, *Communities in Modern Britain* (Penguin Books, 1966).
35. D. H. Lawrence, 'Nottingham and the Mining Country', in *Selected Essays* (Penguin Books, 1950), p. 121. And cf. Fred Inglis: 'The History of English 19th Century art, literature and music, and much of the past 70 years as well, has been the history of a national imagination trying to keep faith with its rural memories and at the same time to make cities it can believe in.' Inglis, 'Townscape', in Denys Thompson (ed.), *Discrimination and Popular Culture* (2nd edn, Penguin Books, 1973), p. 25.
36. Raphael Samuel, 'Comers and Goers', in H. J. Dyos and M. Wolff (eds.), *The Victorian City: Images and Realities* (2 Vols., Routledge & Kegan Paul, 1973), Vol. 1, pp. 123–60.
37. ibid., p. 152.
38. ibid., p. 153.
39. R. C. K. Ensor, *England 1870–1914* (Oxford University Press, 1936), p. 137.
40. H. Trevor-Roper, 'Apologia Transfugae', Presidential Address

delivered at the annual meeting of the Joint Association of Classical Teachers, Leicester, 19 May 1973. Reprinted in the *Spectator*, 14 July 1973.

41. ibid.
42. Marx's speech at the Hague Conference is reported by Karl Kautsky, *The Dictatorship of the Proletariat* (Ann Arbor, University of Michigan Press, 1964; first published 1918), pp. 9–10. The remark quoted occurs in a letter to Kugelmann of 12 April 1871. See Marx and Engels, *Selected Correspondence* (Foreign Languages Publishing House, Moscow, 1953), p. 318.
43. Engels, Preface to the English translation of Vol. 1 of *Das Kapital* (Swann Sonnenschein, London, 1886).
44. Lenin, *The State and Revolution* (Foreign Languages Publishing House, Moscow, n.d.), p. 61.
45. Neal Blewett, 'The Franchise in the United Kingdom 1885–1918', *Past and Present*, No. 32, December 1965, pp. 27–56. Generalizing the point for other industrial societies, Ralf Dahrendorf calculates that 'before World War I, only between 10 and 15 per cent of the population of Europe had a realistic chance to take part at all in the political life of their countries'; while for the United States, 'in the presidential election of 1912, for example, little more than 16 per cent of the population took part.' Dahrendorf, 'Recent Changes in the Class Structure of European Societies', *Daedalus*, Vol. 92, No. 1, 1964, p. 229.
46. Landes, *The Unbound Prometheus*, pp. 187–92, 330.
47. Marx and Engels, *Manifesto of the Communist Party*, in *Selected Works in 2 Vols.* (Foreign Languages Publishing House, Moscow, 1962), Vol. 1, p. 46.
48. G. Therborn, 'The Working Class and the Birth of Marxism', *New Left Review*, No. 79, May–June 1973, p. 8. Engels in 1892 had described the Chartists as 'the first working-men's party of modern times'. See the special introduction to the English edition of *Socialism: Utopian and Scientific*, in Marx and Engels, *Selected Works in 2 Vols.*, Vol. 2, p. 110.
49. Marx and Engels, *The German Ideology* (International Publishers, New York, 1947), p. 204.
50. Marx and Engels, *The Holy Family* (Foreign Languages Publishing House, Moscow, 1956), p. 53. And cf. the similar account in *The Poverty of Philosophy* (International Publishers, New York, 1963), pp. 172–3, where the evolution of the political consciousness of the English working class is discussed.

51. For Marx's constant expectation of a revolutionary crisis in the 1850s, see David McLellan, *Karl Marx: His Life and Thought* (Macmillan, 1973), pp. 281–2.
52. Therborn, 'The Working Class and the Birth of Marxism', p. 9.
53. On this see the brief but powerful article by H. Lubasz, 'Marx's Conception of the Revolutionary Proletariat', *Praxis*, Vol. 5, 1970, pp. 288–90.
54. For the Chartists, see D. J. Rowe, 'The London Working Men's Association and the "People's Charter" ', *Past and Present*, No. 36., April 1967, pp. 73–86; for the period of the First International, H. Collins and C. Abramsky, *Karl Marx and the British Labour Movement* (Macmillan, 1965), *passim.* Collins and Abramsky comment: 'What is undoubtedly relevant is the fact that in the lifetime of the First International efforts to organise the unskilled majority of the working class failed almost completely . . . Paradoxically, the men who allied themselves with Marx in the period of the International came from the privileged stratum of the working class' (p. 48). This is not, of course, a paradoxical fact at all, but the common experience of all radical and revolutionary movements of the last 150 years in Europe.
55. This list is but a selection of groups, almost all of the same craft-like complexion, taken from the list of English societies affiliated to the First International by 1867. See Collins and Abramsky, op. cit. Ch. 5, Appendix 3, p. 81.
56. Dobb, *Studies in the Development of Capitalism*, p. 265.
57. Marx, 'Critical Notes on "The King of Prussia and Social Reform" ' (1844), in L. D. Easton and K. H. Guddat (eds.), *Writings of the Young Marx on Philosophy and Society* (Anchor Books, New York, 1967), p. 353.
58. Lubasz, 'Marx's Conception of the Revolutionary Proletariat', p. 289.
59. This was bound to be the case particularly with those theories, such as in Comte, Spencer, and Durkheim, where the modern, scientific and industrial, character of nineteenth-century European society was seen simply as the first expression of a movement that was worldwide, and which must eventually embrace all societies. In the case of the increasing division of labour, Durkheim, drawing on the evolutionary biology of his time, thought this to be a general law both of the natural and the social worlds, and *a fortiori* the future of all societies: 'The division of labour in society appears to be no more than a particular form of this

general process; and societies, in conforming to that law, seem to be yielding to a movement that was born before them, and that similarly governs the entire world.' *The Division of Labour in Society*, p. 41.

60. There are really two forms of the convergence thesis, a strong and a weak; and they are often confused. The first holds that all societies everywhere are destined to become industrial – that there is a *world* process of convergence onto a uniform industrial type. The second simply says that *once* the process of industrialization gets under way in a particular society, it will tend to develop structural features similar to all other cases of industrialization, i.e., that there is a 'logic' to the industrialization process. It should be clear that the second form of the thesis does not presuppose the first (although the first almost inevitably entails the second): one can believe that the business of getting industrialization started at all is an extraordinarily difficult and by no means inevitable development, while still believing that *if and when* a society 'takes off' it will produce a social structure uniform in almost all important respects with other more developed industrial societies. On the whole the nineteenth-century thinkers held the strong form of the convergence thesis; the tendency in this century among academic sociologists has been to go for the weak.

61. For two especially influential statements of this view, see P. A. Sorokin, 'Mutual Convergence of the United States and the U.S.S.R. to the Mixed Sociocultural Type', *International Journal of Comparative Sociology*, Vol. 1, 1960, pp. 143–76; and Marion J. Levy, *Modernization and the Structure of Societies* (2 Vols., Princeton University Press, Princeton, 1966).

62. Clark Kerr, John T. Dunlop, Frederick Harbison, C. A. Myers, *Industrialism and Industrial Man* (Penguin Books, 2nd edn, 1973), pp. 55–6. And cf. Levy: 'The level of structural uniformity among relatively modernized societies continually increases regardless of how diverse the original basis from which change took place in these societies may have been.' Op. cit., Vol. 11, p. 709.

63. These points are well made, in their defence of the convergence thesis, by E. G. Dunning and E. I. Hopper, 'Industrialization and the Problem of Convergence: A Critical Note', *Sociological Review*, Vol. 14, No. 2, July 1966, pp. 163–86.

64. cf. Feldman and Moore: '. . . Virtually no one rejects the notion that industrial societies share a core set of social structures that together provide a kind of extended operational definition of

industrialism itself.' Arnold S. Feldman and Wilbert E. Moore, 'Industrialization and Industrialism: Convergence and Differentiation', in W. A. Faunce and W. H. Form (eds.), *Comparative Perspectives on Industrial Society*, pp. 59–60. That this is so seems to be accepted by even the sharpest critics of the convergence thesis. See, e.g., T. H. Marshall, 'A Summing-Up', in P. Halmos (ed.), *The Development of Industrial Societies* (University of Keele, *Sociological Review Monograph* No. 8, 1964), p. 144; and A. Giddens, *The Class Structure of the Advanced Societies* (Hutchinson, 1973), p. 141.

65. Feldman and Moore, 'Industrialization and Industrialism', pp. 60, 67–8.
66. Dunning and Hopper, 'Industrialization and the Problem of Convergence', pp. 181–2. For other evidence of convergence, see the works cited in Ian Weinberg, 'The Problem of the Convergence of Industrial Societies' *Comparative Studies in Society and History*, Vol. 11, No. 1, Jan. 1969, p. 4, n. 1. For later work, see D. J. Treiman, 'Industrialization and Social Stratification', *Sociological Inquiry*, 40, Spring 1970, pp. 207–34.
67. There is an excellent extended discussion of these points in Reinhard Bendix, 'Tradition and Modernity Reconsidered' (see note 16, above).
68. J. Schumpeter, *Capitalism, Socialism, and Democracy* (4th edn, Allen & Unwin, 1954), pp. 136–7 (Schumpeter's italics). For the extent of this pattern, and the length of its persistence, in the various European societies, see the individual chapters in Margaret Scotford-Archer and Salvador Giner (eds.), *Contemporary Europe: Class, Status, and Power* (Weidenfeld & Nicolson, 1971). For Britain, see especially W. G. Guttsman, *The British Political Elite* (MacGibbon & Kee, 1963). And cf. Giddens: 'Any analysis of the development of modern capitalism from the latter part of the 19th century up to the present time must recognise the protracted significance of "traditional" land-owning groups within the class structure.' *The Class Structure of the Advanced Societies*, p. 165; and the helpful discussion, pp. 164–7.
69. Engels, Preface (1892) to the English edition of *Socialism: Utopian and Scientific*, in Marx and Engels, *Selected Works in 2 Vols.* (Foreign Languages Publishing House, Moscow, 1962), Vol. 2, p. 112. The whole of this preface is a brilliant account of the paradoxes of English social and political development since the seventeenth century – with the compromise between the old

aristocracy and the new bourgeoisie seen as the principal feature of that development. Later accounts have not added much to this sketch; see, e.g., P. Anderson, 'Origins of the Present Crisis', in P. Anderson and R. Blackburn (eds.), *Towards Socialism* (Collins, 1965), pp. 11–52; and cf. E. P. Thompson's splendid polemic against this, 'The Peculiarities of the English', in J. Saville and R. Miliband (eds.), *The Socialist Register 1965* (The Merlin Press, 1965), pp. 311–62.

70. Portraits of the specifically industrial, as opposed to the generally commercial, English bourgeois are hard to come by either in sociology or in fiction. But one of the most convincing of these is the character of the industrialist Thornton in Elizabeth Gaskell's novel *North and South* (1855). For some interesting reflections on the split English middle class, and the constant pull of the gentlemanly ideal, see D. C. Coleman, 'Gentlemen and Players', *Economic History Review*, Vol. 25, No. 1, 1973, pp. 92–116; and J. P. Nettl, 'Consensus or Elite Domination: The Case of Business', *Political Studies*, Vol. XIII, No. 1, 1965, pp. 22–44. A more bizarre twist to the hold of the 'gentility principle' was Alfred Marshall's hope and expectation that not only the middle class but the working class would be 'gentled'. See A. Marshall, 'The Future of the Working Classes' (1873), in A. C. Pigou (ed.), *Memorials of Alfred Marshall* (Macmillan, 1925), pp. 101–18.

71. The different role of the banks in the various cases of European industrialization is succinctly discussed in Gerschenkron 'Economic Backwardness in Historical Perspective' (see note 23, above).

72. D. Landes, 'French Business and the Businessman: A Social and Cultural Analysis', in E. M. Earle (ed.), *Modern France* (Russell & Russell, New York, 1964), p. 336. (Reprint of 1951 edition, published by Princeton University Press.)

73. Schumpeter, *Capitalism, Socialism, and Democracy*, pp. 12–13.

74. For some representative contemporary responses illustrating what he calls 'the exemplary significance of Manchester' for the new industrial system, see Steven Marcus, *Engels, Manchester, and the Working Class* (Vintage Books, New York, 1975). Ch. 2, 'The Town'.

75. Sidonia, in Benjamin Disraeli's novel *Coningsby* (1844).

5 Reculer Pour Mieux Sauter: The Climax of Industrialism

1. Quoted Margaret Cole, *The Story of Fabian Socialism* (Heinemann, 1961), p. 1.
2. Quoted S. Pollard, *The Idea of Progress* (Penguin Books, 1971), p. 149.
3. H. G. Wells, *The Discovery of the Future*, A Discourse delivered to the Royal Institution on 24 January 1902 (T. Fisher Unwin, 1902), pp. 90–93.
4. H. G. Wells, *The War in the Air* (first published 1907; reprinted, with new prefaces, 1921 and 1941). New reprint, including all the prefaces, Penguin Books, 1967, pp. 228–30. In the preface of 1921, Wells pointed out with justifiable satisfaction that the book was written 'before the days of the flying machine; Bleriot did not cross the Channel until July 1909; and the Zeppelin airship was still in its infancy.' This dating incidentally mars Fred Iklé's otherwise apt observation, that Wells' predictions straddled two sets of values, 'the nineteenth century technology optimism of the Crystal Palace expositions and the end-of-this-world experience of World War I'. Wells clearly did not have to wait for the war to develop his apolcalyptic vision. See Iklé, 'Can Social Predictions be Evaluated?' *Daedalus*, Vol. 96, No. 3, Summer 1967, p. 746.
5. The intellectual currents of the period are well analysed in H. Stuart Hughes, *Consciousness and Society: The Reorientation of European Social Thought 1890–1930* (Vintage Books, New York, 1958).
6. A. R. Radcliffe-Brown, 'The Present Position of Anthropological Studies', *The Advancement of Science: 1931* (British Association for the Advancement of Science, 1931), p. 22. For the reaction against evolutionism see particularly I. C. Jarvie, *The Revolution in Anthropology* (Routledge & Kegan Paul, 1964). In the Foreword to Jarvie's volume, Ernest Gellner consisely sums up the shift of direction accomplished by Malinowski and his followers: 'In substance, this consists of a shift of attention *from* speculative genetic theories of human society, and the associated attempt to use contemporary simple societies as surrogate time-machines, *to* intensive, thorough and accurate field work, and a style of explanation which concentrates on exploring the interrelations of activities and institutions at any one given time, and refrains from invoking the passage of time as a facile and often vacuous *deus ex machina*. To paraphrase a remark of Dr Zhivago's, the life of soci-

eties is something which has point in itself – it is not made up of left-overs of which they have somehow forgotten to divest themselves, or, for that matter, of anticipations of the future. Properly understood, this approach involves a disregard neither of history nor of change.'

7. As Sidney Pollard emphasizes throughout his book, *The Idea of Progress.*
8. See T. H. Huxley's Romanes Lecture of 1893, reprinted together with that of his grandson Julian Huxley, in *Evolution and Ethics 1893–1943* (The Pilot Press, 1947).
9. For these changes, see Eric Hobsbawm, *Industry and Empire* (Weidenfeld & Nicolson, 1968), pp. 144–9: and Hobsbawm, *Labouring Men: Studies in the History of Labour* (Weidenfeld & Nicolson, 1964), pp. 179–203. See also F. H. Hinsley in *The New Cambridge Modern History Vol. XI: Material Progress and World-Wide Problems 1870–98* (Cambridge University Press, 1962), pp. 11–25; D. Landes, *The Unbound Prometheus* (Cambridge University Press, 1969), pp. 235–48; M. Dobb, *Studies in the Development of Capitalism* (Routledge & Kegan Paul, 1963), pp. 309 ff.; Harry Braverman, *Labour and Monopoly Capital* (Monthly Review Press, New York, 1974), pp. 85 ff.
10. Landes, *The Unbound Prometheus*, p. 289.
11. ibid., pp. 322–3.
12. ibid., p. 307.
13. ibid., p. 307. See also Braverman, *Labour and Monopoly Capital*, p. 126, and, generally, pp. 85–137; and cf. Hobsbawm's comment on automation:

> There was nothing revolutionary in it, in principle. The original cotton factory already strove after the ideal of becoming a gigantic, complex and 'self-acting' (as it was then called) automaton, and each technical innovation brought it a little closer towards this object. With some exceptions like the Jacquard loom it remained pretty remote from it, by modern standards, because the incentives to eliminate skilled labour were not strong enough, but above all because the implications in terms of labour management and the organization of production were not yet systematically thought out. But it was visibly mass-production and on the road to automation, and certain forms of early chemical production, with their continuous operation, automatic control of temperature (a thermostat was patented in 1831) and virtual elimination of all process-work were even closer. [*Industry and Empire*, p. 146.]

14. Landes, *Unbound Prometheus*, p. 248. And cf. Keynes' confident assertion, uttered during the period of the slump in the 1930s, quoted at the head of this chapter.
15. For theories of progress and evolution in the United States at this time, see L. Sklair, *The Sociology of Progress* (Routledge & Kegan Paul, 1970), pp. 88ff.
16. S. M. Lipset, *Political Man* (Heinemann, Mercury Books edn 1963; first published in 1959), p. 406.
17. R. Aron, *The Industrial Society* (Weidenfeld & Nicolson, 1967), pp. 45–6. A similar view, that the industrial society, once created, can 'manage' the stresses to which it gives rise, underlies the argument in E. Gellner, *Thought and Change* (Weidenfeld & Nicolson, 1964).
18. In addition to the works by Lipset and Aron cited above, see also Daniel Bell, *The End of Ideology* (Collier Books, New York, 1961), and R. Aron, *The Opium of the Intellectuals* (Secker & Warburg, 1957). For Lipset's later thoughts on the subject, and a defence of his earlier position, see S. M. Lipset, 'Ideology and No End: The Controversy Till Now', *Encounter*, Dec. 1972, pp. 17–22.
19. Aron, *The Industrial Society*, pp. 179–80.
20. For a critical discussion of the thesis of the 'incorporation' of the western working class, see M. Mann, *Consciousness and Action Among the Western Working Class* (Macmillan, 1973).
21. This defence of mass society has become something of a commonplace among American sociologists. See Leon Bramson, *The Political Context of Sociology* (Princeton University Press, Princeton, 1961), pp. 96ff.; and E. Shils, 'Mass Society and its Culture', in N. Jacobs (ed.), *Culture for the Millions?* (Beacon Press, Boston, 1964), pp. 1–27.
22. Keynes' political essays of the inter-war years serve as an admirable pendant to the more extreme assertions of Burnham. They put, in a cooler and more measured tone, substantially the same argument as Burnham about a new economic age (which in one place Keynes called 'the period of stabilization'), and which was characterized by the large managerial corporation and active state intervention in economic and social life. In a direct anticipation of Burnham's analysis Keynes even wrote in an essay of 1925: 'The abuses of this epoch [the epoch of stabilization] in the realm of Government are Fascism on the one side and Bolshevism on the other.' The essays are conveniently reprinted in Vol. IX:

Essays in Persuasion, of *The Collected Writings of John Maynard Keynes* (Macmillan, for The Royal Economic Society, 1972).

23. The original formulation of the modern 'pluralist' concept of democracy is to be found in J. Schumpeter, *Capitalism, Socialism, and Democracy* (Allen & Unwin, 1954), pp. 269ff. Among many advocates one can cite A. Kornhauser, *The Politics of Mass Society* (The Free Press, Glencoe, 1959). For a review and a criticism of the approach, see the first part of R. Miliband, *The State in Capitalist Society* (Weidenfeld & Nicolson, 1969).
24. Lipset, *Political Man*, pp. 414–15.
25. The common destiny of all industrial societies as mapped out by Clark Kerr *et al.*, in *Industrialism and Industrial Man* (Penguin Books, 1973).
26. J. K. Galbraith, *Economic Development* (Harvard University Press, Cambridge, Mass., 1964), p. 3.
27. Pollard, *The Idea of Progress*, pp. 191–2. So powerful was the euphoria created by the era of economic growth after 1945 that even erstwhile prophets of doom, such as Arnold Toynbee in his *Study of History*, managed to convert their earlier cyclical formulations into a scheme that now emphasized the underlying unilinear and progressive direction of human history (but in religious rather than material or intellectual terms). For Toynbee's post-war reformulation, see Sklair, *The Sociology of Progress*, pp. 82–4.

6 A Post-Industrial Society?

1. Aron, quoted D. Bell, 'The Study of the Future', *The Public Interest*, No. 1, Fall 1965, p. 119.
2. See H. Kahn and A. Wiener (eds.), *The Year 2000* (The Macmillan Co., New York, 1967); R. Jungk and J. Galtung (ed.), *Mankind 2000* (Allen & Unwin, 1969); N. Calder (ed.), *The World in 1984* (2 Vols., Penguin Books, 1964); M. Vassiliev and S. Gouschev (eds.), *Life in the Twenty-First Century* (Penguin Books, 1961); A. Toffler, *Future Shock* (Random House, New York, 1970); Wendell Bell and James A. Mau (eds.), *The Sociology of the Future* (Harper & Row, New York, 1972); Ciba Foundation Symposium, *The Future as an Academic Discipline* (Elsevier, Amsterdam, 1975). The number of institutes, organizations, and individuals currently engaged in systematic analysis of future trends runs into thousands, although most of these are concerned with fairly short-term technological forecasting. For comprehen-

sive listings, see the annotated bibliography by Bettina Huber in Bell and Mau (eds.), op. cit., pp. 339–454; the P.E.P. survey of future studies, ... *And Now the Future*, edited by Charles de Hoghton, W. Page, and G. Streatfeild (P.E.P., London, 1971); and E. Jantsch, *Technological Forecasting in Perspective* (O.E.C.D., Paris, 1967). For a general discussion of some of the literature, see the review article by K. Kumar, 'The "Sociology of the Future" ', *Sociology*, Vol. 7, No. 2, 1973, pp. 277–80.

3. Bell, 'The Study of the Future', p 122.
4. Toffler, *Future Shock*, p. 11.
5. This was the basic procedure of the widely used 'Delphi' method of social forecasting. For an account, see Olaf Helmer, *Social Technology* (Basic Books, New York, 1966), who also surveys various of the other methods currently used.
6. For some valuable reflections on the futurological enterprise, see R. Nisbet, 'The Year 2000 And All That', *Commentary*, Vol. 45, No. 6, June 1968, pp. 60–66; A. Shonfield, 'Thinking About the Future', *Encounter*, Feb. 1969, pp. 15–26; R. Heilbroner, 'Futurology', in his *Between Capitalism and Socialism* (Vintage Books, New York, 1970), pp. 259–68; J. Goldthorpe, 'Theories of Industrial Society: Reflections on the Recrudescence of Historicism and the Future of Futurology', *European Journal of Sociology*, Vol. XII, No. 2, 1971.
7. See on this especially K. Bock, 'Evolution, Function, and Change', *American Sociological Review*, Vol. 28, No. 2, 1963, pp. 229–37; and J. D. Y. Peel, *Herbert Spencer, The Evolution of a Sociologist* (Heinemann, 1971).
8. The most significant and interesting case is that of Talcott Parsons, whose rhetorical question at the opening of his book *The Structure of Social Action*: 'Who now reads Herbert Spencer?' is now clearly answered: Parsons himself. See, e.g., his *Societies: Evolutionary and Comparative Perspectives* (Prentice Hall, Englewood Cliffs, 1966); and cf. the following comment on the attempt to set out the main structural features of industrial societies:

> Its validity ... rests not only on its empirical correctness with reference to the facts of known industrial society, but also on the way in which it fits into a broader scheme of comparative structural analysis, including many nonindustrial cases. Such a scheme, in my opinion, to be adequate must include an explicit and well organized evolutionary dimension. It is quite clear that no 'primitive' society (defined, for instance, as nonliterate) could develop a full-fledged

industrial economy. In the long run, our ability to handle this type of problem will depend on the level of comparative evolutionary theory of social structures that we are able to work out. [T. Parsons, 'Some Principal Characteristics of Industrial Societies', in C. E. Black (ed.), *The Transformation of Russian Society* (Harvard University Press, Cambridge, Mass., 1960), p. 39.]

9. For the parallels, see K. Kumar, 'The Industrializing and the Post-Industrial Worlds: On Development and Futurology', in E. de Kadt and G. Williams (eds.), *Sociology and Development* (Tavistock Publications, 1974), pp. 329–60.
10. See especially, D. Bell, *The Coming of Post-Industrial Society* (Basic Books, New York, 1973); Kahn and Wiener (eds.), *The Year 2000*; Z. Brzezinski, *Between Two Ages: America's Role in the Technetronic Era* (The Viking Press, New York, 1970); P. Drucker, *The Age of Discontinuity* (Pan Books, 1971); R. E. Lane, 'The Decline of Politics and Ideology in a Knowledgeable Society', *American Sociological Review*, Vol. 31, No. 5, 1966, pp. 649–62. For the ideological and historical 'situating' of this group, see K. Kumar, 'Futurology', *Listener*, 18 Feb. 1971
11. The fullest statement from western Europe is A. Touraine, *The Post-Industrial Society* (Random House, New York, 1971). See also Jungk and Galtung (eds.), *Mankind 2000*; R. Dahrendorf, 'Recent Changes in the Class Structure of Contemporary Europe', *Daedalus*, Vol. 93, No. 1, 1964, pp. 225–70. The differences between the American and European approach are neatly brought out in the exchange between Daniel Bell and Robert Jungk in *The Times-Europa Supplement*, Jan. 1975. British sociology characteristically has kept a low profile on all this – but cf. T. Bottomore's welcome to the post-industrial idea and his comment that 'if this conception can be fruitfully elaborated it may come to occupy the central place which the notion of industrial capitalism as a social system had in 19th century sociology.' Bottomore, *Sociology as Social Criticism* (Allen & Unwin, 1975), p. 53. See also Russell Lewis, *The New Service Society* (Longman, 1973).

It is generally true that the radical perspective on the post-industrial thesis has a European provenance – especially in European social theory but also in European events, as in 'May '68' – even where the elaborations are carried out in the United States. Such is the case, e.g., with Herbert Marcuse and many of the theorists of the American 'New Left'. For a discussion of these within the context of the post-industrial idea, see Norman Birnbaum,

'Is there a Post-Industrial Revolution?' in his *Toward a Critical Sociology* (Oxford University Press, New York, 1971), pp. 393–415.

12. R. Richta *et al.*, *Civilization at the Crossroads: Social and Human Implications of the Scientific and Technological Revolution* (3 Vols., Czechoslovak Institute of Arts and Sciences, Prague, 1967. Also published in one volume, International Arts and Sciences Press, Prague, 1968). See also the contributions to the 'Special Issue on Prognostication and Planning' of the *World Marxist Review*, Vol. 14, No. 1, 1971; P. Apostol, 'Marxism and the Structure of the Future', *Futures*, Vol. 4, No. 3, 1972, pp. 201–10; M. Drobyshev, 'Sociology of the Tension between Culture and Science Today', Paper delivered to UNESCO conference on *Culture and Science*, Paris, 1971. Many of the East European scholars involved in 'futurology' revealed themselves at the Seventh World Congress of Sociology, Varna, Bulgaria, 14–19 September 1970. For résumés of papers, see *Sociological Abstracts* (1970). The East European contribution, especially the Richta volumes, is discussed in K. Kumar, 'Futurology – The View from Eastern Europe', *Futures*, Vol. 4, No. 1, 1972.
13. See A. Etzioni, *The Active Society* (The Free Press, New York, 1968); G. Lichtheim, *The New Europe: Today and Tomorrow* (Basic Books, New York, 1963); Kahn and Wiener, *The Year 2000*; M. Bookchin, *Post-Scarcity Anarchism* (The Ramparts Press, Berkeley, 1971); Kenneth Boulding, *The Meaning of the Twentieth Century: The Great Transition* (Harper & Row, New York, 1964); Bell, *The Coming of Post-Industrial Society*; Drucker, *The Age of Discontinuity*; P. Halmos, *The Personal Service Society* (Constable, 1970); Dahrendorf, 'Recent Changes in the Class Structure of Contemporary Europe'; Brzezinski, *Between Two Ages*.
14. See J. Habermas, *Toward a Rational Society* (Heinemann, 1971); P. Anderson and A. Cockburn (eds.), *Student Power* (Penguin Books, 1969); N. Chomsky, *American Power and the New Mandarins* (Penguin Books, 1969); R. Flacks, 'Revolt of the Young Intelligentsia: Revolutionary Class-Consciousness in a Post-Scarcity Society', in R. Aya and N. Miller (eds.), *The New American Revolution* (The Free Press, New York, 1971), pp. 223–59; J. K. Galbraith, *The New Industrial State* (Penguin Books, 1969); C. Kerr, *The Uses of the University* (Harvard University Press, Cambridge, Mass., 1963); Drucker, *The Age of Discontinuity*.
15. As shown by the frequent engagement by the post-industrial

theorists with the technocratic theories of J. Ellul, *The Technological Society* (Knopf, New York, 1964), and J. Maynaud, *Technocracy* (Methuen, 1968).

16. See H. Marcuse, *One Dimensional Man* (Sphere Books, 1968); C. Lasch, 'Toward a Theory of Post-Industrial Society', in M. D. Hancock and G. Sjoberg (eds.), *Politics in the Post-Welfare State* (Columbia University Press, New York, 1972), pp. 36–50; Kahn and Wiener, op. cit ; Bookchin, op. cit.
17. J M. Keynes, 'Economic Possibilities for our Grandchildren', in his *Essays in Persuasion* (Macmillan, 1972. The essay was written in 1930), p. 326.
18. See R. Hoggart, *Speaking To Each Other*, (2 Vols., Penguin Books, 1973); D. Riesman, 'Leisure and Work in Post-Industrial Society', in E. Larrabee and R. Meyersohn (eds.), *Mass Leisure* (The Free Press, Glencoe, 1958); R. Dubin, 'Industrial Workers' Worlds: A Study of the "Central Life Interests" of Industrial Workers', in E. O. Smigel (ed.), *Work and Leisure* (College and University Press, New Haven, 1963), pp. 53–72; J. Goldthorpe, D. Lockwood, J. Platt, and F. Bechhofer, *The Affluent Worker in the Class Structure* (Cambridge University Press, 1969). For the cultural criticism associated with the May events, the writings of the Paris Situationists are especially important. For a selection of their writings, see C. Gray (ed.), *Leaving the 20th Century: The Incomplete Work of the Situationist International* (Free Fall Publications, London, 1974).
19. Halmos, *The Personal Service Society*; Ivan Illich, *De-schooling Society* (Calder & Boyars, 1971), *Medical Nemesis: The Expropriation of Health* (Calder & Boyars, 1975); P. Rieff, *The Triumph of the Therapeutic* (Penguin Books, 1973), *Fellow Teachers* (Faber & Faber, 1975).
20. See Richta *et al*, op. cit.
21. Bell, *The Coming of Post-Industrial Society*, pp. 12–33.
22. There are naturally differences of emphasis, but accounts substantially in agreement with Bell can be found in Brzezinski, op. cit.; Galbraith, op. cit.; Kahn and Wiener, op. cit.; Drucker, op. cit.; Lane, op. cit.; Touraine, op. cit.; Galtung, 'On the Future of the International System', in Jungk and Galtung (eds.), *Mankind 2000*, pp. 12–41; Lichtheim, op. cit.; Richta *et al*, op. cit.
23. Touraine, op. cit., pp. 64–9.
24. V. Fuchs, *The Service Economy* (Columbia University Press, New York, 1968), p. 7. The evolution is as follows: In 1929 the service

sector's share of total employment was 40 per cent; by 1967 it was over 55 per cent, and by 1975 it was expected to be 60 per cent (pp. 1–2).

25. For the general movement towards services in all industrial societies, see especially Fuchs, op. cit., *passim*; Dahrendorf, 'Recent Changes in the Class Structure of European Societies'; M. Lengellé, *The Growing Importance of the Service Sector in Member Countries* (O.E.C.D., Paris, 1966); Richta *et al.*, op. cit., Vol. III, Tables 2–4; Galbraith, *The New Industrial State*, pp. 238 ff. For the British case, see *Social Trends 1974* (Central Statistical Office, London), p. 98, and subsequent annual issues.
26. R. M. Hartwell, *The Industrial Revolution and Economic Growth* (Methuen, 1971), p. 205. Commenting further on the English case he remarks that the trend towards a service economy 'becomes obvious quantitatively as soon as there are statistical records, and from the first Census of 1801 there is a secular tendency for the percentage of employment in services to rise. The trend indeed is one of the best known, most obvious statistical aspects of English economic growth.' ibid., p. 210. We might note that over a third of the workforce was employed in services throughout the first half of the nineteenth century. Victor Fuchs similarly remarks, for the United States, that 'for as long as we have records on the industrial distribution of the labour force, we find a secular tendency for the percentage accounted for by the service sector to rise.' Fuchs, op. cit., p. 22.
27. Hartwell, op. cit., p. 212. For the development of services in nineteenth-century Europe as a whole, see Hartwell, 'The Service Revolution: The Growth of Services in Modern Economy', in C. M. Cipolla (ed.), *The Industrial Revolution* (Collins, 1973), pp. 358–394. And cf. also Landes' comment on the general European pattern, that 'as productivity rose and the standard of living with it, the administrative and service sector of the economy – what some economists have called the tertiary sector – grew – more rapidly than industry itself.' D. Landes, *The Unbound Prometheus: Technological Change and Industrial Development in Western Europe from 1750 to the Present* (Cambridge University Press, 1969), p. 9.
28. R. Heilbroner, 'Economic Problems of a "Post-Industrial" Society', in D. Potter and P. Sarre (eds.), *Dimensions of Society* (University of London Press, 1974), pp. 226–7. The table on p. 226 gives the movements of the employed population over the last fifty years

for the U.S., U.K., France and Germany. The Japanese case, in addition, is a forceful example of the generality of this pattern as against the English one. Japan supplanted the primary sector not first with the secondary sector but with the tertiary sector: the secondary sector expanded fast with industrialization but the tertiary sector expanded even faster *at the same time*. See K. Tominaga, 'Post-Industrial Society and Cultural Diversity', *Survey*, Vol. 16, No. 1, 1971, pp. 68–77.

29. Such a movement, for instance, links phenomena as apparently disparate as the Chicago school of sociology, Italian and German Fascism, French Poujadism, American McCarthyism, and Communism in Central and Eastern Europe. Indeed the only industrial country significantly absent from this list is Britain, the oldest of the industrialized and urbanized societies.
30. Fuchs, *The Service Economy*, p. 189.
31. Bell, *The Coming of Post-Industrial Society*, p. 163.
32. See Fuchs, op. cit., pp. 190–92. Fuchs states that in the U.S. a third of the employees in the service sector are engaged in 'non-profit' operations.
33. P. Clarke, *Small Businesses: How They Survive and Succeed* (David & Charles, Newton Abbot, 1972), pp. 23–4.
34. For the U.S., see Heilbroner, op. cit., p. 233. For Britain, J. Westergaard and H. Resler, *Class in a Capitalist Society: A Study of Contemporary Britain* (Heinemann, 1975), p. 152, n.
35. As with, for instance, Fuchs, op. cit., p. 32. And cf. Birnbaum's remark '. . . the general role of white-collar workers – of the tertiary sector, as it is called . . .' 'Is there a Post-Industrial Revolution?', p. 394.
36. Heilbroner, op. cit., p. 235.
37. In the United States between 1950 and 1960, the proportion of white-collar workers in manufacturing rose from 25·6 per cent to 30·5 per cent – and this is reckoned as an underestimate, since many such workers in manufacturing are classified as 'Industry'. Fuchs, op. cit., pp. 34–6. For Britain, between 1951 and 1974 the proportion of white-collar workers in manufacturing moved from 17·6 per cent to 27 per cent; and in the construction industry, from 9·7 to 17·2 per cent. T. Noble, *Modern Britain: Structure and Change* (Batsford, 1975), p. 137; *Department of Employment Gazette*, H.M.S.O., July 1974, p. 623. Postan further notes for the U.K. that of the 1·1 million increase of workers in the manufacturing industries between 1948 and 1962, 745,000 of these were

'salaried' workers, mainly clerical and technical personel. M. M. Postan, *An Economic History of Western Europe* (Methuen, 1967), p. 101.

38. Bell, *The Coming of Post-Industrial Society*, pp. 134–5; Galbraith, *The New Industrial State*, pp. 241–3; G. Sayers Bain *et al.*, 'The Labour Force', in A. H. Halsey (ed.), *Trends in British Society Since 1900* (Macmillan, 1972), p. 98. For the other European countries see the chapters for individual countries in M. Scotford-Archer and S. Giner (eds.), *Contemporary Europe: Class, Status, and Power* (Weidenfeld & Nicolson, 1971). For a general review and discussion of the growth of the white-collar groups, see A. Giddens, *The Class Structure of the Advanced Societies* (Hutchinson, 1973), pp. 177ff.
39. Bell, *The Coming of Post-Industrial Society*, p. 125.
40. Lichtheim, *The New Europe*, p. 194. And cf., as an example of a widely shared view, Alexander Carr-Saunders' observation of 1944 that 'the labourer is becoming a figure of the past.' A. M. Carr-Saunders and P. A. Wilson, 'The Emergence of the Professions', *Encyclopaedia of the Social Sciences* (Macmillan, New York, 1944).
41. For some of the more impressive attempts, see C. Wright Mills, *White Collar* (Oxford University Press, New York, 1951); D. Lockwood, *The Blackcoated Worker* (Allen & Unwin, 1958); M. Crozier, *The World of the Office Worker* (Chicago University Press, Chicago, 1971); Dahrendorf, 'Recent Changes in the Class Structure of Contemporary Europe'.
42. H. Braverman, *Labour and Monopoly Capital: The Degradation of Work in the Twentieth Century* (Monthly Review Press, New York, 1974), p. 350.
43. For the U.K., the growth in clerical employment was easily the most rapid and voluminous among white-collar workers, increasing by 292 per cent during the period 1911–66. In 1911, clerical occupations made up 4·5 per cent of the total labour force; by 1966 they constituted 13·2 per cent. And it is quite clear that it is women who have taken up much of the new employment. By 1966 women, who made up 29·8 per cent of the white-collar occupations in 1911, constituted 46·5 per cent of *all* white-collar employees; by 1971, they formed a clear majority. And since 1951 they have also formed a clear majority among the grades that are the most numerous, the clerical workers, shop assistants, and certain lower professional occupations such as teaching and nursing.

See Sayers Bain *et al.*, 'The Labour Force', pp. 98–9; and Westergaard and Resler, *Class in a Capitalist Society*, pp. 291–6, who rightly comment (p. 291):

> It is quite misleading to point – as so many commentators do – to the fact that nearly half the working population now are in non-manual jobs. For while a majority of working women have jobs that can be so described, over three in every five men are still manual workers, ' blue-collar' workers in American terminology, even by conventional definitions of job boundary lines. And it is still men's occupational positions far more than women's that set the essential circumstances of life for most households, however much one may deplore this.

For the similar American picture, Braverman, op. cit., p. 296.

44. Braverman, op. cit., pp. 293–358, gives a comprehensive and convincing account of the main changes in white-collar work consequent upon increasing mechanization and specialization.
45. Cf. this apposite comment of Braverman's:

> In the beginning, the office was the site of mental labour and the shop the site of manual labour. This was even true *after* Taylor (F. W.) and in part *because* of Taylor: scientific management gave the office a monopoly over conception, planning, judgement, and the appraisal of results, while in the shop nothing was to take place other than the physical execution of all that was thought up in the office. Insofar as this was true, the identification of office work with thinking and educated labour, and of the production process proper with unthinking and uneducated labour, retained some validity. But once the office was itself subjected to the rationalization process, this contrast lost its force. The functions of thought and planning became concentrated in an ever smaller group within the office, and for the mass of those employed there the office became just as much a site of manual labour as the factory floor. With the transformation of management into an administrative labour process, manual work spreads to the office and soon becomes characteristic of the tasks of the mass of clerical workers. [*Labour and Monopoly Capital*, pp. 315–16.]

None of this implies, of course, that white-collar workers will see or make common cause with the group of traditional manual workers whose conditions they now share in so many respects.

46. Fuchs, *The Service Economy*, pp. 4–8; Braverman, op. cit., pp. 382–4.
47. Bell, *The Coming of Post-Industrial Society*, p. 127.
48. Halmos, *The Personal Service Society*, p. 46. And see also, for the same view confidently stated, E. Freidson, 'Professionalization

and the Organization of Middle-Class Labour in Post-Industrial Society", in P. Halmos (ed.), *Professionalization and Social Change* (University of Keele, Sociological Review Monograph No. 20, 1973) pp. 47–60.

49. Richta *et al.*, *Civilization at the Crossroads*, Vol. 1, pp. 32–6.
50. Bell, op. cit., pp. 135–7.
51. G. Sayers Bain *et al.*, 'The Labour Force', p. 98 and Table 4.2, p. 114; 'A view of Occupational Employment in 1981', *Department of Employment Gazette*, H.M.S.O., July 1975, pp. 619–22. And cf. this finding of the British *Strategic Plan for the South-East*, that while there was a great growth of the service sector as a whole in London and S.E. England throughout the period 1951–68, 'within the service industries there were significant increases in the number of workers in professional and scientific services and in insurance, banking and finance, while clerical employment in general declined.' *Report of Economic Consultants*, Vol. 5, *Strategic Plan for the South East* (H.M.S.O. 1970), p. 13.
52. Galbraith, *The New Industrial State*, pp. 238–43, 271.
53. Bell, op. cit., p. 153.
54. H. Wilensky, 'The Professionalization of Everyone?', *American Journal of Sociology*, Vol. 70, No. 2, 1964, p. 146.
55. As even Bell's figures make plain: op. cit., p. 176. See also Birnbaum, 'Is there a Post-Industrial Revolution?', p. 399; and S. Rosenbaum, 'Social Services Manpower', *Social Trends 1971* (H.M.S.O.), pp. 6–12.
56. See W. S. Bennett, Jr, and M. C. Hokenstad, Jr, 'Full-Time People Workers and Conceptions of the "Professional" ', in Halmos (ed.), *Professionalization and Social Change*, pp. 38–9.
57. See, e.g., Freidson, op. cit.
58. On all this, see M. Oppenheimer, 'The Proletarianization of the Professional', in Halmos (ed.), *Professionalization and Social Change*, pp. 213–28; Braverman, op. cit., pp. 241–47, 403–9; A. Gorz, 'Technical Intelligence and the Capitalist Division of Labour', *Telos*, Vol. 12, Summer 1972; H. Wilensky, 'Work, Careers, and Social Integration', *International Social Science Journal*, Vol. XII, Fall, 1960, esp. pp. 557–8.
59. M. Cooley, 'Contradictions of Science and Technology in the Productive Process', in H. Rose and S. Rose (eds.) *The Political Economy of Science* (Macmillan, 1976), pp. 72–95.
60. A. Gorz, 'On the Class Character of Science and Scientists', in Rose and Rose (eds.), op. cit., pp. 59–71.

61. On this see especially Oppenheimer, op. cit. Let it be said, again, that what is loosely called the 'proletarianization' of professionals does not in the least entail that professionals will make common cause with non-professionals against their common enemies. Indeed the militant action among professionals is largely in *defence* of their traditional status and conditions, and is meant either to maintain or to restore their privileges and distinctive position as compared with the other groups in the population.
62. Bell, *The Coming of Post-Industrial Society*, p. 378.
63. See, e.g., Landes, *Unbound Prometheus*, pp. 61–3. And cf. Braverman:

> The contrast between science as a generalized social property incidental to production and science as capitalist property at the very centre of production is the contrast between the Industrial Revolution, which occupied the last half of the eighteenth and the first third of the nineteenth centuries, and the scientific and technical revolution, which began in the last decades of the nineteenth century and is still going on. [*Labour and Monopoly Capital*, p. 156.]

64. Richta *et al.*, *Civilization at the Crossroads*, Vol. I, p. 28.
65. For an extended account of this view, see A. Etzioni, *The Active Society* (The Free Press, New York, 1968).
66. Bell, *The Coming of Post-Industrial Society*, p. 20.
67. Drucker, *The Age of Discontinuity*, p. 52.
68. Touraine, *The Post-Industrial Society*, p. 97.
69. Ernest Mandel, quoted in Anderson and Cockburn (eds.), *Student Power*, p. 31.
70. Bell, op. cit., p. 164.
71. Touraine, op. cit., p. 101.
72. Toffler, *Future Shock*, p. 27; D. Price, *Science Since Babylon* (Yale University Press, New Haven, 1961), *passim*, esp. p. 102. And cf. the similarly unrevealing assertion of the American economist J. J. Spengler in his 1966 Presidential Address to the American Economic Association: 'Today more economists are practising than lived and died in the past four thousand years, and their number is growing even faster than the world's population.' Quoted Bell, op. cit., p. 199.
73. The United States, predictably, is ahead of most other industrial societies in this. Whereas those enrolled in college in 1900 constituted only 4 per cent of the age group 18–21, by 1970 over 50 per cent of this age group were in college. Bell, op. cit., pp. 216–17.

For expansion in the number of Ph.D.'s, etc., see ibid., pp. 220–21. For the United Kingdom see *Social Trends* (1970, annually), which includes comparisons with earlier periods.

74. For a discussion of the Solow–Denison argument, see K. Green and G. Morphet, *Research and Technology as Economic Activities* (SISCON, Manchester, 1975), pp. 12–14.
75. Heilbroner, 'Economic Problems of the "Post-Industrial" Society', p. 228.
76. Cybernetic ideas, and cybernetic technology, play an important part in the post-industrial argument. For a critical account of the ideas and influence of the cyberneticians and systems theorists, see R. Boguslaw, *The New Utopians* (Prentice-Hall, Englewood Cliffs, N.J., 1965).
77. Fritz Machlup, *The Production and Distribution of Knowledge in the United States* (Princeton University Press, Princeton, 1962), pp. 361–2.
78. Bell, *The Coming of Post-Industrial Society*, p. 212. For the figures quoted, see ibid., p. 250. For the rapid increase in R. & D. expenditure in the U.S. during this century, see Heilbroner, op. cit., p. 229. For comparison with other O.E.C.D. countries see L. Sklair, *Organized Knowledge* (Paladin Books, 1973), pp. 17–21, and C. Freeman, *The Economics of Industrial Innovation* (Penguin Books, 1974).
79. See Heilbroner, op. cit., p. 229.
80. J. Jewkes *et al.*, *The Sources of Invention* (Macmillan, 1958).
81. See especially J. Langrish *et al.*, *Wealth From Knowledge: A Study of Innovation in Industry* (Macmillan, 1972). And see the summary of other work by Freeman, op. cit., p. 208.
82. D. S. Greenberg, *The Politics of Pure Science* (2nd edn., New American Library, New York, 1971), p. 9.
83. Freeman, op. cit., p. 195.
84. Langrish *et al.*, op. cit., p. 18.
85. ibid., p. 41.
86. S. R. Williams, *Technology, Investment and Growth* (Chapman & Hall, 1967).
87. Langrish *et al.*, op. cit., p. 41. For the importance of market factors rather than scientific or inventive creativity, see Freeman, op. cit., pp. 164ff., who emphasizes especially the political and military nature of the demands.
88. Heilbroner, 'Economic Problems of the "Post-Industrial" Society', p. 230. Similar observations are powerfully made in Braverman,

op. cit., pp. 430–43. The theme, suitably generalized, is a major part of the critique of the radical 'de-professionalizers', such as Paul Goodman and Ivan Illich.

89. For these figures, see Bell, op. cit., p. 253: Sklair, op. cit., pp. 19–20.
90. For some useful remarks in this direction, see J. Floud, 'A Critique of Bell', *Survey*, Vol. 16, No. 1, 1971, pp. 25–37; and N. Chomsky, 'The Welfare/Warfare Intellectuals', *New Society*, 3 July 1969.
91. Bell, *The Coming of Post-Industrial Society*, pp. 268–98.
92. For examples, see D. Griffiths, 'Science and Technology: Liberation or Oppression', *Impact of Science on Society*, Vol. XXV, No. 4, 1975, pp. 295–305.
93. See Freeman, op. cit., p. 279. For a general discussion of the implications of the post-industrial theory for the rest of the non-industrial world, see K. Kumar, 'The Industrializing and the "Post-Industrial" Worlds: On Development and Futurology', in E. de Kadt and G. Williams (eds.), *Sociology and Development* (Tavistock Publications, 1974), pp. 329–60.
94. See the remarks at the end of Chapter 4 on the ambiguous legacy of the sociological image of industrialism. Clearly, as I have laid out the elements of that image in Chapter 3, it should have been apparent to many sociologists how closely the allegedly post-industrial tendencies in fact *continued* the deepest tendencies of industrialism (especially at the level of 'rationalization' and 'secularization'). And of course sociological critics of post-industrialism have pointed out just this (see e.g., the review of Bell by George Ross in R. Miliband and J. Saville (eds.), *The Socialist Register 1974*, Merlin Press, London, 1974). But there was an important cross-cutting influence, arising out of the English experience and the reflection upon it, which has allowed the sociological tradition to hold what one might call both a specifically sociological and 'esoteric' model of industrialism (and where Weber is most likely to be the key figure), and a more popular but still profoundly influential model, taken originally from England but powerfully developed by Marx. It is in this latter image that factories, industrial workers, etc., figure so prominently. Given the significance of the Marxist tradition in the later sociology of industrialism, it is not difficult to see how this image might lead sociologists to entertain the idea of a 'post-industrial' society – even if, on other occasions, they are prepared to stress certain continuities. It is part of the power – as well as the ambiva-

lence – of Bell's presentation, in particular, that he draws heavily on both aspects of the sociological image of industrialism.

95. For a good examination of Marx's handling of the 'new middle class', see A. Harris, 'Pure Capitalism and the Disappearance of the Middle Class', *Journal of Political Economy*, June 1939, pp. 328–56.
96. For this development, see P. Stearns, 'Is there a Post-Industrial Society?', *Society*, Vol. 11, No. 4, pp. 10–25. For the case of England, see W. J. Reader, *Professional Men: The Rise of the Professional Classes in Nineteenth Century England* (Weidenfeld & Nicolson, 1966).
97. Landes, *Unbound Prometheus*, pp. 323–6.
98. As Bell acknowledges at several points – e.g., 'it is clear that in the society of the future . . . the scientist, the professional, the *technicien*, and the technocrat will play a prominent role in the political life of the society'. op. cit., p. 79.
99. Following Comte, I am taking the word 'industry' in a broad, not narrow sense – to include any kind of collective effort transformed by the application of scientific method or the scientific spirit . . . the type of society which . . . I have called industrial, could also be called scientific . . . The qualitative difference between present-day and earlier science and technology is *obviously* the indispensable pre-condition of all the other features usually attributed to modern societies' [Aron's emphasis]. [R. Aron, *The Industrial Society* (Weidenfeld & Nicolson, 1967), pp. 98–9.]
100. A. Giddens, *The Class Structure of the Advanced Societies*, p. 262.
101. See R. Pahl and J. Winkler, 'The Coming Corporatism', *New Society*, 10 October 1974.
102. See, e.g. R. Dahrendorf, *Society and Democracy in Germany* (Weidenfeld & Nicolson, 1968), for the argument that the Nazi period in Germany accomplished the 'bourgeois revolution' that had for so long been staved off by the persisting dominance of the feudal-military Junker class.
103. E. Shils, 'Tradition, Ecology, and Institutions in the History of Sociology', *Daedalus*, Fall 1970, p. 825. See also, but from a different point of view, John Goldthorpe (note 6, above).

7 Continuities and Discontinuities in Social Development

1. T. H. Marshall, 'A Summing Up', in P. Halmos (ed.), *The Development of Industrial Societies* (University of Keele, *Sociological Review Monographs* No. 8, 1964), p. 141.

2. Ivan Illich, *Tools for Conviviality* (Calder & Boyars, 1973), p. 82.
3. A. C. Pigou, *The Economics of Welfare* (Macmillan, 1920).
4. The point has been frequently made. See, e.g., R. Heilbroner, 'Economic Problems of a "Post-Industrial" Society', in D. Potter and P. Sarre (eds.), *Dimensions of Society* (University of London Press, 1974), p. 227.
5. For the figures and a good critical discussion, see Ian Gough, 'State Expenditure in Advanced Capitalism', *New Left Review*, No. 92, July–August 1975, pp. 53–92; and J. O'Connor, *The Fiscal Crisis of the State*, (St Martin's Press, New York, 1973). See also R. E. Pahl, ' "Collective Consumption" and the State in Capitalist and State Socialist Societies', in R. Scase (ed.), *Industrial Society: Class, Cleavage, and Control* (Allen & Unwin, 1977), pp. 153–71.
6. Quoted E. P. Thompson, 'Time, Work Discipline, and Industrial Capitalism', *Past and Present*, No. 38, Dec. 1967, p. 84.
7. Quoted D. Landes, *The Unbound Prometheus: Technological Change and Industrial Development in Western Europe from 1750 to the Present* (Cambridge University Press, 1969), pp. 341–2.
8. ibid., p. 342.
9. Quoted Raphael Samuel, 'The Struggle against School in 19th Century London', University of Kent at Canterbury, Open Lecture, 1972 (*mimeo.*). For official opinion on the functions of education during this period, see also R. Johnson, *The Blue Books and Education 1816–1896* (University of Birmingham, Centre for Contemporary Cultural Studies, 1976). It is interesting that well before the 1867 Reform Act opened the way to universal suffrage, Walter Bagehot was already foreseeing its consequences and proposing (in effect) school as the remedy. As he remarked in 1848: 'The only effective security against the rule of an ignorant, miserable and vicious democracy, is to take care that the democracy shall be educated, and comfortable and moral.' Quoted by R. H. S. Crossman in his Introduction to W. Bagehot, *The English Constitution* (Fontana Library, 1963), p. 10.
10. See R. Williams, *The Long Revolution* (Penguin Books, 1965), esp. pp. 145 ff.
11. Samuel, op. cit. And cf. this comment of Young and Willmott: 'To begin with, it was the family that paid the price for the recognition of a new right to education that almost no one wanted except those who already had it. The parents finally lost the income their children might have earned and had thenceforth to contend with a

rival in the teacher for the educational role which had once been theirs alone.' M. Young and P. Willmott, *The Symmetrical Family: A Study of Work and Leisure in the London Region* (Routledge & Kegan Paul, 1973), p. 75.

12. Samuel, op. cit.
13. For these figures and projections, see *The Times*, 23 July 1976; *Education Statistics for the United Kingdom 1973* (H.M.S.O., 1975); *Social Trends 1974* (H.M.S.O., 1974); the articles by Halsey *et al.* on schools and higher education in A. H. Halsey (ed.), *Trends in British Society Since 1900* (Macmillan, 1972), pp. 148–226. Westergaard and Resler give a figure of '19 or 20 per cent' of the age group 'going into some form of fulltime higher education' in 1971, but it is unclear what levels of higher education this covers. It is certainly higher than the figure quoted in most other sources. See J. Westergaard and H. Resler, *Class in a Capitalist Society* (Heinemann, 1975), p. 320.
14. T. C. Cochran, *Social Change in Industrial Society: Twentieth Century America* (Allen & Unwin, 1971), p. 66.
15. J. S. Coleman, *Selected Educational Statistics for the United States* (The Ditchley Foundation, Oxford, 1970), p. 4. For the other figures in this paragraph: J. and M. Rowntree, 'Youth as a Class', *International Socialist Journal*, No. 5, 1968, pp. 25–58; Bell, *The Coming of Post-Industrial Society* (Basic Books, New York, 1973), pp. 216–21.
16. Quoted J. and M. Rowntree, 'Youth as a Class', p. 33.
17. ibid., p. 33.
18. Bell, *The Coming of Post-Industrial Society*, p. 215.
19. See, e.g., U.S. Dept of Health, Education, and Welfare: *Educational Research and Development in the United States* (Government Printing Office, Washington, 1970), p. 38.
20. 'Public Sector Employment, June 1974', *Department of Employment Gazette*, Dec. 1974 (H.M.S.O., 1974), p. 1141.
21. Quoted M. J. Bowman, 'The Human Investment Revolution in Economic Thought', *Sociology of Education*, Vol. 39, 1966, pp. 111–37, who also provides a convenient summary of the literature and arguments.
22. See the report in *The Times*, 15 December 1975. And see also the report of the evidence to the House of Commons sub-committee on the attainments of secondary school pupils and school-leavers, *The Times*, 7 December 1976.
23. The Committee's report is summarized in *The Times*, 23 March 1976.

24. For brief details see Everett Reimer, *School is Dead* (Penguin Books, 1971), pp. 129 ff. A major American educational research project underlined this point by concluding that it was impossible to find any correlation between schooling and occupational attainment. See C. Jencks, *Inequality: A Re-assessment of the Effect of Family and Schooling in America* (Basic Books, New York, 1972).
25. Ivar Berg, *Education and Jobs: The Great Training Robbery* (Penguin Books, 1973).
26. ibid., p. 110.
27. ibid., p. 110.
28. Quoted in Berg, op. cit., p. 91. And cf. the comment of Herbert Bienstock, New York regional director of the Bureau of Labour Statistics:

> The completion of a high school education has become an important requirement for entry into the labour market of today. Employers, finding persons with high school diplomas becoming more available in a period of rising education attainment, have come to use the diploma as a screening device, often seeking people with higher levels of education even when the job content is not necessarily becoming more complex or requiring higher levels of skill. This has been true in many of the rapidly growing job categories in the clerical, sales, and service fields. [Quoted H. Braverman, *Labour and Monopoly Capital: The Degradation of Work in the Twentieth Century* (Monthly Review Press, New York, 1974), p. 438.]

29. Quoted Braverman, op. cit., pp. 442–3.
30. Ralf Dahrendorf, in *The Times Higher Educational Supplement*, 19 November 1976.
31. Braverman, op. cit., p. 439.
32. J. and M. Rowntree, 'Youth as a Class', pp. 34–5. The authors make it clear that these figures are not 'artificially' swollen by enrolment in the Vietnam war: 'To keep our historical perspective and to avoid the problems of the statistical short run, we have brought our data only up to 1965. Our case does not rest on current war spending and we do not wish to confuse our analysis of the long run problems of U.S. capitalism by introducing data collected under the influence of the most recent imperialist war' (p. 32, n. 5).
33. Berg, op. cit., p. 24.
34. For the American evidence, see *Trends in Higher Education: Demand and Supply* (The Ditchley Foundation, Oxford, 1971), Conference Report on Education and Youth, Feb. 1971, p. 2.

For the renewed rise in the number of students in Britain, following a period of stagnant demand, see *Committee of Vice-Chancellors and Principals of the Universities of the United Kingdom: Report on the Period 1972–76* (London, 1976); and *The Times*, 23 December 1976.

35. A. H. Halsey, 'The Sociology of Education', in N. J. Smelser (ed.), *Sociology* (John Wiley & Sons, New York, 1967), pp. 398–9.
36. See A. V. Cicourel and J. I. Kitsuse, *The Educational Decision-Makers* (Bobbs-Merrill, Boston, 1963).
37. M. D. Shipman, 'Education and Social Control'. Paper presented at the British Sociological Conference on *Knowledge and Social Control*, University of Durham, March 1969.
38. Braverman, *Labour and Monopoly Capital*, pp. 439–40. For a similar argument about the function of the educational system, see Ivan Illich, *De-Schooling Society* (Calder & Boyers, 1971); and Herbert Gintis, 'The New Working Class and Revolutionary Youth', Supplement to *Continuum*, Vol. 8, Nos. 1–2, Spring-Summer 1970, pp. 151–74; Gintis, 'Education, Technology, and the Characteristics of Worker Productivity', *American Economic Review*, May 1971. Gintis emphasizes in particular the role of the educational system in inculcating attitudes conducive to the regular performance of economic tasks in a work environment which is alienating.
39. Illich, *Tools for Conviviality*.
40. ibid., p. 8.
41. The more particular proposals are set out in *De-Schooling Society*, *Energy and Equity* (Calder & Boyars, 1974), and *Medical Nemesis* (Calder & Boyars, 1975).
42. Peter Harper, 'What's *Left* of Alternative Technology', *Undercurrents*, No. 6, March–April 1976, p. 35. For a critical exposition of the alternative technology movement, see D. Dickson, *Alternative Technology and the Politics of Technical Change* (Collins/Fontana, 1974).
43. Some of the more interesting contributions, apart from those already listed, were: M. Bookchin, *Post-Scarcity Anarchism* (The Ramparts Press, Berkeley, 1971); T. Roszak, *The Making of the Counter-Culture* (Faber & Faber, 1970); T. Roszak, *Where the Wasteland Ends: Politics and Transcendence in Post-Industrial Society* (Faber & Faber, 1973); E. F. Schumacher, *Small is Beautiful* (Blond & Briggs, 1973); the reissue of Peter Kropot-

kin's classic of 1899, *Fields, Factories and Worshops* (e.g. in Colin Ward's edition, Allen & Unwin, 1974).

44. K. Marx, 'The Economic–Philosophical Manuscripts of 1844', in T. B. Bottomore (trans. and ed.), *Karl Marx: Early Writings* (Watts & Co., 1963), p. 122.
45. Braverman, *Labour and Monopoly Capital*, p. 430.
46. G. Barraclough, 'The Great World Crisis', *New York Review of Books*, 23 Jan. 1975, p. 22; Schumacher, *Small is Beautiful*, p. 115. For Barraclough's powerful reflections on the historic significance of the oil crisis, see also the following articles by him in the *New York Review of Books:* 'The End of an Era', 27 June 1974; 'Wealth and Power: The Politics of Food and Oil', 7 August 1975; 'The Haves and the Have Nots', 13 May 1976.
47. Barraclough, 'The Great World Crisis', p. 21.
48. Quoted ibid., p. 21.
49. R. Bacon and W. Eltis, *Britain's Economic Problem: Too Few Producers* (Macmillan, 1976), p. 6.
50. ibid., pp. 14–15, 84–5.
51. See especially Illich, *Medical Nemesis, passim.* And for the loss of service entailed through the increasing bureaucratization of the health service, see Max Gammon, *Health and Security: Report on Public Provision for Medical Care* (St Michael's Organization, London, 1976).
52. H. Wilensky, *The Welfare State and Inequality* (University of California Press, Berkeley, 1975), p. 30. Wilensky gives only figures for health and social security; the figure for education previously given – about 6 per cent of G.N.P. – is added to this.
53. *The Times*, 7 July 1975.
54. A simple example illustrates the grotesque situation that can come about through the multiplication of agencies involved in a particular social problem. The Campaign for the Homeless and Rootless sent a memorandum to the Manpower Services Commission in August 1976, complaining about re-training provision for the 'socially disadvantaged' – disabled people, unskilled manual labourers, homeless people, etc. In making its appeal the group had to address itself not only to the Commission, but to the Training Services Agency, the Employment Services Agency, the Department of Health and Social Security, and a whole host of voluntary organizations (for a report see *The Times*, 20 August 1976). It is not surprising that many 'socially disadvantaged' people find that the hand stretched out to help is palsied with bureaucratic

overkill. The situation of poor families seems to be especially tough in this respect. Westergaard and Resler say 'there are today probably over forty separate types of service – national or local, each with its own test or tests of poverty – a considerable number of which may be relevant for an individual family with a low income.' *Class in a Capitalist Society*, p. 179.

55. Max Weber, 'Bureaucracy', in H. H. Gerth and C. Wright Mills (eds.), *From Max Weber: Essays in Sociology* (Routledge & Kegan Paul, 1948), p. 229.
56. Quoted J. L. Bower, 'On the Amoral Organization', in R. Marris (ed.), *The Corporate Society* (Macmillan, 1974), p. 178.
57. For a discussion and elaboration, see E. Goodman, *The Impact of Size* (The Acton Society Trust, London, 1969); and M. Slater, *Economies of Scale: Sources and Measurement* (Acton Society Trust, London, 1975).
58. For the managerial philosophy in government, see T. Smith, *Anti-Politics* (Charles Knight, 1972); and S. Thorn, *A Study of the Size Implications of Recent Public Policies* (Acton Society Trust, London, 1974).
59. See A. Sampson, *The New Anatomy of Britain* (Hodder & Stoughton, 1971), p. 570. See also L. Hannah, *The Rise of the Corporate Economy* (Methuen, 1976), p. 216, Table A2, which shows the share of the 100 largest firms in manufacturing net output in Britain over the century to be as follows: 1909, 15 per cent; 1970, 45 per cent.
60. G. Newbould, *Management and Merger Activity* (Guthstead, Liverpool, 1970). This finding is supported by Siekman's study of takeovers in the same period. See his article in J. M. Samuels (ed.), *Readings in Mergers and Takeovers* (Elek Books, London, 1972).
61. T. Burns, 'On the Rationale of the Corporate System', in R. Marris (ed.), *The Corporate Society*, p. 174.
62. ibid., p. 171.
63. ibid., pp. 172–4.
64. ibid., p. 165.
65. Schumacher, *Small is Beautiful*, p. 17.
66. 'A Blueprint for Survival', *Ecologist*, Vol. 2, No. 1, Jan. 1972, p. 2.
67. Schumacher, op. cit., p. 13.
68. ibid., p. 14.
69. See the letter by F. Arnold Robinson in *The Times*, 25 August 1976. The possibility of conversion to solar energy use is per-

suasively argued in an earlier letter by Prof. J. O'M. Bockris, *The Times*, 14 August 1976. The British Government is belatedly recognizing the importance of solar energy, and in February 1977 announced a much expanded programme of research. In a report published in that month the Department of Energy calculated that even within the short term solar energy could make a significant contribution to the country's energy needs – perhaps as much as 20 per cent over the next fifty years. See *Solar Energy: Its Potential Contribution Within the United Kingdom* (Dept of Energy, Energy Paper No. 16, H.M.S.O., 1977).

The question of salvation through nuclear energy, too, will inevitably be raised here. This is clearly not the place to attempt a detailed discussion. But one can at least say that the transfer to nuclear energy *on the scale necessary* for it to supply most of the world's energy needs poses problems of a dimension scarcely ever contemplated by its proponents. Not to mention the likelihood of industrial accidents, or industrial sabotage, the problems of the storage, transportation, and disposal of waste materials remain intractable (as, to their great credit, the Swedish electorate realized in turning out, in the election of 1976, the Social Democratic Party after forty-four years in power, when Prime Minister Olaf Paalme proposed going ahead with a massive nuclear programme). As a Working Party on the Control of Pollution put it in its report to the British Secretary of State for the Environment,

> the biggest cause of worry for the future is the storage of the long-lived radioactive wastes . . . Unlike other pollutants, there is no way of destroying radioactivity . . . so there is no alternative to permanent storage . . . In effect, we are consciously and deliberately accumulating a toxic substance on the offchance that it may be possible to get rid of it at a later date. We are committing future generations to tackle a problem which we do not know how to handle. [Quoted Schumacher, *Small is Beautiful*, pp. 133–4.]

See also Schumacher's own persuasive case against the reliance on nuclear energy as a way out of the energy dilemma, ibid., pp. 124–35. The debate about nuclear power has been most instructively re-opened in Britain following the publication, late in 1976, of the Sixth Report of the Royal Commission on Environmental Pollution (the Flowers Report), and its recommendation that the Government consider very carefully before committing itself to a programme of fast breeder nuclear reactors. For a powerful attack on the whole nuclear energy strategy, and the advocacy of alternative energy use (especially wind and water), see the review of the Flowers Report by Lord Rothschild, *The Times*, 27 September 1976; and Sir Martin Ryle, *The Times*, 14 December 1976.

70. E. J. Mishan, *The Costs of Economic Growth* (Penguin Books, 1969), p. 119.
71. ibid., p. 104.
72. As shown by Martin Slater in his review of the evidence. See note 57, above.
73. Dennison's findings are quoted by Colin Ward in his edition of Kropotkin, *Fields, Factories, and Workshops*, p. 160.
74. F. Engels, *The Condition of the Working Class in England*, trans. and eds., W. O. Henderson and W. H. Chaloner (Basil Blackwell, 1958), pp. 133–4.
75. Marx, 'The Economic-Philosophical Manuscripts of 1844', in Bottomore, *Karl Marx: Early Writings*, p. 125.
76. First quotation, from an American car worker, in C. R. Walker and R. H. Guest, *The Man on the Assembly Line* (Harvard University Press, Cambridge, Mass., 1952), p. 176; the second, from an English car worker, in Huw Beynon, *Working for Ford* (Allen Lane The Penguin Press, 1973), p. 114.
77. Clerical worker quoted in *On the Quality of Working Life*, Manpower Papers No. 7, Department of Employment (H.M.S.O., 1973), p. 9.
78. For some of the evidence, and an interesting discussion of the deceitful nature of the Utilitarian bargain of work ('pain') for leisure ('pleasure'), see A. Clayre, 'Improving the Quality of Work', *Universities Quarterly*, Vol. 30, No. 4, Autumn 1976, pp. 433–43. As Clayre puts it:

    > Since the Utilitarians . . . it has been usual to think of work as 'pain', and of pay and time away from work as adding up to 'pleasure'; thus it has been 'economically rational' for people to do long, unpleasant and boring work for the sake of higher pay. But if the relation between work and leisure is not of this kind at all – if nothing can repay a man in leisure for the capacities of enjoyment that depriving work has destroyed – then the monotonous work is paid for in a coinage which work itself debases, and the entire notion of a fair wage-bargain for depriving work becomes suspect' [p. 441].

79. There is a useful historical survey in H. Wilensky, 'The Uneven Distribution of Leisure: The Impact of Economic Growth on "Free Time" ', *Social Problems*, Vol. 9, Summer 1961, pp. 32–56.

For Britain, see M. A. Bienefeld, *Working Hours in British Industry: An Economic History* (Weidenfeld & Nicolson/L.S.E. Research Monographs, 1972). For the United States, see J. S. Zeisel, 'The Workweek in American Industry 1850–1956', in E. Larrabee and R. Meyersohn (eds.), *Mass Leisure* (The Free Press, Glencoe, 1958), pp. 145–53; and P. Henle, 'Recent Growth of Paid Leisure for U.S. Workers', in E. O. Smigel (ed.), *Work and Leisure* (College and University Press, New Haven, 1963), pp. 182–203.

80. For some recent assessments see, Young and Willmott, *The Symmetrical Family*, pp. 128 ff.; *Social Trends 1975* (H.M.S.O., 1975), p. 86, Table 3.14; A. F. Sillitoe, *Britain in Figures* (Penguin Books, 1971), pp. 106–7. These figures are for male workers only – women do less overtime and hence have a shorter working week on average.
81. Reported in Ward's edition of Kropotkin, op. cit., p. 189.
82. ibid., p. 189. For the 'moonlighting' phenomenon in the United States, see H. Swados, 'Less Work – Less Leisure', in Larrabee and Meyersohn (eds.), *Mass Leisure*, pp. 353–63.
83. J. M. and R. E. Pahl, *Managers and Their Wives* (Penguin Books, 1972), pp. 252–8.
84. Young and Willmott, *The Symmetrical Family*, pp. 133–42.
85. Reported by Young and Willmott, op. cit., p. 146.
86. Wilensky, 'The Uneven Distribution of Leisure', p. 39. For further evidence and discussion of the long hours of managers and professionals, see also D. Riesman, 'Leisure and Work in Post-Industrial Society', in Larrabee and Meyersohn (eds.), *Mass Leisure*, pp. 363–85; and D. Riesman and R. Weiss, 'Some Issues in the Future of Leisure', in E. O. Smigel (ed.), *Work and Leisure*, pp. 168–81.
87. For Britain, see 'A View of Occupational Employment in 1981', *Department of Employment Gazette*, July 1975 (H.M.S.O., 1975), pp. 619–22; Young and Willmott, *The Symmetrical Family*, p. 25. For the U.S., Bell, *The Coming of Post-Industrial Society*, p. 135. And see also notes 50–51 to Chapter 6.
88. Although there could be a significant growth of 'enforced leisure' as a result of mass unemployment. This would continue the pattern of today where much of the shorter working week or working year is 'enjoyed' by those who least want or can use this free time – unskilled workers, older workers, young black school-leavers, etc. See Wilensky, 'The Uneven Distribution of Leisure', *passim.*

89. For an extended discussion, see K. Kumar, 'Revolution and Industrial Society: An Historical Perspective', *Sociology*, Vol. 10, No. 2, 1976, pp. 245–69.
90. For these figures see, Department of Employment, Manpower Papers No. 4, *Absenteeism* (H.M.S.O., 1971); A. Clayre, 'Improving the Quality of Work'; Braverman, *Labour and Monopoly Capital*, pp. 32–3.
91. These three authors are quoted by R. Hyman, *Strikes* (Collins/Fontana, 1972), p. 116 – although it must be said that Hyman himself interprets these findings differently. One also has to note the renewed concern with the wages issue in the first half of the 1970s – but this is hardly surprising in a period of extraordinarily rapid inflation, and does not affect the main inference from the evidence of the earlier period.
92. For an account of the Lordstown plant and the strike, see David Wilson, 'The Cruel Industry', *Observer* (Business Section), 3 Sept. 1972. It might be worth mentioning here that some writers have interpreted even direct wages strikes as fundamentally about the nature of work and work satisfaction: e.g., André Gorz:

> In fact, the majority of wage claims are revolts against oppression – revolts against the systematic mutilation of the worker's personality, against the stunting of his professional and human faculties, against the subordination of the nature and content of his working life to technological developments which rob him of his powers of initiative, control and even foresight. Wage claims are much more frequently motivated by *rebellion against working conditions* than by a revolt against the economic *burden of exploitation* borne by labour. They express a demand for *as much money as possible to pay for the life wasted, the time lost, the freedom alienated* in working under these conditions. The workers insist on being paid as much as possible *not because they put wages* (money and what it can buy) *above everything else* but because . . . workers can fight the employer only for *the price* of their labour, not for control of the conditions and content of their work' [Gorz's emphases]. [Gorz, 'Work and Consumption', in P. Anderson and R. Blackburn (eds.), *Towards Socialism* (Collins/Fontana, 1965), p. 319.]

93. L. Taylor and P. Walton, 'Industrial Sabotage: Motives and Meanings', in S. Cohen (ed.), *Images of Deviance* (Penguin Books, 1971), p. 219.
94. Quoted ibid., p. 221.

95. H. Swados, 'The Myth of the Happy Worker', in M. Stein, A. J. Vidich and D. M. White (eds.), *Identity and Anxiety* (The Free Press, New York, 1960), p. 204.
96. Quoted Braverman, *Labour and Monopoly Capital*, pp. 34–5.
97. For brief accounts of these schemes, see *On the Quality of Working Life*, Department of Employment, Manpower Papers No. 7 (H.M.S.O., 1973); Clayre, 'Improving the Quality of Work'; and the articles collected together in Mary Weir (ed.), *Job Satisfaction* (Collins/Fontana, 1976).
98. Weir, Introduction to *Job Satisfaction*, pp. 19–20.
99. Robert Taylor, 'The Volvo Way of Work', *New Society*, 15 April 1976.
100. Findings reported in *On the Quality of Working Life*, pp. 34–40; and Taylor, op. cit.
101. *On the Quality of Working Life*, pp. 41–2. With this judgement Clayre, above, n. 97, concurs, as does Weir, op. cit., p. 21.
102. See the spirited attack in the pamphlet *Job Enrichment: It's a Con . . .* (Industrial Sociology Unit, Imperial College, University of London, 1972, mimeo.), prepared by a group of trade unionists and industrial sociologists. Acknowledging this, a group of shop stewards at Lucas Aerospace in Britain have prepared a 'Corporate Plan' which goes beyond demands for job enrichment, worker-directors, and the like, and which suggests a fundamental re-direction in the industry's use of its resources of advanced technology and skilled technical manpower. The plan includes detailed proposals for 150 new products and processes. The intention is that these are all products which are socially useful (e.g. various safety devices for North Sea Oil exploration), and that will continue to use to the fullest extent the scientific and technical skill of the workforce, thus avoiding redundancies. See M. Cooley, 'Socially Useful Work', *Universities Quarterly*, Vol. 32, Dec. 1977.
103. Braverman, *Labour and Monopoly Capital*, p. 39.
104. K. Marx and F. Engels, *The German Ideology*, ed. R. Pascal, (International Publishers, New York, 1947), p. 22.
105. Riesman, 'Leisure and Work in Post-industrial Society,' pp. 364, 376.
106. J. M. and R. E. Pahl, *Managers and their Wives*, esp. pp. 252 ff; J. Child and B. Macmillan, 'Managers and their Leisure', in M. Smith, S. Parker, and C. Smith (eds.), *Leisure and Society in Britain* (Allen Lane The Penguin Press, 1973), pp. 111–26.

107. Quoted A. Sampson, *The New Anatomy of Britain*, p. 597.
108. See R. Williams and D. Guest, 'Are the Middle Classes Becoming Work-Shy?' *New Society*, 1 July 1971. For a general discussion of the attitudes and outlook of these middle-class groups, see further, K. Kumar, 'The Salariat', *New Society*, 21 October 1976.
109. B. Heraud, 'Professionalism, Radicalism, and Social Change', in P. Halmos (ed.), *Professionalization and Social Change* (University of Keele, *Sociological Review Monograph* No. 20, 1973), p. 86.
110. For a discussion of some of these movements in Britain see Heraud, op, cit.; P. Leonard, 'Professionalization, Community Action and the Growth of Social Service Bureaucracies', in Halmos (ed.), op. cit., pp. 103–118; for the United States, R. Perrucci, 'In the Service of Man: Radical Movements in the Professions', in Halmos (ed.), op. cit., pp. 179–94.
111. Needless to say this too is by no means new – is anything truly so? – in the history of the industrial societies. Other periods – notably that immediately preceding the First World War and that following it – have shown a strong ideological hostility to science and technology. But again the matter is one of degree. I would argue that the penetration of the anti-science ideology is much greater today than it ever was in the earlier periods – much of this, of course, having to do with the 'nationalization' of consciousness brought about by the mass media.
112. For an all-out attack on scientific reason (in the Newtonian tradition), see T. Roszak, *Where the Wasteland Ends* (see note 43 above); for the dismissal of the idea of any privileged methodology, see P. Feyerabend, *Against Method: Outline of an Anarchist Theory of Knowledge* (New Left Books, 1975). See also H. Marcuse, *One Dimensional Man* (Sphere Books edn, 1968), who is careful not to attack science as such, but the dominant 'bourgeois' (Weberian) interpretation of it, the 'technical reason' which has become, Marcuse argues, institutionalized, in the theory and practice of modern industrial societies. So also – but more cautiously – J. Habermas, 'Technology and Science as "Ideology" ', in his *Toward a Rational Society* (Heinemann, 1971), pp. 81–122.
113. Johan Galtung, *Images of the World in the Year 2000* (European Co-ordination Centre for Research and Documentation in Social Sciences, Vienna, 1930), p. 25. For similar findings about the Netherlands, see M. Abrams, 'Mass View of the Future: A Report from the Netherlands', *Futures*, Vol. 3, No. 2, June 1971, pp. 103–15.

114. See, e.g. University of Kent at Canterbury, Appointments Service, *Ninth Annual Report 1974–5*; and, more generally, the report in *The Times*, 17 July 1976. In the case of Britain, the whole phenomenon may perhaps be seen as a resurgence of the anti-industry, anti-'trade' cultural attitude that is of such long standing in British history, and which in retrospect may be seen to have been offset only temporarily by the successes of the early Industrial Revolution. See Ch. 4., note 70, above.

115. See D. Bell, *The Cultural Contradictions of Capitalism* (Heinemann, 1976).

116. Clark Kerr *et al.*, *Industrialism and Industrial Man* (2nd edn, Penguin Books, 1973), pp. 302–4.

8 Progress and Industrialism

1. Saint-Simon, 'Letters of Henri de Saint-Simon to an American' (1817), in F. Markham (ed. and trans.), *Henri de Saint-Simon: Social Organization, The Science of Man, and Other Writings* (Harper Torchbooks, New York, 1964), p. 69.
2. See further, Chapter 7, note 89, above.
3. What I have been describing here will be easily recognizable to many as the process of Darwinian evolution. For a brief attempt to apply Darwinian concepts to a theory of progress and social change, see K. Kumar, 'Sociological Darwinism', *Biology and Human Affairs*, Vol. 40, No. 2, 1975, pp. 71–6, and Vol. 40, No. 3, 1975, pp. 146–53.
4. E. Gellner, 'Our Current Sense of History', *European Journal of Sociology*, Vol. XII, No. 2, 1971, p. 178. For further consideration of the industrial societies' sense of historical dispossession, see J. H. Plumb, *The Death of the Past* (Penguin Books, 1973); and Golo Mann, 'The History Lesson', *Encounter*, August 1972.
5. Cf. Harold Lasswell's remark of 1966, 'Mankind is passing from the primacy of the past to the primacy of expectations of vast future change.' Quoted Wendell Bell and James A. Mau (eds.), *The Sociology of the Future* (Harper & Row, New York, 1972), p. 2. Cf. also the claim of Bell and Mau: 'A reorientation of social research is in order because the rise of human mastery is ushering in new dynamics of change, under which man is increasingly liberated from the bonds of the past and is increasingly able to transcend the limitations of the present.' ibid., p. 12.
6. G. Barraclough, *An Introduction to Contemporary History* (Watts & Co., 1964). And see also Chapter 7, note 45.

7. J. Schumpeter, *Capitalism, Socialism, and Democracy* (2nd edn, Allen & Unwin, 1947), p. 139. The exceptional nature of the century of peace *between* nations is the subject of Karl Polanyi, *The Great Transformation: The Political and Economic Origins of our Time* (Beacon Press, Boston, 1957; first published in 1944).
8. George Steiner, 'The Many Faces of Violence', *Listener*, 9 October 1975, p. 460.
9. E. Gellner, 'A Social Contract in Search of An Idiom', *Political Quarterly*, Vol. 46, No. 2, April–June 1975, pp. 127–52.
10. ibid., p. 140.
11. See R. E. Pahl and J. T. Winkler, 'The Coming Corporatism', *New Society*, 10 October 1974, pp. 72–6; J. T. Winkler, 'The Corporatist Economy: Theory and Administration', in R. Scase (ed.), *Industrial Society: Class, Cleavage and Control* (Allen & Unwin, 1977), pp. 43–58; G. Newbould and A. Jackson, *The Receding Ideal* (Guthstead Ltd, Liverpool, 1972); J. Robertson, *Profit or People? The New Social Role of Money* (Calder & Boyars, 1974). An interesting earlier version of the late industrial/pre-industrial parallel saw the growth and power of the large corporations as similar in many ways to the emergence of 'bastard feudalism' in fifteenth-century England. See R. Samuel, '"Bastard" Capitalism', in E. P. Thompson (ed.), *Out of Apathy* (Stevens & Sons, London, 1960), pp. 19–55. The difference between 'bastard capitalism' and 'corporatism' marks the passage from a condition of weak state power *vis-à-vis* the private corporation to one of preponderant power.
12. For the steady growth, in practice, of functional representation in recent British politics, see T. Smith, 'Trends and Tendencies in Re-ordering the Representation of Interests in Britain', Paper delivered to the Annual Conference of the Political Studies Association, Nottingham, 22–4 March 1976.
13. Lord Hewart of Bury, *The New Despotism* (Ernest Benn, London, 1929). The parallel has become a commonplace since.
14. It is easy enough to see, from the accounts of the earlier chapters, how readily movements towards 'corporatism', etc., fit into the basic trends of rationalization and centralization implicit in industrialism from the very beginning. But it is, for certain purposes, important also to see nineteenth-century industrial society from another angle, as a *liberal* polity and economy; and from this point of view corporatism and the 'new despotism' express discontinuities. For further discussion of this point, see K. Kumar,

'Continuities and Discontinuities in the Development of Industrial Societies', in R. Scase (ed.), *Industrial Society*, pp. 29–42.

15. Penty's book was called *Old Worlds for New: A Study of the Post-Industrial State* (London, 1917). It is quoted by Bell, *The Coming of Post-Industrial Society* (Basic Books, New York, 1973), p. 37, n. 45.
16. M. Young and P. Willmott, *The Symmetrical Family: A Study of Work and Leisure in the London Region* (Routledge & Kegan Paul, 1973), esp. pp. 263 ff.
17. ibid., p. 269.
18. ibid., p. 267. The view of the increased importance of family life, of a move towards 'family-centredness' is supported by J. H. Goldthorpe, D. Lockwood, F. Bechhofer, J. Platt, *The Affluent Worker* (3 Vols., Cambridge University Press, 1968–69). And cf. Rosalind Mitchison: 'The family has survived much better as an institution than any other competitor . . . compulsory family togetherness is a dominant feature of our world.' 'The Family', *Listener*, 22 February 1973, p. 234.
19. In April 1974, nearly a quarter of male manual workers in manufacturing industry were working shifts, with a much higher proportion in such industries as metals, coal mining, and petroleum products. In June 1974 one in four women in manufacturing industry were working part-time. See P. J. Sloane, 'Changing Patterns of Working Hours', Department of Employment, *Manpower Paper No. 13* (H.M.S.O., 1975), p. 1.
20. British schemes are described and discussed in Sloane, op. cit.; American schemes in Riva Poor (ed.), *4 Days, 40 Hours* (Pan Books, 1972). For similar developments on the European continent, see *The Times-Europa* Report, 1 April 1975. At the time of the report, between 30 and 40 per cent of all employees in Switzerland were working flexible hours; about 800 firms and organizations in France had adopted the system; 500 in Britain, accounting for about 100,000 employees; one out of three private firms in West Germany, and six out of ten government organizations. The biggest single experiment in flexible working hours has been conducted at the Fiat works in Italy, affecting 25,000 employees since Feb. 1973.
21. Quoted Sloane, op. cit., p. 3; see also ibid., pp. 36–7 for similar responses to other schemes of flexible working hours.
22. Young and Willmott, *The Symmetrical Family*, p. 284.
23. Philippe Lamour and Jacques de Calendar, *Prends le temps de*

Vivre (Seuil, Paris, 1974), quoted in *The Times-Europa Report*, above.

24. See E. P. Thompson, 'Time, Work Discipline, and Industrial Capitalism', *Past and Present*, No. 38, Dec. 1967, pp. 56–97.
25. J. Langdon Goodman, *Man and Automation* (Penguin Books, 1959), p. 101.
26. Young and Willmott, op. cit., p. 285.
27. J. Martin and A. R. D. Norman, *The Computerized Society* (Prentice-Hall, Englewood Cliffs, N.J., 1970), p. 32. For the further discussion of the decentralizing potential of the computer and more generally the new electronic media of communication, see Stafford Beer, *Designing Freedom* (John Wiley & Sons, London and New York, 1974); Marshall McLuhan, *Understanding Media: The Extensions of Man* (Sphere Books, 1967); Hans Magnus Enzensberger, 'Constituents of a Theory of the Media', *New Left Review*, Vol. 64, Nov.–Dec. 1970, pp. 13–36.
28. Young and Willmott, op. cit., p. 285.
29. C. H. Waddington, 'Work and Leisure' (mimeo., *School of the Man-Made Future*, University of Edinburgh, 1972).
30. I know of several examples of this phenomenon, but unfortunately not of any study of it that I can cite.
31. R. E. Pahl, 'Patterns of Urban Life in the Next Fifteen Years', *Universities Quarterly*, Vol. 30, No. 4, Autumn 1976, p. 403.
32. For an interesting account of how these values have been literally built into English landscape and 'townscape', see F. Inglis, 'Nation and Community: A Landscape and its Morality', *Universities Quarterly*, Vol. 30, No. 4. Autumn 1976, pp. 444–61.
33. *The Times*, 14 October 1976. There is of course a long tradition of foreigners pointing out the virtues of England to the incurious or uncaring English – Tocqueville and, in a different way, Benjamin Disraeli, being good nineteenth-century examples (not to mention a host of Scotsmen). For other examples at the present time, cf. this remark of the American economist John Kenneth Galbraith: 'Your real problem is that you were the first of the great industrialized nations, and so things happen here first – you are living out the concern for some more leisurely relationship with industrial life that other people have been discussing for 50 years or more.' *Sunday Times*, 2 January 1977; and see the interview with another distinguished foreigner resident in London, Arthur Koestler, in *The Times*, 21 February 1977.
34. F. Engels, 'On Authority', in K. Marx and F. Engels, *Selected*

Works in Two Volumes (Foreign Languages Publishing House, Moscow, 1962), Vol. I, p. 637.

35. Robert Heilbroner, 'Men at Work', *New York Review of Books*, 23 Jan. 1975, p. 8.
36. K. Marx, *The Poverty of Philosophy* (International Publishers, New York, 1963. First published 1847), p. 137.
37. ibid., p 167–8.
38. Andrew Ure, quoted by Marx, op. cit., pp. 140–41.
39. S. A. Marglin, 'What Do Bosses Do? The Origins and Functions of Hierarchy in Capitalist Production', *The Review of Radical Political Economics*, Vol. 6, No. 2, Summer, 1974, p. 186.
40. ibid., pp. 87–8.
41. ibid., p. 84.
42. Cf. Marx's comment: 'As the concentration of instruments [of labour] develops, the division of labour develops also, and *vice versa*. This is why every big mechanical invention is followed by a greater division of labour, and each increase in the division of labour gives rise in turn to new mechanical inventions.' *The Poverty of Philosophy*, p. 139.
43. Marglin, op. cit., p. 95.
44. Francis Bacon, *Novum Organum*, Aphorisms, Book 1, VI.

Bibliography

ABRAMS, M., 'Mass View of the Future: A Report from the Netherlands', *Futures*, Vol. 3, No. 2, 1971, pp. 100–115.

ABRAMS, P., 'The Sense of the Past and the Origins of Sociology', *Past and Present*, No. 55, May 1972, pp. 18–32.

ALMOND, G., and COLEMAN, J. S. (eds.), *The Politics of the Developing Areas*, Princeton University Press, Princeton, 1960.

ANDERSON, P., 'Origins of the Present Crisis', in P. Anderson and R. Blackburn (eds.), *Towards Socialism* (q.v., below), pp. 11–52.

ANDERSON, P., and BLACKBURN, R. (eds.), *Towards Socialism*, Collins, 1965.

ANDERSON, P., and COCKBURN, A. (eds.), *Student Power*, Penguin Books, 1969.

APOSTOL, P., 'Marxism and the Structure of the Future', *Futures*, Vol. 4, No. 3, 1972, pp. 201–10.

ARENDT, H., *On Revolution*, Faber & Faber, 1963.

ARMENGAUD, A., 'Population in Europe 1700–1914', in C. Cipolla (ed.), *The Industrial Revolution* (q.v., below), pp. 22–76.

ARON, R., *The Opium of the Intellectuals*, Secker & Warburg, 1957.

ARON, R., *The Industrial Society*, Weidenfeld & Nicolson, 1967.

AVINERI, S. (ed.), *Karl Marx on Colonialism and Modernization*, Doubleday & Co., New York, 1969.

BACON, R., and ELTIS, W., *Britain's Economic Problem: Too Few Producers*, Macmillan, 1976.

BAIN, G. SAYERS, BACON, R., and PIMLOTT, J., 'The Labour Force', in A. H. Halsey (ed.), *Trends in British Society Since 1900* (q.v., below), pp. 97–128.

BARRACLOUGH, G., *An Introduction to Contemporary History*, Watts, 1964.

BARRACLOUGH, G., 'The End of An Era', *New York Review of Books*, 27 June 1974.

BARRACLOUGH, G., 'The Great World Crisis', *New York Review of Books*, 23 January 1975.

BARRACLOUGH, G., 'Wealth and Power: The Politics of Food and Oil', *New York Review of Books*, 7 August 1975.

BARRACLOUGH, G., 'The Haves and the Have Nots', *New York Review of Books*, 13 May 1976.

BECKER, C., *The Heavenly City of the Eighteenth Century Philosophers*, Yale University Press, New Haven, 1932.

BECKER, H., 'Sacred and Secular Societies', *Social Forces*, Vol. 28, No. 4, 1950, pp. 361–76.

BEER, S., *Designing Freedom*, John Wiley & Sons, London and New York, 1974.

BELL, D., *The End of Ideology*, Collier Books, New York, 1961.

BELL, D., 'The Study of the Future', *The Public Interest*, No. 1, Fall 1965, pp. 119–30.

BELL, D., 'Notes on the Post-Industrial Society', *The Public Interest*, No. 6, 1967, pp. 24–35, and No. 7, 1967, pp. 102–118.

BELL, D. (ed.), *Towards the Year 2000: Work in Progress*, Beacon Press, Boston, 1968.

BELL, D., *The Coming of Post-Industrial Society: A Venture in Social Forecasting*, Basic Books, New York, 1973.

BELL, D., *The Cultural Contradictions of Capitalism*, Heinemann, London, 1976.

BELL, W., and MAU, J. A. (eds.), *The Sociology of the Future*, Harper & Row, New York, 1972.

BENDIX, R., 'Tradition and Modernity Re-considered', *Comparative Studies in Society and History*, Vol. IX, 1967, pp. 292–346.

BENNETT, W. S., Jr, and HOKENSTAD, M. C., Jr, 'Full-Time People Workers and Conceptions of the "Professional" ', in P. Halmos (ed.), *Professionalization and Social Change*, (q.v., below), pp. 21–46.

BERG, I., *Education and Jobs: The Great Training Robbery*, Penguin Books, 1973.

BERGER, P. L., *The Social Reality of Religion*, Faber & Faber, 1969.

BERGER, P. L., BERGER, B., and KELLNER, H., *The Homeless Mind*, Penguin Books, 1974.

BERNSTEIN, H., 'Modernization Theory and the Sociological Study of Development', *Journal of Development Studies*, Vol. 7, No. 2, 1971, pp. 141–60.

BEYNON, H., *Working for Ford*, Allen Lane The Penguin Press, 1973.

BEZANSON, A., 'The Early Use of the Term "Industrial Revolution" ', *Quarterly Journal of Economics*, Vol. XXXVI, 1921–2, pp. 343–49.

BIENEFELD, M. A., *Working Hours in British Industry: An Economic History*, Weidenfeld & Nicolson/L.S.E. Research Monographs, 1972.

BIRNBAUM, N., *Toward a Critical Sociology*, Oxford University Press, New York, 1971.

BLEWETT, N., 'The Franchise in the United Kingdom 1885–1918', *Past and Present*, No. 32, Dec. 1965, pp. 27–56.

BOCK, K., 'Darwin and Social Theory', *Philosophy of Science*, Vol. 22, No. 2, 1955, pp. 123–34.

BOCK, K., 'Evolution, Function, and Change', *American Sociological Review*, Vol. 28, No. 2, 1963, pp. 229–37.

BOGUSLAW, R., *The New Utopians*, Prentice-Hall, Englewood Cliffs, New Jersey, 1965.

BOOKCHIN, M., *Post-Scarcity Anarchism*, The Ramparts Press, Berkeley, 1971.

BOTTOMORE, T. B., *Sociology as Social Criticism*, Allen & Unwin, 1975.

BOULDING, K., *The Meaning of the Twentieth Century: The Great Transition*, Harper & Row, New York, 1964.

BOWMAN, M. J., 'The Human Investment Revolution in Economic Thought', *Sociology of Education*, Vol. 39, 1966, pp. 111–37.

BRAMSON, L., *The Political Context of Sociology*, Princeton University Press, Princeton, 1961.

BRAVERMAN, H., *Labour and Monopoly Capital: The Degradation of Work in the Twentieth Century*, Monthly Review Press, New York, 1974.

BRIGGS, A., *Victorian Cities*, Penguin Books, 1968.

BRZEZINSKI, Z., *Between Two Ages: America's Role in the Technetronic Era*, The Viking Press, New York, 1970.

BURCKHARDT, J., *Reflections on History*, trans. M. D. Hottinger, Allen & Unwin, 1943.

BURNHAM, J., *The Managerial Revolution*, Penguin Books, 1962. (First published in 1941.)

BURNS, T. (ed.), *Industrial Man*, Penguin Books, 1969.

BURNS, T., 'On the Rationale of the Corporate System', in R. Marris (ed.), *The Corporate Society* (q.v., below), pp. 121–77.

BURROW, J. W., *Evolution and Society: A Study in Victorian Social Theory*, Cambridge University Press, 1966.

BURY, J. B., *The Idea of Progress*, Macmillan, 1923.

CALDER, N. (ed.), *The World in 1984*, 2 vols., Penguin Books, 1964.

CARLYLE, T., 'Signs of the Times' (1829), in *Thomas Carlyle: Selected Writings*, ed. A. Shelston, Penguin Books, 1971.

CHAMBERS, J. D., 'Enclosure and the Labour Supply in the Industrial Revolution', *Economic History Review*, 2nd Series, Vol. 5, 1953, pp. 318–43.

CHILD, J., and MACMILLAN, B., 'Managers and their Leisure', in M. Smith, S. Parker, and C. Smith (eds.), *Leisure and Society in Britain* (q.v., below), pp. 111–26.

CHOMSKY, N., *American Power and the New Mandarins*, Penguin Books, 1969.

CHOMSKY, N., 'The Welfare/Warfare Intellectuals', *New Society*, 3 July 1969.

Ciba Foundation Symposium, *The Future as an Academic Discipline*, Elsevier, Amsterdam, 1975.

CIPOLLA, C. (ed.), *The Industrial Revolution*, Collins/Fontana, 1973.

CLARK, G. KITSON, *The Making of Victorian England*, Methuen, 1962.

CLARKE P., *Small Businesses: How They Survive and Succeed*, David & Charles, Newton Abbot, 1972.

CLAYRE, A., 'Improving the Quality of Work', *Universities Quarterly*, Vol. 30, No. 4, 1976, pp. 433–43.

COCHRAN, T. C., *Social Change in Industrial Society: Twentieth Century America*, Allen & Unwin, 1971.

COLEMAN, D. C., 'Gentlemen and Players', *Economic History Review*, 2nd Series, Vol. 26, No. 1, 1973, pp. 92–116.

COLLINS, H., and ABRAMSKY, C., *Karl Marx and the British Labour Movement*, Macmillan, 1965.

COOLEY, M., 'Contradictions of Science and Technology in the Productive Process', in H. Rose and S. Rose (eds.), *The Political Economy of Science* (q.v., below), pp. 72–95.

CROZIER, M., *The World of the Office Worker*, Chicago University Press, Chicago, 1971.

DAHRENDORF, R., 'Recent Changes in the Class Structure of European Societies', *Daedalus*, Vol. 92, No. 1, 1964, pp. 225–70.

DAHRENDORF, R., *Society and Democracy in Germany*, Weidenfeld & Nicolson, 1968.

DAVIS, K., 'Population', in G. Hardin (ed.), *Science, Conflict, and Society*, W. H. Freeman, San Francisco, n.d.

Department of Employment (U.K.), 'Public Sector Employment, June 1974', *Department of Employment Gazette*, Dec. 1974, p. 1141.

Department of Employment, 'A View of Occupational Employment in 1981', *Department of Employment Gazette*, July 1975, pp. 619–22.

Department of Employment, *Absenteeism*, Manpower Papers No. 4, H.M.S.O., 1971.

Department of Employment, *On the Quality of Working Life*, Manpower Papers No. 7, H.M.S.O., 1973.

Department of Employment, *Employment Prospects for the Highly Qualified*, Manpower Papers No. 8, H.M.S.O., 1974.

Department of Employment, *Changing Patterns of Working Hours*, Manpower Papers No. 13, H.M.S.O., 1975.

Department of Energy, *Solar Energy: Its Potential Contribution Within the United Kingdom*, Energy Papers No. 16, H.M.S.O., 1977.

DICKSON, D., *Alternative Technology and the Politics of Technical Change*, Collins/Fontana, 1974.

DOBB, M., *Studies in the Development of Capitalism*, rev. edn, Routledge & Kegan Paul, 1963.

DRUCKER, P., *The Age of Discontinuity*, Pan Books, 1971.

DUBIN, R., 'Industrial Workers' Worlds: A Study of the "Central Life Interests" of Industrial Workers', in E. O. Smigel (ed.), *Work and Leisure* (q.v., below), pp. 53–72.

DUNNING, E. G., and HOPPER, E. I., 'Industrialization and the Problem of Convergence: A Critical Note', *Sociological Review*, Vol. 14, No. 2, 1966, pp. 163–86.

DURKHEIM, E., *The Division of Labour in Society*, trans. G. Simpson, The Free Press, New York, 1933. (First published, in French, 1893.)

DURKHEIM, E., *Socialism*, trans. C. Sattler, Collier Books, New York, 1962. (First given as lectures, 1895–6.)

DURKHEIM, E., *The Elementary Forms of the Religious Life*, trans. J. Swain, Allen & Unwin, 1915. (First published, in French, 1912.)

DYOS, H. J., *Urbanity and Suburbanity*, Leicester University Press, 1973.

DYOS, H. J., and WOLFF, M. (eds.), *The Victorian City: Images and Realities*, 2 Vols., Routledge & Kegan Paul, 1973.

Ecologist, 'A Blueprint for Survival', Vol. 2, No. 1, 1972.

ELLUL, J., *The Technological Society*, Knopf, New York, 1964.

ENGELS, F., *The Condition of the Working Class in England in 1844*, trans. and eds., W. O. Henderson and W. H. Chaloner, Basil Blackwell, 1958. (First published, in German, in 1845.)

ENGELS, F., 'On Authority', in K. Marx and F. Engels, *Selected Works in 2 Vols.* (q.v., below), pp. 636–39.

ENSOR, R. C. K., *England 1870–1914*, Oxford University Press, 1936.

ETZIONI, A., *The Active Society*, The Free Press, New York, 1968.

FAUNCE, W. A. (ed.), *Readings in Industrial Sociology*, Appleton-Century-Crofts, New York, 1967.

FAUNCE, W. A., and FORM, W. H., 'The Nature of Industrial Society', in Faunce and Form (eds.), *Comparative Perspectives on Industrial Society*, Little, Brown & Company, Boston, 1969, pp. 1–18.

FELDMAN, A. S., and MOORE, W. E., 'Industrialization and Industrialism: Convergence and Differentiation', in W. A. Faunce and W. H. Form (eds.), *Comparative Perspectives On Industrial Society* (q.v. above), pp. 55–71.

FISCHER, W., 'Social Tensions at Early Stages of Industrialization', *Comparative Studies in Society and History*, Vol. 9,1966–7, pp. 64–83.

FLACKS, R., 'Revolt of the Young Intelligentsia: Revolutionary Class-Consciousness in a Post-Scarcity Society', in R. Aya and N. Miller (eds.), *The New American Revolution*, The Free Press, New York, 1971, pp. 223–59.

FLOUD, J., 'A Critique of Bell', *Survey*, Vol. 16, No. 1, 1971, pp. 25–37.

FORSTER, P. G., 'Secularization in the English Context: Some Conceptual and Empirical Problems', *Sociological Review*, Vol. 20. May 1972, pp. 153–68.

FRANKENBERG, R., *Communities in Modern Britain*, Penguin Books, 1966.

FREEMAN, C., *The Economics of Industrial Innovation*, Penguin Books, 1974.

FREUDENBERGER, H., and REDLICH, F., 'The Industrial Development of Europe: Reality, Symbols, Images', *Kyklos*, Vol. XVII, 1964, pp. 372–401.

FREUND, J., *The Sociology of Max Weber*, Allen Lane The Penguin Press, 1968.

FUCHS, V., *The Service Economy*, Columbia University Press, New York, 1968.

GABOR, D., *Inventing the Future*, Penguin Books, 1964.

GALBRAITH, J. K., *The New Industrial State*, Penguin Books, 1969.

GALTUNG, J., 'On the Future of the International System', in R. Jungk and J. Galtung (eds.) *Mankind 2000* (q.v., below), pp. 12–41.

GALTUNG, J., *Images of the World in the Year 2000*, European Co-ordination Centre for Research and Documentation in Social Sciences, Vienna, 1970.

GELLNER, E., *Thought and Change*, Weidenfeld & Nicolson, 1964.

GELLNER, E., 'Our Current Sense of History', *European Journal of Sociology*, Vol. XII, No. 2, 1971.

GELLNER, E., 'A Social Contract in Search of An Idiom', *Political Quarterly*, Vol. 46, No. 2, 1975, pp. 127–52.

GERSCHENKRON, A., *Economic Backwardness in Historical Perspective*, Harvard University Press, Cambridge, Mass., 1962.

GERSCHENKRON, A., *Continuity in History, and Other Essays*, The Belknap Press, Cambridge, Mass., 1968.

GIDDENS, A., *The Class Structure of the Advanced Societies*, Hutchinson, 1973.

GINSBURG, N., 'The City and Modernization', pp. 122–37 in M. Weiner (ed.), *Modernization: The Dynamics of Growth*, Basic Books, New York, 1966.

GINTIS, H., 'The New Working Class and Revolutionary Youth', Supplement to *Continuum*, Vol. 8, Nos. 1–2, Spring–Summer 1970, pp. 151–74.

GINTIS, H., 'Education, Technology, and the Characteristics of Worker Productivity', *American Economic Review*, May 1971.

GOODMAN, E., *The Impact of Size*, Acton Society Trust, London, 1969.

GOODMAN, E., *A Study of Liberty and Revolution*, Duckworth, 1975.

GOODMAN, J. LANGDON, *Man and Automation*, Penguin Books, 1959.

GOLDTHORPE, J. H., 'Theories of Industrial Society: Reflections on the Recrudescence of Historicism and the Future of Futurology', *European Journal of Sociology*, Vol. XII, No. 2, 1971, pp. 263–88.

GOLDTHORPE, J. H., LOCKWOOD, D., BECHHOFER, F., and PLATT, J., *The Affluent Worker*, 3 Vols., Cambridge University Press, 1968-9.

GORER, G., *Exploring English Character*, The Cresset Press, 1955.

GORZ, A., 'Work and Consumption', in P. Anderson and R. Blackburn (eds.), *Towards Socialism* (q.v., above), pp. 317–53.

GORZ, A., 'Technical Intelligence and the Capitalist Division of Labour', *Telos*, Vol. 12, Summer 1972.

GORZ, A., 'On the Class Character of Science and Scientists', in H. Rose and S. Rose (eds.), *The Political Economy of Science* (q.v., below), pp. 72–95.

GOUGH, I., 'State Expenditure in Advanced Capitalism', *New Left Review*, No. 92, July–August 1975, pp. 53–92.

GREEN, K., and MORPHET, G., *Research and Technology as Economic Activities*, SISCON, Manchester, 1975.

GREENBERG, D. S., *The Politics of Pure Science*, 2nd edn, New American Library, New York, 1971.

GRIFFITHS, D., 'Science and Technology: Liberation or Oppression', *Impact of Science on Society*, Vol. XXV, No. 4, 1975, pp. 295–305.

GRUNER, S. M., *Economic Materialism and Social Moralism*, Mouton, The Hague, 1973.

GUTTSMAN, W. G., *The British Political Elite*, MacGibbon & Kee, 1963.

HABAKKUK, H. J., 'The Historical Experience on the Basic Conditions of Economic Progress', pp. 29–45 in S. N. Eisenstadt (ed.), *Compara-*

tive Perspectives on Social Change, Little, Brown & Co., Boston, 1968.

HABAKKUK, H. J., *Population Growth and Economic Development since 1750*, Leicester University Press, 1971.

HABERMAS, J., *Toward a Rational Society*, Heinemann, 1971.

HALMOS, P. (ed.), *The Development of Industrial Societies*, University of Keele, Sociological Review Monograph No. 8, 1964.

HALMOS, P., *The Personal Service Society*, Constable, 1970.

HALMOS, P. (ed.), *Professionalization and Social Change*, University of Keele, Sociological Review Monograph No. 20, 1973.

HALSEY, A. H., 'The Sociology of Education', in N. J. Smelser (ed.), *Sociology*, John Wiley & Sons, New York, 1967.

HALSEY, A. H. (ed.), *Trends in British Society Since 1900*, Macmillan, 1972.

HANNAH, L., *The Rise of the Corporate Economy*, Methuen, 1976.

HARPER, P., 'What's *Left* of Alternative Technology', *Undercurrents*, No. 6, March–April 1976, pp. 35–8.

HARRIS, A., 'Pure Capitalism and the Disappearance of the Middle Class', *Journal of Political Economy*, June 1939, pp. 328–56.

HARRISON, J. F. C., *The Early Victorians 1832–51*, Panther Books, 1973.

HARTWELL, R. M., *The Industrial Revolution and Economic Growth*, Methuen, 1971.

HARTWELL, R. M., 'The Service Revolution: The Growth of Services in Modern Economy', in C. Cipolla (ed.), *The Industrial Revolution* (q.v., above), pp. 358–94.

HARVEY, D., *Social Justice and the City*, Edward Arnold, 1973.

HAYEK, F. A., *The Counter-Revolution of Science*, The Free Press, New York, 1955.

HEILBRONER, R. L., *Between Capitalism and Socialism*, Vintage Books, New York, 1970.

HEILBRONER, R. L., 'Economic Problems of a "Post-Industrial" Society', in D. Potter and P. Sarre (eds.), *Dimensions of Society*, University of London Press, 1974, pp. 225–44.

HEILBRONER, R. L., *An Inquiry into The Human Prospect*, W. W. Norton & Co., New York, 1974.

HEILBRONER, R. L., 'Men at Work', *New York Review of Books*, 23 January 1975.

HELMER, O., *Social Technology*, Basic Books, New York, 1966.

HENLE, P., 'Recent Growth of Paid Leisure for U.S. Workers', in E. O. Smigel (ed.), *Work and Leisure* (q.v., below), pp. 182–203.

HERAUD, B., 'Professionalism, Radicalism, and Social Change', in P. Halmos (ed.), *Professionalization and Social Change* (q.v., above), pp. 85–102.

HEWART OF BURY, LORD, *The New Despotism*, Ernest Benn, 1929.

HINSLEY, F. H. (ed.), *Material Progress and World-Wide Problems 1870–98*, The New Cambridge Modern History, Vol. XI, Cambridge University Press, 1962.

HOBSBAWM, E. J., *The Age of Revolution 1789–1848*, The New American Library, New York, 1964.

HOBSBAWM, E. J., *Labouring Men: Studies in the History of Labour*, Weidenfeld & Nicolson, 1964.

HOBSBAWM, E. J., *Industry and Empire: An Economic History of Britain Since 1750*, Weidenfeld & Nicolson, 1968.

HOGGART, R., *Speaking to Each Other*, 2 Vols., Penguin Books, 1973.

HOSELITZ, B. F., and MOORE, W. E. (eds.), *Industrialization and Society*, UNESCO, Mouton, The Hague, 1966.

HOUGHTON, W. E., *The Victorian Frame of Mind 1830–70*, Yale University Press, New Haven, 1957.

HUGHES, H. STUART, *Consciousness and Society: The Reorientation of European Social Thought 1890–1930*, Vintage Books, New York, 1958.

HUXLEY, J. S. and T. H., *Evolution and Ethics, 1893–1943*, The Pilot Press, London, 1947.

HYMAN, R., *Strikes*, Collins/Fontana, 1972.

IKLÉ, F. C., 'Can Social Predictions Be Evaluated?', *Daedalus*, Vol. 96, No. 2, 1967, pp. 733–58.

ILLICH, I., *De-Schooling Society*, Calder & Boyars, 1971.

ILLICH, I., *Tools for Conviviality*, Calder & Boyars, 1973.

ILLICH, I., *Energy and Equity*, Calder & Boyars, 1974

ILLICH, I., *Medical Nemesis: The Expropriation of Health*, Calder & Boyars, 1975.

INGLIS, F., 'Townscape', in D. Thompson (ed.), *Discrimination and Popular Culture*, 2nd edn, Penguin Books, 1973.

INGLIS, F., 'Nation and Community: A Landscape and its Morality', *Universities Quarterly*, Vol. 30, No. 4, 1976, pp. 444–61.

IONESCU, G., 'Saint-Simon and the Politics of Industrial Societies', *Government and Opposition*, Vol. 8, No. 1, 1973, pp. 24–47.

JANTSCH, E., *Technological Forecasting in Perspective*, O.E.C.D., Paris, 1967.

JARVIE, I. C., *The Revolution in Anthropology*, Routledge & Kegan Paul, 1964.

JENCKS, C., *Inequality: A Re-assessment of the Effect of Family and Schooling in America*, Basic Books, New York, 1972.

JEWKES, J., SAWERS, D., and STILLERMANN, R., *The Sources of Invention*, Macmillan, 1958.

JOHNSON, R., *The Blue Books and Education 1816–96*, University of Birmingham, Centre for Contemporary Cultural Studies, 1976.

JUNGK, R., and GALTUNG, J. (eds.), *Mankind 2000*, Allen & Unwin, 1969.

KAHL, J., 'Some Social Concomitants of Industrialization and Urbanization', in W. A. Faunce (ed.), *Readings in Industrial Sociology* (q.v., above), pp. 28–67.

KAHN, H., and WIENER, A., *The Year 2000*, The Macmillan Co., New York, 1967.

KAUTSKY, K., *The Dictatorship of the Proletariat*, Ann Arbor, University of Michigan Press, 1964. (First published 1918.)

KERR, C., *The Uses of the University*, Harvard University Press, Cambridge, Mass., 1963.

KERR, C., DUNLOP, T., HARBISON, F., and MYERS, C. A., *Industrialism and Industrial Man*, 2nd edn, Penguin Books, 1973. (First published in 1960.)

KEYNES, J. M., 'Economic Possibilities for our Grandchildren' (1930), in his *Essays in Persuasion*, Macmillan, for The Royal Economic Society, 1972.

KLEIN, V., *Samples from English Culture*, 2 Vols., Routledge & Kegan Paul, 1965.

KLINGENDER, F. D., *Art and the Industrial Revolution*, Paladin Books, 1972.

KORNHAUSER, A., *The Politics of Mass Society*, The Free Press, New York, 1959.

KROPOTKIN, P., *Fields, Factories and Workshops*, ed. C. Ward, Allen & Unwin, 1974. (First published 1899.)

KUMAR, K. (ed.), *Revolution: The Theory and Practice of a European Idea*, Weidenfeld & Nicolson, 1971.

KUMAR, K., 'Futurology', *Listener*, 18 Feb. 1971.

KUMAR, K., 'Futurology – The View from Eastern Europe', *Futures*, Vol. 4, No. 1, 1972, pp. 90–94.

KUMAR, K., 'The "Sociology of the Future" ', *Sociology*, Vol. 7, No. 2, 1973, pp. 277–80.

KUMAR, K., 'The Industrializing and the Post-Industrial Worlds: On Development and Futurology', pp. 329–60 in E. de Kadt and G. Williams (eds.), *Sociology and Development*, Tavistock Publications, 1974.

KUMAR, K., 'Sociological Darwinism', *Biology and Human Affairs*, Vol. 40, No. 2, 1975, pp. 71–6, and Vol. 40, No. 3, 1975, pp. 146–53.

KUMAR, K., 'Revolution and Industrial Society: An Historical Perspective', *Sociology*, Vol. 10, No. 2, 1976, pp. 245–69.

KUMAR, K., 'Industrialism and Post-Industrialism: Reflections on a Putative Transition', *Sociological Review*, Vol. 24, No. 3, 1976, pp. 439–78.

KUMAR, K., 'The Industrial Societies and After', *Universities Quarterly*, Vol. 30, No. 4, 1976, pp. 383–401.

KUMAR, K., 'The Salariat', *New Society*, 21 October 1976.

KUMAR, K., 'Continuities and Discontinuities in the Development of Industrial Societies', in R. Scase (ed.), *Industrial Society* (q.v., below), pp. 29–42.

KUZNETS, S., 'Consumption, Industrialization, and Urbanization', in B. F. Hoselitz and W. E. Moore (eds.), *Industrialization and Society* (q.v., above), pp. 99–115.

LAMPARD, E. E., 'The Social Impact of the Industrial Revolution', pp. 302–21 in M. Kranzberg and C. W. Pursell (eds.), *Technology in Western Civilization*, Madison, Wisconsin, 1967.

LAMPARD, E. E., 'The Urbanizing World', in H. J. Dyos and M. Wolff (eds.), *The Victorian City* (q.v., above), Vol. I, pp. 3–57.

LANDES, D. S., 'French Business and the Businessman: A Social and Cultural Analysis', pp. 334–53 in E. M. Earle (ed.), *Modern France*, Russell & Russell, New York, 1964.

LANDES, D. S., *The Unbound Prometheus: Technological Change and Industrial Development in Western Europe from 1750 to the Present*, Cambridge University Press, 1969.

LANE, R. E., 'The Decline of Politics and Ideology in a Knowledgeable Society', *American Sociological Review*, Vol. 31, No. 5, 1966, pp. 649–62.

LANGRISH, J., GIBBONS, M., EVANS, W. G., and JEVONS, F. R., *Wealth From Knowledge: A Study of Innovation in Industry*, Macmillan, 1972.

LARRABEE, E., and MEYERSOHN, R. (eds.), *Mass Leisure*, The Free Press, Glencoe, 1958.

LASCH, C., 'Toward a Theory of Post-Industrial Society', pp. 36–50 in M. D. Hancock and G. Sjoberg (eds.), *Politics in the Post-Welfare State*, Columbia University Press, New York, 1972.

LAWRENCE, D. H., 'Nottingham and the Mining Country', pp. 114–22 in *Selected Essays*, Penguin Books, 1950.

LENGELLÉ, M., *The Growing Importance of the Service Sector in Member Countries*, O.E.C.D., Paris, 1966.

LENIN, V. I., *The State and Revolution*, Foreign Languages Publishing House, Moscow, n.d.

LENIN, V. I., 'Frederick Engels', pp. 18–19 in R. Pollitt (ed.), *Lenin on Britain*, Martin Lawrence, 1934.

LEONARD, P., 'Professionalization, Community Action, and the Growth of Social Service Bureaucracies', in P. Halmos (ed.), *Professionalization and Social Change* (q.v., above), pp. 103–18.

LERNER, D., *The Passing of Traditional Society*, The Free Press, New York, 1958.

LEVY, M. J., *Modernization and the Structure of Societies*, 2 Vols., Princeton University Press, Princeton, 1966.

LEWIS, R., *The New Service Society*, Longman, 1973.

LICHTHEIM, G., *The New Europe: Today and Tomorrow*, Basic Books, New York, 1963.

LICHTHEIM, G., *The Origins of Socialism*, Weidenfeld & Nicolson, 1969.

LIPSET, S. M., *Political Man*, Heinemann, Mercury Books, 1963.

LIPSET, S. M., 'Ideology and No End: The Controversy Till Now', *Encounter*, Dec. 1972, pp. 17–22.

LOCKWOOD, D., *The Blackcoated Worker*, Allen & Unwin, 1958.

LUBASZ, H., 'Marx's Conception of the Revolutionary Proletariat', *Praxis*, Vol. 5, 1970, pp. 288–90.

LUKACS, G., *Studies in European Realism*, Grosset & Dunlap, New York, 1964.

MACHLUP, F., *The Production and Distribution of Knowledge in the United States*, Princeton University Press, Princeton, 1962.

MACINTYRE, A., *Secularization and Moral Change*, Oxford University Press, 1967.

MCLELLAN, D., *Karl Marx: His Life and Thought*, Macmillan, 1973.

MAINE, SIR HENRY, *Ancient Law*, Dent & Sons, 1917. (First published 1861.)

MANN, G., 'The History Lesson', *Encounter*, August 1972.

MANN, M., *Consciousness and Action Among the Western Working Class*, Macmillan, 1973.

MANUEL, F. E., *The New World of Henri Saint-Simon*, University of Notre Dame Press, Indiana, 1963.

MANUEL, F. E., *The Prophets of Paris*, Harper Torchbooks, New York, 1965.

MARCUS, S., *Engels, Manchester, and the Working Class*, Vintage Books, New York, 1974.

MARCUSE, H., 'Industrialization and Capitalism in the Work of Max Weber', *New Left Review*, No. 30, March–April 1965, pp. 3–17.

MARCUSE, H., *One Dimensional Man*, Sphere Books, 1968.

MARGLIN, S. A., 'What Do Bosses Do? The Origins and Functions of Hierarchy in Capitalist Production', *The Review of Radical Political Economics*, Vol. 6, No. 2, Summer 1974, pp. 60–112.

MARRIS, R. (ed.), *The Corporate Society*, Macmillan, 1974.

MARSHALL, A., 'The Future of the Working Classes', pp. 101–18 in A. C. Pigou (ed.), *Memorials of Alfred Marshall*, Macmillan, 1925.

MARSHALL, T. H., 'A Summing-Up', in P. Halmos (ed.), *The Development of Industrial Societies* (q.v., above).

MARTIN, J., and NORMAN, A. R. D., *The Computerized Society*, Prentice-Hall, Engelwood Cliffs, New Jersey, 1970.

MARX, K., 'Critical Notes on "The King of Prussia and Social Reform" ' (1844), in L. D. Easton and K. H. Guddat (eds.), *Writings of the Young Marx on Philosophy and Society*, Anchor Books, New York, 1967.

MARX, K., 'The Economic–Philosophical Manuscripts of 1844', in T. B. Bottomore, trans. and ed., *Karl Marx: Early Writings*, Watts & Co., 1963.

MARX, K., *The Poverty of Philosophy*, International Publishers, New York, 1963. (First published in 1847.)

MARX, K., and ENGELS, F., *The Holy Family*, Foreign Languages Publishing House, Moscow, 1956. (First published 1845.)

MARX, K., and ENGELS, F., *The German Ideology*, International Publishers, New York, 1947. (Written 1845–6.)

MARX, K., and ENGELS, F., *Selected Works in Two Volumes*, Foreign Languages Publishing House, Moscow, 1962.

MARX, K., and ENGELS, F., *Selected Correspondence*, Foreign Languages Publishing House, Moscow, 1953.

MARX, K., *Capital*, trans. Eden and Cedar Paul, 2 Vols., Dent & Sons, 1910.

MERRINGTON, J., 'Town and Country in the Transition to Capitalism', *New Left Review*, No. 93, Sept.–Oct. 1975, pp. 71–92.

MEYNAUD, J., *Technocracy*, Methuen, 1968.

MILIBAND, R., *The State in Capitalist Society*, Weidenfeld & Nicolson, 1969.

MILL, J. S., 'On Liberty' (1859), in *The Essential Works of John Stuart Mill*, ed. M. Lerner, Bantam Books, New York, 1961.

MILLER, S. M., 'Notes on Neo-Capitalism', *Theory and Society*, Vol. 2, No. 1, 1975, pp. 1–35.

MILLS, C. W., *White Collar*, Oxford University Press, New York, 1951.

MISHAN, E. J., *The Costs of Economic Growth*, Penguin Books, 1969.

MOORE, B., Jr, *The Social Origins of Dictatorship and Democracy*, Allen Lane The Penguin Press, 1967.

MOORE, W. E., 'The Attributes of an Industrial Order', in S. Nosow and W. H. Form (eds.), *Man, Work, and Society*, Atherton, New York, 1962.

MUMFORD, L., *The City in History*, Penguin Books, 1966.

NETTL, J. P., 'Consensus or Elite Domination: The Case of Business', *Political Studies*, Vol. XIII, No. 1, 1965, pp. 22–44.

NEWBOULD, G., *Management and Merger Activity*, Guthstead, Liverpool, 1970.

NEWBOULD, G., and JACKSON, A., *The Receding Ideal*, Guthstead, Liverpool, 1972.

NISBET, R., *The Sociological Tradition*, Heinemann, 1967.

NISBET, R., 'The Year 2000 and All That', *Commentary*, Vol. 45, No. 6, June 1968, pp. 60–66.

NISBET, R., *Social Change and History: Aspects of the Western Theory of Development*, Oxford University Press, 1969.

NOBLE, T., *Modern Britain: Structure and Change*, Batsford, 1975.

O'CONNOR, J., *The Fiscal Crisis of the State*, St Martin's Press, New York, 1973.

OPPENHEIMER, M., 'The Proletarianization of the Professional', in P. Halmos (ed.), *Professionalisation and Social Change* (q.v., above), pp. 213–28.

PAHL, R. E., *Patterns of Urban Life*, Longman, 1970.

PAHL, R. E., 'Patterns of Urban Life in the Next Fifteen Years', *Universities Quarterly*, Vol. 30, No. 4, 1976, pp. 402–19.

PAHL, R. E., '"Collective Consumption" and the State in Capitalist and State Socialist Societies', in R. Scase (ed.), *Industrial Society* (q.v., below), pp. 153–71.

PAHL, R. E. and J. M., *Managers and their Wives*, Penguin Books, 1972.

PAHL, R. E., and WINKLER, J., 'The Coming Corporatism', *New Society*, 10 October 1974.

PARSONS, T., 'Some Principal Characteristics of Industrial Societies', pp. 13–42 in C. E. Black (ed.), *The Transformation of Russian Society*, Harvard University Press, Cambridge, Mass., 1960.

PARSONS, T., *Societies: Evolutionary and Comparative Perspectives*, Prentice-Hall, Englewood Cliffs, New Jersey, 1966.

PEEL, J. D. Y., *Herbert Spencer: The Evolution of a Sociologist*, Heinemann, 1971.

PELLING, H., *Popular Politics and Society in Late Victorian Britain*, Macmillan, 1968.

PERKIN, H., *The Making of English Society 1780–1880*, Routledge & Kegan Paul, 1969.

PERRUCCI, R., 'In the Service of Man: Radical Movements in the Professions', in P. Halmos (ed.), *Professionalisation and Social Change* (q.v., above), pp. 179–94.

PICKVANCE, C. G. (ed.), *Urban Sociology: Critical Essays*, Tavistock Publications, 1976.

PIGOU, A. C., *The Economics of Welfare*, Macmillan, 1920.

PLUMB, J. H., *The Death of the Past*, Penguin Books, 1973.

POLANYI, K., *The Great Transformation: The Political and Economic Origins of our Time*, Beacon Press, Boston, 1957.

POLLARD, S., *The Idea of Progress: History and Society*, Penguin Books, 1971.

POOR, R. (ed.), *4 Days, 40 Hours*, Pan Books, 1972.

POPPER, K., *The Poverty of Historicism*, Routledge & Kegan Paul, 1957.

POSTAN, M. M., *An Economic History of Western Europe*, Methuen, 1967.

PRICE, D., *Science Since Babylon*, Yale University Press, New Haven, 1961.

RADCLIFFE-BROWN, A. R., 'The Present Position of Anthropological Studies', *The Advancement of Science: 1931*, British Association for the Advancement of Science, 1931.

RAISON, T. (ed.), *The Founding Fathers of Social Science*, Penguin Books, 1969.

READER, W. J., *Professional Men: The Rise of the Professional Classes in Nineteenth Century England*, Weidenfeld & Nicolson, 1966.

REDFIELD, R., 'The Folk Community', *American Journal of Sociology*, Vol. LII, No. 4, 1947, pp. 293–308.

REIMER, E., *School is Dead*, Penguin Books, 1971.

RICHTA, R., *et al.*, *Civilization at the Crossroads: Social and Human Implications of the Scientific and Technological Revolution*, 3 Vols., Czechoslovak Institute of Arts and Sciences, Prague, 1967.

RIEFF, P., *The Triumph of the Therapeutic*, Penguin Books, 1973.

RIEFF, P., *Fellow Teachers*, Faber & Faber, 1975.

RIESMAN, D., 'Leisure and Work in Post-Industrial Society', in E. Larrabee and R. Meyersohn (eds.), *Mass Leisure* (q.v., above), pp. 363–85.

RIESMAN, D., and WEISS, R., 'Some Issues in the Future of Leisure', in E. O. Smigel (ed.), *Work and Leisure* (q.v., below), pp. 168–81.

ROBERTSON, J., *Profit or People? The New Social Role of Money*, Calder & Boyars, 1974.

ROSE, H. and S. (eds.), *The Political Economy of Science*, Macmillan, 1976.

ROSENBAUM, S., 'Social Services Manpower', *Social Trends 1971*, pp. 6–12.

ROSTOW, W. W., *The Stages of Economic Growth*, Cambridge University Press, 1960.

ROSZAK, T., *The Making of the Counter-Culture*, Faber & Faber, 1970.

ROSZAK, T., *Where the Wasteland Ends: Politics and Transcendence in Post-Industrial Society*, Faber & Faber, 1973.

ROWE, D. J., 'The London Working Men's Association and the "People's Charter" ', *Past and Present*, No. 36, April 1967, pp. 73–86.

ROWNTREE, J. and M., 'Youth as a Class', *International Socialist Journal*, No. 5, 1968, pp. 25–58.

SAINT-SIMON, H., *Social Organization, The Science of Man, and Other Writings*, trans. and ed., F. Markham, Harper Torchbooks, New York, 1964.

SAMPSON, A., *The New Anatomy of Britain*, Hodder & Stoughton, 1971.

SAMUEL, R., ' "Bastard" Capitalism', in E. P. Thompson (ed.), *Out of Apathy*, Stevens & Sons, 1960, pp. 19–55.

SAMUEL, R., 'The Struggle Against School in Nineteenth Century London', University of Kent at Canterbury, 1972, mimeo.

SAMUEL, R., 'Comers and Goers', in H. J. Dyos and M. Wolff (eds.), *The Victorian City* (q.v., above), Vol. I, pp. 123–60.

SAMUELS, J. M. (ed.), *Readings in Mergers and Takeovers*, Elek Books, London, 1972.

SCASE, R. (ed.), *Industrial Society: Class, Cleavage, and Control*, Allen & Unwin, 1977.

SCHUMACHER, E. F., *Small is Beautiful*, Blond & Briggs, 1973.

SCHUMPETER, J., *Capitalism, Socialism, and Democracy*, 4th edn, Allen & Unwin, 1954.

SCOTFORD-ARCHER, M., and GINER, S. (eds.), *Contemporary Europe: Class, Status, and Power*, Weidenfeld & Nicolson, 1971.

SCOTT, J. W., and TILLEY, L. A., 'Women's Work and the Family in Nineteenth Century Europe', *Comparative Studies in Society and History*, Vol. 17, No. 1, 1975, pp. 36–64.

SERVAN-SCHREIBER, J. J., *The American Challenge*, trans. R. Steel, Atheneum, New York, 1968.

SHILS, E., 'Tradition, Ecology, and Institutions in the History of Sociology', *Daedalus*, Fall 1970, pp. 761–825.

SHONFIELD, A., 'Thinking About the Future', *Encounter*, Feb. 1969, pp. 15–26.

SILLITOE, A. F., *Britain in Figures*, Penguin Books, 1971.

SIMMEL, G., 'The Metropolis and Mental Life', in K. Wolff (trans. and ed.), *The Sociology of Georg Simmel*, The Free Press, New York, 1950.

SKLAIR, L., *The Sociology of Progress*, Routledge & Kegan Paul, 1970.

SKLAIR, L., *Organized Knowledge*, Paladin Books, 1973.

SLATER, M., *Economies of Scale: Sources and Measurement*, Acton Society Trust, London, 1975.

SMELSER, N., *Social Change in the Industrial Revolution*, Routledge & Kegan Paul, 1959.

SMELSER, N., 'Mechanisms of Change and Adjustment to Change', in B. Hoselitz and W. E. Moore (eds.), *Industrialization and Society* (q.v., above), pp. 32–54.

SMIGEL, E. O. (ed.), *Work and Leisure*, College and University Press, New Haven, 1963.

SMITH, A., *The Wealth of Nations*, 2 Vols., Dent & Sons, 1910. (First published 1776.)

SMITH, M., PARKER, S., and SMITH, C. (eds.), *Leisure and Society in Britain*, Allen Lane The Penguin Press, 1973.

SMITH, T., *Anti-Politics*, Charles Knight, 1972.

Social Trends, H.M.S.O., annually from 1970.

SOROKIN, P. A., 'Mutual Convergence of the United States and the U.S.S.R. to the Mixed Socio-Cultural Type', *International Journal of Comparative Sociology*, Vol. 1, 1960, pp. 143–76.

SPENCER, H., *Social Statics*, John Chapman, 1851.

SPENCER, H., *The Principles of Sociology*, 3 vols., Williams & Norgate, 1876–97.

SPENCER, H., 'Progress: Its Laws and Causes' (1857), in *Essays, Scientific, Political, and Speculative*, 3 vols., Williams & Norgate, 1891.

STEARNS, P., 'Is there a Post-Industrial Society?' *Society*, Vol. 11, No. 4, 1974, pp. 10–25.

STEINER, G., 'The Many Faces of Violence', *Listener*, 9 October 1975.

SWADOS, H., 'The Myth of the Happy Worker', pp. 198–204 in Stein, M., Vidich, A. J., and White, D. M. (eds.), *Identity and Anxiety*, The Free Press, New York, 1960.

SWADOS, H., 'Less Work, Less Leisure', in E. Larrabee and R. Meyersohn (eds.), *Mass Leisure* (q.v., above), pp. 353–63.

TAYLOR, L., and WALTON, P., 'Industrial Sabotage: Motives and Meanings', pp. 219–45 in S. Cohen (ed.), *Images of Deviance*, Penguin Books, 1971.

TAYLOR, R., 'The Volvo Way of Work', *New Society*, 15 April 1976.

THERBORN, G., 'The Working Class and the Birth of Marxism', *New Left Review*, No 79, May–June 1973.

THOMPSON, E. P., 'The Peculiarities of the English', pp. 311–62 in J. Saville and R. Miliband (eds.), *The Socialist Register 1964*, The Merlin Press, London, 1965.

THOMPSON, E. P., 'Time, Work Discipline, and Industrial Capitalism', *Past and Present*, No. 38, Dec. 1967, pp. 56–97.

TOCQUEVILLE, A., DE, *Democracy in America*, 2 Vols., trans. H. Reeve, Schocken Books, New York, 1961. (First published, in French, 1835–40.)

TOCQUEVILLE, A., DE, *The Ancien Régime and the French Revolution*, trans. S. Gilbert, Collins/Fontana, 1966. (First published in 1856.)

TOFFLER, A., *Future Shock*, Random House, New York, 1970.

TOMINAGA, K., 'Post-Industrial Society and Cultural Diversity', *Survey*, Vol. 16, No. 1, 1971, pp. 68–77.

TÖNNIES, F., *Community and Society*, trans. and ed. C. P. Loomis, Harper & Row, New York, 1963. (First published as *Gemeinschaft und Gesellschaft*, 1887.)

TOURAINE, A., *The Post-Industrial Society*, Random House, New York, 1971.

TREVOR-ROPER, H. R., 'Apologia Transfugae', *Spectator*, 14 July 1973.

United Nations, *Post-War Demographic Trends in Europe and the Outlook Until the Year 2000*, U.N. Economic Commission for Europe, Paris, July 1975.

VASSILIEV, M., and GOUSCHEV, S. (eds.), *Life in the Twenty-First Century*, Penguin Books, 1961.

WADDINGTON, C. H., 'Work and Leisure', University of Edinburgh, School of the Man-Made Future, 1972, mimeo.

WALKER, C. R., and GUEST, R. H., *The Man on the Assembly Line*, Harvard University Press, Cambridge, Mass., 1952.

WATSON, J. S., *The Reign of George III 1760–1815*, Oxford University Press, 1960.

WEBER, M., 'Science as a Vocation', in H. Gerth and C. W. Mills (eds.), *From Max Weber: Essays in Sociology*, Routledge & Kegan Paul, 1948.

WEBER, M., 'Bureaucracy', in Gerth and Mills (eds.), *From Max Weber* (above).

WEBER, M., *The Protestant Ethic and the Spirit of Capitalism*, trans. T. Parsons, Unwin Books, 1930. (First published in German 1904–5.)

WEINBERG, I., 'The Problem of the Convergence of Industrial Societies: A Critical Look at the State of a Theory', *Comparative Studies in Society and History*, Vol. 11, No. 1, 1969, pp. 1–15.

WEINER, M. (ed.), *Modernization: The Dynamics of Growth*, Basic Books, New York, 1966.

WEIR, M. (ed.), *Job Satisfaction*, Collins/Fontana, 1976.

WELLS, H. G., *The Discovery of the Future*, T. Fisher Unwin, 1902.

WELLS, H. G., *The War in the Air*, Penguin Books, 1967. (First published 1907.)

WESTERGAARD, J., and RESLER, H., *Class in a Capitalist Society: A Study of Contemporary Britain*, Heinemann, 1975.

WILENSKY, H., 'Work, Careers, and Social Integration', *International Social Science Journal*, Vol. XII, Fall 1960, pp. 543–60.

WILENSKY, H., 'The Uneven Distribution of Leisure: The Impact of Economic Growth on "Free Time"', *Social Problems*, Vol. 9, Summer 1961, pp. 32–56.

WILENSKY, H., 'The Professionalization of Everyone?', *American Journal of Sociology*, Vol. 70, No. 2, 1964, pp. 137–58.

WILENSKY, H., *The Welfare State and Inequality*, University of California Press, Berkeley, 1975.

WILENSKY, H., and LEBEAUX, C. N., *Industrial Society and Social Welfare*, 2nd edn, The Free Press, New York, 1965.

WILLIAMS, R., *Culture and Society 1780–1950*, Penguin Books, 1963.

WILLIAMS, R., *The Long Revolution*, Penguin Books, 1965.

WILLIAMS, R., *The English Novel from Dickens to Lawrence*, Chatto & Windus, 1970.

WILLIAMS, R., *The Country and the City*, Chatto & Windus, 1973.

WILLIAMS, R., and GUEST, D., 'Are the Middle Classes Becoming Work-Shy?', *New Society*, 1 July 1971.

WILLIAMS, S. R., *Technology, Investment and Growth*, Chapman & Hall, 1967.

WILSON, B., *Religion in Secular Society*, Penguin Books, 1969.

WILSON, D., 'The Cruel Industry', *Observer* (Business Section), 3 Sept. 1972.

WINKLER, J. T., 'The Corporatist Economy: Theory and Administration', in R. Scase (ed.), *Industrial Society* (q.v., above), pp. 43–58.

WIRTH, L., 'Urbanism as a Way of Life', *American Journal of Sociology*, Vol. XLIV, July 1938, pp. 1–24.

WOLIN, S. S., *Politics and Vision*, Allen & Unwin, 1961.

World Marxist Review, 'Special Issue on Prognostication and Planning', Vol. 14, No. 1, 1971.

WRIGLEY, E. A., 'The Process of Modernization and the Industrial Revolution in England', *Journal of Interdisciplinary History*, Vol. III, No. 2, 1972, pp. 225–59.

YOUNG, M., and WILLMOTT, P., *The Symmetrical Family: A Study of Work and Leisure in the London Region*, Routledge & Kegan Paul, 1973.

ZEISEL, J. S., 'The Workweek in American Industry 1850–1945', in E. Larrabee and R. Meyersohn (eds.), *Mass Leisure* (q.v., above), pp. 143–53.

Index